Sheffield
Learning
Collegiat
Collegiate Crescent Campus
Sheffield   S10 2BP

D1376018

101 872 246 7

ONE WEEK LOAN

-9 NOV 2010

Sheffield Hallam University
Learning and Information Services
Withdrawn From Stock

AUSTRALIA
The Law Book Company
Sydney

CANADA and USA
Carswell
Toronto

HONG KONG
Sweet & Maxwell Asia

NEW ZEALAND
Brookers
Wellington

SINGAPORE and MALAYSIA
Sweet & Maxwell Asia
Singapore and Kuala Lumpur

Michael Freeman

UNDERSTANDING
FAMILY LAW

First Edition

LONDON
SWEET & MAXWELL
2007

Published in 2007 by Sweet & Maxwell Limited
of 100 Avenue Road, Swiss Cottage, London NW3 3PF
(*http://www.sweetandmaxwell.co.uk*)

First Edition 2007

Michael Freeman asserts the moral right to be
identified as the author of this work.

ISBN 978-0-421-90170-4

Typeset by YHT Ltd, London

Printed in Great Britain by
Athenaeum Press Ltd., Gateshead, Tyne & Wear

All rights reserved. Crown copyright material is reproduced
with the permission of the Controller of HMSO and the
Queen's Printer for Scotland.

No part of this publication may be reproduced or transmitted
in any form or by any means, or stored in any retrieval system
of any nature, without prior written permission, except for
permitted fair dealing under the Copyright, Designs and
Patents Act 1988, or in accordance with the terms of a licence
issued by the Copyright Licensing Agency in respect of
photocopying and/or reprographic reproduction. Application
for permission for other use of copyright material including
permission to reproduce extracts in other published works
shall be made to the publishers. Full acknowledgment of
author, publisher and source must be given.

Copyright © Michael Freeman, 2007

SHEFFIELD HALLAM UNIVERSITY
WIL
346·015
FR
COLLEGIATE LEARNING CENTRE

You may think this is a convincing argument. I did (Freeman and Lyon, 1983) and to some extent still do. But let us look at it critically. First, do people choose cohabitation rather than marriage? There are all sorts of reasons for cohabiting.[394] Some cohabit because they reject marriage. The autonomy view is particularly persuasive in their case. Others cohabit because they cannot, or cannot presently, get married. To treat them as if they are married seems particularly perverse. Others cohabit because of past experiences, bad marriages, difficult divorces. Cohabitation is also often a preliminary to marriage (a postponement of a final decision, a "trial marriage", etc.). Many also drift into cohabitation. And many, as we have already seen, do not know the differences between cohabitation and marriage. For how many of these couples is there a true choice? There may also be inequality of bargaining power: one party may have greater knowledge (and knowledge is power[395]), the other may be vulnerable. She may, for example, be pregnant. We talk of autonomy and assume both want the same thing. But one may want marriage, and the other cohabitation. There may be all sorts of reasons for differences of opinion. It takes "two to tango": it also takes two to go through a ceremony of marriage. Cohabitation can "just happen". Herring points out (2004, pp.74–75) that some of the legal consequences of marriage do not reflect the couple's decision but

"rather the justice of the situation or the protection of a state interest (for example, protecting the interests of children). One might take the view that it should not be possible to choose not to have justice or not to protect a state interest".

It is at the end of the relationship that these considerations come into focus. One can imagine couples who reject intervention during a functional relationship but appreciate it when it becomes dysfunctional.

COHABITATION CONTRACTS

How much autonomy do we give cohabiting couples? What is the status of a cohabitation agreement?[396] There is no doubt that once such contracts were illegal and contrary to public policy.[397] Authorities going back to the eighteenth century are clearly of the view that such contracts were for an immoral purpose.[398] In

1938 Lord Wright stated: "the law will not enforce an immoral purpose, such as a promise between a man and a woman to live together without being married ...".[399] Cohabitation contracts also caused problems because English law was reluctant to recognise domestic contracts.[400] Public policy has changed. But cohabitation contracts may still be challenged on the ground that there was no intention to create legal relations, or, of course, if there is duress, undue influence, misrepresentation (and also where there is lack of independent advice). A cohabitation agreement which was an agreement about sexual relations is still regarded as unlawful.[401] Not many cohabitation contracts are made, though they may become more common. Those that are more likely focus on property and money issues than on sex.[402] And even where sex is the primary concern, solicitors drafting the agreement will make sure that property and financial issues appear squarely on the face of the contract.

REFORMING COHABITATION

It is accepted by most that the law of cohabitation is in need of reform. The courts have attempted to rectify injustice through the law of trusts and proprietary estoppel (on which see Lowe and Douglas, 2006, pp.153–169). Suggestions that this jurisprudence should be codified were rejected by the Law Commission in 2002.[403] It believed that this would frustrate development of these rules and deprive the courts of the flexibility needed to do justice between cohabitants.

The 2002 report achieved nothing. It was both too broad in its ambitions—it looked not just at cohabitants but at any home-sharers—and too narrow—concentrating only on homes. The Law Commission identified a number of key problems: searching for parties' common intention is unrealistic, the line between contributions to property which count and those which do not is not clear; looking after children appears not to count; quantification of shares is difficult[404] with the result that decisions are inconsistent and difficult to reconcile; the uncertainty of the law can lead to lengthy and costly litigation.[405]

The Law Commission favoured a scheme based on contributions, rather than one based on intentions (except where there was an express declaration of trust). Contributions can be judged objectively; intentions relate back to what is (dimly) remembered and to imputed agreements. The Commission was, however, unable to arrive at a workable set of proposals.

The Law Society, also in 2002, produced a report with rather more focused recommendations.[406] It proposed giving courts the power to redistribute the property of couples who have cohabited for two years[407] or had shown the required degree of commitment by having had a child together. This power to redistribute would only arise where there was not a cohabitation contract which provides for financial issues in the event of a breakdown of the relationship. The Family Law (Scotland) Act 2006 has implemented an adjustive regime similar to this Law Society proposal.[408] Australia and New Zealand (see Pawlowski, 2001 and Atkin, 2003) too have legislation addressing this issue.

In 2006, the Law Commission returned to cohabitation. It has issued a consultation paper,[409] which recommends a scheme not unlike that proposed by the Law Society. It would limit cohabitants' claims to circumstances where "the applicant can establish that the economic effects of the relationship, positive and negative, are not fully shared between the parties on separation".[410] This would involve examining any economic advantage retained by the respondent on separation which arose from the applicant's contributions, and/or any economic disadvantage the applicant has sustained as a result of contributions made during the relationship, or to be sustained as a result of continuing child-care responsibilities following separation. Whether these proposals, which do not meet with universal approval, far from it, will be taken any further remains to be seen.

LIVING APART TOGETHER

Marriage, civil partnership and cohabitation have been discussed. We need now to address the relatively recent phenomenon known as "living apart together" (LAT). It is a recognised sociological concept (for example, Bawin-Legros and Gauthier, 2001), and also a term used in demographic literature (for example, by Haskey, 2005). The legal and social policy implications of LAT are also now being explored (see Haskey and Lewis, 2006). According to Haskey, (2005), about one-in-three persons in the age range 16–59 who are neither cohabiting nor married (and living with their spouse) are in an LAT relationship. The key element is the maintenance of independence.

People may live apart together for numerous reasons: employment may force them to live in different places, one of them (or both) may be caring for an elderly parent or they may not be able to afford a home and continue to live with parents or they may choose to preserve their own space. They may already have their own home and be used to paying for their own home expenses (Levin, 2004, pp.236–237). Is their relationship "conjugal"? Can they be considered a "couple"? We associate cohabitation with a common residence. Should LAT make us reconsider whether this is a necessary feature? If so, what else should be look to? Many of those who live apart together will have children in common. Some will organise their financial affairs together. Just as cohabitation may be a prelude to marriage, so LAT may also be a postponement device, with those who live apart together coming to live together or even marrying. As Diduck hypothesises, "like cohabitants did years ago, those living in a committed, sexually exclusive, intimate yet non-co-residential relationship must learn to manage their version of autonomous intimacy with external norms of what it means to be a 'couple'".[411] And, as cohabitants have made us rethink the norms of relationship, those living apart together may continue this process.

NON-CONJUGAL RELATIONSHIPS

Discussion of cohabitation has made us reflect on why relationships matter. But what of relationships outside conjugality (whether this takes the form of marriage, civil partnership, cohabitation or living apart together)? What of persons who are not "a couple", but who live together for mutual support, caring and companionship? They may be related, for example siblings; they may be friends. One of them may have special needs, and require the care and attention of the other, or the relationship may be one of adult child and elderly parent. There may be two or more of them. There may be sexual intimacy, or more likely, not. They may be ex-lovers who have continued to reside together and remain "friends". We may look for separate institutions but boundaries may be blurred. We are not talking about a homogenous group. Their financial affairs may be "inextricably intertwined".[412]

English law has taken tentative steps to accommodate non-conjugal relationships, within the context of domestic violence, by constructing the concept of the "associated person".[413] This embraces a wide, and widening, group including relatives,[414] fiancé(e)s and ex-fiancé(e)s, and those who have had "an intimate personal relationship" (without cohabiting).[415] But neither legislation nor blueprints for change (Law Commission reports, for example) extend the homesharer concept beyond domestic violence.

By contrast, the Law Commission of Canada[416] has urged that we go back to the drawing board and ask why relationships matter. Such an examination would make us think "outside the marital and conjugal box".[417] Marriage is one way, perhaps the most important way, of regulating personal relationships, but it is not the only way. But, rather than starting with this, with the inevitable consequence that everything else gets measured against the yardstick of marriage, the Canadian report starts with the fundamental values which it believes should guide the development of government policies: these are pre-eminently equality and autonomy.[418] In the light of these principles, it concluded that the distinction between conjugal and non-conjugal relationships is inconsistent with the value of equality, and that autonomy is furthered if "the state's stance is one of neutrality regarding the individual's choices whether to enter into personal relationships".[419]

3

UNDERSTANDING DOMESTIC VIOLENCE

INTRODUCTION

Domestic violence was rediscovered in the early 1970s. That is to say, it emerged as a recognised social problem then. But violence against women has always been with us: only rarely (the latter part of the nineteenth century being the foremost previous instance: see Doggett, 1992 and Cobbe, 1878) is the objective condition interpreted as a problem worthy of attention. It was Erin Pizzey's *Scream Quietly or The Neighbours Will Hear* in 1974[1] which brought domestic violence to public attention. Pizzey was, initially,[2] extremely influential, but she was speaking to an audience already sensitised by the Women's Movement.[3] The problem of violence against women tends to be perceived as a problem in periods when there is an active feminist movement.[4] But for much of history it has remained hidden; a state of denial has often prevailed. However, as Jalna Hanmer has written; "the use of force and its threat ... is ... a major component in the social control of women by men".[5]

Domestic violence is defined by the Home Office as "any violence between current and former partners in an intimate relationship, wherever and whenever the violence occurs. The violence may include physical, sexual, emotional and financial abuse".[6] It is primarily a problem of men's abuse of women, though it does exist in same-sex relationships,[7] and there is also evidence of men being abused by women.[8] The abuse of men is much less common (though government statistics suggest that in nearly one in five reported incidents men are the victims).[9] Men are also less likely to be seriously injured,[10] less likely to be a repeat victim and are not usually fearful of being at home. It may be that men tend to report more trivial incidents[11] Much violence by women, it is thought, may be acts of self-defence.[12] Differences according to gender are thus marked. The law treats victims of both genders identically. In this chapter, there will be no further consideration of male victims specifically, and the language used will assume domestic violence against women.

Though once described as "le vice anglais", domestic violence is not unique to this country. A study of ten European countries found that one in four women will experience domestic violence in their lifetime and one in eight annually.[13] UK government statistics reveal the extent of the problem, with an estimated 635,000 annual incidents in England and Wales (81 per cent of the victims being women).[14] A national "Day To Count" in 2000 revealed that the police receive a call for assistance every minute from domestic violence victims: 85 per cent of these calls are from women assaulted by men.[15] The true extent of domestic violence is not known because, for various reasons, there is widespread under-reporting. Levels of reporting may be rising: there is increased awareness of the problem and the availability of remedies. Even so, according to Home Office figures, only 35 per cent of incidents are reported.[16]

It should be stressed that domestic violence has serious implications for the safety and well-being of children. Indeed, it may be said to be a form of child abuse.[17] From 40 to 70 per cent of children who witness abuse against their mothers are themselves likely to be physically abused by the same men (who may, or may not, be their fathers).[18] Domestic violence often occurs during contact visits: contact indeed may be used as an opportunity to continue harassment or abuse.[19] Some 25,000 children stay in Women's Aid refuges annually.

CAN IT BE EXPLAINED?

How is domestic violence to be explained? There are a number of myths,[20] which can easily be disposed of. Thus, it has frequently been asserted that it is a working-class phenomenon and is attributable to a sub-culture of violence thought to reside in such a population.[21] But domestic violence crosses all social class barriers. It is also said that violence in sexual relations is directly related to violence against wives because marriage is the main outlet for legitimating sexual intercourse. But there is little biological linkage between sex and violence, though the two may be linked in particular cultures, such as our own. It does not have to be so: Mead reports on the Arapesh of New Guinea who know nothing of rape and have no "conception of male nature that might make rape understandable to them".[22] There is also the "catharsis myth",[23] discredited elsewhere but occasionally still propagated to explain domestic violence. Severe violence, it suggests, can be reduced if "normal aggression is allowed to be expressed" and "tension is released". Myths are a form of defence mechanism: the family is an important social institution, and the myths have grown up as shields to protect it.[24]

Domestic violence has been explained in a number of ways. The earlier interpretations emphasised pathology: the men were sick, suffered from mental illness, were alcohol or drug abusers, or had inadequate personalities.[25] But this view individualises the problem: it treats it as "exceptionalistic" (Ryan, 1976, p.17). Another interpretation attributes domestic violence to frustration, stress and blocked goals. It locates the sources of battering in social-structural factors: poverty and unemployment are commonly cited.[26] For Richard Gelles (1972, p.185), "violence is an adaptation or response to structural stress". This produces frustration which is often followed by violence. The lower socio-economic classes are most likely to suffer from the stressful conditions depicted here, through the better-off have other stressful conditions to contend with. Violence may be an adaptation to stressful structural conditions, but the theory does not explain why: what the casual relationship is, if any, between economic conditions and domestic violence.[27]

Some try to explain abuse by blaming the victim. Pizzey and Shapiro (1982) even suggested victims are addicted to violence, so that they will seek out violent relationships. Women who are bad housekeepers and women who "nag" are said to provoke violence, even perhaps deserve it.

What all these explanations ignore is patriarchy.[28] Domestic violence is about power. It is not, any more than is rape, an "explosion of testosterone" (Wilson, 1983, p.199). In these terms violence by men against women in the home should not be seen as a breakdown in the social order, as orthodox interpretations have perceived it, but as an affirmation of a particular sort of social order.[29] Looked at in this way domestic violence is not dysfunctional; quite the reverse, it appears functional. And, of course, the law has played a part, perhaps a major part, not just in reproducing this social order, but in actually constituting and defining that order (Freeman, 1984). As Freeman noted:

"The legal form is one of the main modalities of social practice through which actual relationships embodying sexual stratification have been expressed. Law defines the character and creates the institutions and social relationships within which the family operates. The legal system is constantly recreating a particular ideological view of relationships between the sexes, best expressed as an ideology of patriarchalism". (1984, p.55)

Thus, the law not only permitted a husband corporally to chastise his wife, but expected him to do so.[30] Blackstone (1765, p.444) argued that the husband's liberties to chastise (and confine) his wife arose out of the doctrine of coverture. He explained:

"As he is to answer for her misbehaviour, the law thought it reasonable to entrust him with this power of restraining her, by domestic chastisement, in the same moderation that a man is allowed to correct his apprentices or children. ... This power of correction was confined within reasonable bounds, and the husband was prohibited from using any violence towards his wife ...".

Nevertheless, he had the liberty to beat her with a stick so long as it was no thicker than his thumb: the origins of the so-called "rule of thumb".[31] Though doubts have been cast on the authority and authenticity of such a rule, it was believed and doubtless employed by centuries of men.[32] The rule, if such it be, could not really survive the ruling in *R v Jackson* in 1891[33] that a husband could not enforce the "general dominion" he had over his wife by imprisoning her if she refused him the conjugal rights to which a court had declared him entitled. (This decision caused riots in Blackburn, where Mrs Jackson had been detained!; see Rubinstein, 1986.) But the liberty to chastise was only finally judicially disapproved in 1978.[34]

The marital rape immunity survived even longer, until 1991.[35] John Stuart Mill (in 1869, p.32) was savagely critical.

"A female slave has (in Christian countries) an admitted right ... to refuse to her master the last familiarity. Not so the wife ... her husband can claim from her and enforce the lowest degradation of a human being, that of being made the instrument of an animal function contrary to her inclination".

It may be assumed that the origin of the marital rape immunity is in the writings of the seventeenth-century judge, Sir Matthew Hale.[36] He argued: "... the husband cannot be guilty of rape committed by himself upon his lawful wife, for by their mutual matrimonial consent and contract the wife hath given up herself in this kind unto her husband, which she cannot retract". Since married women could not then make contracts—and could not do so until 1935[37]—what Hale was in effect saying was that a woman's last exercise of contractual autonomy was agreeing to marriage, with all that is entailed.

The marital rape immunity was removed in the landmark House of Lords decision of *R v R*.[38] The Lords held that to say a woman consented irrevocably to sexual intercourse with her husband was "unacceptable" in modern times; marriage was now "a partnership of equals".[39]

In a patriarchal society "male dominance must be maintained at all costs, because the person who dominates cannot conceive of any alternative but to be dominated in turn".[40] And, according to Bell and Newby (1976, p.154), "the belief on the part of many wives that not only do their husbands possess greater power but in the last analysis, they *ought* to do so, is the kind of belief that occurs in other highly stratified social situations". Deference derives from power but in time becomes a moral position. Sex-role socialisation and the ideologies associated with the home (and see Oakley, 1974) are sufficiently effective strategies to have turned might into right in marriages. But, as Bell and Newby point out:

"'might' remains very close to the surface. Deference stabilizes the hierarchical nature of the husband–wife relationship, but ... the relationship is embedded in a system of power—the naked use of this power can be, and is, resorted to if the relationship threatens to break down. Two sorts of power ... form the constant background to the deferential dialectic between husbands and wives. These are the power of the hand and the power of the purse." (1976, p.164)

The Dobashes (1980, pp.22–24) argue that men who use violence are merely conforming to cultural norms that endorse dominance and the enforcement of that dominance. Violence often occurs when women do not fulfil their expected traditional roles: violence being used to reassert authority. Burton and Kitzinger (1998) found that almost one in four young men thought it was right to hit a woman who slept with someone else. Forcing a wife or girl friend to have sex was also deemed to be acceptable, and "disrespectful" women also were thought to deserve "punishment".[41] In Hearn's research male violence is seen by perpetrators as "being a man" and symbolically showing "being a man" (1998, p.37).

EARLY LEGAL RESPONSES

The law is never going to conquer domestic violence. Only a cultural revolution will achieve that.[42] There were a few stuttering attempts in the nineteenth century, including the development of the separation order.[43] But nothing really happened until the mid–1970s.[44] Until the Domestic Violence and Matrimonial Proceedings Act 1976, victims had had to rely on the law of tort (which few did)[45] or the criminal law, and here they encountered an unsympathetic police response. The police view of domestic violence (or as they preferred to call it, "domestic disturbances") in the mid–1970s can be neatly summarised by quoting the Association of Chief Police Officers' evidence to the House of Commons Select Committee:

"Whilst such problems take up considerable Police time ... in the majority of cases the role of the Police is a negative one. We are, after all, dealing with persons 'bound in marriage', and it is important, for a host of reasons, to maintain the unity of the spouses ...".[46]

The 1976 Act, followed by another in 1978,[47] took the civil law approach to domestic violence. Before the Act it was impossible to obtain an injunction (prohibiting violence) unless a substantive remedy such as damages was also sought. Some women did sue violent partners in tort and claim damages (usually 40 shillings) even though all they really wanted was an injunction. The 1976 Act provided that a spouse or a cohabitant could seek either a non-molestation or an exclusion injunction from the county court without having to seek another remedy at the same time. It will be observed that the term used is "molestation", not domestic violence. "Molestation", which was not defined then nor since in later legislation, is clearly wider in scope than violence. It has been interpreted to include not just violence, but harassment, pestering and threatening behaviour.[48]

The exclusion injunction could have had even greater significance. Rather than a victim having to leave the home and seek refuge in a shelter, it enabled her to evict the abuser and return in safety. An exclusion injunction excluded the abuser from part or all of the matrimonial (or quasi-matrimonial)[49] home or from the area in which it was situated, or required him to permit her to return to it. There was initial reluctance by courts to exclude an abuser who wasn't a spouse:[50] this was conceded in an important House of Lords decision in 1978.[51] Lord Denning M.R had proclaimed (in the Court of Appeal) that where justice required it "personal rights ... should be given priority over rights of property".[52] But the courts remained unhappy at giving exclusion orders. They saw them as "draconian"[53] and were most reluctant to grant them where there was no proof of violence.

The other novelty of the 1976 legislation gave a judge the power to attach a power of arrest to an injunction provided the abuser had caused actual bodily harm to his spouse or cohabitant or a child, and he considered he was likely to do so again.[54] This was a valuable innovation because injunctions are frequently broken and, before the 1976 Act, this meant returning to the court. However, the Court of Appeal quickly ruled that the power of arrest was not to be regarded as a "routine remedy".[55] It soon became apparent that they regarded powers of arrest (a quasi-criminal remedy for a civil order) as "draconian" as well.[56]

So the 1976 Act (and similar powers given to magistrates in 1978) did not work as well as was hoped. In particular, because of a House of Lords ruling in *Richards v Richards* in 1984,[57] courts considering whether to issue an exclusion injunction were required to have regard among other things to the conduct of the spouses in relation to each other. This placed too much emphasis on conduct and too little on the effects of this as felt by the victims.

THE FAMILY LAW ACT 1996: CIVIL REMEDIES

As a result of a Law Commission report in 1992,[58] the civil law was reformed in 1996. With a few additions this remains the law today.

The Family Law Act 1996 provides for two categories of orders. Non-molestation orders[59] and, what are now called, occupation orders.[60] All three levels of courts, the High Court, county courts and magistrates' courts have jurisdiction to make these orders.[61] There are also powers to grant orders *ex parte*,[62] to accept undertakings in lieu of making orders[63] and to enforce orders.[64] There is also a remarkable power, provided for but never brought into operation, which would have enabled a third party (in practice the police) to apply for an order where they had attended at an incident of molestation and had reasonable cause to believe that abuse had occurred.[65] There are dangers in adopting this approach. First, it may disempower victims, so that private violence is replaced by a form of public paternalism; second, it could lead the police into redefining domestic violence as a civil rather than a criminal matter (see further Burton, 2003).

The non-molestation order

Non-molestation orders are made much more frequently than occupation orders.[66] They are less intrusive; they do not require anyone to leave his home.

A non-molestation order is an order containing either or both of the following provisions—

(a) provision prohibiting ... the respondent from molesting another person who is associated with the respondent;

(b) provision prohibiting the respondent from molesting a relevant child.[67]

As already indicated, "molestation" is not defined. There are a number of cases which illustrate the meaning and scope of molestation without confining it. There was always a danger that legislating a meaning would have done just this. According to Ormrod L.J. "it applies to any conduct which can properly be regarded as such a degree of harassment as to call for the intervention of the court".[68] Rifling through a woman's handbag,[69] writing abusive letters and shouting obscenities,[70] and giving photographs of a former lover to the press[71] have all been held to be molestation.

To apply for a non-molestation order the applicant must be an "associated person".[72] This concept could have been avoided.[73] It would have been possible to open up this protection to anyone, for example neighbours, tenants and victims of sexual harassment. It might have been possible to protect against the workplace bully by means of a non-molestation order (see Barmes, 2006). But the Law Commission reasoned that a domestic relationship justified special remedies and procedures. Those included within the associated person concept are wide, and the list was further extended by the Civil Partnership Act 2004[74] and the Domestic Violence, Crime and Victims Act 2004.[75]

"A person is 'associated with' another person if—

(a)   they are, or have been, married to each other;

(aa)   they are or have been civil partners of each other;

(b)   they are cohabitants or former cohabitants;

(c)   they live or have lived in the same household, otherwise than merely by reason of one of them being the other's employee, tenant, lodger or boarder;

(d)   they are relatives;

(e)   they have agreed to marry one another (whether or not that agreement has been terminated);

(eza) they have entered into a civil partnership agreement (whether or not that agreement has been terminated);

(ea)   they have or have had an intimate personal relationship with each other which is or was of significant duration;

(f)   in relation to any child, they are both persons falling within subsection (4); or

(g)   they are parties to the same family proceedings."

Subsection (4) provides that a person falls within this subsection in relation to a child if he is a parent of the child or has or has had parental responsibility for the child. A child under 16 may apply for an order, with leave of the court: this may only be granted if the court is satisfied that the child has sufficient understanding to make the application.[76]

The "associated persons" concept is broad, perhaps too broad (Cretney, 2003, p.254). There are few family relationships omitted (cousins are not included—one wonders why!). The courts have adopted a purposive construction of the concept and shown a willingness to include rather than exclude in borderline situations. Thus, in *G v G (Non-Molestation Order: Jurisdiction)*[77] a woman who spent two nights a week with a man, had a sexual relationship with him and a joint bank account was cohabiting within the meaning of (b) ((ea) was not then in the list). It is not even necessary that the dispute be a family dispute: brothers with a business dispute have been held to be within the jurisdiction.[78] Once it is accepted that a purposive interpretation is to be adopted, it is difficult to see a case for excluding any applicants. The list of "associated persons" has already been extended twice. Why not just allow anyone to seek a non-molestation order?

A non-molestation order may be made on a free-standing application, or where an application is made in other family proceedings.[79] The court may also make an order of its own motion if it considers that the order should be made for the benefit of any other party or of any relevant child.[80] When considering whether to make an occupation order, a court must also consider whether to make a non-molestation order of its own motion.[81] The reason for this is that the police may arrest without warrant for breach of a non-molestation order, but not for breach of an occupation order.

Before the 1996 Act there were no criteria laid down indicating when a non-molestation order should be granted. Section 42(5) now requires the court to focus on "the need to secure the health, safety, and well-being" of the applicant and any relevant child. It is thus the victim's need for protection, rather than the abuser's conduct,[82] which is important. This raises the question as to whether a non-molestation order can be made against a respondent who cannot help it: one who suffers from mental illness or dementia.[83] Despite the decision in *Banks v Banks*[84] (which was only a county court decision) it is possible to make a non-molestation order against such a person (Mrs Banks was a 77-year-old manic depressive unable to control her behaviour), but enforcement is difficult. A person can only be guilty of contempt of court if s/he has sufficient mental capacity to understand the effects of the court order.[85] Cases of troublesome teenagers and of alcoholics and drug addicts will test the courts. Perhaps, the family courts are the wrong place to deal with them.[86]

A non-molestation order can refer to molestation in general and/or to particular acts of molestation (for example, telephoning the victim).[87] It may be made for a specified period or until further order.[88] Under the the pre–1996 law it was understood that non-molestation orders were to give a breathing space to the parties.[89] This is no longer so, and an order can now be made of indefinite duration in appropriate circumstances.[90] A non-molestation order made in other family proceedings, for example on an application for a contact order, ceases to have effect if those proceedings are withdrawn or dismissed.[91] This provision passed uncontentiously, but is unfortunate: the non-molestation order may still be required; indeed, the application for contact may have been dismissed because of the applicant's domestic violence.[92]

Instead of making an order, the court may accept an undertaking from any party to the proceedings.[93] This is enforceable as if it were a court order.[94] It can no longer accept an undertaking instead of making a non-molestation order where it appears the respondent has used or threatened violence against the applicant or a relevant child, and a non-molestation order is necessary so that any breach may be punishable as a criminal offence.[95]

Under the 1996 Act, continuing the policy of the 1976 Act, a power of arrest could be attached to a non-molestation order.[96] The Domestic Violence, Crime and Victims Act 2004 has removed the power of arrest for non-molestation orders (it is retained for occupation orders). Breaches of non-molestation orders are now dealt with either in civil proceedings for contempt of court (as previously) or as a criminal offence.[97] This is a new and controversial offence introduced by the Domestic Violence, Crime and Victims Act 2004.[98]

Breach of a non-molestation order is, as is any other breach of a court order, contempt of court. The contemnor can be fined or imprisoned for up to two years. The courts are ever more willing to impose prison sentences today to send out the message that domestic violence will not be tolerated. In *H v O (Contempt of Court: Sentencing)* the court thought "Parliament and society generally now regard domestic and other violence associated with harassment and molestation as demanding rather more condign deterrent punishment than formerly".[99] The father received a nine-month sentence. The court stressed the importance of passing comparable sentences to those a criminal court would impose, while paying regard to the maximum sentence available for contempt of court. This was approved more recently in *Murray v Robinson*,[100] where there was a non-violent breach of a non-molestation order. The lack of violence, held the court, was not sufficient to reduce the gravity of the breach, particularly where, as here, the conduct occurred in or close to the victim's home, when the feeling of insecurity created might be very considerable. The court acknowledged that imprisonment was not a long-term solution in the context of the breakdown of a family relationship. It noted the paucity of alternative punishments: many more are available to criminal courts. It also observed that if a case warranted a sentence near the top of the range, the appropriate course was to bring proceedings under the Protection from Harassment Act 1997,[101] where greater powers of punishment were available to the court.

The 2004 Act makes breach of a non-molestation order a criminal offence: "a person who without reasonable excuse does anything that he is prohibited from doing by a non-molestation order is guilty of an offence".[102] The breach does not have to involve violence. The maximum sentence on indictment is imprisonment for five years plus a fine. This is three years more than the maximum sentence for contempt of court. There is a choice between the two methods of enforcement—only one procedure can be used since the defendant cannot be punished twice over[103]—but we may predict that the criminal route will be preferred, certainly by the police. Whether it will make victims reluctant to seek non-molestation orders because of the potential involvement in criminal proceedings (see Bessant, 2005) remains to be seen.

The occupation order

Occupation orders are much more complicated. Their rationale is simple. The victim of domestic violence may consider that her safety in the home can only be secured by excluding her abuser. Or she may have fled the home but, with nowhere better to stay, may wish to return. The order has more serious consequences than a non-molestation order: it interferes with the enjoyment of property rights. The goal of applicants may depend upon who they are: so-called "entitled" applicants may be seeking long-term regulation of the property (perhaps a place to bring up children in a safe environment); non-entitled applicants may be looking for a short-term solution. The Act does not use the "associated person" concept when dealing with occupation orders. Rather it distinguishes between applicants in terms of their property rights.

Entitled applicants are persons who are entitled to occupy the house by virtue of a beneficial estate or interest or contract or enactment giving the right to remain in occupation or have home rights.[104] Such an applicant may seek an order where the house is, or at any time has been, the home of the applicant and a person with whom he is associated, or was intended by them to be their home.[105]

There are declaratory orders[106] and, more significantly regulatory orders.[107] These may enforce entitlement to remain as against the respondent; require the respondent to permit the applicant to enter and remain in the house or part of it; regulate the occupation by either or both; prohibit, suspend or restrict the exercise by the respondent of his right to occupy the house; if the respondent has home rights in relation to the house, and the applicant is the other spouse or civil partner, restrict or terminate those rights; require the respondent to leave the house or part of it; or exclude the respondent from a defined area in which the house is included (this may be a few hundred yards or conceivably a large area).[108]

When should a regulatory order be made? As we have seen, under previous legislation there was too much emphasis on the conduct of the respondent, rather than upon the needs of the applicant and any children. The Law Commission, in addressing this, proposed a "balance of harm" test. The object is to be fair to respondents and also to offer protection to victims. And, where the effects on the victims are sufficiently grave, to give the courts a duty to make an order. Section 33(7) accordingly provides that if it appears to the court that the applicant or any relevant child is "likely to suffer significant harm attributable to the conduct of the respondent" if an order is not made, the court "shall" make the order unless it appears that "the respondent or any relevant child is likely to suffer harm if the order is made", and "the harm likely to be suffered by the respondent or child ... is as great as, or greater than, the harm attributable to conduct of the respondent which is likely to be suffered by the applicant or child if the order is not made". The term "significant harm" is taken from the Children Act 1989,[109] and will be discussed in a later chapter.[110] "Harm" is defined (in s.63(3)) to mean, in relation to an adult, ill-treatment or the impairment of health or development. "Ill-treatment" includes sexual abuse, but only in relation to children. Can this be intentional (are adult women not sexually abused)? If it is a slip, there have been opportunities to correct it, and nothing has been done (and see Diduck and Kaganas, 2006, p.468).

A good illustration of the "balance of harm" test in practice is *B v B (Occupation Order)*[111] The case concerned a married couple with two children: the husband's son, aged six, from a previous marriage, and their baby. The husband was violent and the wife left with the baby and was rehoused—by the local authority in bed and breakfast accommodation. The husband stayed with his son in the council flat (of which he and the wife were joint tenants). The court was satisfied that if it made no order, the mother and baby would continue to live in unsatisfactory temporary accommodation, and would suffer significant harm, attributable to the husband's violence. But the court also accepted that if the husband and his son were excluded from the flat they too would suffer significant harm: the local authority would not be under any obligation to house them, since they would be characterised as intentionally homeless[112] (the child would go into care). The mother, however, would eventually be rehoused in suitable accommodation (she had a "priority need").[113] So no occupation order was made. The court was concerned to stress that "the message" of the case was not that fathers who treat their partners violently and cause them to leave home can expect to remain in occupation of previously shared accommodation. It was important that this was pointed out, because many would take just that message from the court's reasoning.

If the balance of harm test is satisfied, the court must make an order. If it is not, it does not follow that an order will not be made. It may, after considering factors listed in s.33(6). Under s.33(6) the court is required to have regard to all the circumstances including:

"(a)   the housing needs and resources of each of the parties and of any relevant child;

(b)   the financial resources of each of the parties;

(c)   the likely effect of any order, or of any decision by the court not to exercise its powers ... on the health, safety or well-being of the parties and of any relevant child; and

(d)   the conduct of the parties in relation to each other and otherwise".

The courts have continued to stress that occupation orders are "draconian".[114] They override property rights, and can therefore be justified only in exceptional circumstances. Nevertheless, it would seem that more occupation orders are being made (there were more than three times as many in 2003 as in 1996, the last year of the old law).[115]

Until the 1976 legislation orders were generally limited to three months' duration.[116] Under the 1996 Act they may be made for a specified period, until the occurrence of a specified event, or until further order. Orders of unlimited duration may thus be made.[117]

An occupation order may also be obtained by a non-entitled applicant but only one who is a cohabitant (protected by the 1976 Act as well, through critics in 1995–1996 did not appreciate this!),[118] a former cohabitant,[119] former spouses[120] and, since the Civil Partnership Act 2004, former civil partners.[121] The order must be sought in respect of a house which is the home they are living in, or have at any time lived in or intended to live in together (as their married home or civil partnership home).[122] The court may make both declaratory provisions and regulatory

ones. They provide the same protection to non-entitled applicants as entitled applicants have.

The criteria governing the making of an order in favour of a
former spouse or former civil partner are the same four listed in
s.33(6) (for entitled applicants), plus three additional ones:
namely, the length of time that has elapsed since the parties
ceased to live together; the length of time that has elapsed since
the marriage or civil partnership was dissolved or annulled; and
the existence of any pending proceedings between them.[123] For
cohabitants and former cohabitants, the court must consider, in
addition to the factors common to entitled applicants and former
spouses and former civil partners, the nature of the parties'
relationship and in particular the level of commitment involved
in it; the length of time during which they have cohabited;
whether there are or have been any children who are children of
both parties or for whom both parties have or have had parental
responsibility; the length of time that has elapsed since the
parties ceased to live together; and, the existence of any pending
proceedings between them over property.[124]

The most interesting of these factors refers to the nature of the
parties' relationship and their commitment. It can be traced to,
and replaces, the provision in s.41 of the 1996 Act, discussed in
Chapter 2.[125] It is doubtful whether s.41 achieved anything and
unlikely that the reference to relationship and commitment will
assist courts over-much. They do not need to be told the difference between a Mrs Burns[126] or Mrs Kokosinski[127] and the
secretary who moves into her boss's house for a couple of
months and then tries to exclude him from the property.

Unlike the provision for entitled applicants, where orders can
be made for an unlimited period, non-entitled applicants are
offered only short-term protection. In the case of former spouses
and former civil partners, the order must not exceed six months,
although it may be extended on one or more occasions.[128] In the
case of cohabitants and former cohabitants, the maximum period
is also six months and only one extension is permitted.[129]

The final category is where neither party is entitled to remain
in occupation of the home: that is neither spouse nor civil partner
has a property right in respect of the family home. Similarly,
former spouses, civil partners or cohabitants may be living in
property in which neither has the right to remain (perhaps as
squatters or bare licensees).[130] The law pre-1996 permitted
spouses and cohabitants to obtain ouster injunctions in these
circumstances, and the 1996 Act continues this policy and

extends it to other non-entitled applicants. As far as spouses, civil partners, former spouses and former civil partners are concerned, the criteria for making an occupation order are the same as apply to entitled applicants, including the balance of harm presumptions. The maximum duration of an order is six months: one extension only is permitted. When the applicant is a cohabitant or former cohabitant, the court must have regard to housing needs, financial resources, the likely effect of any order on the health, safety or well-being of the parties or a relevant child, and the parties' conduct, and then consider the balance of harm test (though here as a presumption). The maximum duration of an order is six months: one extension is permitted.

On or after making an occupation order—except where it is made in the case of neither party having entitlement to occupy— the court has a number of ancillary powers.[131] It can impose repair and maintenance obligations, require a party to pay the rent, mortgages or other outgoings, and impose obligations in respect of the furniture or other contents of the house. This is important because it may be that an ousted respondent may wish to take revenge by stripping the house bare before he leaves.[132] When considering whether and, if so, how to exercise these ancillary powers, the court must consider all the circumstances of the case, including the parties' financial needs and resources, present and future financial obligations, including those to any relevant child. These are important powers but there is, apparently, no way of enforcing ancillary orders. The Court of Appeal thought this a serious omission requiring urgent parliamentary attention.[133] That was in 2000: nothing has been done, through the opportunity to plug the gap clearly presented itself in 2004.

As we saw, breach of a non-molestation order is now a criminal offence: breach of an occupation order is not. However, when a court is deciding whether to make an occupation order, it must decide whether to make a non-molestation order of its own motion.[134] In many cases it is as a result likely that breach of an occupation order will amount to a criminal offence: the same acts being breaches of both orders. An occupation order can still have a power of arrest attached to it. A non-molestation order cannot. However, the court may attach a power of arrest to a non-molestation order when making an occupation order.[135]

The court can attach a power of arrest to an occupation order.[136] The power differs depending on whether the occupation order was made with notice or *ex parte* (without notice).[137] As far as orders on notice are concerned, if it appears to the court that the respondent has used or threatened violence against the applicant or a relevant child, it *must* attach a power of arrest unless it is satisfied that the applicant or any child will otherwise be adequately protected.[138] The Court of Appeal has held that a power of arrest can be imposed for a shorter period than the other provisions in the order.[139] This is an odd disjuncture: why weaken the enforcement procedure in the middle of an order? Does this indicate that the duration of the order may itself be too long? On the other hand, it may be thought unjust to expose the respondent to arrest for a longer period than is strictly necessary.

Where the order is made *ex parte*, the court *may* attach a power of arrest, but only if the respondent has used or threatened violence against the applicant or a relevant child, and there is a risk that the applicant or child will suffer significant harm as a result of the respondent's conduct if the power of arrest is not attached immediately.[140]

A power of arrest permits a constable to arrest without warrant a person whom he has reasonable cause to suspect is in breach of any provision in an order to which the power of arrest is attached.[141] The person arrested must be brought before a judge or justice of the peace within 24 hours.[142] If the matter is not disposed of, he may be remanded in custody or on bail. A person arrested for breach of an order must be bought before the relevant court for contempt. A minor cannot be committed to contempt, but a power of arrest may still be attached to an occupation order in respect of him. This may be useful in order to remove him from premises where he is causing concern to the occupants. In *Re H (Respondent Under 18: Power of Arrest)*,[143] an occupation order was made, with a power of arrest attached, ordering a 17-year-old son, who had been violent and abusive to his parents, to leave the house where he was living with his parents and not to return, to enter, or attempt to enter it. He challenged the decision to attach a power of arrest. The Court of Appeal held that one could be attached. The court was concerned with the limited powers it has to deal with persons under 18 who are in contempt of court, but who cannot be committed. Ironically, if the order were a non-molestation order breach by a 17-year-old could prosecuted as a criminal offence.

Where there is serious domestic violence it may be necessary to proceed swiftly, so swiftly in fact that the respondent is not given an opportunity to defend himself before the order is made. There are civil liberties issues here and Art.6 of the European

Convention on Human Rights is particularly pertinent. Section 45 of the 1996 Act permits courts to make both non-molestation and occupation orders *ex parte*. It is arguable that an *ex parte* occupation order infringes a person's rights under Art.6. To fall within Art.6, removal from one's home would have to be interpreted as a punishment. It could be argued that it is not, since the application is brought by an individual, not the state, and the purpose is not to punish the respondent but protect the applicant (see Herring, 2004, p.264).

A court may make both non-molestation and occupation orders *ex parte* where "it considers it just and convenient to do so".[144] It must have regard to any risk of significant harm to the applicant or a relevant child, attributable to the conduct of the respondent, if the order is not made immediately. It must also have regard to whether the applicant will be deterred or prevented from pursuing the application if an order is not made immediately, and whether there is any reason to believe the respondent is aware of the proceedings but is deliberately evading service and that an applicant or relevant child will be seriously prejudiced by the delay involved in effecting service.[145] A power of arrest can be attached to an *ex parte* occupation order, which may last for a shorter period than other provisions in the order.[146] The court must give the respondent the opportunity of a full hearing as soon as is just and convenient.

OTHER CIVIL REMEDIES

Civil remedies for domestic violence are also found elsewhere. The Protection from Harassment Act 1997, as well as creating new criminal offences (to be discussed below), created a statutory tort of harassment.[147] A person who is, or may be, the victim of harassment—broadly defined, as we shall see in our discussion of the criminal offence—may seek damages for anxiety caused by harassment and any financial loss which results.[148] The High Court and county courts are also able to grant injunctions to prohibit further harassment, and the claimant may apply for a warrant of arrest to be issued where s/he considers that the defendant has broken the terms of the injunction.[149] If the injunction is breached, the defendant is in contempt of court: he has also committed an offence under the 1997 Act if there is no reasonable excuse.[150] Despite the fact that breach of such an injunction amounts to a criminal offence, the standard of proof required for the injunction remains the civil standard. The Divisional Court in so holding distinguished seeking an injunction under s.3 from an anti-social behaviour order sought by a public authority—where the criminal standard applies[151]—since an application for an injunction is a private remedy sought by an individual.[152] This is far from convincing, and a challenge using the European Convention on Human Rights can be expected, sooner rather than later.

The possibility also exists of obtaining injunctions in other civil proceedings. There is little need or scope for this, but it is always possible that a situation will fall outside the jurisdiction of both the Family Law Act 1996 and the Protection from Harassment Act 1997. The High Court and county courts may grant an injunction "in all cases in which it appears to the court to be just and convenient to do so".[153] In *Richards v Richards*,[154] the House of Lords held that an injunction under this jurisdiction can only be granted to support an existing legal or equitable right. It might therefore be open to a victim of domestic violence to sue in tort, for assault or battery for example, and claim an injunction to restrain further violence. But this is exactly where we were before 1976. What is the point? "Harassment" (in the 1997 Act) and "molestation" (in the 1996 Act) are both wider in scope anyway. It was also considered in *Richards v Richards* that where Parliament had laid down a statutory regime, this should govern, rather than any common law jurisdiction.

Whether there remains, in addition, inherent jurisdiction is debatable. Wall J. in *C v K (Inherent Powers; Exclusion Order)*[155] pointed to "a substantial degree of confusion, both about the nature of the inherent jurisdiction and the extent of the powers exercisable under it".[156] *C v K* antedates both the 1996 Act and 1997 Act: both would now cover it (the parties were former cohabitants, there was a relevant child to protect, and there was "harassment"). Wall J. held there was inherent jurisdiction to protect children from harm, as well as co-existing statutory jurisdiction (s.37 of the Supreme Court Act 1981 and s.38 of the County Courts Act 1984) to grant injunctive relief in support of legal and equitable rights. But can these co-exist or is the better view that inherent jurisdiction is now subsumed in statute? After *Richards v Richards* the latter looks the better interpretation. It may be that this is a wholly academic debate. Or it may be that there are cases which will fall outside all the protective nets listed, and where the only recourse will be to inherent jurisdiction. A reading of *C v K* might reveal such a situation. If the grandmother had not been granted a residence order, powers under ss.37 and 58 could not have been invoked. If her abusive joint tenant had not been a former cohabitant (and also someone with whom she had had an intimate personal relationship) the 1996 Act would have been a non-starter in relation to herself (though clearly her grandson was a relevant child). If the joint tenant had not been violent, but had only brought prostitutes on to the premises, it is doubtful whether there would have been "harassment" within the 1997 Act. As can be seen, it is not easy to construct a scenario where inherent jurisdiction might remain valuable, but, it is submitted, it might well exist.

THE CRIMINAL JUSTICE RESPONSE

We must now consider the criminal law. It would be possible to construct a distinct crime of "wife-beating".[157] English law has never considered this. Rape of a wife was not considered a crime until the immunity from prosecution was removed by the House of Lords in 1991,[158] and subsequently by legislation.[159] The law on assault had inbuilt ambivalence: of course, assaulting a wife was criminal, but for a long time the view persisted that husbands had the right to correct wives (and they weren't expected to do so by setting them "lines"!).

It is now the case that a husband or wife (as obviously a cohabitant and civil partner) can be prosecuted for any of the offences against the person that a stranger can, ranging from common assault to murder. Of course, some acts widely regarded as domestic violence, such as withholding money and belittling, are not crimes. If criminal proceedings are brought the spouse is both competent to give evidence and compellable to do so.[160] Although there is no empirical data, it seems that only rarely will a wife be compelled to give evidence against her husband.

The criminal justice system was little used by victims of domestic violence until recently. There are a number of reasons for this. There was the attitude of the police. They didn't see domestic violence as truly criminal. In their eyes it was "a family matter" or a "private affair". Police attitudes were in part shaped by assumptions about the role of women in society, the importance attached to "family life" and the perceived need for families to stay intact.[161] But they were also influenced by concerns that victims would change their minds, refuse to press charges and, therefore, waste police time. The occasional police officer had been injured on a domestic violence call: stories about such incidents nourished police negative attitudes towards it.[162] Policing is a macho institution and sexist attitudes to women, even to female police officers, will die very slowly.

In 1990 the Home Office reminded police officers of "their responsibility to respond ... to requests from victims for help, and of their powers to take action in cases of violence".[163] Gradually, the police have become more interventionist. Following a North American model, particularly associated with Duluth and Minneapolis, pro-arrest and no drop policies developed.[164] Domestic violence units were established and domestic violence officers were appointed.[165] Despite these important initiatives, there was still evidence of a reluctance to arrest, even of failures to record domestic violence incidents as crimes (they were "no-crimed"). In 2000 the Home Office issued another circular.[166] This introduced a presumption of arrest: if an arrest was not effected the officer has to record in writing the reasons. The circular instructs officers to speak to the victim and alleged assailant separately. The victim is to be asked if she wants the matter to be taken to court. It makes it clear that the police role is not conciliation.

By 2004 an inspection report noted that strides had been made, but that "the priority given to domestic violence locally was variable".[167] Thus, arrests were made in 13 to 63 per cent of cases where, potentially, there could have been arrests. The inspectors were also concerned that there was a significant under-recording of domestic violence crime.[168] Where a crime was recorded, only 21 per cent of offenders were charged.[169] Decisions as to whether a crime should be recorded or a charge bought usually depended on the victim's wishes and her willingness to co-operate.[170]

This poses a dilemma. There are good reasons for endorsing a pro-arrest policy.[171] It provides the victim with immediate protection, and if the assailant is held in custody, with time to make plans for her safety. It gives the police "a tangible product" for work conventionally regarded as a waste of time (Morley and Mullender, 1992, p.270). And it sends important messages to all that domestic violence is a serious crime which will not be tolerated. On the other hand, it may not be in the victim's interest. If, as a result the assailant/partner loses his job, her economic security may be threatened. Unless other measures are put in place, arrest may endanger her safety; she may find herself subject to reprisals, and this may be a major reason why she decides to withdraw from the criminal justice process.

Questions have been raised as to whether tough criminal justice responses empower the victim. It may support her sense of human dignity. On the other hand "it may simply entail a transfer of control from the private realm: an individual male batterer; to the public: a largely male coercive institution. Both may be experienced as abusive" (Morley and Mullender, 1992, p.272; see also Coker, 2001, p.807).[172] As indicated already, the law was changed in 1984 to make a spouse a compellable witness in court.[173] There is some concern that this may give women a "choice" between testifying and risking more violence and not testifying and exposing themselves to punishment for contempt of court.[174] The evidence on whether tougher criminal justice responses deters is ambivalent.[175] It would be unrealistic to put our faith in the police as the answer to domestic violence. Much more needs to be done. Perpetrator programmes are required: batterers need to be worked with therapeutically so that they confront their own violence and address it.[176] But therapists who fail clearly to attribute sole responsibility to the batterer, as is the danger, may "collude with batterers by not making their violence the primary issue or by implicitly legitimizing men's excuses for the violence" (Adams, 1988, p.177). This may result in the abuse continuing.

It is the Crown Prosecution Office which decides whether a person arrested should face trial. It was common for it to downgrade charges (Paradine and Wilkinson, 2004, para.6.1). Inspections now suggest that charging has become more appropriate.[177] The CPS has to be satisfied that there is enough evidence to provide "a realistic prospect of conviction". It must also be satisfied that a prosecution is in the public interest. This includes account being taken of "the consequences for the victim of the decision whether or not to prosecute, and any views expressed by the victim or victim's family".[178] The CPS now says that, if the test is satisfied and the victim is willing to give evidence, a prosecution will "almost always" be initiated.[179] If the victim says she does not wish the prosecution to go ahead, and there is a suspicion that she has been pressured to so do, the police will be asked to investigate.[180] In a serious case, she may be compelled to give evidence, but this rarely happens.[181] It is possible for a statement to be admitted without the witness having to appear.[182] This power, in the law since 1988, has rarely been invoked. In addition, the Youth Justice and Criminal Evidence Act 1999 introduced "special measures" which can be taken where a court is satisfied that the quality of a witness's evidence

is "likely to be diminished by reason of fear or distress".[183] These
include enabling a witness to give evidence from behind a screen
so that she is not face-to-face with her assailant;[184] providing a
video-link to give evidence from outside the court;[185] excluding
persons from the court where there are reasonable grounds to
believe they will seek to intimidate the witness (for example the
assailant's family, but not the assailant or his representatives).[186]
It is also proposed that cross-examination may take place by
means of video recording.[187] There is no evidence as yet as to
how much use is being made of these special measures, or as to
their impact. The assumption being made, rightly in the majority
of cases, is that she does not want to drop charges but is inti-
midated. But she may genuinely wish to halt the prosecution
process, having used it, as she sees it positively to renegotiate her
relationship, perhaps to "bring him to his senses".

Criticisms continue to be made of the way the CPS acts. The
Inspectorate report in 2004 found that prosecutors accepted bind-
overs in cases where criminal proceedings were more appropriate.[188] It also found the practice of requiring a victim to appear
in court to explain why she did not wish to proceed persisted.[189]

Very few incidents of domestic violence reported to the police
end in a conviction. The Inspectorate report indicates it is no
more than 5 per cent.[190] There is a high rate of acquittal. But even
when there is a conviction, there has been a tendency for the
sentence to be lenient. Plea-bargaining remains common. Twenty
years ago the Court of Appeal (Criminal Division) ruled that the
fact that a serious assault has occurred in a domestic context is
no mitigation whatsoever. The judge described the way that
serious assaults were rendered "trivial" because of a relationship
of marriage as "completely outdated".[191] Hester *et al.*, in 2003,
found sentences to be more lenient when reference was made to
contact between offenders and their children.[192] The Court of
Appeal (Criminal Division) continues to emphasise that an
incident of violence is not mitigated because it takes place in a
domestic environment.[193] But the task of the courts is not easy:
imprisonment may not benefit the victim if she loses the assailant's income. And, unless his violence is addressed in prison, he
may come out no less violent than when he was incarcerated. On
the other hand, a non-custodial sentence may leave the victim
open to further abuse. It is not surprising that there is a widespread use of binding over in domestic cases. The Sentencing
Guidelines Panel is currently consulting on sentencing in
domestic violence cases. Its task is complex.[194]

As already indicated, the assailant can be charged with the whole range of offences from assault to murder. Police confusion about common assault and their powers in relation to it led to the Police and Criminal Evidence Act 1984 being amended in 2004 to add common assault to the list of offences arrestable without a warrant.[195] This reform was hardly needed, since within a year the distinction between arrestable and non-arrestable offences was abolished: all offences are now arrestable (even dropping litter).[196]

THE PROTECTION FROM HARASSMENT ACT

One piece of legislation of particular relevance to victims of domestic violence is the Protection from Harassment Act 1997. The Act was passed to deal with "stalking",[197] not specifically domestic violence. Section 1 of the Act provides that:

"(1) A person must not pursue a course of conduct—

    (a) which amounts to harassment of another; and

    (b) which he knows or ought to know amounts to harassment of the other.

(2) For the purpose of this section, the person whose course of conduct is in question ought to know that it amounts to harassment of another if a reasonable person in possession of the same information would think the course of conduct amounted to harassment of the other."

"Harassment" is not defined, but s.7(2) provides it includes alarming or causing distress. It also provides that a course of conduct must involve conduct on at least two occasions.[198] A person who pursues a course of conduct in breach of s.21 is guilty of the offence of harassment, and is liable on summary conviction to imprisonment for up to six months or a fine not exceeding level 5 on the standard scale, or both. A course of conduct must involve conduct on at least two occasions: there must be a link between the incidents complained of.[199] Where a link cannot be proved, it may be necessary to fall back on the law of assault, and charge the two instances of this. Harris's research (2000) found police reluctance to reply upon a course of conduct until there were at least three complaints made by the victim.

Section 4 creates a more serious offence, that is to pursue a course of conduct which puts a person in fear of violence. The offence is committed if the person "knows or ought to know that his course of conduct will cause the other so to fear on each of those occasions". The maximum sentence on indictment is five years' imprisonment, a fine or both; on summary conviction six months' imprisonment, the statutory maximum fine or both. Where a person is tried on indictment, the jury may return a verdict under section 2 where they find the accused not guilty under section 4.

Courts also have the power to make a restraining order.[200] As originally enacted they could only do this when the person was convicted under the 1997 Act. The Domestic Violence, Crime and Victims Act 2004 has extended this power to conviction for any offence.[201] A restraining order is like a civil injunction and prohibits the defendant from doing anything which amounts to further harassment or will cause a fear of violence on the part of the victim of the offence or any other person, for example a child. The order can be of fixed or indefinite duration,[202] and can have conditions attached, for example not to contact the victim. It is a civil order: the standard of proof is the civil standard and the civil rules on admissibility of evidence apply. But breach of the order, or any of its terms, without reasonable cause is a criminal offence punishable by imprisonment of up to five years and/or a fine (on summary conviction for up to six months and/or the maximum statutory fine). The 2004 extends the power to make a restraining order to cases where the defendant has been acquitted, if the court considers it necessary to do so to protect a person from harassment by the defendant.[203] This is an example of what is being called, "future law" (Zedner, 2007): feared offenders being made subject to criminal sanctions before they have been convicted of anything. An ECHR challenge is inevitable.

The Court of Appeal (Criminal Division) has given some guidance on sentencing for offences under s.2, s.4 and for breach of a restraining order.[204] It thinks that for a first offence "a short, sharp sentence" may be appropriate, and for a second offence 15 months on a plea of guilty is an appropriate starting point. It lists a number of factors to take account of, including the seriousness of the conduct, the effect on the victim, the offender's mental health and whether he is prepared to undergo treatment and whether he has shown remorse and a recognition that he needs help. Harris's research (2000) found that a conditional discharge and binding over are the most commonly used sentences. The courts are more realistic than the legislature. However, leniency may in part explain the legislature's return to the subject in 2004, and the introduction of restraining orders on an acquittal.

The 1997 Act is being used much more than was anticipated.[205] Harris (2000) found support for its use among the police, the CPS and magistrates. The judiciary, however, thought harassment should be seen as a civil, rather than a criminal, matter. Some magistrates were also concerned that criminalising harassment could lead to malicious accusations. And police and prosecutors were also alert to women they considered to be "paranoid" (Harris, 2000, p.42). Nevertheless, nearly half of the victims in Harris's study had "endured the unwanted behaviour for a significant period before they decided to report it" (2000, p.19). The proportion of harassment cases dropped by the CPS (39 per cent) is much higher than the average for other offences. One-third were terminated because of a reluctance of the victim to proceed.[206] This mirrors findings in the criminal justice system generally. The law's bark looks worse than its bite. The courts have powers to impose severe sentences—according to Court of Appeal (Criminal Division) guidelines, too severe—but sentences are relatively low, and restraining orders are frequently breached (some 40 per cent are).[207] Since only about one-third of those in breach receive custodial sentences,[208] it may be thought that neither offenders nor the courts take the orders very seriously.

There are thus both civil and criminal law responses to domestic violence. There is an increasing shift in emphasis by policy-makers towards tacking domestic violence through the criminal justice system. The value of this is that it emphasises that violence is criminal, no matter whom the victim is. On the other hand, there is a danger that resolution is taken away from victims and that her needs are subsumed in the state's impera- tive to punish the offender, with whom she may wish to have a continuing relationship. She may also be in conflict with him over contact with their children. And domestic violence is child abuse as well.[209] So, the new emphasis on the criminal nature of domestic violence should not deflect us from appreciating it is a "family" matter.

A DOMESTIC VIOLENCE COURT?

The Court of Appeal has drawn attention to the "unsatisfactory nature of the present interface between the criminal and family courts". It points out that it is "expensive, wasteful of resources and time-consuming" and that it is "stressful for the victim to move from court to court in order to obtain redress and protection from the perpetrator".[210] Is the answer integrated courts, with criminal and civil jurisdiction in the same court? This model is to be found in several states in the USA, as well as in Canada and parts of Europe. From the victim's perspective the case for one court is convincing: everything would be addressed in one setting. On the other hand, concern has been expressed that the criminal side of such a court would be dominant and the victim might be encouraged to take the criminal route when she preferred a family law remedy. It might deter her from using the court at all.

Whilst there is no active initiative to create an integrated court we have seen since 1999 the development of specialist domestic violence courts. The first was established in Leeds magistrates' court, and since then a number of courts have piloted their own versions. These courts operate only in the criminal jurisdiction. They are specialist courts. They set aside a dedicated session just for domestic violence cases. The personnel are trained and will build up experience to ensure domestic violence criminal justice meets the highest standards. It is likely that the introduction of such courts will become national policy in due course. It is too early to say whether new practices will emerge: in the USA there is evidence that in such courts there is more plea-bargaining, but that is a feature of American criminal justice anyway, and may not be replicated here. Specialist courts may also lead to better multi-disciplinary work between the different support services.

PREVENTION

It is imperative that we also turn our attention to prevention. This involves addressing the reasons why domestic violence occurs. On one level this requires us to tackle substance abuse: there is a clear link, or at least an association, between alcohol misuse and domestic violence. Almost one-third of victims say their assailant has been drinking. Thirty per cent of domestic violence, perhaps more, starts during pregnancy, and existing violence often escalates during it. Routine ante-natal questioning may reveal the extent of this, though there may be a reluctance to report it. The reason why men are violent to their pregnant partners needs investigation (jealousy, suspicion the child is not theirs, the refusal of sex, fear that they will no longer be her primary concern may be some of the reasons or rationalisations), and tackling. This is part of an agenda to change attitudes. Far too many male role-models, well-known footballers for example, are violent towards women. Canteen-culture encourages images of women as submissive sex-objects. Pornography encourages this too. Education must redress this: at school level, with offenders (the most obvious risk factor for domestic violence is previous domestic violence), in prisons.

4

UNDERSTANDING DIVORCE

THE DEVELOPMENT OF DIVORCE LAW

The law puts few obstacles in the way of those who wish to get married. Ending a valid marriage has always been more difficult. Until 150 years ago it required an Act of Parliament.[1] This meant that divorce was only open to the wealthy and to husbands (only four women ever divorced their husbands using this complicated procedure). But the poor were not to be outdone and their marriages sometimes ended in husbands (or less often wives) deserting, and even in wife-sales, a practice believed by the rural poor to terminate marriage.[2] Hardy immortalised this folk custom in *The Mayor of Casterbridge*.[3]

Judicial divorce was introduced by the Divorce and Matrimonial Causes Act 1857. This did not change the law: it merely simplified the procedure. The law of divorce still discriminated against women, who had to prove their husband's adultery was aggravated by one of incest, bigamy, rape, sodomy, bestiality, cruelty or desertion for two years.[4] It did nothing to promote accessibility to the courts and so the poor were hardly better off.[5] It was another 50 years before divorce re-emerged as a political issue. Women's suffrage was being debated, and resisted. Greater equality between the classes was also being discussed.[6] The Gorell Royal Commission, which reported in 1912, was a remarkable document for its day.[7] The Majority Report set out three principles: equality of access between rich and poor and men and women; divorce to be seen as "merely a legal mopping-up operation after the spiritual death of a marriage" (Stone, 1990, p.393); there is no necessary connection between the number of divorces and the level of sexual immorality.[8]

The only reform that came of this was (in 1923) making the adultery ground the same for men and women.[9] The extension of the grounds of divorce beyond adultery to include desertion for three years, cruelty, habitual drunkenness and incurable insanity required a Private Member's Bill in 1937. To succeed, A.P.

Herbert, the Bill's sponsor, had to agree to a three years' bar on divorce, unless exceptional hardship or exceptional depravity could be proved.[10] Until then divorce was, in theory, available immediately after a marriage. In 1938 the number of divorces granted was 6092. The Second World War stimulated a demand for greater access to the divorce courts. The Poor Persons' Procedure, established in 1914 at the start of the previous World War, could no longer cope with the pressure, and a number of war-time solutions (see Cretney, 2003b, pp.311–312 for the details) were introduced to assist the forces and their wives. The introduction of legal aid in 1949 was more significant in creating equality between men and women in divorce than the substantive reforms of 1923 and 1937. Unfortunately, because of an economic crisis, while legal aid was introduced to help finance divorce proceedings, the provisions for making legal advice available were never brought in as envisaged. It thus became easier to divorce than to get advice about counselling and conciliation, which might have saved some of these marriages.

The first attempt to move away from fault-based divorce came in 1951 with Eirene White's Bill.[11] It would have added seven years' separation to the existing grounds of divorce, requiring the courts in such cases to be satisfied that there was no reasonable prospect of cohabitation being resumed. Irretrievable breakdown would have become an additional ground of divorce. The Bill got a Second Reading by 131 votes to 60. The Government responded by setting up a Royal Commission under Lord Morton, a Lord of Appeal in Ordinary, and with an over-representation of lawyers. The Commission reported in 1956.[12] The 19 Commissioners were split three ways on the way ahead. One (Lord Walker, a Scottish judge) favoured irretrievable breakdown, though the court would need to be satisfied by proper evidence that the alleged breakdown was indeed irretrievable. He did not favour divorce by consent, which would "destroy the concept of marriage as a life-long union".[13] Nine others supported the status quo: the proper function of the law was to give relief for a wrong. Accordingly, the matrimonial offence should remain "the determining principle of the divorce law".[14] The remaining nine ("liberals") accepted that the law should make provision for divorce where there was irretrievable breakdown, even in the absence of a matrimonial offence, but five of this group would have refused divorce for separation if the other party objected, and even the four prepared to accept separation-divorce against the will of the other party would have insisted on the applicant demonstrating in such a case that the separation was attributable to "unreasonable conduct of the other spouse".[15] It is not surprising that little by way of divorce reform came of the Morton Commission. In McGregor's judgment, it obfuscated "a socially urgent but politically inconvenient issue" (McGregor, 1957, p.187).

In 1962 Leo Abse's Private Member's Bill[16] resurrected Mrs White's proposal of 1951: it would have added seven years' separation to the grounds of divorce. Although he focused on the hardship caused to children by laws which prevented their parents marrying, his proposal foundered on Church opposition.[17] However, it did pave the way for the Divorce Reform Act 1969. And two provisions in Abse's Bill did find their way to the statute book. The law of condonation was amended to allow couples to resume cohabitation for one period of up to three months without this constituting condonation.[18] And, collusion was converted from being an absolute bar to divorce to a discretionary one.[19] As Cretney notes (2003b, p.351)

"apparently technical changes in the law played their part in creating a climate of opinion in which only a few years later legislation allowing divorce for irretrievable breakdown (effectively including divorce by consent) and consigning the doctrines of condonation and collusion to the history books seemed to command general support".

Change was beginning to look inevitable: the courts sensed this and also contributed to reform. Thus, decisions in 1964 held that a respondent who was not morally blameworthy could nevertheless be cruel.[20] It was not far from this to ask whether the petitioner could be expected to tolerate the respondent's behaviour and from there to asking whether the marriage had irretrievably broken down.

The catalyst for change, however, came from an unexpected source, a group set up by the Archbishop of Canterbury. Its report, *Putting Asunder*,[21] published in 1966, supported the case for irretrievable breakdown as the ground for divorce. Breakdown was not to be introduced as an additional ground to the existing offence-based ones. It saw decrees as more like death certificates: pronouncing on a relationship, rather than in favour of one spouse and against the other.[22] It favoured the concept of a joint petition.[23] In these ways *Putting Asunder* is astonishingly radical, particularly given the attitudes of the Church in the past.

In other ways its radicalism struck a sour note. For example, since irretrievable breakdown was to be the sole ground, the court would need to be convinced that a marriage was indeed beyond repair, and to this end it recommended the employment of "forensic social workers".[24] It would be their job to determine whether a marriage was beyond repair and to report to the court. There would then be a judicial enquiry and the court would have to satisfy itself that the marriage had broken down irretrievably.

Putting Asunder was referred to the Law Commission which produced, also in 1966, *Reform of the Grounds of Divorce: The Field of Choice*.[25] This set out what it considered the aims of a good divorce law, which are:

"To buttress, rather than undermine, the stability of marriage, and when, regrettably marriage has irretrievably broken down, to enable the empty legal shell to be destroyed with the maximum fairness and the minimum bitterness, distress and humiliation".[26]

It regarded *Putting Asunder*'s model of breakdown established by inquest as impracticable. It saw two alternatives as practicable: breakdown without inquest proved by separation (it envisaged this would be no longer than six months); if so short a period were not acceptable, separation as a ground "would be practicable only as an addition to the existing grounds based on matrimonial offence".[27] Despite the seeming chasm between the models in the two reports, an agreement (Cretney calls it a "concordat") (2003b, p.364) was reached between the Archbishop's Group and the Law Commission (with only the Archbishop himself dissenting). Irretrievable breakdown should replace the matrimonial offence as the sole ground of divorce but in place of inquest the court would infer breakdown on proof of a matrimonial offence or separation for two years if the respondent consented and five years if s/he did not.[28]

DIVORCE LAW TODAY

It took Private Members' Bills introduced twice and the overcoming of considerable opposition to get this compromise on the statute book as the Divorce Reform Act 1969 (Lee, 1974). With a few changes it remains the law today.[29] There was, as we shall see, an attempt to overturn it in 1996, but legislation passed then has not, and will not, be implemented.

The Matrimonial Causes Act 1973 consolidated the Divorce Reform Act 1969 together with reforms relating to the financial and property consequences of divorce.

Adultery and intolerability

Section 1(1) of the 1973 Act lays down that there is only one ground for divorce: that the marriage has broken down irretrievably. Irretrievable breakdown, however, can only be established by proving one or more of the five facts set out in s.1(2). Proof of irretrievable breakdown without proof of one of the five facts is insufficient.[30] It is not, however, necessary to show that the "fact" relied upon caused the irretrievable breakdown.[31] More puzzling is the question whether a decree can be granted when a "fact" is established but irretrievable breakdown is not. The answer, it seems, lies in s.1(4): once a "fact" has been proved, the court "shall" grant a decree unless it is "satisfied on all the evidence that the marriage has not broken down irretrievably". In other words, proof of one of the five facts raises an almost irrebuttable presumption that the marriage has irretrievably broken down. There has been no reported instance of a respondent succeeding in rebutting the presumption that proof of one of the "facts" establishes breakdown. Does this mean that, despite s.1(1), the ground for divorce is either a matrimonial offence or separation? That it is an illusion to believe English divorce is based on irretrievable breakdown?

The first fact on which the petitioner may rely is that the respondent has committed adultery and the petitioner finds it intolerable to live with him.[32] Before the Divorce Reform Act, adultery by itself was a ground for divorce. Now adultery as such is insufficient. There are two limbs to s.1(2)(a): adultery and the petitioner finding living with the respondent intolerable. The meaning of adultery is clear: it may be defined as voluntary sexual intercourse between two persons of the opposite sex, one or both of whom are married but not to each other.[33] If a married woman is raped, she does not commit adultery.[34] Nor is it adultery if she receives donor insemination without her husband's consent.[35] There must be penile–vaginal penetration: anal intercourse is not sufficient for adultery, nor is masturbation or other non-penetrative sex.[36] The law is clear as to what adultery means: whether ordinary people are is less certain; among misconceptions is (or was) apparently that it is not adultery if the woman is over 50 and it is not adultery in the daytime (and see Lawson, 1988, pp.40–41).

Whether or not the petitioner finds it intolerable to live with the respondent is a question of fact. The test is subjective: does this petitioner find it intolerable to live with this respondent?[37]

The two limbs of the adultery fact are linked by the word "and". "And" can be used conjunctively and disjunctively. If it is used here conjunctively, a causal link between the two limbs would be required. If disjunctively, the petitioner can rely not just on the adultery but on any other matter to show s/he finds it intolerable with the respondent. An example, given cynically by one judge, was the wearing of pink knickers.[38] Different views were initially expressed[39] but the Court of Appeal in *Cleary v Cleary*,[40] and subsequently in *Carr v Carr*,[41] ruled that the two limbs were "independent",[42] "separate and unrelated".[43] Accordingly, the petitioner is not under an obligation to show that it is in consequence of the adultery that s/he finds it intolerable to live with the respondent. This interpretation may be criticised: it is difficult to reconcile it with the provision in the Act which stipulates that cohabitation for a period not exceeding six months after the petitioner discovers the respondent's adultery shall be disregarded in determining whether s/he finds it intolerable to live with the respondent.[44] "Whether" seems to imply that it must be the adultery which makes cohabitation intolerable. (Freeman, 1972; Lowe and Douglas, 2006, p.267).

Behaviour

The second "fact" is that the respondent has behaved in such a way that the petitioner cannot reasonably be expected to live with the respondent.[45] This replaces the old ground of cruelty. It is frequently called "unreasonable behaviour".[46] But this is not correct: what is important is not the behaviour as such, but the effect of it on the petitioner.[47] Whether the respondent's behaviour is such that the petitioner can no longer reasonably be expected to live with him is a question of fact, and one for the court, not the petitioner, to answer.[48] The test is objective. It was formulated in *Livingstone-Stallard v Livingstone-Stallard* as:

"Would any right-thinking person come to the conclusion that this husband has behaved in such a way that this wife cannot reasonably be expected to live with him, taking into account the whole of the circumstances and the characters and personalities of the parties?"[49]

It is not enough to show incompatibility. Thus, in *Buffery v Buffery*,[50] the parties had "just grown apart"; they could not communicate and had nothing in common. In *Pheasant v Pheasant*[51] the husband alleged that his wife had not been able to give him the spontaneous, demonstrative affection for which he craved and so it was impossible for him to live with her any longer, but he alleged nothing in the wife's behaviour that could be regarded as a breach of any of the obligations of marriage or as effectively contributing to the break-up of the marriage.

Divorces are granted for a wide range of behaviour. This can be illustrated though clearly no definitive list can be given. Violence is an obvious example,[52] but we should bear in mind what Bagnall J. said in *Ash v Ash*: a violent petitioner can reasonably be expected to live with a respondent who is also violent.[53] Subjecting a wife to a constant atmosphere of criticism, boorish behaviour and disapproval has been held to be "unreasonable behaviour".[54] So has "improving" the matrimonial home—this included mixing cement on the living room floor and leaving the lavatory door off for eight months—but this husband also unjustifiably alleged that the two teenage girls were not his.[55] Dogmatic and chauvinistic behaviour towards a sensitive wife has also held to be behaviour such that she could not reasonably be expected to live with him.[56] So has financial irresponsibility.[57] An affair in which there was no adultery, or none that could be proved, has also been held to come within the behaviour fact:[58] the implication of this is that if the association falls short of adultery it is not necessary for the petitioner to show s/he finds it tolerable to live with the respondent; if adultery takes place, s/he is. Behaviour is more than a mere state of affairs or state of mind. It is "action or conduct by one which affects the other".[59] It may take the form of acts or omissions or may be a course of conduct. It must have "some reference to the marriage".[60] The whole history of the marriage must be looked at. Incidents, which may be trivial, when looked at cumulatively can amount to behaviour that comes within this provision.[61]

A particularly difficult problem arises when the respondent, because of mental or physical ill-health, cannot help his/her behaviour.[62] Thus, in *Katz v Katz*[63] the husband suffered from manic-depressive illness accompanied by paranoid or schizophrenic features. He was a rigid, obsessive man who would sit glued to a transistor radio. He would also flare up, and accuse his wife unreasonably of sexual misconduct. She was driven to an attempted suicide. The wife was granted a decree. To determine whether such behaviour on the part of a respondent who is mentally ill and lacks the capacity to form any intention reaches the quality and standard envisaged by the behaviour fact, the test to be applied, held the court, is whether, after making allowances for his disabilities and the temperaments of both parties, the character and gravity of his behaviour is such that, in the opinion of the court, the petitioner cannot be reasonably expected to live with him. In *Thurlow v Thurlow*,[64] the wife was an epileptic who, in addition, suffered increasingly from a severe neurological disorder. She was bedridden, incontinent, and, as her condition deteriorated, she displayed bad temper, aggression and became destructive. She was now in hospital, the prognosis being that she would require indefinite institutional care. The husband was given a decree. It was said that "behaviour" included negative conduct, for example prolonged silences or total inactivity, as well as positive conduct. It included conduct which was involuntary and resulted from mental or physical illness or injury. It was important that the court took account of the obligations of marriage ("in sickness and in health") but it had to take account also of the effect on the health of the petitioner and his capacity to bear the stresses imposed.

Desertion

The third "fact" is that the respondent has deserted the petitioner for a continuous period of at least two years immediately preceding the presentation of the petition.[65] Desertion has the following four elements. First, de facto separation between the spouses. Although this will usually involve one leaving the matrimonial home, it is possible for desertion to occur with both living under the same roof but in two households rather than one.[66] Desertion is not "the withdrawal from place, but from a state of things".[67] Second, there must be an *"animus deserendi"*, an intention to remain separated from the other.[68] There is no intention to desert, necessarily, when one goes away on business, or is posted away by the armed services or is imprisoned, or is ill and in hospital.[69] But there can be an intention to desert even when they cannot live together: in *Beeken v Beeken*,[70] husband and wife were in separate Japanese POW camps, but she communicated to him that she had met a Norwegian man and intended to live with him on release. She was held to be in desertion from that moment. Third, there is no desertion if the separation is by consent.[71] Fourth, if one has a reasonable cause or reasonable excuse for leaving the other, s/he is not in desertion. Finding a man in the wife's bedroom and other men in the house gave, it was held, the husband every ground for supposing that she had committed adultery, and that this reasonable belief justified his leaving her.[72] More recently, when a Muslim man took a second wife against the will of the first one, it was held that she had a reasonable cause for leaving him, and was not in desertion.[73]

Separation with consent

The fourth "fact" is that the parties to the marriage have lived apart for a continuous period of at least two years immediately before the presentation of the petition and the respondent consents to a decree being granted.[74] The parties are to be treated as living apart unless they are living with each other in the same household.[75] This is not the same thing as living together in the same house, as the case of *Fuller (Orse Penfold) v Fuller*[76] amply illustrates. The wife had left the husband to live with another man. But when the husband became seriously ill and unable to look after himself, she took him in as a paying lodger. It was held they were "living apart". The words "with each other" (in s.2(6)) connoted a matrimonial relationship. But Mrs Fuller was living with Mr Penfold, not her husband. Contrast *Mouncer v Mouncer*,[77] where a husband and wife continued to take their meals together and shared cleaning duties. The only reason why the husband continued to live in the house was his wish to live with and continue to care for his children. It was held they were sharing the same household: a rejection of a normal physical relationship coupled with an absence of normal affection was not sufficient to constitute "living apart". Even if the spouses are physically separated, it does not follow they are living apart. According to the Court of Appeal in *Santos v Santos*,[78] before they can be said to be living apart one of them at least must regard the marriage as at an end. The wife petitioner in this case had returned to her husband, and his bed, on three occasions. Although these visits did not together exceed six months,[79] they indicated that she recognised the marriage as subsisting. It is, so the court held, not necessary for the spouse who believes the marriage to be at an end to communicate that decision to the other. A long-term prisoner could, therefore, be regularly visited by his wife and he would not have to tell her that he intended to divorce her upon his release (this interpretation of "living apart" applies to the five years' "separation fact" as well, where her consent is not necessary).

The respondent must consent to the decree. In *McG (formerly R) v R*,[80] the wife's solicitors had failed to elicit whether the husband consented, though there was evidence in a letter that he "simply wants this affair to be brought to finality as soon as possible". That he did not object to a decree did not mean he thereby consented. Consent is thus a positive requirement. If the respondent cannot be found, it is impossible to rely on this fact. The mental capacity required to give consent to a divorce is the same as that required for marriage: that is, does the respondent understand the nature of his consent, and appreciate the effect and result of giving it?[81] If the respondent cannot consent, no one can consent for him. Respondents must be given such information as to enable them to understand the effect of the decree.[82]

Separation and no consent

The fifth "fact" on which the petitioner may rely is that the spouses have lived apart for a continuous period of at least five years immediately preceding the presentation of the petition.[83] This "fact" is similar to the fourth "fact". The period of time is five years, not two, and the respondent's consent is not required. This means that a spouse can be divorced against his/her will, even where she is blameless and even where she does not believe in divorce. Critics dubbed this provision "Casanova's Charter",[84] but since, at least initially, just as many petitions were brought by wives, it could equally well, or just as ineptly, be referred to as "Messalina's Charter".[85] Whatever, it is not much used now, and the interest lies in the way Parliament has tried to protect the respondent and, in practice, the courts have failed to do so.

Section 5 of the 1973 Act permits the respondent to oppose the grant of a decree on the ground that the dissolution of the marriage will result in grave financial or other hardship to him/her and that it would in all the circumstances be wrong to dissolve the marriage.

The hardship must result from the divorce, and not, as it frequently will, from the breakdown of the marriage.[86] Most divorces result in hardship. The hardship must be grave, that is

to say exceptional.[87] Although this must be considered in relation
to the particular marriage, whether it is "grave" will depend
upon what "sensible people" knowing the facts would think.[88]
Thus, in *Rukat v Rukat*,[89] where grave "other" hardship was in
issue, a woman who kept up the pretence of a subsisting marriage for 25 years was held to be sincere in her belief that divorce
would cause her grave hardship, but was not entitled to reply on
the defence.

Hardship includes the loss of the chance of acquiring any
benefit which the respondent might acquire if the marriage were
not dissolved.[90] There are two main sources of such hardship.
First, the former wife (since it will usually be the woman putting
forward this defence it is convenient to assume it will be the
former wife, but exactly the same principles apply to former
husbands) will no longer be able to claim certain social security
benefits by virtue of her former husband's contributions (for
example, retirement pension and bereavement allowance).
However, a former wife in such circumstances and in need
would be entitled to income support. If what she would receive
from this is not substantially less than what she would get from
contribution-based benefits, she will not suffer grave financial
hardship.[91] On the other hand, if she is in paid employment after
her husband's retirement or death, she will not be entitled to
income support but would, in the absence of a divorce, be entitled to benefits which are the result of her husband's contributions. Of course, in many cases it will not be easy to determine
her circumstances in what may be a distant future: her
employment prospects are dependent on numerous con-
tingencies including her health and her skills, as well as those
likely to need her care. It is thus very difficult to determine grave
financial hardship when this loss is in issue.

The main potential loss which has featured in litigation is the
loss of a pension accruing to an employee's widow. The problem
is less than it is used to be because of reforms which enable
courts to allocate either pension payments or pension rights to
the divorced spouse as part of the financial provision package.[92]
Before these reforms it was rare to refuse a divorce on grounds of
loss of a pension. There is just one reported case, in which the
husband, an ex-police officer was refused a divorce when he
could only offer an annuity to the wife of £215 per annum.[93] In
most cases the wife was able to use the s.5 defence as a bargaining counter. Thus, in *Parker v Parker*[94] the contingent loss of a
police widow's pension was offset by the husband agreeing to

purchase a deferred annuity, and by taking out a second mortgage on his house to secure this. In the past proceedings have sometimes been adjourned to enable the husband to come up with proposals to recompense the wife for a loss she may sustain in the future. The pension reforms on divorce should make this less necessary in future, and may see the demise of the s.5 defence altogether.

However, the defence may remain useful in other areas. In another case[95] in which the defence succeeded—at least initially—the wife satisfied the court that she would suffer grave financial hardship if she could not buy a flat in which she would be able to look after her seriously ill adult son, while his wife was at work. The sum offered by the husband was not sufficient to buy a flat in the area. Shortly after, the son died, and a divorce was granted.[96]

The defence has also been raised a number of times in relation to "other" hardship. These cases all involve women from cultures outside this country. The defence is that divorce is anathema to them on religious grounds, or that it will lead to social ostracism in the communities in which they live. In *Banik v Banik*,[97] the parties were Hindus. They married in India and the husband came to England, leaving his wife behind. Twelve years later he sought a divorce on the five years' separation "fact". The wife's defence was that she would be a social outcast in India if divorced. Ormrod J. "pooh-poohed" her claim. The Court of Appeal, however, ruled it a possible defence. It was heard a second time,[98] and Hollings J concluded the divorce would only cause inconvenience.[99] When wives have said they do not believe in divorce, courts have, somewhat uncharitably, responded that a divorce should not affect their beliefs.[100] Courts have also distinguished between what they consider to be sophisticated cities like Mumbai and Delhi and more remote parts of India.[101] The suggestion, though there is no case in which it has succeeded, is that it is more realistic to mount a s.5 defence on ostracism grounds if the wife lives in rural India rather than in a major centre of population.

Even if the respondent establishes that a decree of divorce will cause her grave financial or other hardship, the court must still pronounce a decree unless it would be wrong in all the circumstances to do so.[102] It is not clear what "wrong" means, and Davies L.J. has hardly assisted our understanding by telling us it means "unjust" and "not right".[103] The court has to consider all the circumstances including the conduct of the parties to the marriage (including the respondent's conduct), the interests of those parties and of any children (including adult children)[104] or other persons concerned (including the petitioner's new partner). A balancing exercise is then undertaken, weighing these interests against hardship that the divorce will cause the respondent.[105] Where the wife is young or the marriage was a short one, a divorce is likely to be granted.[106] In *Brickell v Brickell*,[107] one was granted despite the grave financial hardship the wife would suffer, because the court took account of her misconduct in ruining the husband's nursing home business. In deciding whether it is wrong to grant a divorce, the courts have said that a balance has to be maintained between upholding the sanctity of marriage and burying empty shells of marriages.[108]

Section 10 Protection

Further protection for the respondent—in both cases based on two years' and five years' separation—is offered by s.10. It is provided that if a decree nisi is granted on one of the separation facts, the respondent may apply for it not to be made absolute unless the court is satisfied: (a) that the petitioner should not be required to make financial provision for the respondent; or (b) that the financial provision made is reasonable and fair, or the best that can be made in the circumstances.[109] This provision dates from a time when courts had less extensive powers than they now have, and it is rarely invoked. But, like s.5, it can be used as a bargaining device. In one case[110] the husband was anxious to remarry—indeed wedding invitations were already printed—and he did not need much encouragement to make a better offer. In another,[111] a husband had failed to make payments under a Spanish maintenance agreement, and the court held it had power to refuse to make absolute the decree nisi granted to the husband on five years' separation. In the past applications under s.10 were sometimes used to provide protection for wives who would lose pension entitlements as a result of divorce. For reasons briefly noted (see below for a fuller discussion), it is no longer necessary to use s.10 for this purpose.[112]

The role of the court

On a petition for divorce it is the duty of the court to "inquire"— a legacy perhaps of *Putting Asunder*—into the facts alleged by the petitioner and any facts alleged by the respondent.[113] Since nearly all petitions are undefended, the respondent is silent and the contest is a thing of the past. In 1973 a special procedure was established for undefended petitions (Elston *et al.*, 1975). This originally applied only to petitions based on two years' separation, but was extended to all undefended petitions from 1977. This major reform got very little attention, which is as well because far less dramatic reform in divorce have provoked hostile opposition. But it constitutes a "silent revolution" (Jacob, 1988, ch.10). It has meant that divorce has become an administrative rather than a judicial procedure (Freeman, 1976). The law outlined above is now just a backdrop and little hinges on it. Most divorces use the adultery and behaviour facts, but who knows whether adultery has taken place or whether the allegations about behaviour are true—and it is tempting to ask "who cares?" There is no judicial scrutiny save in a miniscule number of cases. The documentation is checked but we may assume this is cursory: certainly, it is unlikely to reveal defects of substance. Nothing is achieved by a judge (or district judge) pronouncing the decree absolute in open court: it is an absurd waste of resources that this practice continues. The day when divorce will be announced on the web is surely close.

The divorce decree is in two stages: the decree nisi and the decree absolute.[114] The petitioner may apply for the decree nisi to be absolute after the expiration of six weeks, unless the court fixes a shorter time.[115] If the petitioner fails to apply for a decree absolute, the respondent may do so after the expiration of three months from the date upon which the petitioner could have applied.[116] There is discretion whether to permit the respondent's application, and it may be deferred where financial matters are outstanding.[117] It was refused in one case where the husband was "devious", even going through a ceremony of remarriage that would not be recognised;[118] but allowed in another where there was no evidence that the respondent was likely to obstruct financial proceedings.[119]

The reason for the gap between decree nisi and decree absolute is to give an unsuccessful respondent an opportunity to appeal against the granting of the decree nisi. It also enables the Queen's Proctor—or any one else—to show cause why the decree should not be made absolute. In the past the Queen's Proctor investigated allegations of collusion. Now the occasional contemporary abuse—immigration fraud, for example[120]—will surface after a decree nisi. There must be a strong suspicion that many more will not.

Promoting reconciliation

Although, as we have seen, divorce law is still firmly wedded to the matrimonial offence, in theory the emphasis is now on irretrievable breakdown. There are thus provisions in the law designed to promote reconciliation between the spouses and thus forestalling divorce.

First, no petition for divorce may be presented to the court before the end of the first year of the marriage.[121] This is an absolute bar. Between 1937[122] and 1984[123] the bar lasted three years but was discretionary. A petitioner who could establish exceptional hardship or show exceptional depravity by the respondent was permitted to institute proceedings within the three-year period. What was meant by "exceptional" was illustrated, notably by Denning L.J. in *Bowman v Bowman*,[124] but never defined. Having to parade intimate details before a court was thought[125] to be embarrassing and unseemly. A shorter, but absolute, bar was substituted. This is interpreted strictly. Is it necessary? Is it any more than a symbol, there to uphold the state's interest in the stability and dignity of marriage? Does it really prevent ill-considered marriage and hasty and ill-thought-out exits therefrom? If not, why insist on it? Why shouldn't the woman who is beaten up on her wedding night obtain an immediate divorce? That she can obtain a non-molestation order immediately, indeed, can petition for judicial separation without waiting for a year to expire,[126] is no answer.

Second, the five "facts" in s.1 of the Matrimonial Causes Act are all accompanied by provisions in s.2 which purport to encourage reconciliation. Thus, a petition based on adultery is not permitted if the parties lived together for more than six months after the petitioner discovered the adultery,[127] but the period of living together is disregarded by the court when it is determining whether the petitioner finds it tolerable to live with the respondent.[128]

Where there is a petition based on behaviour, the spouses may live with each other for a period or periods after the occurrence of the final incident, and the court must disregard this in determining whether the petitioner cannot reasonably be expected to live with the respondent, if the length of that period (or periods) was six months or less.[129] The language in the adultery provision and in the behaviour one are different. Six months' cohabitation after adultery means it cannot be relied upon by the petitioner. Periods longer than six months do not bar a petition based on behaviour. Of course, the longer the period of living together the more likely it is that the court will draw the inference that the petitioner can reasonably be expected to tolerate the respondent's behaviour. But if, for example, she goes on living with him because she has nowhere else to go, a court may conclude that it remains open to her to use the behaviour fact well after the six months' period has elapsed. In *Bradley v Bradley*,[130] a wife (and the seven children) remained in the matrimonial home despite his violence. She even had sexual intercourse with him because she was frightened of what might happen if she did not submit. She was in a "Catch-22" situation: the council would only rehouse her on divorce, but she had nowhere to go in the meantime.

There are reconciliation provisions in the desertion and separation facts as well. In considering whether the period of desertion or living apart is continuous, no account is to be taken of any one period, not exceeding six months, or of any two or more periods, not exceeding six months in all, during which the parties resumed living with each other. No period during which the parties lived with each other is counted as part of the period of desertion or of the period for which the parties lived apart.[131] There is no information as to how successful these "kiss and make up" provisions have been.

Third, if a petitioner instructs a solicitor to act for him or her in divorce proceedings, the solicitor is required to certify whether s/he has discussed with the petitioner the possibility of a reconciliation and given the names and addresses of persons qualified to help effect a reconciliation.[132] A solicitor is not obliged to discuss reconciliation with the client. Most petitioners do not consult solicitors, and the provision is thought to serve little purpose if it ever did.

Fourth, the court can adjourn divorce proceedings at any stage if there is a reasonable possibility of a reconciliation between the parties.[133] This provision is little used. Once the special procedure was introduced, there was little opportunity to do so.

Couples may stay together for reasons other than reconciliation. They may have learnt "to make the best of imperfect circumstances". That they continue to live together (or rather persist in co-residence) is not necessarily an indicator that the marriage has been "saved". These findings emerge from a recent study which found that nearly a fifth of those contemplating divorce were still living with their spouse two years later.[134] The divorce statistics do not tell us the whole story: they do not reveal either those who split up without divorcing or those who stay together (perhaps after attempts at reconciliation) whose marriages have broken down.[135]

ITS OBJECTIVES

The law of divorce today finds few supporters. As we shall see, there was an attempt to reform it in 1996, but this failed. Before this abortive attempt is discussed, it is worth briefly appraising the current law in terms of the objectives set out in *Field of Choice* 40 years ago. The current law was devised to put these into operation. Of course, the Law Commission could not anticipate the introduction of the special procedure.

Objective 1 is to "buttress, rather than undermine the stability of marriage".[136] Can divorce law make a positive contribution towards upholding marriage? The Law Commission thought it could. First, by ensuring that divorce was not "so easy" that spouses would have no inducement to make a success of their marriage.[137] Second, by ensuring every encouragement was given to reconciliation. But there is no doubt that divorce is "easy".[138] By way of parenthesis, this is not to suggest, as Deech (1994) has, that the divorce rate increases after law reform. As Phillips (1988, p.25) points out, "in almost all countries divorce rates had begun to rise before legal reform". The reforms are partly a response to increased divorce, not a cause of it. Divorce has been made easier than was perhaps intended by judicial interpretation of "facts" like adultery and behaviour. Thus, when the courts rejected the causal link between adultery and intolerability, the "fact" was diluted.[139] When they moved away from expecting a spouse to put up with "the fair wear and tear" of marriage, the behaviour "fact" became easier to prove.[140] It is hardly surprising that petitioners continue overwhelmingly to rely in these two "facts": why should they wait two years to construct a "civilised" divorce?

One of the ways that divorce law was supposed to buttress the stability of marriage was through the bar on divorce petitions being presented within the first three years of marriage.[141] *Field of Choice* saw this as a "useful safeguard against irresponsible or trial marriages and a valuable external buttress to the stability of marriages during the difficult early years".[142] Why anyone thought a bar should have this effect is incomprehensible. It is unlikely that many couples were even aware of its existence. It was obvious in the 1970s that the bar was not working: there were nearly 2000 applications every year for leave to petition within three years. In 1984, as already discussed, the bar was reduced to an absolute one of one year. There is no evidence that it enhances marriage in any way.

A further way, it was supposed, of buttressing marriage is through encouraging reconciliation. But none of the provisions designed to achieve this has had any noticeable effect. It may even be doubted whether they were intended to do so. Thus, for example, all a solicitor has to do is to certify that s/he has not discussed reconciliation: there is no obligation even to explain why not.

Objective 2 is enabling empty legal shells of marriages to be destroyed with maximum fairness, and minimum bitterness, distress and humiliation.[143] The reform undoubtedly enabled a large number of dead marriages to be buried and many children to be legitimated (more of a concern in the early 1970s than it is now). Nearly 30,000 petitions in 1971 were brought on the five years' separation fact: relatively few now are, or were once the backlog was cleared. If, eventually, bitterness, distress and humiliation were taken out of the divorce process, it was by the introduction of the special procedure,[144] not by divorce law reform. It may have been an aspiration of the reformers that couples would divorce consensually using the two years' separation provision, but this has not happened. Most divorces use a fault-based "fact" (adultery or behaviour), and barely one in five divorce petitions use the two years' separation provision.[145] There is a gender difference, with women most commonly citing their husbands' behaviour, and men petitioning on the two years' separation "fact".[146] Most defended divorces remain bitter mud-slinging affairs with allegations and counter-allegations. Few would want these intimate details of the marriage exposed, but the facts about the most torrid divorces are widely reported in the media and the law reports.

There was an air of optimism at the time of the 1969 Act. It fitted the era. But, as Smart (1999, p.9) has pointed out, by the 1980s "the optimistic scenario in which families happily reconstituted themselves did not materialize". Instead, a moral panic about the number of divorces and the effect of this substantial increase on the family—the number of decrees absolute doubled between 1971 and 1981 and continued to rise—set in.[147] The Booth report in 1985 recommended a number of changes to take recrimination out of divorce.[148] Nothing came of the recommendations, though some found their way into reforms recommended by the Law Commission.

THE PROBLEMS WITH THE CURRENT LAW

After issuing a Discussion Paper in 1988,[149] the Law Commission published its report *The Ground for Divorce Law* in 1990.[150] It identified six problems with the law.

First, it is confusing and misleading. The behaviour "fact" is cited as particularly confusing. Above all, "the present law pretends it is conducting an inquiry into the facts of the matter, when in the majority of cases it can do no such thing".[151]

Second, it is discriminatory and unjust. It is hardly surprising that the two years' separation "fact" is relied upon more commonly by those who are better off: it is easier for them to establish two households to satisfy the separation precondition. This leaves poorer people, who do not have this luxury, to rely on the fault-based "facts". The fault "facts" do not necessarily reveal the truth: the petitioner may also be blameworthy, but it may not be in the respondent's interests to defend or to cross-petition.[152]

Third, it distorts the parties' bargaining positions. Negotiations about the future care of children and distribution of family assets may be distorted by whichever of the parties is in a stronger position in relation to the divorce itself.[153]

Fourth, it provokes unnecessary hostility and bitterness. The system "encourages one to make allegations against the other".[154] The legal process may compound unhappiness. It does nothing to relieve it.

Fifth, it does nothing to save the marriage. The law, despite its avowed intention, "makes it extremely difficult for estranged couples to become reconciled",[155] and gives them every incentive to obtain a "quickie" decree based on behaviour or adultery.

Sixth, it can make things worse for the children. "Children who suffer most are those whose parents remain in conflict".[156] The law may exacerbate this conflict.

THE 1996 ACT: AN ABORTIVE ATTEMPT AT REFORM

These criticisms persuaded the Law Commission to recommend major reforms to divorce law. As with its predecessor in 1966, it set out what it considered to be the objectives of a good divorce law. In part this reproduced the 1966 formulation—the emphasis on supporting marriage and the goal of ending the unsalvageable ones with as little distress, bitterness and hostility as possible—but there was a new emphasis on children. The law should seek:

"To minimize the harm that the children of the family may suffer, both at the time and in the future, and to promote as far as possible the continued sharing of parental responsibility for them".[157]

The Law Commission rejected a return to a fault-based system.[158] (But would it have been a "return"?) It rejected also divorce by demand of one party as providing "no safeguard against precipitate divorce".[159] It did not see divorce by consent as an option, because there would be cases where one party adamantly refused to consent.[160] It also rejected divorce just on separation: it was alert to the discriminatory nature of this.[161]

It proposed divorce after a period for the consideration of future arrangements and for reflection.[162] This initiative was taken up by the Major Government. Its 1993 Consultation Paper set out what it saw as its objectives for a better divorce process. These were

"... to support the institution of marriage; to include practicable steps to prevent the irretrievable breakdown of marriage; to ensure the parties understand the practical consequences before taking an irreversible decision; where divorce is unavoidable, to minimize the bitterness and hostility between the parties and reduce the trauma for the children; and to keep to a minimum the cost to the parties and to the taxpayer".[163]

The Government accepted the model of divorce after a period for reflection and consideration and much else in the Law Commission's report. But the Government emphasised the role of mediation: "bitterness and hostility would be reduced through the mediation process and couples are helped to manage conflict to the benefit of their children and themselves".[164] Added to which, mediation is considerably cheaper than the legal process.[165] It also took the view that there should be no divorce until financial and other arrangements had been finalised.[166] In an era when there was an emphasis on "family values"[167] we should not be surprised to find the argument that "people who marry should discharge their obligations undertaken when they contracted their earlier marriage, and also their responsibilities which they undertook when they became parents, before they became free to remarry".[168]

There was an attempt to reform divorce law in 1996.[169] It failed for reasons which will be given. The Family Law Act 1996 does, however, contain a statement of general principles. Though these are designed to apply to one part of the Act, which will never be brought into operation, and another, which has been superseded, they remain on the statute book, and are of interest as a policy statement. They are:

"(a) that the institution of marriage is to be supported;
 (b) that the parties to a marriage which may have broken down are to be encouraged to take all practicable steps, whether by marriage counselling or otherwise, to save the marriage;
 (c) that a marriage which has irretrievably broken down and is being brought to an end should be brought to an end—

    (i) with minimum distress to the parties and to the children affected;
   (ii) with questions dealt with a manner designed to promote as good a continuing relationship between the parties and any children affected as is possible in the circumstances; and
  (iii) without costs being unreasonably incurred in connection with the procedures to be followed in bringing the marriage to an end; and

 (d) that any risk to one of the parties to a marriage, and to any children, of violence from the other party should, so far as is reasonably practicable, be removed or diminished".[170]

Of these principles only (d), relating to domestic violence, is new. It is, of course, also very significant.

Much has been written about the divorce law in the Family Law Act 1996, including about its ideology (Reece, 2003; see also Freeman, 2006). The outline which follows is offered as one example of what a divorce law could look like. Whether reform when it comes—and it will inevitably come at some time—will resemble this model remains to be seen. The complete package proved a non-starter, and, it is believed, will remain so.

To get a divorce "order", as it was to be called, it would first have been necessary to attend an "information meeting".[171] It was originally envisaged that these would be group meetings.

When accepted that this would be demeaning and embarrassing, though it is difficult to see why, it was proposed that they would be conducted on a one-to-one basis.[172] This could have led to something like 300,000 such meetings a year. The information to be given was to range over a large number of issues (marriage counselling, mediation, the welfare, wishes and feelings of children, domestic violence, the divorce process).[173] We were never told how long the meeting was to last: cynics (or students) might think several months were needed!

Before a statement of marital breakdown could be made to the court, a further three months would have to elapse.[174] This was to provide a cooling-off period and an opportunity to explore the scope for reconciliation. The statement would declare that the person or persons who made it believed that the marriage had broken down,[175] not, it should be noted, that it had broken down irretrievably, because the period of reflection and consideration was there to establish whether this was so. A statement of marital breakdown could not be filed until a marriage had lasted one year.[176]

The period for reflection and consideration was to last 9 months,[177] unless there was a child of the family under 16, in which case it was extended for another 6 months.[178] Never before had English law put additional obstacles in the way of spouses with children divorcing. The period could also be extended where the parties wanted to attempt a reconciliation,[179] and where one party who did not accept the marriage was over applied to the court for an extension of time.[180] The 9-month period could not in any circumstances be reduced.[181]

When the 9-month (or 15-month) period was over, either or both of the parties would have been able to apply for a divorce order.[182] There was also a provision, modeled on s.5 of the Matrimonial Causes Act 1973, for the court to make orders preventing divorce on hardship grounds.[183] But this provision was wider than its model: it applied to all applications for divorce orders; hardship included hardship to a child of the family; and to qualify the hardship needed to be only "substantial", and not "grave", as in the earlier legislation.[184]

Before the divorce order could be made, future arrangements would have to be finalised: questions relating to money and property,[185] and the welfare of any dependent children. As far as children were concerned, the Act set out a checklist of factors to which the court would have had to have had particular regard including the wishes and feelings of the child considered in the light of his age and understanding and the circumstances in which those wishes were expressed.[186] This emphasis on the child is considerably greater than exists under the current law. The reference to the wishes and feelings of the child in particular was a recognition of the personality and integrity of the child and the need to take children's rights seriously, something that rarely happens now[187] (and see Smart *et al.*, 2001; Butler *et al.*, 2003).

There was a change of government shortly after the 1996 Act was passed. The Labour Government was anxious to ensure that the Act would work before it brought into operation. It accordingly set up pilots, one to look at information meetings, the other at mediation.

The information meeting pilot cast doubt on the project (Walker *et al.*, 2001). People had different problems and needed information packs and meetings tailored to them. They also wanted advice which meetings were not empowered to give. But most disappointing was the finding that only 7 per cent of those attending meetings said divorce was now less likely. On the contrary, the meeting "tended to tip those who were uncertain about their marriage into divorce mode". Government had wished to deflect people away from lawyers towards counselling and mediation: nearly three-quarters of those in the research study made it clear that they valued solicitors as more important sources of information and advice. As if information meetings were not expensive enough! It was hardly surprising when the information meeting idea was dropped.

The mediation pilot was more successful (Davis *et al.*, 2001). About 70 per cent of those using mediation found it helpful (or very helpful). And it did lead to agreements (45 per cent mediating about children and 34 per cent mediating financial disputes reached an agreement). Nevertheless, it was clear that participants in the study preferred solicitors, and the evidence did not indicate that mediation was having a significant impact on legal costs. The government concluded that mediation was unlikely to diminish legal aid expenditure sufficiently.

The Government announced in January 2001 that it would not implement the divorce part of the Family Law Act 1996. To critics, including myself (and see Freeman, 1996c and 1997) this was a welcome conclusion. But a balanced appraisal of the Act is called for. The abolition of fault was long over-due[188]: our experience with the matrimonial offence suggests that, certainly in modern times, there are limits to the power of the law to control private behaviour. The emphasis on children's welfare, particularly on their wishes and feelings, is a recognition of the impact of divorce on children, and it is a salutary reminder of divorce's true innocents. The information meeting was ill-thought out and badly designed, but we can learn from it that people can profit from possession of information that most of them would not otherwise have. The upgrading of the risk of domestic violence into a general principle is also to be welcomed.

On the other hand, making divorce a lengthier process—for those with children it would have taken getting on for two years—would have caused problems if not hardship. True, they would not have to have lived apart—the ground was marital breakdown, not separation—but if they did not do so some may indeed have reflected and considered, but others would have indulged in cruelty and violence. There would have been greater demand for non-molestation and occupation orders. Children would have been born.[189] And was the discriminatory nature of this recognised? It would be much easier for the better-off to separate—to reflect in new surroundings—while the poor were condemned to perpetuate dead relationships. One wonders how many marriages would have been saved by "reflection and consideration": it is more likely that this would confirm the importance of getting divorced. Given the alertness elsewhere in the provisions to the welfare of the child, it is sad that the impact of reflection and consideration on children was overlooked.

There was discussion at the time as to whether the 1996 Act made divorce easier or harder. If lengthier is harder than the 1996 law made divorce harder. Removing fault arguably made divorce easier—but in practice, and given that most divorces were undefended, this was rarely difficult to establish. Even when the courts tried to complicate the separation grounds in *Santos v Santos*[190] they failed. Inserting a mental element into separation could have proved a brake on the separation ground, but there is no evidence that it has had any impact whatsoever. In one sense the law was making it much harder. It was asking people to "reflect". It was never made entirely clear what they were supposed to reflect upon. The general principles in s.1 perhaps? Or Lord Mackay's statement—he was the Lord Chancellor at the time—that marriage is a "divinely appointed arrangement fundamental to the well-being of our community"[191] (stay together—that's what God wants). And in this speculation we cannot overlook the fact that this divorce law was as much about marriage, as about divorce (and see Hasson, 2003).

Divorce reform is no longer on the agenda. What we now have

instead are tentative steps to improve the process. The work which went into producing information leaflets, when information meetings were being piloted, have not come to naught. The information remains available, and there are different leaflets tailored to adults and children.

A Family Advice and Information Services (FAInS) has also been established. Among its objectives are

"(a) To bring together expert services to protect children from harm and the risk of social exclusion;

 (b) To facilitate the dissolution of broken relationships, in ways which minimize distress to parents and children, and which promote family relationships and co-operative parenting;

 (c) To provide tailored information and access to services that may assist in resolving disputes, or may assist those who are trying to save their relationship."[192]

FAInS is premised upon the need for holistic solutions: marriage support, counselling, mediation, legal services may all need to be accessed by someone with marital problems. Referral from one to the other needs to be made as smooth as possible. Lawyers have an important role to play in this. Indeed, they may survive as major players in the divorce process despite the attempts in recent years to marginalise them (and see Walker, 2004).

Divorce reform must go back on to the agenda. No one can be satisfied with the status quo, where more than two-thirds of divorces are rooted in "offence" facts, and where the culture thus remains one of blame, guilt and recrimination. The 1996 route is clearly unacceptable. Cretney (2002) is surely right to question whether the "routine processing of marriage break-down" is an appropriate judicial function. Should we take divorce away from the courts? Did we not in reality do most of this when we introduced Special Procedure? Should we not think through the implications of the "administrative divorce"? Are we prepared to contemplate divorce on demand? These questions must be addressed.

DISSOLVING CIVIL PARTNERSHIPS

This chapter has been about divorce. The Civil Partnership Act 2004 applies similar rules to ending civil partnerships as currently govern divorce. The opportunity to rethink was thus lost. Just as civil partnership is not marriage, so its termination is not by divorce but by dissolution.

An application to dissolve a civil partnership may not be brought within one year of its formation.[193] The ground for dissolution is the irretrievable breakdown of the civil partnership, to be established by the proof of one or more of four "facts".[194] These are the same as for divorce, with the omission of adultery plus intolerability. Infidelity in gay and lesbian relationships will presumably constitute behaviour such that the other partner cannot be reasonably expected to continue to live with him/her (and see Harper and Landells, 2006). There are provisions in the 2004 Act designed to facilitate reconciliation: for example living with the other partner for six months after "behaviour" is disregarded.[195] There is the equivalent of s.5 of the 1973 Act to protect a partner who believes dissolution will result in grave financial or other hardship.[196] All other provisions which could possibly apply to a civil partnership are also extended by analogy to marriage and divorce.

There have not been any dissolutions yet: the first ones are forecast for 2007. We therefore do not know what procedure will apply: it may be assumed that something like special procedure will be introduced.

The "dissolution order" will have two stages: "conditional" and "final", with six weeks between them.[197] The Queen's Proctor will be able to investigate any abuses or other issues arising during the proceedings.[198] Presumably, other developments like mediation will be made available to civil partners as to couples going through divorce.

JUDICIAL SEPARATION

The ecclesiastical courts, which were not able to grant divorces, did grant decrees of divorce *a mensa et thoro* (from bed and board). This relieved parties of the duty to cohabit.[199] In 1857 these were renamed judicial separation.

Judicial separation may be sought as an alternative to divorce. It does not however dissolve the marriage. It tends to be sought by those who have religious or other objections to divorce and by those who cannot yet get a divorce because they have not been married for a year. Obviously, when the bar on divorce was set at three years, there were more applicants for judicial separation. In 2004 there were 724 petitions, and 419 decrees were granted.

The five facts for divorce are the grounds upon which a judicial separation may be obtained. It is not necessary to prove that the marriage has irretrievably broken down.[200]

The main consequences of a decree of judicial separation are (i) the court may make orders relating to money and children and (ii) neither spouse has a right to succeed to property on the other spouse's intestacy.

Civil partners may now get separation orders. One of the four facts must be proved. Irretrievable breakdown need not be established. Since it is not clear whether civil partners have a duty to cohabit, the order has no effect on the obligation, if it exists.[201]

IS MEDIATION THE ANSWER?

Mediation is "a process in which an impartial third person, the mediator, assists couples considering separation or divorce to meet together to deal with the arrangements which need to be made for the future". In recent years there have been attempts to encourage divorcing couples to make more use of mediation. It is a precondition of public funding to meet with a mediator to assess whether the assistance of a mediator will be valuable. The Legal Services Commission is now funding many more mediations than a decade ago. Mediating services are cheaper than lawyers and this is a major reason for the emphasis on them. But it is also thought that mediation copes with the problems of divorce better than does the legal system. It encourages the parties to find their own decisions rather than having one imposed upon them by a court.

Mediation is not about reconciliation. Mediation is not directed at bringing the parties back together again. This may be an incidental result but the primary objective of mediation is to settle arrangements for the future. It is forward-looking and it is not judgmental. There are different types of mediation. Out-of-court mediation can be used before the legal process has even begun. If it results in an agreement, this can be put to a court which may make it the basis of a consent order (discussed in Chapter 5). In-court mediation integrates mediation with the process of the court. The district judge may direct the parties to attend a mediation meeting with a court welfare officer with a view to seeing whether an agreement can be reached. If one is, it can be embodied in a consent order. It is easy for the line between adjudication and mediation to be blurred: certainly, the parties may feel that the law is directing them towards an agreement.

The mediator can play a number of different roles (Roberts, 1988). S/he can offer minimal intervention, assisting the parties to communicate and equipping them with resources that they lack, but leaving the content of any agreement to them. S/he can take a more directive role, influencing the content of the decision, trying to ensure that it is fair. S/he can also see their role as therapeutic : the emphasis is then on rebuilding relationships which may be particularly valuable in promoting contact arrangements subsequently.

Mediation is controversial. There are particular concerns in using it where there has been domestic violence (Kaganas and Piper, 1994; Grillo, 1991; Bryan 1992). There are concerns too that the interests of children may not be adequately protected. Children over nine may be involved in a mediation meeting (Parkinson, 2006) but even older children may find themselves marginalised. Parents will represent children's interests, as they perceive them. There is concern also that mediators will lack necessary skills, for example for dealing with complex financial arrangements, tax issues and pensions (Dingwall and Greatbatch, 2001). But the most serious concerns relate to the mediator's impartiality. Piper (1996) found that mediators often excluded from their summaries what they considered irrelevant. And mediators can over-influence the content of an agreement, by suggestions, by comments, by how s/he conducts the mediation, even by body language. Mediation is likely to work best where there is equality of bargaining power. But if, for example, the husband is a businessman and the wife a homemaker, his experience and knowledge are likely to give him greater negotiation skills. Mediation may work against the interests of women for other reasons as well. The wife's concern may so focus on keeping the children that she will sacrifice anything to achieve this. She may be keener to come to an amicable agreement than her husband is. Women may be socially conditioned to avoid conflict and men to fight their corner. Women it is thought (but compare Davis and Roberts, 1989) may lose out in mediation (Bryan, 1992).

When parties bargain they do so "in the shadow of the law" (Mnookin and Kornhauser, 1979). They also do so in the shadow of societal norms (Neale and Smart, 1997), for example that mothers should be the primary carers of children. The agreements they reach are therefore not entirely theirs, though these influences will vary in intensity.

So what are the benefits of mediation? It may be more effective. Certainly, the government thinks this (HM Government 2004, para.2). Much depends upon what "effective" means. The parties will have invested much in achieving an agreement and so may be more committed to it. If it fails they may be in a better position to renegotiate. But do mediated agreements last or last longer than court orders? There is no evidence that they do (Walker, 2004). It may also be that the emotional issues of breakdown are better resolved in mediation. Mediation is often portrayed as having the capacity to remove conflict and reconstitute at least some of the functions of the ideal family. Martha Fineman (1988, p.732) notes the way mediators describe divorce, not as the termination of a marital relationship, but "as a process which, through mediation, restructures and reformulates the spouses' relationship". Mediation is claimed to have the capacity to preserve the family unit for the children. Thus, Landau *et al.* (1987, p.183) argue that "as mediation continues to develop, integrative work is being done that is blending family therapy objectives with family mediation". And this, we are told (*ibid.*), leads to an awareness that "both parents from broken marriages continue to function in important ways in the lives of their children". But we should not forget that women are typically the primary caretakers before and after divorce and have a great fear of losing their children. This may be especially so in marriages when there has been violence. As Geffner and Pagelow (1990, pp.152–153) point out : "Batterers have already demonstrated their willingness to use violence as a response to anger, stress or frustration, and to control the behaviour of others. Thus, the children in these cases are at risk of being abused after divorce even if they have not been abused before".

Mediation (certainly out of court mediation) is a private affair. The parties can negotiate over what most concerns them and may include matters a court would find trivial (Herring, 2003, p.18, gives the example of a dispute about who should keep the goldfish!). The mediator can look at the complete picture, unconstrained by the narrow perimeters imposed by legal doctrine (Menkel-Meadow, 1984), though it inevitably casts a shadow. Mediation can search for creative solutions that no court could impose. Adjudication is formalised and highly structured, with strict procedural stages and steps. What evidence can be put to courts is controlled: mediation by contrast is informal and unstructured. There are no constraints on the presentation of evidence or argument.

Courts judge. They look at past behaviour and measure it against a normative standard. One party is then found to be in the wrong, the other in the right. They deal in winners and losers. Relationships as such are no business of adjudication: they rarely survive it.

COLLABORATIVE LAW

Collaborative law developed in the USA during the 1990s, and is beginning to take root here. Parties have their own lawyers but they sign a participation agreement which commits them not to take their dispute to court. Should one of them decide to take court action a different lawyer will need to be instructed. The parties and their lawyers then hold settlement meetings to attempt to solve the issues before them. Other experts (accountants, for example) may assist the process.

Collaborative law is similar to mediation. Its distinguishing feature is the parties' commitment not to go to court. An increasing number of practitioners are participating (Pirrie, 2006). It is too early to assess its success. Reports from the USA are encouraging (Fretwell, 2003). Resolution has embraced the concept: by 2006 nearly 600 professionals had trained as collaborative practitioners, nearly 10 per cent of its membership.

UNDERSTANDING THE FINANCIAL CONSEQUENCES OF DIVORCE

Most husbands are in a much more powerful financial position than their wives. The division of labour in the family adversely affects the economic viability of women, particularly when they have children (Smart, 1984). There is considerable evidence, in this country and elsewhere, that on divorce it is women who suffer most: men, indeed, the research finds, come out of marriage better-off.[1]

The law is attempting more than ever to redress this imbalance. A number of appellate decisions, particularly two from the House of Lords,[2] and statutory reforms of pension law in 1995 and 1999[3] have addressed these inequities. But the law, and in particular the private law associated with marriage, divorce and its consequences, can only achieve so much. As long as women's earnings are less,[4] and their working lives are punctuated by having and bringing up children, as long as they remain the primary homemakers, many of them will suffer if their marriages break down. We cannot concentrate exclusively upon private support law: we cannot avoid "asking the more basic questions around the division of responsibilities among men, women and society, and around the greater issues of sex equality in the economy generally" Diduck and Orton, 1994, p.686). Pamela Symes (1985, p.51) points out that in very few cases will financial provision on divorce "adequately recompense an ex-wife for the many disadvantages she suffers when her marriage ends and distinguishing between specifically marriage-related disabilities and the more general ones is not always a simple exercise". The law must deal, Diduck and Orton quite rightly note (1994, p.687), with "the society it has helped to create and play its part in shaping ideologies it helps to support". These are big issues and must be returned to after we have looked at the current state of the law.

First, we need to examine briefly its development.

THE ORIGINS OF FINANCIAL PROVISION

The ecclesiastical courts offered wives some financial protection: they could order the husband to pay alimony pending suit and permanent alimony after granting a divorce *a mensa et thoro*.[5] With the introduction of divorce in 1857, this power was vested in the Divorce Court, which was given the additional power to order the husband to secure maintenance for the wife's life.[6] But the court had no power under the 1857 Act to make a maintenance order against a man who lacked assets upon which periodical payments could be secured. As Cretney notes (2003b, p.397) this legislation was framed "primarily in the context of the wealthier families who had at least some capital". It also reflected the "Victorian belief that capital was to be used to provide income and not to be spent". It is for this reason that the Act did not confer power on the court to order a husband to pay or transfer capital to the wife. As Cretney remarks (2003b, p.397), "maintaining the ex-wife was one thing, but dissipating the family capital was quite another". It was 1907 before the court was given an effective power to order a divorced husband to make unsecured weekly or monthly payments for the wife's maintenance and support.[7]

The court's powers were thus limited. It was only in 1963 that the concept of a lump sum order was accepted.[8] This enabled the courts to move way from thinking about income maintenance and to emphasise rather capital adjustment. But this did not happen immediately, the Court of Appeal expressing a view in 1967 that a lump sum order was not likely to arise "except in relatively rare cases".[9] At the time of the passing of the Divorce Reform Act in 1969 there was real concern at the financial plight of wives, particularly innocent wives divorced against their will. There was much talk of the five years' separation divorce as "Casanova's Charter".[10] The loss of pension expectations was a particular concern. One response, now forgotten by almost everyone, was an attempt to introduce community of property: a Bill to enact this got a Second Reading in the House of Commons.[11]

The Government's response to concern about divorce reform and to the community of property initiative was to promise reform of the law relating to financial provision. It did so by means of the Matrimonial Proceedings and Property Act 1970. Important reforms to this were made in 1984,[12] and subsequently by pensions legislation. But the essential structure of the financial provision regime remains that established in 1970, which came into operation with the Divorce Reform Act in 1971. The law is now in the Matrimonial Causes Act 1973, into which the 1984 Act reforms are incorporated.

THE SETTLEMENT CULTURE

Most couples do not go to court but settle the financial arrangements on divorce by agreement. They do, of course, "bargain in the shadow of the law" (Mnookin, 1979). Since the divorce reform of the early 1970s it has been the policy of the law to encourage couples to settle their affairs between themselves. What has been described (see Davis *et al.*, 1994, p.211) as a "settlement culture" now characterises the divorce process. For many lawyers going to court is seen as an admission of professional failure. Because of the discretionary nature of the system, the scope for negotiation is "almost infinite" (Davis *et al.*, 1994, p.256). But, as Davis *at al.* point out, (p.256):

"...along with discretion goes *uncertainty*; the *elevation of professional judgment* (because only lawyers ... have the necessary knowledge and skill to weigh up the competing factors); *an almost limitless need for information about family finances* (because discretion, if it is to be justified at all, has to be based on a minute examination of differing circumstances), and *the demand for large amounts of professional time* (because discretion, if it is not to be exercised arbitrarily, takes time)".

There are strong arguments "against settlement" (Fiss, 1984). The terms of the settlement may reflect an imbalance of power between the parties. This may be in particular to the disadvantage of women, who may do better with trials. This was certainly the impression Davis *et al.* came away with (1984, p.262). Second, in a settlement culture it is lawyers who decide, not the parties. These lawyers are often overburdened and underpaid: many are skilled and dedicated, others "inexperienced ... ineffectual and ... doubtfully competent" (Davis *et al.*, 1994, p.257). We cannot be sure there will be a parity between the solicitors who represent parties.

Whatever the criticisms and they are substantial, as Lord Scarman stated in 1979, "the law ... encourages spouses to avoid bitterness after family breakdown and to settle their money and property problems".[13] The emphasis on settlement does not mean that spouses are free to make their own financial arrangements. The courts can scrutinise an agreement and may refuse to uphold it.[14] Further, the parties may intend an agreement to be final, but this does not stop one of them seeking to reopen it if s/he becomes dissatisfied with its terms. In *Xydhias v Xydhias*,[15] the parties reached an agreement and draft consent orders were produced by counsel. The husband subsequently sought to withdraw his consent and wanted the case to be fully fought in court. The wife wanted an order to reflect the agreement that had been reached. Her application was accepted by the Court of Appeal, which nevertheless made clear that the normal rules of contract do not apply: an agreement for the compromise of an ancillary relief application does not give rise to a contract enforceable in law.

What cannot be done by private agreement can be achieved by asking the court to embody the agreement in a consent order. It is not then the agreement, but the court order which is the source of subsequent rights and obligations. But the court does not act as a "rubber stamp". Indeed, in *Livesey (formerly Jenkins) v Livesey*,[16] the House of Lords held it could not make a consent order unless it possessed information about all the circumstances of the case so as to be able to satisfy itself that the order would comply with all the criteria laid down by the Matrimonial Causes Act 1973. This ruling caused consternation. How many consent orders would be vulnerable? The result was to include within the Matrimonial and Family Proceedings Act 1984 a provision that the court may make a consent order for financial relief on agreed terms on the basis only of prescribed information furnished with the application.[17] The rules, reflecting this, provide that every application for a consent order must be accompanied by two copies of the draft order and a statement of information, including duration of the marriage, an estimate of the parties' means, the arrangements to be made for the accommodation of the parties and any children, whether either party has a present intention to marry or cohabit, and "any other especially significant matters".[18]

The role of the court is controversial. It has been said that these provisions "confine the paternal function of the court ... to a broad appraisal of the parties' financial circumstances ... without descent into the valley of detail".[19] Is it confined enough? Cretney (2003a, pp.403–405) does not think so. He says that the "family justice system still seems reluctant to accept that it should shed its 'paternal' role in purporting to supervise or assess the arrangements a married couple makes when they have concluded that their relationship has broken down". It is "far from clear what purpose (save, perhaps, a symbolic one)" supervision and assessment serves. In his view it is better that the courts distance themselves from unnecessary intervention into family life.

Since 1990 the courts have been instrumental in procedural reforms designed to facilitate settlements. In *F v F (Ancillary Relief: Substantial Assets)*[20] Thorpe J. expressed the opinion that it was "incumbent upon us to develop systems for the determination of financial disputes at a much more realistic cost".[21] He made this statement in a case in which the parties' costs amounted to almost £1.5 million. After a pilot scheme was tested in some courts in the mid-1990s, reforms were introduced nationwide in 2000.[22] There were two innovations. The introduction of the so-called Form E—the details of which are outside the remit of a text such as this. In short, it requires parties to provide information about their circumstances to enable the case to be disposed of justly and proportionately. A full, frank and up-to-date disclosure of assets and circumstances is required.[23] Second, a financial dispute resolution appointment (FDR) has been introduced.[24] At this a district judge will assist the parties to reach an agreement. The judge may make an "early neutral evaluation" of the likely outcome if the case goes to court. The FDR is "an invaluable tool for dispelling unreal expectations".[25] If the case settles, the court will make a consent order. If it does not, there will be a court hearing: the parties will have been warned about the costs implications of not settling.

THE ORDERS: MONEY

What orders can the court make?

First, there is maintenance pending suit.[26] The courts have power, on a petition for divorce to order either spouse to make such periodical payments to the other pending suit as they think reasonable. No guidelines to govern the court's discretion are laid down. There was a practice to bring the wife's income— maintenance pending suit is invariably sought by wives—up to one-fifth of the spouses' joint income.[27] This practice has died out. The order exists to provide for immediate needs of the spouse and children. The sum awarded can be substantial. It can include a sum to fund the costs of the proceedings.[28] This conclusion is supported (in the view of Holman J.) by reference to Art.6 of the ECHR, and the need for there to be "equality of arms" in relation to legal representation.[29] Disputes about the amount of maintenance pending suit in "big money" cases are "almost unknown".[30]

Second, the court has the power to make orders for periodical payments.[31] These can be secured or unsecured. Most are unsecured. When unsecured, the order directs a spouse to make payments (weekly, monthly or annually). If they are not paid, enforcement proceedings can be brought. It is not easy to enforce unsecured payments. In accordance with the "clean break" philosophy of the 1984 legislation (discussed below) on an application for periodical payments, the court may dismiss the application, or dismiss the application with a direction that the applicant shall not make any further application.[32] It can also consider making a "deferred clean break order" under which periodical payments continue for a fixed period only: this is to give the payee time to adjust "without undue hardship" to the termination of financial dependence on the former spouse.[33]

Secured periodical payments are much more attractive to the payee. They are protected even if the payer becomes bankrupt, and they can continue even after the payer's death (even death does not "part" the spouses!).[34] There is no problem of enforcement since payments are secured on specified assets which are transferred to trustees. At one stage it seemed there was an increased willingness to make a secured periodical payments order. Now it is clear that there are few cases in which such an order can be made—in those a commuted capital payment is more common[35]—and it has been said the secured orders "have been virtually relegated to the legal history books".[36]

Periodical payments cease to have effect on the payer's death (unless secured), and on the remarriage of the payee.[37] They do not cease automatically on the payee's cohabitation, even if it is settled and long-term. In *Atkinson v Atkinson*,[38] the Court of Appeal refused to make qualitative judgments about what constituted settled cohabitation. The Court of Appeal had an opportunity to reconsider this ruling in 2003.[39] Although cohabitation was now more common and more accepted, the court did not think it was necessary to do so. Whether periodical payments should automatically cease on remarriage is debatable. It is a disincentive to marry. It may mean that a divorced woman will lose by remarriage, if she marries a man less well-off than her first husband. Her children will also suffer if her standard of living abruptly declines. What has been overlooked are the ways inequality and dependency continue not only after divorce but also in many cases after remarriage. As Symes explains (1985, p.57):

"The accumulation of responsibilities and obligations, the consequences of an unequal partnership based on dependency—all mean that an absolute severance of the bond without massive adjustment would be manifestly unjust, more likely impossible".

Third, the court may order either party to pay a lump sum or sums to the other.[40] It can be made to be paid to a specified person for the benefit of any child of the family or to the child him or herself.[41] Lump sums can be ordered to be paid by instalments, in which case they may be secured, and interest may attract.[42] A lump sum may be ordered to enable the payee to meet any liabilities or expenses already incurred in maintaining herself or any child of the family before an application is made.[43]

As has been pointed out,[44] there was initial reluctance to make lump sum orders. This changed after the implementation of the divorce legislation in 1971. The decision of the Court of Appeal in *Wachtel v Wachtel*[45] was the watershed. It upheld a decision to allocate to the wife a sum sufficient to enable her to fund the purchase of a house for herself. In doing so, it proclaimed that the 1970 Act was not a codifying statute but a "reforming statute designed to ... accord to the courts the widest possible powers in readjusting the financial position of the parties and to afford the courts the necessary machinery to that end",[46] and that it was intended to "remedy the injustice" whereby a wife's contributions to the welfare of the family were given little recognition in determining entitlement to family property.[47] Shortly afterwards, in *Trippas v Trippas*,[48] the Court of Appeal stressed that a lump sum is not simply another way of quantifying financial provision. "It is a separate provision on its own".[49] There was no point going back to cases decided under the 1963 Act. It has come to be seen that the most important use of lump sums is to adjust the parties' capital assets. It is an "equitable redistribution of property".[50] It will not be ordered if it will deprive the payer of his livelihood,[51] nor where there is no prospect of his being able to comply with it.[52]

Lump sum orders are now routine in cases where the husband is wealthy. But they may also be ordered where he has some capital but not a great deal of income. A lump sum payment may also be ordered if the wife needs a capital sum, for example in order to purchase a house.

In *Calderbank v Calderbank*[53]—the case in which it was first stressed that husbands and wives come to the "judgment seat upon the basis of complete equality"[54]—the husband was awarded a lump sum to enable him to buy a house in which to live and where the children could stay when he had contact with them. Lump sums have also been ordered to enable wives to set up a business: in *Gojkovic v Gojkovic*[55] to buy a hotel.

One advantage of a lump sum is that it can used to effect a clean break between the parties. It is a final order and cannot be varied, though a court can suspend or remit future instalments, a power which is exercised "particularly sparingly".[56] Because it is a final order there is also potential injustice where the payer would be in a position to make a lump sum payment (or a larger one than at present) were the application to have been made in the near future. The court thus has the power to adjourn proceedings where there is a real possibility of capital from a specific source becoming available quite soon.[57] The contingency is often an inheritance expectancy. The court will not adjourn the application where this is too remote. An example is *Michael v Michael*,[58] in which the court explained that there was a difference between the foreseeable future and the near future. The contingency was the mother's death but, as Nourse L.J. so rightly remarked, "the world is full of women in their eighties who had high blood pressure in their sixties".[59] Where a lump sum application has been adjourned, the court can order a lump sum to be paid, even though the former spouse who is to receive it has remarried in the interim.[60] Singer J. justified this by emphasising that the remarriage did not affect or diminish her ongoing contributions to the welfare of the children. Of course, exactly the same argument could be made where a former wife in receipt of periodical payments remarries, and, as we have seen, statute bars her from continuing to receive them.

THE PENSIONS QUESTION

The fourth type of order is in relation to pensions, and was introduced, in relation to pension attachment in 1995, and, in relation to pension sharing, in 1999. Pensions are obviously an important financial asset. The loss of a pension as a result of divorce can cause hardship, particularly for women who may have inadequate pension arrangements.

Legislation in 1995 has given the courts the power to make a pension attachment order.[61] If one is made, then once the pension becomes payable the person responsible for the pension arrangement must pay part of the pension income and/or lump sum available under the arrangement to the other party to the marriage. This "earmarking" has a number of disadvantages. No part of the pension is payable, whatever her age and her needs, until he decides to retire. He may decide not to retire: recent policy changes encourage this. The court cannot force him to retire. Nor can it compel him to continue to make payments to the pension arrangement. It is difficult also for the court to predict what her needs will be when the pension becomes payable. Since it is a financial provision order under s.23, and not a new or distinct species of order, it can also be varied during the payer's lifetime and terminates should the payee remarry (or die). It obstructs the goal of a clean break as well. As Wilson J. put it: "notwithstanding divorce, the wife who has the benefit only of an attachment order remains hitched to the husband's wagon".[62]

Because of some of these concerns, pension sharing was introduced.[63] A pension sharing order is an order which provides that one party's shareable rights under a specified pension arrangement, or shareable state scheme rights, be subject to pension sharing for the benefit of the other party, and specifies the percentage value to be transferred. The effect of the order is to credit the transferee with a percentage of the transferor's pension arrangement. This is reduced accordingly. The basic state pension cannot be shared, but the state earnings related pension (SERPS) and shared additional pension can. The order cannot be made if there is already a pensions attachment order. It can be made in respect of a pension which is already being paid.

These two pension-related orders co-exist and pension attachment may still accordingly be chosen. In most cases pension sharing will be found the preferable solution.

THE ORDERS: PROPERTY

The next orders relate specifically to property.

There is first the transfer of property order.[64] The court may order that specified property be transferred to the other spouse.

Most commonly this will be the matrimonial home or an interest in it. But other property, for example shares, may be subject to this order. The order may also transfer property to any child of the family or to a specified person for the benefit of such a child. The property to be transferred must be in the power of the transferor to transfer. Where, as in *TL v ML*,[65] the assets in question were controlled by his parents, it was held inappropriate to regard them as available for transfer. It must also be within the effective control of the court: if the property is abroad, an order can only be made if it can be effectively enforced.[66]

Second, the court may direct that property to which a party to the marriage is entitled be settled for the benefit of the other party and/or the children of the family.[67] The most common use of this power is the so-called *Mesher* order.[68] This grapples—it is debatable how successfully—with the need to preserve the investment interest of both spouses, while the same time providing a house in which to bring up the children. It orders that the home be settled on trust for one or both of the spouses in specified shares, with sale postponed until a future event (for example the children reaching a certain age or finishing full-time education, or until death, remarriage or cohabitation of the other spouse). The *Mesher* order has a number of drawbacks.[69]

It is a property transfer order and is therefore not variable. But it may last for many years, and circumstances change. Upon the triggering event, the wife (now most probably in her 40s or 50s) will have to rehouse herself without the capital—her share of the proceeds of sale are likely to be reduced by virtue of having had occupancy for a number of years—or probably the income to do so adequately. She may have to move to a cheaper area, away from friends and employment, at just the time she is having to adjust to the children leaving home. She will have, moreover, to co-operate with her former husband to organise the sale, revisiting past acerbities. *Mesher* orders do nothing for the "clean break". If she wants to move before the triggering event— perhaps she gets a job in another part of the country—there will also be difficulties. There was even a suggestion at one time that she ought to pay rent to her former husband: little was heard about this after it became apparent that for some women this would mean paying back or foregoing periodical payments, a blow not softened by the realisation that he would have to pay tax on the rent received. When the *Mesher* order was formulated, too little attention was paid to the interests of children. It is all-too-common for adult children to remain in the matrimonial home and to remain dependent. What happens to them once the triggering event comes into operation?

After *White v White* (discussed below),[70] some thought there might be more use of *Mesher* orders, because of its emphasis on fairness (Fisher, 2002; Hodson *et al.*, 2003). But if women will struggle to rehouse themselves when the sale is triggered, *White v White* with its "yardstick of equality",[71] should lead to less reliance on the *Mesher* order. In *B v B (Mesher Order)*,[72] the court refused a *Mesher* order when it was clear that the wife's prospects of being able to generate capital of her own between the time of the case and the triggering event were small whereas there was every reason to believe the husband would generate such capital. This inequality of outcome was the result of her having to bring up a two-year-old.

Another form of settlement order is the *Martin* order.[73] This gives one spouse the right to occupy the house until death, remarriage or cohabitation. The wife's position—it will normally be the wife upon whom the property is settled—will thus be secured. In *Martin v Martin*, the couple were childless and the husband, who had left to live with another woman, enjoyed secure council housing. The wife was left in the former matrimonial house which belonged to both of them beneficially in equal shares. The Court of Appeal upheld the judge's order that the house should be held in trust for the wife during her life or until her remarriage or such earlier date as she should cease to live there, and thereafter on trust for both of them in equal shares. The Court of Appeal approved the *Martin* order in *Clutton v Clutton*[74] (it was in slightly different form, referring to death, remarriage or cohabitation). This case was complicated by the fact that the order would encourage the husband to spy upon the wife to establish that she was cohabiting, and thus trigger a sale. The court thought the bitterness which would be felt by the husband if he discovered she was living with a cohabitant in the former matrimonial home outweighed the bitterness she would feel if she sensed she were under "perpetual supervision".[75] A *Martin* order would protect the interests of both of them (but see Hayes, 1994).

Third, the court may make an order varying any "ante-nuptial or post-nuptial" settlement made on the parties to the marriage for their benefit and/or the children of the family.[76] This power dates from 1857, and was until the modern reforms the only way in which the courts could deal with capital on the breakdown of a marriage. The concept of a "settlement" was broadly interpreted. A purchase of a house in joint names was regarded as a "settlement".[77] In *Brooks v Brooks*[78] it was held to extend to a personal pension scheme a businessman had established under which he and his spouse were beneficiaries. This was before the pension reforms of 1995 and 1999, and it is no longer possible or necessary to use the settlement provision in this way. Another recent example of this expansive use of the concept is *C v C (Variation of Post-Nuptial Settlement: Company Shares)*[79]: a husband's shareholding in his company was transferred into a settlement in the Cayman Islands, with his wife as a beneficiary. Now that wide powers exist under the 1973 Act, this order is little used. Ormrod L.J. said as much in 1974,[80] and in *Brooks v Brooks* Lord Nicholls of Birkenhead spoke of the language as "archaic".[81] It cannot be long before the order itself is consigned to the history books: what it achieves can now be effected by other more matrimonial-oriented methods.

Fourth, the court has the power to order the sale of any property in which, or in the proceeds of sale of which, both or either of the parties has or have a beneficial interest (in possession or reversion).[82] The order may be made notwithstanding that a third party is also interested in the property. This power was not in the 1970 legislation but was added, following the Law Commission's recommendation,[83] in 1981.[84] This order can only be made where the court makes a secured periodical payments order, a lump sum order or a property adjustment order.

The courts' powers to redistribute the spouses' property upon divorce are thus extremely wide. There are nevertheless actions which cannot be taken. Thus, there is no power to deal with property which does not belong to either of the spouses, where, for example, the matrimonial home belongs to a parent or is tied accommodation. There is no power to order a third party—a new partner for example—to provide for the applicant or the children of the family.[85] And a limited company is a third party—though if this is no more than a spouse's "alter ego" an order may be made.[86] There is no power to grant financial relief which does not come within the terms of the legislation.[87] Thus, there is no power to order one party to pay out of the proceeds of sale of the matrimonial home the debts of either party which are not connected to the interest in the property.[88]

THE GOVERNING PRINCIPLES: WHITE AND MILLER/ MCFARLANE

We must now examine the principles which are applied in determining the orders. Various principles have been adopted at various times and dropped: for example, the so-called "one-third rule", which was still offering guidance in the 1970s.[89]

The 1970 Act laid down general principles, now in s.25 of the Matrimonial Causes Act. There were reforms effected by the Matrimonial and Family Proceeding Act 1984 (Freeman, 1984). And there have since been important House of Lords rulings in *White v White*[90] and in *Miller v Miller; McFarlane v McFarlane*.[91] The principles established in these overarch those laid down in legislation, and for this reason will be considered first. The legislation gives the courts discretion. This has long been acknowledged, and was re-emphasised in *White v White*.[92]

In *White v White* the House of Lords purported to lay down a principle to circumscribe this discretion. Lord Nicholls of Birkenhead stated it thus:

"Everyone would accept that the outcome ... should be fair. More realistically, the outcome ought to be as fair as possible in all the circumstances. But everyone's life is different. Features which are important when assessing fairness differ in each case. And sometimes different minds can reach different conclusions on what fairness requires. ... Fairness, like beauty, lies in the eye of the beholder.

... There is one principle of universal application. ... In seeking to achieve a fair outcome, there is no place for discrimination between husband and wife and their respective roles. ... If, in their different spheres, each contributed equally to the family, then in principle it matters not which of them earned the money and built up the assets. There should be no bias in favour of the money-earner and against the home-maker and the child-carer".[93]

In *White v White*, and in other cases upholding this principle, the parties have not necessarily got equal shares of the assets. Nevertheless, the "yardstick"[94] is equality of division.[95] As Lord Nicholls of Birkenhead went on to point out:

"... equality should be departed from only if, and to the extent that, there is a good reason for doing so. The need to consider and articulate reasons for departing from equality would help the parties and the court to focus on the need to ensure the absence of discrimination".[96]

He insisted that "yardstick of equality" is not the same thing as a "presumption"[97] of equality or even a "starting point".[98] This would transgress the boundaries of permissible interpretations of s.25. But Lord Cooke of Thorndon did not think a "yardstick" would produce results different from a starting point or guidelines,[99] and he is clearly right.

Subsequently, Lord Nicholls has referred to fairness as an "elusive concept".[100] And Baroness Hale of Richmond explained "the ultimate objective is to give each party an equal start on the road to independent living".[101] The yardstick of equality is "an aid, not a rule".[102] In the later case of *Miller v Miller; McFarlane v McFarlane* Lord Nicholls (joined by Baroness Hale) attempted to put some flesh on the concept of fairness. First, there are financial needs. The most common source of need is the presence of children.[103] Their welfare is "always" the first consideration. However, as Baroness Hale pointed out, this can all-too-easily become a "limiting principle",[104] as happened before *White v White* where women's needs ("reasonable requirements") were met but men left marriage often with large surpluses. Hence the imperative for a second strand, namely compensation to redress "any significant prospective economic disparity between the parties arising from the way they conducted their marriage".[105] Mrs McFarlane's situation is a excellent illustration: she had given up a career in a leading firm of city solicitors to bring up three children. Of course, she was able to earn her own living but at nowhere the level of her former husband (at the time of their marriage she was earning more than him). The third strand is sharing the fruits on the basis that marriage is a partnership of equals.[106] There are cases where this is easier than others: Baroness Hale cites the case of *Burgess v Burgess*,[107] a long marriage between a solicitor and a doctor: "although one party might have better prospects than the other in the future, once marriage was at the end there was no reason for one to make further claims upon the other".[108] *White v White* raised questions and provoked criticisms. Of the questions raised, perhaps the most important are discussed here.

(i) When may the principle of equality be departed from?

In the aftermath of *White v White* there were attempts to justify a departure by demonstrating that one party had made a larger contribution to the welfare of the family than the other. There were cases in which husbands were alleged to be exceptionally gifted businessmen, to have made "stellar" contributions.[109] "A domestic goddess self-evidently makes a 'stellar' contribution, but that was not what these debates were about".[110] Rather they were about husbands like Mr Cowan who spotted a niche market for plastic bin-liners![111] Even wives who came up against husbands who were not "geniuses" lost out: you don't have to be a genius to make a special or exceptional contribution to business! Not surprisingly, a "forensic Pandora's box" had been opened. It was firmly closed in *Lambert v Lambert*[112] (which on appeal *L v L*[113] was now called). Thorpe L.J. pointed to the danger of "gender discrimination" since "there is no equal opportunity for the homemaker to demonstrate the scale of her comparable success".[114] The Lords in *Miller v Miller; McFarlane v McFarlane* have confirmed this: for equality to be departed from the contribution must be "so marked that to discard it would be inequitable".[115] But there are still cases where equality is departed from, even though this oozes gender discrimination. For example, in *Sorrell v Sorrell*[116] assets were divided 60:40, leaving the wife with assets of just under £30 million. The husband was an "exceptionally talented" businessman; the wife a 59-year-old who had married for "keeps" (metaphorically, and, cynics might say, literally as well) and had spent the 32 years of marriage as a wife and mother. Only if equality became a presumption—and the Lords in *White v White* specifically said they did not intend this—will cases like *Sorrell v Sorrell* not recur. If there is ever to be a "special contribution" Sir Martin Sorrell's is likely to be it. The judge refrained from calling it "stellar", because rightly this is not a route we should any longer take. On the other hand, it is difficult to see in what way Lady Sorrell could actually match her husband's contribution to business success.

(ii) Does White v White only apply to lengthy marriages?

White v White concerned a long marriage (34 years), and most of the cases which have applied it have also been long. Eekelaar (2001a) has argued that it is through time that the case for a 50 per cent share builds up, that equality is only attainable after a lengthy, but unspecified, period. Of course, it is the length of homemaking to which he is referring: "homemaking for 1 day, however brilliantly done, is in itself of relatively little value" (Eekelaar, 2003, p.831). It is clear that to emphasise duration in this way is discriminatory (Bailey-Harris, 2003, p.388). Diduck and Kaganas (2006, p.261) point out that this "accepts without challenge the hierarchically gendered value placed upon one type of contribution over another". Yet despite these rather obvious problems with emphasising length, it was suggested in *GW v RW (Financial Provision: Departure from Equality)*[117] that an equal division was appropriate where the marriage was over 20 years in length, but more problematic where it was less. This reasoning was followed in *M v M*,[118] but has now been disapproved by the House of Lords. However, Baroness Hale stated that if assets were not "family assets",[119] that is not generated by the joint efforts of the parties, then duration of the marriage might justify a departure from the yardstick of equality. So length of marriage may still be relevant. But what is a long marriage? The judge in *GW v RW* seized upon 20 years as the qualifying criterion but he could equally as well have said 15 or 25. In *Foster v Foster*,[120] the marriage was a short one (only four years) and, although the court departed from the yardstick of equality, it did affirm that where the capital surplus had been generated by joint efforts, it did not matter how long it had taken to build this up. This reasoning was approved by the Lords in *Miller v Miller* (which was a short—three years—childless marriage): "a short marriage is no less a partnership of equals than a long marriage".[121] However, the Lords recognised an "instinctive feeling" that parties will "generally have less call upon each other on the breakdown of a short marriage",[122] so that a 50–50 split is unlikely to be the division laid down.

(iii) Does White v White only apply to the wealthy?

Lord Nicholls, in both *White v White* and in *Miller v Miller; McFarlane v McFarlane*, states categorically that equality is a principle of universal application. "It is applicable to all marriages".[123] Most of the reported cases in which *White v White* has been applied are "big money" cases, but there are examples of its principles applied to couples who are less well-off. There is no problem upholding the principle in all cases, so long as it is realised that it will be difficult, sometimes impossible, to apply it in practice to the many divorcing couples who have very little in the way of assets. Many of them will have substantial debts. The only "fruits" they will share will be bitter ones. *White and Miller/ McFarlane* are blueprints for the wealthy, not the "have nots". For the latter it is arguable that the discredited goal of meeting "reasonable requirements" fits circumstances better. For them the priority of the divorce justice system must be to ensure that whoever takes the children—and this will usually be the woman—also has adequate accommodation in which to house them.

(iv) What of conduct?

It was to be expected that questions would be asked after *White v White* about the impact of conduct on equality. As we shall see, the general rule is that conduct is only taken into account when it would be inequitable to disregard it.[124] Would there be circumstances when a lesser standard might displace the equality yardstick? In *Miller v Miller* the Court of Appeal agreed with the trial judge that the husband's conduct in leaving the wife for another woman entitled the court to attach less weight to the shortness of the marriage than otherwise it might.[125] But this conclusion has been firmly rejected by the House of Lords: "in most cases fairness does not require consideration of the parties' conduct".[126] Only where such conduct is "obvious and gross"[127] will it displace the principle of equality.

(v) Equality when?

An issue left open by *White v White* relates to the date of calculating equality. Are assets as at the date of the divorce to be divided or is the homemaker (whose homemaking role may well continue after the divorce, particularly if there are children to bring up) to share in what the breadwinner acquires in the future? To achieve equality now is one thing: to maintain equality quite another. As has already been stressed, the effects of being married are perpetuated by divorce. Should the yardstick of equality then apply to income as well as capital? In *McFarlane v McFarlane; Parlour v Parlour* before the Court of Appeal[128] it was argued for two non-working wives of high-income earning husbands, one an accountant, the other a Premier league footballer, that the yardstick of equality rather than reasonable requirements should apply to the determination of the quantum of their maintenance by way of periodical payments. This would allow them to accumulate capital for their future support. For the husbands it was argued that the purpose of periodical payments was to maintain. Bennett J.'s conclusion that needs should not constitute a "glass ceiling"[129] was approved by the Court of Appeal.[130] Thorpe L.J. stated:

"Clearly in the assessment of periodical payments, as of capital provision, the overriding objective is fairness. Discrimination between the sexes must be avoided. The cross-check of equality is not appropriate for a number of reasons. First, in many cases the division of income is not just between the parties, since there will be children with a priority claim for the costs of education and upbringing. Secondly, Lord Nicholls of Birkenhead suggested the use of the cross-check in dividing the accumulated fruits of past shared endeavours. In assessing periodical payments the court considers the division of the fruit of the breadwinner's future work in a context where he may have left the child-carer in the former matrimonial home, where he may have to meet alternative housing costs and where he may have in fact or in contemplation a second wife and a further child".[131]

The Court of Appeal held that the overriding objective laid down in *White v White* could apply to periodical payments—in an exceptional case, such as here, where there was a huge surplus of available income after the needs of the parties had been met. The House of Lords in the *McFarlane* appeal (the *Parlour* case was not appealed to the Lords) reasoned that once it was established that "compensation" was a basis for achieving fairness, it could not be right to limit a wife's periodical payments to what she needed.[132] The Court of Appeal had imposed a limited term order of five years on Mrs McFarlane.[133] The Lords did not think this right: it was "most unlikely to be sufficient to achieve a fair outcome".[134] If circumstances changed, the husband could apply for a variation. Clean breaks may be important but they are not to be achieved at "the expense of a fair result".[135] A difficult balance has to be struck between the two (but see Cooke, 2004). This will be discussed further in the context of the clean break.

The timing of the assessment also an issue when the husband acquires a large bonus after the marriage breakdown. In *Rossi v Rossi*[136] it was said that if the bonus "relates to a period immediately following separation. ... It is too close to the marriage to justify categorisation as non-matrimonial".[137] The judge drew the line at 12 months. But in *H v H*,[138] Charles J. disagreed. The relevant date was when the "mutual support between the parties ended. Since that time, the husband had acquired two bonuses of £2,380,538 and £2,347,284 respectively. Neither of these were accordingly included as part of the matrimonial assets.

White v White is not without its critics, and criticisms have continued since the later Lords' ruling in *Miller v Miller*; *McFarlane v McFarlane*. Cretney, writing about *White*, thought it "simplistic" to equate home-making contributions and com-mercially-motivated money-making activity. Even if, he thought, right-thinking people now wanted to make such an equation, this was "a matter of social judgment for Parliament rather than the courts" (2001, p.3). To argue that the equation is simplistic is to fail to understand gender discrimination. To limit the judicial function in this way is to give the courts too narrow a role.

Others, for example Bailey-Harris (2001a) have pointed to the narrow focus of *White v White* on contributions. And, as Eekelaar points out (2001), this suggests a shift in emphasis from a wel-fare-based approach (in which the needs of the parties are met) to an entitlement-based approach (under which you get what you have earned). But this is a step towards—and to some critics a step too far—community of property.[139]

The extension of the *White* principles to income also been criticised. Thus, Cooke (2004) argues that it "perpetuates dependency and perhaps animosity". It militates against the acceptance today that marriage "may well not be for life". It discourages a fresh start and may be "particularly damaging to women by discouraging financial independence". But the legacy of dependency will not be turned round by ignoring it, and financial independence may be ultimately more readily attain-able if the base is comfort rather than penury. A further criticism (Moor and Le Grice, 2006) is that the *Miller/McFarlane* decision may encourage the ex-husband to take a less demanding, lower-paying job. No court is going to order him to stop playing golf on Wednesdays! How would a court respond to an ex-wife's application for variation (asking for a higher percentage of his income) because he is now earning substantially less? And what if after separation he had a serious accident or became ill and was unable to work? This issue has yet to be addressed.

THE STATUTORY PRINCIPLES

We must now consider the statutory principles governing financial provision. These principles are laid down in s.25 of the

Matrimonial Causes Act 1973, as amended by the Matrimonial and Family Proceedings Act 1984. The new s.25 has made children's welfare the first consideration in support cases.[140] It also removed the target of attempting to place the parties in the financial position in which they would have been if the marriage had not broken down and each had properly discharged financial obligations and responsibilities to the other. The 1984 Act also added a new s.25A, thus enacting the "clean break" principle. The principle must now be looked at in the light of *Miller v Miller; McFarlane v McFarlane*.

The legislation prioritises the welfare of children. It then lists eight matters to which the court "shall in particular have regard". These are not ranked in hierarchy and which a court will emphasise may depend on the facts of the particular case and their judgment. The factors listed embody no coherent philosophy. Diduck and Kaganas (2006, p.244) point to the way that the first five of the factors are needs-based and the last three contain elements of a compensation model. But, as they point out (pp.244–245), "entitlement is not based on the fact of the marriage, but rather is a reimbursement or compensation for needs that were created by the way in which the parties structured their marital roles". And engrafted is also the clean break model, which reflects yet a different philosophy—moving on to a fresh start and self-sufficiency. Sections 25 and 25A were not, it hardly needs to be said, formulated by philosophers. They reflect rather English pragmatism.

The court is directed, when considering whether to exercise its powers and, if so, in what manner:

"...to have regard to all the circumstances of the case, first consideration being given to the welfare while a minor of any child of the family who has not attained the age of eighteen".

The importance of this emphasis on children's welfare should not be underestimated. Although children's welfare is only the "first consideration", and not as elsewhere in legislation the "paramount consideration",[141] and although this means it is not the overriding consideration,[142] putting children in the forefront of the decision-making process is significant. Thus, it has been held[143] that it would be contrary to a child's interests if a parent were to be left in "straitened circumstances", since this would cause the child distress. It also means that a spouse with a young child may not be expected to go out to work.[144] The particular accommodation needs of a child may justify a substantial capital award, even where the marriage has been short. Having somewhere to be able to have a child stay on a contact visit has been considered important enough to justify an award sufficient to permit the purchase of accommodation.[145] Compare *B v B (Financial Provision: Welfare of Child and Conduct)*,[146] where the need to ensure that a child with a disturbed background has a secure and satisfactory home had the consequence that there was no money to enable his father to purchase a house.

First consideration is only to be given to the welfare of the child during that child's minority. The courts, however, recognise that a child's dependency does not come to an end on the 18th birthday. In *Richardson v Richardson (No.2)*,[147] a periodical payment order in favour of the wife was extended so that she could continue to be financially responsible for the two daughters while they were at college. That they were no longer minor was not decisive. As Thorpe J. put it: "What is decisive is that they are still dependent".[148]

It has already been noted that the court must have regard to all the circumstances of the case. The Act identifies a large number of these. The list is not exhaustive, and there is no hierarchy.

First, the income, earning capacity, property and other financial resources which each of the parties to the marriage has or is likely to have in the foreseeable future.[149] It used to be assumed that all of the spouses' property needed to be taken into account. But with the introduction of the yardstick of equality with its emphasis on achieving a fair settlement,[150] the question has arisen as to the status of assets such as gifts and inheritance and in particular about wealth generated by the efforts of one of the spouses only. In *Miller v Miller; McFarlane v McFarlane* Lord Nicholls and Baroness Hale agreed that the source of capital was relevant, but differed as to the criterion to be applied. For Lord Nicholls it was that which was acquired as a result of the parties common endeavours ("the marital acquest")[151] which should be shared (though in a short marriage like the Millers', fairness might dictate that not even this should be shared). In a longer marriage, such property might be seen as a contribution to the matrimonial assets. Baroness Hale distinguished "family assets" from "business or investment assets generated solely or mainly by the efforts of one party":[152] in the case of the latter it might not be necessary to include them in property to be subjected to the yardstick of equality, particularly where the marriage was short. It is likely that in most marriages the distinction will be unimportant since courts will seek to divide all of the parties' assets. It may be that it will only be in short marriages that a deviation from the yardstick of equality will be ruled.

Gifts and inheritance were not in issue in *Miller v Miller; McFarlane v McFarlane*, but in *White v White* Lord Nicholls did say that in the case of an inheritance the spouse to whom it was given should be allowed to keep it.[153] There is burgeoning case law on this, for example on whether there is a difference between an inheritance received during the marriage and landed property passed down through generations,[154] and the law is not yet settled.

It is clearer on earning capacity, a matter often disputed in the past. Thus, it is expected that an unemployed man will, if he is able, obtain work, even if it is very different from what he has done previously.[155] If he could earn more by doing overtime this is also taken into account.[156] The courts only look to possible increases in earning capacity where it would be reasonable to expect a spouse to take steps to achieve a higher income.[157] In the case of women in particular they will take note of commitments to looking after children before coming to any such conclusion.[158] They are also well aware of the difficulties older women may have in returning to the labour market after time out for home-making and/or childcare.[159] The work environment changes rapidly and often requires new skills.

The existence of a new partner cannot be ignored (Hodson, 1990). As already indicated, periodical payments terminate on remarriage, though not necessarily on cohabitation. Where the wife is living with another man, his financial resources may reduce the need for periodical payments or lead to a reduction in the award made.[160] The financial means of the husband's new partner are also relevant: they reduce his needs thereby releasing more money with which he can support his first family.[161] The court will not, however, make an order which will have the effect of compelling the new partner to make payments from her income or capital.[162]

Second, the financial needs, obligations and responsibilities which each of the parties has or is likely to have in the foresee-able future have to be considered.[163] For about 20 years in so-called "big money" cases the courts interpreted "needs" to mean "reasonable requirements".[164] It led to unseemly squabbles about wives' shopping lists. And in the main it was male judges who had to make the decisions. Questions such as how much did she reasonably require for clothes? Did she really need to buy her furniture at Heal's (wouldn't Habitat suffice?) Did it really require £4000 a year to feed the labrador?[165] It also led to con-clusions which, judged by post-*White* standards, were manifestly unfair. Lady Conran was awarded £10.5 million of Sir Terence's total wealth of some £85 million, and this despite her "out-standing" contributions in helping her husband's business and reputation over 30 years.[166] A consequence of this was the development of the so-called *Duxbury* calculation,[167] which enabled courts to order a capital sum which would, when invested, meet the wife's reasonable requirements. The longer the marriage, the older the wife, the less, of course, this sum had to be.[168] "Reasonable requirements" is no longer the test. As Lord Nicholls explained in *White v White*, "financial needs are only one of the factors to be taken into account in arriving at the amount of an award".[169] And, commenting on the "Duxbury paradox" he added

"The amount of capital required to provide for an older wife's financial needs may well be less than the amount required to provide for a younger wife's financial needs. It by no means follows that, in a case where resources exceed the parties' financial needs, the older wife's award will be less than the younger wife's. Indeed, the older wife's award may be sub-stantially larger".[170]

The emphasis in leading cases on big money divorces should not deflect us from considering "needs" in the more common cases of middle income parties and those at the poverty end.[171] The most obvious needs here are to maintain oneself and those dependent on one, and for a home. Once it is decided with whom the children are to live, ensuring their carer has a home is a principal target. The children's welfare is, we have seen, the first consideration. It is also important, we have also seen, that if the non-resident parent is to have contact he has somewhere for this to take place. The needs of children are most important but the needs of others including a second spouse must also be considered. This is difficult where resources are not abundant, as in a case like *Roberts v Roberts*[172] where a man on low income had the daunting task of trying to maintain his former wife and five children and his new partner, their child and two children she had in a previous relationship. First families come first. It is the husband's choice to assume liability for a second family.[173]

Third, is the standard of living enjoyed by the family before breakdown of the marriage.[174] Of course, there will be cases where a wife's standard of living during marriage has been lower than it should have been, for example because her husband has not revealed to her what he is earning. The argument that "enjoyed" includes "should have enjoyed" was accepted in *Preston v Preston*.[175] The frugal wife has produced different judicial responses: in *H v H (Clean Break: Non Disclosure: Costs)*[176] it was held that the standard of living during the marriage had to be taken into account; in *A v A (Financial Provision)*[177] the court was more concerned that the award should reflect the reality of the husband's wealth.

Fourth, is the age of each party and the duration of the marriage.[178] We have already considered the issue of the short marriage. There are also long marriages which have broken down after a few weeks, or months. The *Krystman*[179] marriage lasted 26 years but the parties cohabited for only two weeks: the court made no order. The more difficult problem is the marriage of a few weeks or months which has followed a substantial period of cohabitation. The courts no longer take the view that it is only marriage which counts. Whether they can do this under this heading (which refers specifically to the duration of "the marriage") is doubtful, but there is no difficulty in seeing pre-marital cohabitation as a "circumstance" or including it within the "welfare" contribution factor or even as "conduct". It was indeed as "conduct" that Wood J. in *Kokosinski v Kokosinski*[180] took account of 24 years of cohabitation: the marriage itself lasted only four months. The wife had given the best years of her life to her husband, had been loving, hard-working and had brought up their son of whom they were justly proud. More recently, Coleridge J. took account of eight years' cohabitation which preceded a four-year marriage.[181] It had, he said, "nothing to do with morality or religious belief and everything to do with striving to achieve financial fairness ... at a particular stage in society's development". He preferred to consider the lengthy cohabitation as a "circumstance" but if he had to include it within one of the factors to view it as a "contribution" or as "conduct".[182]

Fifth, there is any physical or mental disability of either of the parties to the marriage.[183] This may lead to no award where the prospective payer is disabled.[184]

Sixth, is the contributions which each of the parties has made or is likely to make in the foreseeable future to the welfare of the family, including any contribution by looking after the home or caring for the family.[185] This provision was a major breakthrough in the 1970 legislation—it was amended to add the words referring to "foreseeable future" in 1984[186]—because it enabled account to be taken specifically of the wife's contribution to homemaking and child care. The importance of this was stressed by Lord Denning M.R. in *Wachtel v Wachtel* in 1973 and in other early decisions.[187] It has become even more important since *White v White* adopted the yardstick of equality.[188] We have seen already that the immediate reaction to this yardstick were challenges to establish the unevenness of contributions by, for example, showing one (in reality the husband) had made "stellar" contributions. The House of Lords in *Miller v Miller; McFarlane v McFarlane* has now held that equality should only be departed from where it would be inequitable to do otherwise.[189]

The other side of the contribution coin may be addressed briefly. But, like the reasoning in *Miller/McFarlane* it is in effect an application of conduct. A good illustration is *H v H*.[190] A wife left her husband and four children after 15 years to live with another man. Her "contribution" to the welfare of the family was thus less than it should have been: she had "left the job unfinished",[191] and she received accordingly a reduced award. That was a ruling of 30 years ago. Today, it is much more likely that this would be considered under the umbrella of conduct, and distinctly possible, as we shall see, that no account would be taken of it.

Seventh, is the conduct of each of the parties, if that conduct is such that it would be inequitable to disregard it.[192] The extent to which conduct—usually misconduct—should be taken account of it has long been contentious. Even before the reforms of 1969 and 1970 the courts had moved away from insisting that adulterous wives should forfeit their maintenance. The introduction of irretrievable breakdown necessitated a further rethink, both in relation to maintenance and also (what was then called) the custody of children.[193] The only reference to conduct in the 1970 Act was incorporated in the minimal loss principle: the court was to place the parties so far as practicable and "having regard to their conduct just to do so" in the financial position in which they would have been if the marriage had not broken down".[194]

In *Wachtel v Wachtel* the Court of Appeal adopted Ormrod J.'s test at first instance that conduct should only be taken into account where it was "both obvious and gross".[195] Lord Denning M.R. was of the view that "in the financial adjustments consequent upon the dissolution of a marriage which has irretrievably broken down, the imposition of financial penalties ought seldom to find a place".[196] Not surprisingly, the courts were reluctant to take misconduct into account. Adultery without more was said not to get to the "starting gate".[197] It was however taken into account when it was with the wife's father-in-law (she had a child by him),[198] and, less dramatically, when a wife allowed her husband to purchase a home in joint names while she was carrying on an adulterous affair.[199]

In 1984, with the removal of the minimal loss principle, conduct was added to the factors to which a court ought to have regard, but only if, in the opinion of the court, it was such that it would be inequitable to disregard it.[200] Conduct now assumed a greater profile, and it was thought that greater account would be taken of it. But this has not proved so. There is no evidence that conduct is more readily being taken account of post–1984 than before. It was taken account of in *Le Foe v Le Foe and Woolwich plc*:[201] the husband mortgaged the matrimonial home to raise money to buy another house in which he intended to live with his mistress. Also in *Evans v Evans*[202] when the wife hired a "hit-man" to kill her husband—he only wounded him, and Mrs Evans from her prison cell sought an increase in periodical payments which, remarkably, Mr Evans was still paying. The Court of Appeal discharged the periodical payments order completely, with Balcombe L.J. remarking that people would think the courts had "taken leave of [their] senses"[203] if Mr Evans were expected to continue to pay periodical payments. Another example of conduct being taken into account is *Kyte v Kyte*[204] where the wife aided the husband's attempted suicide—she provided drugs and alcohol to assist. She stood to inherit on his death. The wife's behaviour even when looked at in the context of the husband's was such that it would be inequitable to disregard it. The lump sum awarded was reduced by nearly two-thirds. A husband who stabbed the wife so severely that she was lucky to be alive was stripped of all his assets, bar a small lump sum, in order to give her a secure future.[205]

It will have been noted that in the cases where conduct is taken into account it is usually criminal, rather than matrimonial, misconduct that is in issue (this is not to suggest, of course, that criminal acts aimed against a spouse are not also matrimonial misconduct). Does this explain the somewhat lenient approach adopted to a woman who married a wealthy man of nearly 80—she was in her 40s—refused to consummate the marriage and confined him to a caravan?[206] She lived with her lover in the house. Although it was obvious why she had married him and her conduct was said to be inequitable to disregard, she was nevertheless awarded a fifth of his capital. This extraordinary ruling was upheld by the Court of Appeal, though the sum was reduced from half a million to £175,000.

The courts have also occasionally taken into account misconduct towards the spouse in her capacity as parent: for example, abducting a child has been held to be conduct that it would be inequitable to disregard.[207] They have taken into account the mismanagement of financial affairs, for example squandering assets.[208] They have also taken into account misconduct in the conduct of ancillary relief proceedings, both in the order for costs and under this heading.[209] The 1996 Act contained a provision, not now implemented, which permitted conduct to be taken account of whatever its nature and whether it occurred during the marriage or after separation or even after dissolution of the marriage.[210] This might have re-emphasised conduct had it been implemented. It was an odd provision given the emphasis in the Act on irretrievable breakdown and mediation. A more recent attempt to focus on conduct was in the Court of Appeal decision in *Miller v Miller*, but as the House of Lords rejected this there is no need to speculate further on whether conduct has a greater part to play in short marriages than longer ones.

Finally, the value to each of the parties to the marriage of any benefit, for example a pension, which by reason of the dissolution (or annulment) that party will lose the chance of acquiring.[211] This antedates the pensions reforms to which reference has already been made.[212] The loss of a pension can still be taken account of in a financial provision award: the loss of a pension may be offset in determining how the available assets are to be shared. For example, a wife may be awarded the matrimonial home in return for not seeking a share of her husband's pension. There are, of course, other prospective losses. The case of *Trippas v Trippas*[213] illustrates this. After the parties separated the husband came into a large sum as a result of a sale of a family business. Had the marriage continued, she would have shared in this either in cash or in kind, and had the husband predeceased her he would have been expected to leave her a large sum. She was awarded a lump sum to compensate her for this loss.

THE CLEAN BREAK

A goal of the contemporary law relating to ancillary provision is to promote self-sufficiency. This was expressed by Lord Scarman in *Minton v Minton* several years before it was embodied in legislation. As he put it:

"The law now encourages spouses to avoid bitterness after family breakdown and to settle their money and property problems. An object of the modern law is to encourage each to put the past behind them and to begin a new life which is not overshadowed by the relationship which has broken down".[214]

The law on the "clean break" is now contained in the Matrimonial and Family Proceedings Act 1984 (as amended).[215] Courts are under a duty to consider whether it would be appropriate so to exercise their powers that the financial obligations of each party towards the other will be terminated as soon after the decree as it considers just and reasonable.[216] If a periodical payments order is still considered appropriate, the court is directed to consider requiring payments to be made for such term as would be sufficient to enable the payee to adjust without undue hardship to the termination of financial dependence on the other party.[217] There is also power to impose a clean break: the court may, if it considers that no continuing obligation should be imposed on either party to pay periodical payments, dismiss the application with a direction that the applicant shall not be entitled to make any further application.[218] Also (under s.28(1A)) the court may direct that a party is not entitled to apply for an extension of a fixed-term periodical payments order. A clean break order can also now be made on a variation application, even against the will of the payee.[219]

The evidence is that these provisions have had an impact beyond expectations, and spousal maintenance is as a result becoming less common (see Perry *et al.*, 2000; Arthur *et al.*, 2002). There are cases where a clean break is not appropriate, where, for example, the wife will continue to care for young children[220] or where there has been a long marriage during which time she has not worked.[221] There is as yet no presumption in favour of a clean break.[222] The goal post—*White v White*—is to achieve fairness and this may require financial support to continue or to continue for a fixed term. Clean breaks may be indicated where the husband is unreliable and cannot be expected to fulfill his obligations.[223] In such a case if capital is available, a lump sum may make more sense than an order for periodical payments. The imposition of a clean break against a party's will nevertheless remains unusual.[224]

The deferred clean break order was re-examined by the House of Lords in the *McFarlane* appeal.[225] As noted previously, the Lords did not consider a five-year term imposed on the wife of a high-earning accountant to produce a fair outcome. This was not a case where his capital assets were sufficient to achieve a clean break. But he would go on earning and his earnings were likely to increase—they were £753,000 p.a. at the time of the case. She had given up working as a solicitor—at one time earning more than he. When the clean break concept became embedded in the mid–1980s cases like Mrs McFarlane were less common and perhaps not even anticipated. How many high-earning female solicitors were there in the mid–1980s? Lord Hope acknowledged the implication of this: to give up employment as a City solicitor to raise a family "comes at a price which in most cases is irrecoverable".[226]

Before a court makes a limited term order, it must consider whether the party in whose favour the order is made can adjust without undue hardship to the termination of financial dependence on the other party. It is difficult to evaluate when hardship is "undue". There is a danger of orders being made without the evidence to support them. A balance has to be struck between the belief in "fresh starts" and the legacy of dependency. Even before *McFarlane* it was coming to be recognised that we were leaning too readily towards clean breaks. That women, often in their 40s, could resume careers as if nothing had happened is an unrealistic expectation. Mrs McFarlane, the House of Lords recognised, has many abilities and will not find it difficult to resume employment, but she will inevitably be penalised by the many years out and can never hope to achieve what was in prospect at the time she gave up paid employment.

VARYING AN ORDER

Most of the orders we have considered can be varied.[227] Lump sum orders cannot be varied (through an order relating to instalments of lump sum payments can).[228] Transfer of property orders cannot be varied; nor can *Mesher* orders. If the court adds a s.28(1A) direction, fixing the term of periodical payments, this period cannot be extended.[229] When a variation application is made, the court is under a duty to consider making a "clean break" as it is on the making of the original application. On applications to vary periodical payments,[230] the court is to consider whether it would be appropriate to vary the order so that payments are required to be made (in the case of secured periodical payments secured) "for such further period as will ... be sufficient ... to enable the [payee] to adjust without undue hardship to the termination of those payments". The court has the power to direct that an order for variation or discharge of a periodical payments order is not to take effect until the expiry of a specified period.[231] This is in order to enable the payee to adjust. Where it imposes a clean break, it can order a lump sum by way of compensation.[232] It can also make a property adjustment order and a pension sharing order.[233] The power to substitute capital provision for future periodical payments was recommended by the Law Commission.[234] It has been left to the courts to work out how the appropriate sum is to be calculated. In *Pearce v Pearce*,[235] the Court of Appeal held the court's function was to substitute an order (or orders) which would "fairly compensate the payee and at the same time complete the clean break".[236] "First consideration" should be given to the option of carving out of the payer's pension funds a pension for the payee equivalent to the discharged periodical payments order.

What factors should be taken into consideration? The Act provides that, when hearing an application for variation, the court is to look for all the circumstances of the case, first consideration being given to the welfare while a minor of any child of the family, and the circumstances of the case include any change in the matters to which it was required to have regard when making the order in the first place.[237] If the application comes after the death of the payer, the changed circumstance resulting from his death must also be taken into account.[238] The change of circumstances does not have to be exceptional or material: but if it is not, this may affect the exercise of the court's discretion.[239] Consent orders may be varied as any other order. However, since the motivation to agree to a consent order would be reduced if they could be readily varied, the courts are less willing to agree to an application to vary such an order.[240]

AVOIDING AN ORDER

A spouse may wish to defeat an application for financial provision by disposing of his assets before an application is made or even after the court has made an order. The court is given powers to defeat such fraudulent dispositions; it can make such orders as it thinks fit to restrain him and to protect the claim of the other spouse. If the court is satisfied that a disposition has already been made with the intention of defeating the claim of the other spouse, it may make an order setting the disposition aside.[241] If to defeat an application for financial provision a spouse makes himself bankrupt this, it is thought, is a not a disposition which the court can review under s.37.[242] The "cheated" spouse has, in these circumstances, to apply to annul the bankruptcy order on the grounds that it ought not to have been made.[243]

It may not be easy to establish what the spouse's intention was when he made the disposition. To meet this problem the Act distinguishes dispositions made three years or more before the application to set aside from those made less than three years before (or about to be made).[244] In the former case, the applicant must prove affirmatively that the intention is to defeat her claim: in the latter the intention is presumed if the effect of the disposition is to defeat her claim, and the burden shifts to him to prove this was not his intention.[245]

APPEALS

A short comment on appeals is required. They are not encouraged. Given the width of discretion courts have in making orders, it is recognised that a different court might come to a different conclusion. So an appellate court is only entitled to interfere with a decision where it is "plainly wrong".[246] Lord Hoffmann commented in *Piglowska v Piglowski* that "to allow successive appeals in the hope of producing an answer which accords with perfect justice is to kill the parties with kindness".[247]

But what if circumstances change after an order is made? This is to confront conflicting considerations: the need for finality and the imperative to do justice. The problem arises where leave is sought to appeal out of time. A striking illustration is the case of *Barder v Barder (Caluori Intervening)*.[248] There was a consent order and the husband agreed to transfer to his wife his half interest in the matrimonial home. Shortly afterwards, the wife killed both children and committed suicide. The whole rationale for the decision was undetermined, and the House of Lords held it should be set aside. The Lords laid down four conditions to be satisfied before leave to appeal out of time could be granted from an order for financial provision or property adjustment (by consent or otherwise). There must be new events which have invalidated the assumption upon which the order was made. They must occur within a relatively short time of the order being made. The application for leave to appeal must be made reasonably promptly. Third parties who have acquired interests in good faith and for value should not be prejudiced.

These conditions have been satisfied in other cases where one of the spouses has died shortly after the order,[249] as well as in cases where the supervening event is the remarriage and vacating of the home—the subject of the order—by a spouse,[250] and cases where after divorce the parties become reconciled.[251] Other possible reasons for requesting leave to appeal out of time are when the law changes—this was recognised as a possibility in *S v S (Ancillary Relief: Consent Order)*[252]—and when the property valuation used to make the order has turned out to be inaccurate. A good illustration of this is *Hope-Smith v Hope-Smith*.[253] The matrimonial home was valued at £116,000. The husband was ordered to pay to the wife £32,000 out of the proceeds of sale. Two years later, as a result of her husband's "wilful conduct and dilatory tactics" the house, now worth £200,000, remained unsold. The Court of Appeal substituted an order that the wife should get 40 per cent of the proceeds of the sale—two-and-a-half times the original order. The *Barder* conditions had been satisfied through no fault of hers. There have been many attempts to reopen orders on similar facts. Some of these have succeeded, and others have failed. The courts are clearly concerned that the floodgates may open, and are now taking a restrictive approach to these to these applications.[254] As Hale J. said in *Cornick v Cornick* something unforeseen and unforeseeable must have happened to bring about a substantial change in the parties' finances before a case is reopened.[255] The husband's redundancy is, it has been held, not an unpredicted event, but part of life's normal difficulties.[256]

An application can be made to set aside an order if the order has been made where facts material to the making of the order were not disclosed or where there has been fraud, duress or misrepresentation. An example is *Vicary v Vicary*.[257] A consent

order was made on the basis that the husband had assets of
£430,000. The husband knew that negotiations were taking place
for the sale of a company in which he had a substantial shareholding, and, shortly after the consent order, his shareholding
was sold for £2.8 million. It was held that the husband had by
deliberate non-disclosure of the true position led his wife to
agree to the terms of a consent order. It was set aside. Not every
failure of disclosure will lead a court to set aside an order.
Certainly, where knowledge of the true facts would not have led
the court to make a different order, it will not be set aside.[258]

REFORMING FINANCIAL PROVISION

Is the existing system of financial provision on divorce satisfactory? It is, of course, in a state of flux. A number of reform routes
are possible (Eekelaar, 1998; Bailey-Harris, 2001a). Some proposals for reform, for example those in a Government Green Paper
in 1998[259] have been virtually adopted in recent cases. For
example, it proposed to add to the s.25 factors an overarching
objective so that courts would have to exercise their powers in
such a way as "to endeavour to do that which is fair and reasonable between the parties and any child of the family".[260] A set
of guiding principles was proposed. These prioritised the welfare of children, took account of any written agreements about
financial arrangements and then provided that the court should
"divide any surplus so as to achieve a fair result, recognising that
fairness will generally require the value of the assets to be
divided equally between the parties".[261] But it also emphasised a
clean break at the earliest date practicable. We now realise that
this goal is less attainable than we once thought. It also proposed
that pre-nuptial agreements should be binding in certain circumstances.[262] However, these circumstances are so limited that
only wealthy childless couples could comply.

It seems unlikely that, in the near future at least, these proposals will be enacted as legislation. They are not the only proposals. In 2003 the Law Society designed a blueprint: it
suggested some guidelines for the sharing of assets on divorce.[263]
Like the Government Green Paper, it rejected an equal division
of assets. It was concerned with the unfairness of this when the
parent with the care of children needs the former matrimonial
home as a home for the children. The report put needs first, in
particular the housing needs of children. It believed that non-

financial contributions of a homemaker and child carer should be given "a weight and significance appropriate to the circumstances of the case",[264] thus adopting in essence the current statutory formula, and in effect turning the clock back pre-*White v White*.[265] It is almost as if it was unaware of the discriminatory nature of this formulation. However, it did emphasise fairness which, it said, "may frequently require the value of the remaining assets to be divided equally".[266] If a judge were to rule against equality of division he would have to specify "which of the factors in section 25 have led him to that conclusion".[267]

In the aftermath of *White v White* and *Miller v Miller; McFarlane v McFarlane* there is increasing demand for pre-marital and post-marital agreements. As already indicated, the Government (in 1998) saw them as useful, but its proposal built in so many safeguards as to rule them out in most cases. The Family Division judges were divided: most wanted the terms of a pre-nuptial agreement added to the s.25 factors: a minority thought that pre-nuptial and post-nuptial agreements should be presumptively binding.[268] In 2004, *Resolution* have proposed that s.25 be amended to stipulate that agreements be considered binding "unless to do so will cause significant injustice to either party or to any minor child of the family".[269] It looks as if English law will come to embrace the pre-nuptial contract, though there are no plans to so at present. The concept remains fraught with problems. For example, will an agreement terminate on the birth of a child? And what other triggering events will frustrate it?

In the light of *White v White* and *Miller v Miller; McFarlane v McFarlane* increasing attention is paid to the idea of a 50:50 split of matrimonial assets (Barlow *et al.*, 2004). Equal division of matrimonial assets is common in several countries in Europe.[270] New Zealand too operates a system where, if marriage has lasted three years, matrimonial assets are shared equally unless circumstances are such as to render such a decision repugnant to justice. The judges of the Family Division are not in favour.[271] There are those (Cretney, 2003a, for example) who think we have introduced a matrimonial regime of community of property by the back door—through the judicial legislation initiated by *White v White*. The Government Green Paper[272] was not in favour of a presumption of equal division of assets, nor was the Law Society.[273] It reflects a particular view of marriage, one characterised by Milton Regan (1999) as an "external orientation". This emphasises "the discrete individual with his or her own interests and who enters the marriage relationship as a sort of market interaction". By contrast, the internal orientation is a commitment to "a shared purpose that transcends the self" (Regan, 1999, p.30). Typically, men will adopt an external orientation, women an internal one. Regan, with whom (on this) Diduck (2003) agrees, says that women are more likely to be successful in achieving recognition for their homemaking and child care when their claims are "justified on the basis of the external, rights and market-based view, as compensation for services provided".[274] But men, at least wealthy men who may have most to lose, are more likely to express their external orientation by negotiating favourable pre-marital agreements from their position of strength, opting out of marriage itself.

Equal division may be fair, and it has the merit of certainty and therefore saves on litigation. But it lacks the element of flexibility and, therefore, cannot accommodate special needs, for example those of a mother whose children are disabled and require full-time care and attention. Whether it will work in the case of poor families may also be doubted: sharing 50:50 a small amount or accumulated debts will give neither spouse enough to do anything with. Further, although it may be high-minded to exclude conduct considerations, this is out of line with community sentiment. A 50:50 division would insult a man whose wife had attempted to kill him or who was having an affair with his father. There will, in other words, be cases where justice dictates a solution other than equal division (and see Herring, 2003). As we saw earlier, it is also difficult to decide what is being shared: the meaning of matrimonial assets is sufficiently difficult to divide two members of the House of Lords. The view has been expressed (Eekelaar, 1998) that equal sharing should depend on living together for a minimum specified duration and having brought up a child during that period. He suggests that a 50:50 division should take effect after 15 years and that the division should be in different proportions for lesser periods of time, for example 10:90 after 3 years and 40:60 after 12. Interestingly, Eekelaar would extend this approach to cohabiting couples on the breakdown of their relationship.[275]

There is no consensus on reform. The recent House of Lords' decisions have rendered reform both less necessary, though whether judicial legislation is appropriate is questioned by some (for example, Cretney, 2003a), and more so because of the questions the decisions have raised. Reform can only proceed successfully when the issues have been thought through and clear principles and policy articulated. We cannot afford a disastrous experiment like the Child Support Agency again.

CIVIL PARTNERSHIP

This chapter has concentrated on marriage. The Civil Partnership Act provides similar financial relief for civil partners who separate or terminate their relationship to that available for spouses. The parallel provisions are in Sch.5 of the Civil Partnership Act 2004. There are, as yet, no reported cases. When they arise they will raise similar questions, but also it is assumed different ones: the ethics of gay relationships may be different (and see Reece, 2003), and fairness and equality may work out in different ways. It may be that different principles will emerge to decide financial disputes. At this juncture, speculation would be idle.

COHABITATION

And what should be done to tackle post-separation issues when cohabiting relationships break down? The Law Commission does not think cohabiting couples should be treated in the same way as a married couple for financial relief purposes.[276] The notion of "equal partnership" which applies to marriage cannot it says, necessarily apply to cohabitants.[277] It argues:

"Where parties are married, the formal commitment they have entered into may be taken as good evidence that they assumed mutual responsibilities to support each other in cases of need. ... Cohabitants currently have no legal obligation of mutual support. ... Even in long relationships, there may be no clear basis for concluding that the parties have assumed that sort of responsibility towards each other".[278]

The Law Commission proposes that, if "eligibility criteria" are met, a claim can be made. The criteria are having a child or living together for a period of time. They seek views on what this time should be. A claim could be made if it can be shown that "the effects of the contributions and associated economic sacrifices ... made during the relationship would otherwise be unfairly shared on separation".[279] The emphasis is thus not welfare oriented—it is not based on needs[280]—but is related to contributions to the relationship and "sacrifices". There are, of course, different sorts of contributions, financial ones and homemaking and child care ones in particular. The Law Commission accordingly suggest that the emphasis should be on whether either party's economic position at separation is improved by the retention of "some economic benefit arising from contributions made by the other party during the relationship" or "impaired by economic sacrifices made as a result of their party's contributions" or as a result of "continuing child-care responsibilities following separation".[281] This is hardly a simple blueprint. The Law Commission recommends that couples would be able to opt out and enter into cohabitation contracts if they preferred to do so.[282] A final report is awaited.

CONCLUSION

White and *Miller/McFarlane* constitute some progress. We are now talking about equality and fairness. And this is important. But we are still situating these concepts within a private relationship. It is as if it is none of the state's business, as if private adjustment can ignore public inequality. The state takes a greater interest in child support—it runs a (rather poor) collection agency—than it does in maintenance of ex-wives after divorce. There are some who believe that maintenance after divorce should be abolished. The argument is that it perpetuates dependency. But, as Smart (1984, p.223) notes: "abolishing maintenance for ex-wives does not give women their financial independence". However, retaining it "has the deleterious effect of containing the 'problem' within the private sphere, with the consequences that women's dependency remains a private issue and a personal conflict, and does not become a matter of public policy".

Can a private law of maintenance ever be anything but unfair? It is predicated on sex roles and sex ranks. Child-rearing and homemaking are perceived as second-class, and those who fulfill these functions (mainly women) are marginalised. The decisions in *White* and *Miller/McFarlane* are important because they recognise these tasks, but attentive reading of the judgments makes it clear that they are secondary, to be measured against the more primary money-earning role.

The "yardstick of equality" demands more than adjustment of a private relationship. It cannot be achieved without true equality in the workplace, the end of discrimination, equal pay, family-friendly workplaces, affordable, good quality child care. *White* and *Miller/McFarlane* address marriage-related disabilities: they do not address the more general handicaps faced by women.

UNDERSTANDING PARENTS AND CHILDREN

THE RIGHT TO FOUND A FAMILY

Most adults in a heterosexual relationship can if they wish become parents. Parenthood is not licensed by the state.[1] You have to pass a driving test to drive a car: your fitness to become a parent is not examined.[2] The state only interferes with child-rearing practices when they fall below what is minimally accepted.[3] The state has greater control on the creation of the adoptive relationship: prospective adopters are carefully vetted.[4] Those who require fertility services are also scrutinised as to their suitability,[5] and courts have, for example, upheld age restrictions imposed by clinics offering services for the infertile.[6]

These are not the only ways in which parenthood is restricted. Two further examples of restrictions may be given. Courts have sanctioned non-therapeutic sterilisations of learning disabled young women, thus removing from them the opportunity to become mothers.[7] These decisions have been taken in the women's best interests,[8] and despite the ringing endorsement by Heilbron J., in the first case about a forced sterilisation to reach an English court, of the right of a woman to reproduce as a basic human right.[9] There are no reported cases approving the sterilisation of a man: in the one recent case to be referred to a court, his best interests were looked at very differently.[10] He could not, of course, become pregnant.

Courts have also ruled on the procreative rights of prisoners. They have affirmed the legality of a prison policy which denies prisoners facilities artificially to inseminate their wives. If the prisoner is serving a lengthy sentence and his wife's body clock is ticking, this in effect deprives the couple of the ability to become parents. Conjugal visits are not permitted in the United Kingdom. In the first of the cases,[11] the Court of Appeal was concerned that the child would be brought up in a single-parent family. This, it hardly needs to be pointed out, is not uncommon.

The wife in this case was going to be only 31 on her husband's release. In the second case, where the wife was 45 and would be 51 on her husband's release, the Court of Appeal was anxious lest a child be brought into the world where there was "seeming insufficiency of resources to provide independently for welfare".[12] Of course, many children sadly are brought up in poverty.

Both challenges by prisoners were mounted under the Human Rights Act 1998, and invoked Art.12 of the European Convention.[13] This confers on men and women of marriageable age the right to marry and found a family.[14] Article 8, which enshrines respect for private and family life, is also pertinent.

In the cases involving prisoners, both the prisoner and his partner wanted a child. But the state may also find itself involved in disputes when only one person wishes to become a parent. She wishes to terminate her pregnancy but he wants her to have his child. Since women do not have the right to an abortion—the decision rests with the two doctors who have, in good faith, decided that her circumstances fit within the statutory grounds[15]—it follows that men do not have the right to prevent an abortion taking place.[16] And so the courts have held.[17] One argument that could be mounted is that the father is intervening to protect the foetus's right to life. It would then become necessary to decide whether this or the woman's right to respect for her private and family life should prevail.[18] Twice recently, the European Court of Human Rights has denied that a foetus is a person with a right to life which could be protected by Art.2 of the Convention.[19]

The second of these cases raised the controversial question as to whether we could impose fatherhood on an unwilling man.[20] Natallie Evans and her partner had had embryos frozen, using their gametes, when she had been told she had ovarian cancer. But their relationship had broken up and he had withdrawn his consent, as English law allowed him to do,[21] to embryos being implanted in her. She had given assurances that the obligations of fatherhood (support obligations, for example) would not be expected. Since she no longer ovulated, access to these embryos was her only chance of having a child who was genetically related to her. He wanted the embryos destroyed. Wall J. and the Court of Appeal ruled in his favour.[22] Thorpe L.J. acknowledged that "for Ms Evans this is a tragedy of a kind which may well not have been in anyone's mind when the statute was framed".[23] The principles underlying the Act were seen as "female self-determination" and consent: they were articulated "by requiring mutual consent to the point of implantation, but by thereafter giving the woman full control of the pregnancy".[24] For Arden L.J. the interference with Ms Evans' private life was justified under Art.8(2) because were her argument to succeed, it would interfere with "the genetic father's right to decide not to become a parent".[25] The court, it will be observed, judged male and female's rights as equivalent. Whether this is right may be doubted. It is agreed that the man has no rights once his partner has been inseminated. It is arguable that whatever rights he has terminate upon ejaculation. As Overall (1995) explains: "men who want to control their sperm should be careful where they put it". In effect, the court gave men the power of veto. The European Court of Human Rights came to the same conclusion,[26] though it argued differently. It was more appropriate, it believed, to analyse the case as one concerning positive obligations. The question was then whether there was a positive obligation on the state

"to ensure that a woman who has embarked on treatment for the specific purpose of giving birth to a genetically related child should be permitted to proceed to implantation of the embryo, notwithstanding the withdrawal of consent by the former partner, the male sperm provider".[27]

It thought, as did Wall J., that it would not be difficult to imagine an infertile man facing "a dilemma" similar to Ms Evans.[28] But at least he could employ a surrogate, provided, of course, the former partner consented. We have not heard the last of this question.[29]

ENCOURAGING PARENTHOOD

We must now look at some policies pursued by government which encourage parenthood.[30] The percentage of children in the population is in decline.[31] Fertility rates are below replacement rates.[32] Government now recognises the implications of this: "if individuals decide that the challenges of combining work and family are too much, they may choose to have fewer children".[33] Infertility is on the increase,[34] and infertility treatment is expensive.[35] In 2003 it was recommended[36] that infertile couples should be entitled to up to three cycles of IVF at public expense. The government responded by agreeing to fund one cycle per couple.[37] The guidelines restrict access to women under 40 to reflect the rapid decline in fertility and hence success rates in women over that age. Access is restricted to infertile couples, so that lesbians and single women will have to pay the full cost of the treatment themselves. Since the success rate of fertility services for such women, whose inability to conceive is not the result of biological dysfunction, may well be higher (and therefore the treatment is more cost-effective), this restriction can only reflect a moral judgment about who deserves publicity funded treatment.[38]

For those who have children, government until recently did rather little. The assumption was that child care was the private concern of mothers and fathers—predominantly of mothers. There has been a seismic shift in policy thinking. If the Labour Government after the 1939–1945 war is remembered for the establishment of the NHS, it may well be that New Labour's most positive legacy will be its child-care strategy. This has put children and families higher on its agenda than any previous government. Overarching all these new policies is a commitment to eradicate child poverty (which more than trebled under the previous Conservative administration) within 20 years.[39] In the UK, 15.4 per cent of children live in households where income is less than half the national average: it is 2.4 per cent in Denmark, 7.5 per cent in France and 10.2 in Germany.[40] A new element in the package designed to target child poverty is the intention to pay child benefit to expectant mothers from the 29th week of pregnancy.[41]

Child benefit itself was introduced in 1975.[42] Until 1945, when the family allowance was introduced, there was no state financial aid to assist with the bringing up of children. Now a flat-rate sum is paid, currently £18.10 for the first child and £12.10 for each other child.[43] It is a non-means tested benefit and is usually paid to the mother.[44] The Equal Treatment Directive does not apply to child benefit: discrimination against fathers is therefore not contrary to European Law.[45] It may well conflict with Arts 8 and 14 of the European Convention on Human Rights. One challenge has failed[46]—there was insufficient evidence to show indirect discrimination—but evidence may now exist, and a successful challenge seems likely. Until 1998 a small additional payment was payable for the first child of a lone parent, and still is for those who were in receipt of the addition before July 5, 1998.[47]

Support is also offered through tax credits. This started in 1999 as "Working Families Tax Credit" and is now Working Tax Credit.[48] It is payable where the claimant is in paid employment for at least 16 hours a week, and is not dependent on the payee having caring responsibilities.[49] But there are greater benefits for those who do have such responsibilities: there is a lone parent addition and a child care element (which curiously has not been raised in 2007) to help working carers who spend money on "approved" or "registered" child care. This child care element covers 80 per cent of the average weekly child care costs of the claimant to an upper limit of £300 per week for two or more children.[50] The child care element is paid directly to the person— in most cases the mother—mainly responsible for the child care.

There is also Child Tax Credit, claimable by a person who is "responsible" for a child (or young person) under 16 (or 19 if in non-advanced education).[51] If a child lives separately with more than one parent—under a shared residence arrangement for example[52]—only one child tax credit can be paid and it cannot be split. In such circumstances, in default of agreement between the parents, the tax credit is payable to the person mainly responsible. This test looks to such questions as how much time does the child spend with the claimant, who pays for the child's clothes, food, etc., who is the main contact for the school, and who looks after the child when s/he is sick. It is possible that this interpretation will inevitably favour mothers over fathers—as, it must be conceded, it should—and that it might therefore fall foul of the Equal Treatment Directive. This would be most unfortunate: regulations could be designed to be compatible with the Directive, but they would work to the detriment of the true caring arrangement. The child tax credit has a number of elements, including a family element and a child element. The latter is currently £1,845 a year, and there are additions if the child is disabled.

Although the sums involved are hardly generous, and have done little to lift families with children out of poverty, they are more than double the equivalent support given in the first year of New Labour (1997–1998). To take an example: a family with two children and a full-time earner on £16,500 a year receives £110 per week in child tax credit and child benefit.[53] But if those on low pay try to increase their earnings, they will be held back by a combination of tax payments and the withdrawal of benefits equal to a 73p income tax rate. There is a campaign to extend the higher rate of child benefit to subsequent children.[54] It has been urged that single parents on income support should be allowed to keep any of the child maintenance they get from the Child Support Agency (or its successor): this, it is thought, would remove 90,000 children from poverty.[55]

FAMILIES WITH DISABLED CHILDREN

One group of families with children with hitherto a low profile are those with disabled children. There are over three quarters of a million children with a disability or limiting long-standing illness in Britain today.[56] It is estimated that disabled children cost three times as much as other children to bring up, but their mothers are seven times less likely than other mothers to be in work. About half of disabled children grow up in, or on the margins of, poverty.[57] In *Every Child Matters*, the Government set out a programme for every child "whatever their background or their circumstances, to have the support they need to be healthy, stay safe, enjoy and achieve, make a positive contribution and achieve economic well-being".[58] But it has been doubted whether government policies for "every child" are yet addressing the particular issues which affect disabled children and their families.[59] An example, currently being addressed,[60] is the need of families of disabled children to get short breaks from 24/7 caring.

EVERY CHILD MATTERS

The Laming Report into the tragic death of Victoria Climbié recognised that "it is not possible to separate the protection of children from wider support to families". It noted that often "the best protection for a child is achieved by timely intervention of family support services".[61] The Government responded by emphasising the "need to focus both on universal services which every child uses, and on more targeted services for those with additional needs".[62] And it identified risk factors such as poor parenting, poor schooling and low income.[63] A year later a White Paper stressed that the Government wanted

"...to help all children and young people maximise their potential by supporting parents, extending the offer of high quality childcare integrated with nursery education and schools, and ensure that, as they grow up, young people have access to the resources that can help each of them fulfill their potential. This means high quality universal services. ... We need to shift away from associating parenting support with crisis interventions to a more consistent offer of parenting support throughout a child and young person's life".[64]

To implement this Acts have been passed in quick succession. The Children Act 2004 places a duty on all children's services authorities to promote co-operation between themselves and other key agencies to improve the well-being of children in their area.[65] "Well-being" is broadly defined and includes, as well as the obvious,[66] social and economic well-being.[67] And in making arrangements they "must have regard to the importance of parents and other persons caring for children in improving the well-being of children".[68]

The "Every Child Matters" outcomes[69] are reinforced by the Childcare Act 2006. Local authorities are placed under a new duty to improve the well-being of young children from birth to five, and to reduce inequalities between young children as regards the five outcomes: *viz.*, being healthy, staying safe, enjoying and achieving, making a contribution to society, and achieving economic well-being. There is also a duty to secure sufficient childcare for working parents, which is part of the strategy to eradicate child poverty. Among the services promoted by government to enhance children's well-being are Sure Start centres, which are intended to provide a one-stop range of services for pre-school children and their families.

The Sure Start programme has been described by one of its architects (Glass, 1999, p.257) as a "radical cross-departmental strategy to raise the physical, social, emotional and intellectual status of young children through improved services". We were told by the Minister for Children that when all Sure Start projects were in operation (by 2005–2006) 400,000 children would be receiving services. But this is only half the children living in poverty in the targeted areas and ignores those outside these areas. There has been doubt for some time whether Sure Start is working (Jack, 2006). And a National Audit Office study, published in December 2006,[70] confirms these concerns. Sure Start, it found, is failing to identify the most disadvantaged families. Teenage mothers, parents of disabled children, some ethnic minority parents and other particularly needy groups are least likely to visit a children's centre to use services such as healthcare or parenting advice. And it argues these services need to be taken to them. Yet only 9 out of 30 children's centres visited by the NAO actively targeted hard-to-reach groups, and few had a system for identifying those most in need of help. The Government would like to extend Sure Start to all families, and there are plans for 3,500 centres by 2010.

THE CONCEPT OF PARENT

Who is a parent? What is a parent? What, in other words, are we looking for? The second question, although arguably the more difficult, can be answered first (and see Eekelaar, 1991b).

The concept of a parent operates on a number of levels. There are "biological" parents, the man and the woman whose gametes produce the child. What was once simple to understand has been complicated by the new reproductive technologies.[71]

There are "social" parents. With the increase in divorce many more children live with a parent and a step-parent. Most step-parents treat the child as a child of the family.[72] Such children will have a biological carer, a social "parent" and an absent parent with whom they may or may not have contact.

The law has also come increasingly to recognise the "psychological" parent, a concept given currency by Goldstein, Freud and Solnit (1973), respectively a lawyer, a pediatrician and a psychoanalyst. They explain:

"Whether any adult becomes the psychological parent of a child is based ... on day-to-day interaction, companionship, and shared experiences. The role can be fulfilled either by a biological parent or by an adoptive parent or by any other caring adult— but never by an absent, inactive adult, whatever his biological or legal relationship to the child may be" (1973, p.19).

English law, which once spurned such a relationship,[73] now acknowledges its value, if not always convincingly.[74] Goldstein *et al.* also point out that adults' and children's perceptions of parenthood may diverge. Children, they say, have "no psychological conception of blood tie relationship until quite late in their development" (1973, p.12). Children are "emotionally unaware of the events leading to their births". What registers in their minds "are the day-to-day interchanges with the adults who take care of them and who, on the strength of these, become the parent figures to whom they are attached" (1973, pp.12–13).

The law distinguishes parentage, parenthood and parental responsibility (see Bainham, 1999b). Parentage refers to those whose gametes produced the child. Parenthood refers to those who are regarded by the law as parents. In most cases they will be those who have parentage, but not always: for example, a sperm donor is not regarded as the father of a child.[75] Parental responsibility,[76] a bundle of obligations and rights, is conferred on all mothers and, now, most fathers (whether married to the mothers or not) but may also be given to other carers, for example grandparents bringing up a child. Parentage, parenthood and parental responsibility could inhere in three different persons. For example, if a woman has a child by donor insemination, the sperm donor could have parentage, if the woman is not married. If she has a partner, he would be regarded as a parent. If she then splits up with him and marries another man and he applies for and gets a residence order, he will have parental responsibility.

It may be thought that this is unnecessarily complex. It is but, Bainham argues, it is also valuable. As he puts it: "the question [is] not whether to prefer the genetic or social parent but how to accommodate both on the assumption that they both have distinctive contributions to make to the life of the child" (1999b, p.27). But from the child's perspective, this may muddy identity. And from the mother's viewpoint her position may be weakened is she has to negotiate several men with differing claims on her child (and see Herring, 2001).

WHO IS A PARENT? THE MOTHER

We may now turn to the question: who is a parent. First, who is the child's mother?

The question, until relatively recently, admitted of only one answer. Lord Simon explained: "Motherhood, although also a legal relationship, is based on a fact, being proved demonstrably by parturition".[77] The advent of assisted reproduction has raised new questions. If the mother has conceived by artificial insemination or by in vitro fertilisation, she is the legal mother. But what if she gives birth as a result of egg or embryo donation? And what if she is a surrogate and is carrying the child under an arrangement which will see the child handed over to the commissioning parents? And surrogates may be the genetic mother or they may be carrying the fertilised egg of another woman.

The law could say that the woman who carries the child (the gestational mother) is the legal mother. It could regard the genetic mother (woman whose egg it is) as the legal mother. It could, feasibly, hold the intending mother to be the legal parent of the child. An emphasis on genetics would lead to some uncertainty, and to cases where the mother was unknown. An emphasis on intention[78] might be appropriate where there is a surrogacy arrangement (Jackson, 2001), and where it is intended that the child be given up for adoption. But would such a test point to a corollary that legal parenthood and therefore legal obligation didn't exist where there was no intention to create a child but, for example, contraception had failed? (And see Douglas, 1994.) There is no reason why this should follow, and intention is a convincing test. English law, however, has opted for the gestational test. Section 27(1) of the Human Fertilisation and Embryology Act 1990 states:

"The woman who is carrying or has carried a child as a result of the placing in her of an embryo or of sperm and eggs, and no other woman, is to be treated as the mother of the child".

Why this conclusion? Three answers may be given. One, rejected by the Warnock committee in 1984,[79] is that a woman bonds with the foetus inside her womb.[80] A second is that it is easier to ascertain who gave birth to a child than who donated an egg. Third, emphasising the gestational mother, and this relieving the genetic mother not only of legal status but also of responsibilities towards the child, may encourage egg donation and thus assist infertile woman to have children.[81]

A woman who gives birth to a child is automatically accorded legal status. In France, Italy and Luxembourg she can give birth anonymously:[82] in effect she can give birth and reject motherhood. This is not so in England. O'Donovan (2000, 2002; O'Donovan and Marshall, 2006) has waged a single-minded campaign to urge the French model on English law. It is a matter of speculation whether the anonymous model leads to fewer abortions and clandestine births. It clearly prevents the child gaining an insight into his/her identity, and it must lead to many of these children feeling utterly rejected. There is a strong argument for saying that the French law[83] is incompatible with Art.8 of the European Convention on Human Rights. However, the European Court of Human Rights has upheld the woman's right to give birth anonymously.

The court said it would be "plainly inhumane to invoke human rights to force a woman ... to choose between abortion or a clandestine birth; the latter always holds a potential of jeopardising the mother's and/or the child's health ...".[84]

Because it is easier to determine who is a child's mother, particularly with the one-dimensional rule in s.27(1), fewer questions have been raised about motherhood than fatherhood. The increase, however, in the number of lesbian couples bringing up children—the children will thus have two women in the role of mothers—should make us question the way the law insists on only one woman being the legal mother.[85] Of course, with a lesbian couple there will only be one gestational mother and one genetic mother, who will bring the child up, and the child will not distinguish between one woman and the other on the grounds of biological relationship. The child may be equally attached to both, perhaps distinguishing between them (as reported by one psychologist) as "ma" and "mummy".[86] Disputes will arise, as in the recent case of *Re G (Children)*.[87] The House of Lords thought that the "unusual" facts of the case—it was a dispute between two lesbians over the upbringing of two girls, genetically related to only one of them—had deflected the courts below from principles of universal application. Of particular relevance here is that which emphasises the importance of the blood tie. As Lord Scott put it, "mothers are special".[88] But does this not have greater meaning in heterosexual relationships where there is only one woman to play the "mothering role"? Even in such relationships, as anthropologists writing about other cultures inform us, child sharing is commonly found.[89] Where a child is reared by two (or more) women, the child can respond to all of them. Is the law thus being unnecessarily one-dimensional?

WHO IS A PARENT? THE FATHER

To answer the question who is a child's father is more difficult, and more complex.

Where a legal system, such as the English, tied ownership and inheritance of property to descent through the male line, as was long the case, paternity was necessarily a "problem".[90] With the advent of DNA testing it has become possible to establish conclusively who is the father of a child. Before science's assistance the law relied on the presumption of legitimacy (or the presumption of paternity).[91] This presumption—which states that where a married woman gives birth to a child her husband is the father—remains the law. Since 1969 it has been possible to rebut the presumption on the balance of probabilities.[92] But, as Thorpe L.J. observed in 2002 in the case of *Re H and A (Children)*, "the paternity of any child is to be established by science and not by legal presumption or inference".[93] The validity of other, less scientific tests, so-called "anthropological tests", for example, to rebut the presumption has been doubted, but evidence of facial resemblance has been used.[94]

Within marriage the presumption of paternity is based on the presumption of legitimacy. Outside marriage—and more than 40 per cent of births occur outside marriage[95]—there is no presumption of fatherhood. However, it has long been established that if a man's name appears on the child's birth certificate, this is prima facie evidence of his paternity.[96] With this now conferring parental responsibility on him as well,[97] there is in fact if not in law, a presumption of paternity. In some jurisdictions, there is a legal presumption of paternity[98]: the Law Commission is not in favour of its introduction into the law of this country.[99] An unmarried man does not have the right to have his name registered as the child's father: the obligation to register the birth rests with the mother.[100] If the mother does not consent, the father will need to seek a court order.[101] Most do, of course, consent, and court orders are very rare. If she subsequently agrees to make a parental responsibility agreement with him, the better view is that this is prima facie evidence of paternity.[102]

The presumption that the husband of a woman is the father of her child can be rebutted on the balance of probabilities.[103] The use of DNA samples will establish not only that a particular man is not the father, but who is. There is power to give directions for the use of such scientific tests.[104] And

"Public policy no longer requires that special protection should be given ... to the status of legitimacy. ... The interests of justice will normally require that available evidence be not suppressed and that the truth be ascertained whenever possible....

In many cases the interests of the child are ... best served if the truth is ascertained.

... However, the interests of justice may conflict with the interests of the child. In general the court ought to permit a blood test of a young child to be taken unless satisfied that that would be against the child's interests; it does not first need to be satisfied that the outcome of the test will be for the benefit of the child."[105]

The problem arises—as it did in *Re F (A Minor) (Blood Tests: Parental Rights)*, from which this quotation is derived—when the mother has had an affair and where her husband and her then lover could both be the father of the child. What is more important: that a child, now or ultimately, should know his identity—a right emphasised by the UN Convention on the Rights of the Child[106]—or that the stability of a marriage, and with this the child's security, should be protected? In *Re F*, the latter consideration prevailed: it was against the child's interests for a direction to be made. The child's welfare, it was said, depended on the stability of the marriage relationship, which a finding of paternity against the husband would disturb. Contrast *Re H (Paternity: Blood Test)*.[107] The husband probably was not the father (he had had a vasectomy, though he had not checked whether this was successful). The mother had had sexual relations both with him and a lover at the relevant time. Evidence pointed to the lover being the child's father. The Court of Appeal stressed the importance of the child knowing his paternity. It was better, it thought, that he grew up knowing the truth. This would not, it reasoned, undermine his attachment to his father-figure, and he would cope with knowing he had two "fathers". It saw this as preferable to allowing a "time bomb" to tick away. These two decisions cannot, despite the court's protestation, be reconciled. The latter is both more consistent with the Lords' ruling in 1972[108] (when both attitudes and scientific knowledge were different), and it is the decision which has tended to be followed. Thus, in *Re H and A (Paternity: Blood Tests)* Thorpe L.J. stressed that the interest of justice were best served by the ascertainment of truth.[109]

Even so, the court will not always make a direction, and may not do so when the case—perhaps an application for contact—can be resolved without determining paternity.[110] If a direction is made, an adult (this includes persons of 16 and 17) may refuse to submit to scientific tests.[111] If there is a refusal, the court may draw such inferences as appear proper.[112] As Ward L.J. said in *Re G (Parentage: Blood Sample)*, "he who obstructs the truth will have the inference drawn against him".[113] In *Re A (A Minor) (Paternity: Refusal of Blood Test)*, it was said by Waite L.J. that "if a mother makes a claim against one of the possible fathers, and he chooses his right not to submit to be tested, the inference that he is the father of the child should be virtually inescapable."[114]

The ascertainment of paternity requires also that a blood sample be taken from the child. The 1969 legislation provided that a sample could be taken from a child (under 16) "if the person who has care and control agrees",[115] This provision may have been incompatible with Art.8 of the European Convention on Human Rights. It was supplemented in 2000 by a provision that, in the absence of consent, a sample may be taken "if the court considers that it would be in [the child's] best interests for the sample to be taken".[116] This statutory formulation is at odds with what the House of Lords ruled in the leading case of *S v S, W v Official Solicitor*.[117] It has led one judge to reason that we have to weigh the child's best interests against the competing interests of the adults.[118] But how is this to be done? Fortunately, he offered the guidance that the child's right to know his own identity was the weightiest consideration.[119] If that is so, it will follow that in the overwhelming preponderance of disputes a sample should be taken from the child, whatever the adults think.

THE FATHER AND ASSISTED REPRODUCTION

The development of techniques of assisted reproduction has resulted in new rules for the determination of what is a child's father in the eyes of the law. Thus, there are exceptions to the basic rule that the genetic father is the child's legal father, and there are situations where a non-genetic "father" is treated as the legal father.

Each of these situations must be considered.

There are two exceptions to the basic rule that the genetic father is the legal father of the child.

First, a man who donates sperm to a licensed clinic for treatment is not the father of any child born using that sperm as long as his sperm is used in compliance with his consent under Sch.3 of the Human Fertilisation and Embryology Act 1990.[120] Sperm donated outside "licensed treatment"—for example, by answering an advertisement in a magazine or shop window—will render the donor the father of any child conceived as a result. Lesbians apparently prefer informal inseminations (Dunne, 2000). Their donors will then be the legal fathers of their children. Dunne's research suggests that it is not uncommon for such men to act also as social fathers, having regular contact and behaving as "kindly uncles" (2000, p.22). A consequence of the rule is that a child born to a single woman as a result of a sperm donation in a licensed clinic is legally fatherless.

But even where the sperm donation is licensed, if it is then used without consent, as would be the case where it was used to fertilise the wrong woman's eggs, the donor is in law the father of the child. This was the conclusion of the court in *Leeds Teaching Hospitals NHS Trust v A*.[121] Mrs A's eggs were mixed by mistake with the sperm of Mr B, and not with the husband's. Since Mr A had not consented to the treatment of his wife with Mr B's sperm, he was not the father. But, because Mr B's sperm had been used without his consent, he was the father. This accident was only detected because the As are white and the Bs black. It would be surprising if this had never happened elsewhere. These conclusions follow logically from complex statutory pro-visions, but cannot be what Parliament intended. The result was that Mr A would have to apply for a residence order in order to acquire parental responsibility.[122] If he wanted to become the parent of the children,[123] he would need to adopt them.

It was the law that sperm donors retained anonymity. In practice this may still happen if parents do not tell their children about their mode of conception. There is, curiously, no obligation on them to do so. However, children have now been given the right to identifying information when they attain the age of 18.[124] The experience of countries like Sweden, which have long pro-moted this right, is that potential donors are deterred.[125] Fewer children will be born as a result of sperm donations: those that are will have a right to know their identity, though this right may prove somewhat hollow.[126]

Second, it was the law that a man could not be the father of a child if his sperm was used after his death. As a result of the *Blood* litigation,[127] legislation now provides that a man, whose sperm is used after his death will, if he was married to the mother or, if not married, he and the woman had been provided with treatment services together, be treated as the father, pro-vided he consented in writing both to the use of his sperm and to being treated as the father, and the mother elected in writing within six weeks of the child's birth to enable the man's parti-culars to be entered on the birth register, and no other persons are to be treated as the father. If these conditions are not satisfied and sperm is used posthumously, the man will not be the child's father.[128] The child will be fatherless.[129] This is unquestionably an unsatisfactory conclusion.

There are also situations where a non-genetic "father" is

treated as a legal father. At common law, only genetic fathers could be regarded as legal fathers.[130] The law was changed initially in 1987 to accommodate children born as a result of donor insemination.[131] The 1990 Act has a more all-embracing provision. Section 28(2) provides that the husband of a woman who has a child as a result of licensed treatment is to be treated as the father of the child, unless it is shown that he did not consent to his wife's treatment. If he did not consent, a licensed clinic would be in breach of the Code of Practice, established by the Human Fertilisation and Embryology Authority, in providing treatment services.[132] As we have seen,[133] a mistake as to the identity of the embryo being placed in a man's wife vitiates his consent, so that s.28(2) does not apply. However, s.28(5) preserves the common law presumption of paternity. To deny paternity—and either or both might wish to do this—it will be necessary to rebut two presumptions of paternity: that in s.28(5) by a DNA test showing that the man is not the biological father of the child; and that in s.28(2) by proving that he did not consent to his wife's treatment. Can a husband consent retrospectively? In the *Leeds Teaching Hospitals* case, the court refused to accept that this was possible.[134]

Second, if the mother is not married—or at least is not married to her partner—he is the child's father if the child is born as a result of licensed treatment services provided for the two of them together.[135] As Hale L.J. noted, this is "an unusual provision, conferring the relationship of parent and child on people who are related neither by blood nor by marriage".[136] What is meant by "treatment together" has proved troublesome.[137] The test which has emerged is whether the couple are engaged on a "joint enterprise".[138] It will not be "treatment together" if the wrong sperm is used,[139] or, if, as in the Natallie Evans litigation,[140] he withdraws his consent before implantation. If at the time an embryo is placed in the woman the couple has separated, the treatment cannot be considered to be "treatment together", and the man is not regarded as the child's father.[141]

If the woman is married and seeks treatment with a man who is not her husband, her husband would be presumed to be the child's father at common law, and by virtue of s.28(2). Both presumptions could be rebutted (the first by DNA evidence, the second by showing he did not consent to her treatment). Under s.28(3) the man would then be regarded as the child's father, so long as he and the woman were never provided with services as "a couple". The child could well end up with a social father (the husband, if the marriage survived), a genetic father (the sperm donor, whose identity might be revealed in 18 years' time) and a legal father (who might, of course, drop out of the picture, and of whose identity the child might remain blissfully ignorant).

THE PARENTAL ORDER

It is possible to become a child's parents in other ways. One is by adoption, and this is considered in the chapter on adoption.[142] A second, which it is convenient to discuss here, is as a result of a parental order.[143] This order is designed, disingenuously it may be thought, to tackle children born as a result of a surrogacy arrangement. The pros and cons of surrogacy and the law's rather mixed response to it are outside the remit of a text on family law.[144] Questions of parentage are very much within it.

As we have seen,[145] the surrogate, irrespective of whose eggs are used, is regarded as the child's mother. Determining who is the father is more difficult. If the surrogate is married, there is a presumption that her husband is the father, which DNA tests would rebut. If IVF is involved, her husband would be regarded as the father provided that he has consented to her treatment;[146] and if he is an unmarried partner he will be regarded as the child's father if, which seems unlikely, the couple were being "treated together".[147] It is not possible for the commissioning father to argue, using s.28(3), that he is being treated together with the surrogate because this provision only applies where she is being treated with another man's sperm.[148]

If the surrogate's husband does not consent, or if she is unmarried, or if she is not being "treated together" with her partner, the child will have no legal father.[149]

This problem may be partially resolved by examining the child's birth certificate. The birth must be registered within 42 days[150] and presumably this will be done by the surrogate.[151] There is a presumption that the man registered as the father is the child's father. If she registers her husband or partner, the presumption that he is the father will be easily rebutted by DNA evidence; if she registers the commissioning father, DNA tests will confirm his paternity. He will also automatically then acquire parental responsibility.[152] The evidence suggests (see Dodd, 2003) that different practices are observed (no name, husband's name, commissioning father's name). It is not surprising that ordinary people should be puzzled.

Even if the commissioning father's name is registered on the birth certificate, the surrogate will still be the mother. The commissioning parents can only become the legal parents by adoption[153]—a lengthy process—or by being granted a parental order.[154] Adoption may be difficult as well if the surrogate decides she does not wish to consent to the child's adoption. Her consent can be dispensed with if the court is satisfied that "the child's welfare [so] requires".[155] Further, any payment or reward made in consideration of the adoption of a child is a criminal offence.[156] This could be a real obstacle, but courts, concerned more with the welfare of children than illegality, have retrospectively authorised such payments.[157]

The parental order is therefore the preferable route to take to regularise the relationship of commissioning parents and their child.

A parental order can be made if the following conditions are satisfied:

(i) the child must have born to a surrogate as a result of assisted procreative techniques (the procedure is not available where DIY has been used or the commissioning father has had sexual intercourse with the surrogate[158]);

(ii) the gametes of at least one of the commissioning couple[159] have been used to bring about the creation of the embryo (so the child must be genetically related to at least one of the commissioning couple);

(iii) the applicants for the order must be husband and wife (cohabitants and gay couples, even those with a registered civil partnership) cannot take advantage of the s.30 procedure);[160]

(iv) the applicants must apply within 6 months of the birth of the child;

(v) the child must have his/her home with the applicants both at the time of the application and at the time of the order, which may prove difficult to establish where the surrogate refuses to hand over the child. It also means that persons with no parental responsibility are required to look after the child prior to the order being made;[161]

(vi) the husband and wife must be at least 18 years old;

(vii) at least one of the applicants must be domiciled in a part of
      the UK (or Channel Islands or Isle of Man);

(viii) the court must be satisfied that the child's father (where he
       is not the husband) and the surrogate freely agree to the
       making of the order. The agreement must be uncondi-
       tional, and with full understanding of what is involved.[162]
       The surrogate is not permitted to agree until six weeks
       have elapsed since the child's birth. The surrogate's
       agreement cannot be dispensed with on the ground that
       the child's welfare requires this (as is the case with
       adoption[163]). If the surrogate, who has agreed to an
       application being made, withdraws her consent, the court
       can still make a residence order;[164]

(ix) the court must be satisfied that no money or other benefit
     (other than for expenses reasonably incurred) has been
     given or received by the husband or wife in connection
     with the making of the order, any agreement required, the
     handing over of the child to the applicants or the making
     of any arrangements with a view to the making of the
     order. Courts can, and do, authorise payment of expenses
     retrospectively.[165] The sums involved may be large and
     may be thought to have an uplift beyond what would be
     regarded as expenses.

In deciding to make a s.30 order, the court must "have regard to
all the circumstances, first consideration being given to the need
to safeguard and promote the welfare of the child".[166] When the
1990 Act was passed, this was the test for adoption as well. But in
2002 this was changed to bring adoption into line with other
proceedings relating to a child's upbringing, and hence to make
the child's welfare the paramount consideration.[167] Despite this
change, the test remains as formulated in the 1994 Regulations. It
is rather difficult to see any justification for this.

UNDERSTANDING PARENTAL RESPONSIBILITY

FROM PARENTAL RIGHTS TO PARENTAL RESPONSIBILITIES

Until relatively recently it was common to talk about parental rights or parental power (and see Collier and Sheldon, 2006). But parenthood is a matter of responsibility rather than rights. This was recognised in West Germany in 1970[1] and by a *Justice* report in this country in 1975.[2] It was the Law Commission in 1988 which recommended the introduction of the concept of parental responsibility which, it said, "would reflect the everyday reality of being a parent and emphasise the responsibility of all who are in that position".[3] Rights are redolent of property, whereas responsibility conjures up an image of trust (Beck *et al.*, 1978; Barton and Douglas, 1995, pp.22–28). Before the Law Commission made its recommendation, both Lord Fraser and Lord Scarman in the watershed *Gillick* decision emphasised that parental rights were justified only because they enabled a parent to perform duties towards a child.[4]

PARENTAL RESPONSIBILITIES

English law has since the Children Act 1989 emphasised parental responsibility but, unlike Scottish law, has stopped short of a comprehensive or helpful definition. Section 3(1) provides that parental responsibility means:

"all the rights, duties, powers, responsibility and authority which by law a parent of a child has in relation to the child and his property".

This tells us very little. It requires us to fall back on the common law and seek a meaning within this. And, as we shall see, this offers no definitive list on content or scope. The Scottish Law Commission gave three reasons for enacting a statutory statement of parental responsibilities. To make explicit what is already implicit; to counteract any impression that a parent has rights but no responsibilities; and to make it clear that rights are not obsolete but are conferred to enable parents to meet their responsibilities.[5] Scottish legislation[6] proceeded to give at least some guidance as to what is expected of parents. Significantly, it puts its guidance on responsibilities before it spells out some of the rights parents have. So s.1 states that a parent has the responsibility:

"(a) to safeguard and promote the child's health, development and welfare;
 (b) to provide, in a manner appropriate to the stage of development of the child—

    (i) direction;
    (ii) guidance;

    to the child;
 (c) if the child is not living with the parent, to maintain personal relations and direct contact with the child on a regular basis; and
 (d) to act as the child's legal representative, but only in so far as compliance with this section is practicable and in the interests of the child".

And s.2 states the rights a parent has to enable these responsibilities to be carried out. It is a partial list only.

The Scottish approach is unquestionably preferable. If it does nothing else, it sets parameters for child-rearing.[7] It is important also in that it separates responsibilities, which directly relate to children, from rights which clearly parents retain against third parties and the local state. In a human rights culture—which, of course, has strengthened since both the English and Scottish legislation—this is significant.[8]

The emphasis on parental responsibility rather than on rights conveys a number of messages. First, and most obviously, that responsibility is more important than rights. Even where parents have rights they may have responsibilities not to exercise them.[9] Second, that it is parents, and therefore not children, who are the decision-makers. This and the *Gillick* decision[10] (discussed in Chapter 13) send out conflicting messages. It is therefore of note that the Lord Chancellor responsible for the Children Act 1989 gave assurances that the new emphasis on parental responsibility did not overturn the *Gillick* principle.[11] However, the retreat from *Gillick*, also discussed in Chapter 13, suggests the courts may think otherwise. Third, the emphasis on parental responsibility conveys the all-important message that it is parents, and not the state, who have responsibility for children. The consequences of this are that parents have responsibility in a normative sense even when they act with complete disregard for that responsibility.[12] English law only allows a parent to be divested of parental responsibility when the child is transplanted into another family by adoption[13] (or after a surrogacy arrangement by a parental order[14]). The grossly abusive parent retains parental responsibility even when the child is subject to a care order, and is removed from the parents.[15] Fourth, the increased emphasis on responsibility can be seen in part as reflecting a view that parents do not have independent rights as such. The Law Commission indeed went so far as to describe talk of parental rights as "a misleading use of ordinary language".[16] This fits well with the weight attached to the welfare principle both in domestic legislation[17] and international conventions.[18] And it is found in case law as well.[19] Even so, within the framework of the European Convention on Human Rights there is still reference to parental rights.[20]

WHY RIGHTS AND RESPONSIBILITIES?

It is worth pausing and asking why parents have rights, and why they have obligations. The standard contemporary answer is to relate them, to say, as was said in the *Gillick* decision, that parents have rights to enable them to carry out their duties. But this is no more than a trite answer to why parents have rights, and is no answer at all to why they have obligations.

Why rights? Certainly, our basic intuition tells us that parents of a child should have the right to nurture their child. Lord Templeman saw this when he stated:

"The best person to bring up a child is the natural parent. It matters not whether the parent is wise or foolish, rich or poor, educated or illiterate, provided the child's moral and physical health are not endangered".[21]

The United States Supreme Court has said that parental rights are "far more precious ... than property rights".[22] For a long time in our history children were indeed regarded as property, and parental rights were strikingly similar to property rights.[23] But this similarity has ceased to exist.[24] Even if parents had rights because the child was a product of their gametes, this would only give each parent a half-interest in the child.[25] And, as we saw in the previous chapter,[26] when a child is born as a result of assisted reproduction there are competing claims over parentage, and therefore over rights. Even in relation to questions like the status of a frozen embryo,[27] we would surely analyse any dispute in terms of prospective parenthood rather than property ownership.[28] The surrogacy case is a useful test-bed. Hill (1991) discusses rights specifically in relation to this. In his view the "balance of equities" (1991, p.419) favours the claims of those who intend to be parents over those of the gestational host. Can this be generalised beyond the assisted reproduction context? The objection that it would follow that there were no rights where there was no intention to create a child—sterilisation has not worked or a contraceptive has failed[29]—can be met with two answers. The person who lacks the intention could be designated a parent and parental obligations could attach, for example to maintain, but it would not have to follow that person was vested also with parental rights.[30] And we could deny the application of the supposed corollary: parental rights could inhere upon intention, and, in the absence of intention, intention could be imputed to acts of sexual intercourse.

Intention may be a convincing explanation for parental rights. But for those not convinced or swayed against it because of its difficulties,[31] there is another rationale for parental rights. It is impossible to bring up a child without making a host of decisions: about schooling, religion, healthcare, etc. The competence to make such decisions must hinge on rightful authority: power—having the child in one's possession—is surely not enough. Tying rights to the authority to make essential decisions also brings in the question of discretion, which it is clear parents retain: for example, though parents must ensure their children are educated, they have discretion to choose the manner of this.[32]

Parental obligation is often explained—intuitively also—in terms of natural bonds. But more is needed. The trust concept has been put forward as one explanation.[33] There are arguments in its favour. The trust concept is designed to shield the beneficiary (the child) against abuse of power by the trustee (the parent). Trustees have discretion in ways they make decisions, but there are limits: they cannot make choices which are manifestly wrong, for example to refuse to consent to life-saving treatment for a child.[34] Also, as Herring (2004, p.355) points out, the trust approach means that "the law would not need to see parents' interest and children's interests as in conflict". But it might fail to address situations, such as the "liver transplant" case, where clearly they are.[35] This was a case where critics—I am one (Freeman, 2000a)—would say the parents considered only their own interest. One problem with the trust model is that trustees, far from acting in this way, are supposed to consider only the interests of the beneficiaries and never their own interests. Given the nature of child-rearing, this is surely expecting too much of even the most devoted parents.[36] Another problem is that this model fails to appreciate that children, particularly older children, are able to take decisions for themselves. And it is, of course, much easier to state the duties of a trustee than it is of a parent. This is a further problem with conceiving of parental obligation in terms of a trust.

Eekelaar (1991a) asks "are parents morally obligated to care for their children?" It is an important question. Why should the obligation extend to one's own children but not those next door or "the impoverished children of the world"?[37] He finds contractarian theories of moral obligation inadequate: they are, he rightly notes, all closely bound up with notion of self-interest. He argues, rather, that we should see a parent's obligations as rooted in both a basic moral duty to promote human flourishing[38] and in the social practices which impose particular responsibility on parents rather than others to care for children. Of course, society could choose to impose the obligation to care for children on persons other than parents. Children could be removed from parents at birth and reared by state agencies. We would find this offensive, but there have been, and may still be, societies in which this, or something close to it, is the preferred mode of child-rearing.[39] Indeed, it is because Barton and Douglas (1995) are concerned that a "social practices" argument could legitimate a practice like this that they think that a case for parents' rights being seen as property rights can be made out. If we were asked what was wrong with the state removing a baby from parents—assuming there was no abuse involved—we might well use property language. The child, we might say, is "theirs", and taking him or her away is tantamount to theft.

Barton and Douglas (1995) explain parental obligation in terms of a voluntary assumption of such responsibility by parents. Of course, it is true that parents do not have to rear a child. They can have their baby placed for adoption. But surely it cannot mean that parents only have an obligation to care for their child where they are willing to assume it. And willingness to undertake responsibility without more does not give it. The woman who takes another's baby will, like anyone else with care of a vulnerable child, have some duties, but these will not be the rights and obligations of parenthood.

Thus, there may not be a totally convincing explanation of why parents have rights or obligations. There are other institutions—private property is a good example—where, delve as we might, we cannot find a convincing theoretical explanation.[40] Perhaps parental rights and obligations must just be assumed to exist before we can begin to think of adult–child relations. A hypothesis like God or the *Grundnorm*[41]—a place to begin reasoning, even if its existence cannot be satisfactorily established.

WHO HAS PARENTAL RESPONSIBILITY?

We can now leave this theorising and ask who has parental responsibility.

First, it should be noted that parental responsibility can be possessed by more than one person.[42] It does not terminate merely because another person acquires it,[43] except where the child is adopted. As pointed out already,[44] it is not forfeited when parental responsibility is vested in a local authority as a result of a care order: in such a situation the local authority can control the exercise by parents of parental responsibility, but it is not taken away from them. Parental responsibility continues after divorce (or dissolution of a civil partnership) or if parents separate. It terminates when the child reaches the age of 18.

Mothers always have parental responsibility.[45] When the mother and father are married to each other at the time of the child's birth, they each have parental responsibility.[46] No person, other than the mother and father, can have parental responsibility at the time of the child's birth.

The unmarried father does not automatically have parental responsibility.[47] Most such men understand they have financial obligations to the child, but research by Pickford (1999) found that over 75 per cent did not understand that they lacked parental responsibility.[48] There are many types of unmarried father:

there are those, the vast majority, who are living in stable cohabiting relationships with the mother and sharing the upbringing of the child; there are also men who become fathers as a result of "one-night stands"; and there are rapists. Ironically, more rapists have parental responsibility than men who father children in casual short relationships, because rape exists, of course, within marriage.[49]

There has been a concern, voiced particularly by feminist groups, that to give all fathers parental responsibility would amount to a "rapist's charter". But this could be dealt with by depriving convicted rapists of parental responsibility[50]—of course some husbands would forfeit their parental responsibility as well—or by allowing the mother to apply to a court for parental responsibility to be removed. The problem is that few rapists are convicted, and it seems wrong to put the onus on the mother to initiate proceedings.

It is also argued (Deech, 1993; Wallbank, 2002) that there is no point giving parental responsibility to men who play no part in the child's upbringing. If you do not interact with the child on a daily basis, you do not know the child "sufficiently well to be able sensibly to take decisions about education, religion, discipline, medical treatment, change of abode, adoption, marriage and property" (Deech, 1993, p.30). Another concern is that absent fathers may misuse parental responsibility to snoop on the mother and interfere with her decisions about the child. It may offer him an opportunity to continue to wield power over her, perhaps even to perpetuate a violent relationship.

Another argument against giving all fathers parental responsibility is the uncertainty that this may create. In the absence of biological tests, we do not know who the father is. If he has not already got parental responsibility it is most unlikely that the mother wishes him to have it—she could have entered into a parental responsibility agreement with him—and it is therefore more than likely that she will resist his claims that he is the father. She might well be advised to claim a sexual relationship with several men.

But there is a case for automatically conferring parental responsibility on all fathers. He is liable for child support.[51] Fathers' rights groups are the first to make this association (Collier and Sheldon, 2006). However, it may be argued that there is no correlativity between support obligations and rights (for example to make decisions about a child's education). Children benefit from being financially supported; it is not necessarily to their advantage that an absent parent can interfere in daily decision-making. Deech (1993) goes further: if he wants parental responsibility he should show commitment to the mother by marrying her. This is, it needs hardly be said, the easiest way for a man to acquire parental responsibility. But it will convince even fewer today than in 1993 when Deech made this argument.

It may be argued also that fathers have rights to parental responsibility.[52] The argument could be mounted under Arts 8 and 14 of the European Convention on Human Rights. Certainly, men are discriminated against, and this would seem to be discrimination on grounds of sex—as also on grounds of marital status, which may well come within Art.14, though not listed as such. This argument has been rejected by the European Court of Human Rights:[53] it held that, given the range of possible relationships between unmarried fathers and their children, there was "an objective and reasonable justification for the difference in treatment ... with regard to the automatic acquisition of parental rights". The unmarried father is clearly entitled to respect for his family life,[54] but so long as there are ways for him to acquire parental responsibility, as there are, it seems unlikely that the courts will hold English law to be incompatible with Convention rights.[55]

Could the case for fathers' rights to parental responsibility be argued in terms of children's rights? The United Nations Convention on the Rights of the Child is clear. States Parties are to "use their best efforts to ensure recognition of the principle that both parents have common responsibilities for the upbringing and development of the child".[56] But do "common responsibilities" include rights, or should they be interpreted to cover, principally, support obligations?[57] Would giving the father parental responsibility enhance children's rights in any way or would it rather cut down on them?[58] A child has the right to know his or her identity,[59] and to have contact with both parents,[60] but these rights are independent of conferring parental responsibility on all fathers.

The Scottish Law Commission, after a consultation process which found a majority in favour of conferring parental responsibility, so recommended.[61] They argued: "if in any particular case it is in the best interests of a child that a parent should be deprived of some or all of his or her parental responsibilities and rights, that can be achieved by means of a court order".[62] The Government rejected the recommendation:

Scots law accordingly retains the English position.[63] In 1998 the Lord Chancellor issued a Consultation Paper.[64] No change came of it, and the debate, at least temporarily, is dormant. On balance I think the existing position is satisfactory. But, in general, opinion has shifted in favour of automatic parental responsibility (see Gilmore, 2003). There has even been a suggestion (Herring 2004, p.325) that the law develops two categories of parental responsibility, one to reflect commitment, the other contribution to day-to-day upbringing. But can there be commitment without a real caring contribution? Does the former cater only for the father in prison or living far away: if such a father's case were genuine he would be granted a parental responsibility order on application.[65] Herring's proposal would unduly complicate the law.

A father will have parental responsibility if he is married to the mother,[66] or is registered as the father of the child on the birth certificate,[67] or enters into a parental responsibility agreement with the mother,[68] or obtains a parental responsibility order from the court,[69] or obtains a residence order,[70] in which case a separate parental responsibility order must be made,[71] or is appointed the child's guardian on the mother's death,[72] or adopts the child,[73] or obtains a special guardianship order.[74] And, if not married to the mother, he can acquire parental responsibility by marrying her.

Once a father has acquired parental responsibility, he has the same rights, duties, etc. as a married father. But, where he acquires parental responsibility as a result of birth registration, a parental responsibility agreement or parental responsibility order, his parental responsibility can be terminated by the court.[75] In revocation applications, the child's welfare is the paramount consideration,[76] and making a revocation must be better than making no order at all.[77] The court will rarely revoke parental responsibility: it did so in one case where the father had inflicted appalling injuries on the child.[78] If it revokes a residence order in his favour, it should not necessarily follow that parental responsibility should also be revoked. Since a married father's parental responsibility cannot be revoked, there is obvious discrimination.

Most unmarried fathers will now acquire parental responsibility by registration as the father on the birth certificate. About 80 per cent of births outside marriage are registered by both parents (and 75 per cent live at the same address).[79] It is to be expected that the number of agreements and orders will decline:

the number of orders having increased in recent years, surprisingly even after the registration provision came in.[80] The father's name can only appear on the birth certificate if the mother agrees to this: in effect the registration provision extends the parental agreement concept. The concern has been expressed (Eekelaar, 2001b) that mothers may be reluctant to register the father's name because of fear that he will interfere with their rearing of the child. There is no evidence of this happening. Whether fathers will shy clear of registration because it may be easier then to trace them for child support is another possible concern, also not substantiated.

A father can also acquire parental responsibility by agreement with the mother. The agreement must be on a prescribed form,[81] which must be signed by both parties, witnessed and then registered in the Principal Registry of the Family Division. No fee is charged. Nevertheless, there is concern that the formalities involved deter parents from using what should be a simple procedure. Of greater concern is the virtually total absence of any scrutiny. A couple could agree on parental responsibility when he is not the father (he may or may not know this). The agreement can confer parental responsibility where this is not in the best interests of the child. Of course, it may be retorted that lots of men with parental responsibility are not the fathers, and that it is not in the best interests of children for many people who currently have parental responsibility to have it vested in them. At least now the agreement must be signed in court and witnessed by a court official: this should prevent the mother's signature being forged[82] and should give us greater assurance that the mother is genuinely agreeing. Not many parental responsibility agreements are made.[83] Where things are amicable, there seems to be no need for an agreement; where there is conflict, it may be impossible to come to an agreement. And few know of the procedure (Pickford, 1999).

A father, not so registered on the birth certificate, who cannot persuade the mother to make a parental responsibility agreement, may apply for a parental responsibility order. In deciding whether or not to make the order the court must regard the child's welfare as the paramount consideration[84] and be satisfied that making the order is better for the child than making no order at all.[85] The Court of Appeal has stated there is no presumption in favour of making an order.[86] However, most applications (90 per cent plus) succeed: in 2004 only 2 per cent of applications were refused.[87]

The Act does not indicate when an order should be made. An early case, however, established guidelines which have, despite more recent suggestions to the contrary,[88] virtually statutory force. They are quoted in nearly every case. At the very least, therefore, Balcombe L.J.'s formulation in *Re H (Minors) (Local Authority: Parental Responsibility) (No.3)* is the inevitable starting point. He emphasised three factors:

"(1) the degree of commitment which the father has shown towards the child; (2) the degree of attachment which exists between the father and the child; (3) the reasons of the father for applying for the order".[89]

Courts have also asked "has he behaved, or will he behave, with parental responsibility for the child?"[90] A little more content was injected into the test by Waite J. in *Re C (Minors)*:

"... was the association between the parties sufficiently enduring, and has the father by his conduct during and since the application shown sufficient commitment to the children to justify giving the father a legal status equivalent to that which he would have enjoyed if the parties had married...?"[91]

It has been said since that the "*Re H* requirements" are not the only factors and even if they are satisfied the court has an overarching duty to apply the paramountcy test and determine whether making an order is for the child's welfare.[92]

Thus, in the case in which this was said,[93] the requirements were satisfied, but the father had caused injuries to the child which indicated deliberate cruelty and possibly sadism. The Court of Appeal agreed with the judge who had refused an order. The judge had commented most aptly: "A responsible parent does not abuse his child".[94] Another case where an order was refused is *Re T (Minor) (Parental Responsibility)*[95] where there was "cruel and callous behaviour in respect of a young child" (keeping a two-year-old girl away from her mother for nine days when access was for two hours). He also failed to maintain the child—an act which in itself might be thought to undermine an application for an order but which, as we shall see, is not always determinative. And he had been violent to the mother when she was pregnant, and had head-butted her when she was carrying a very young baby.

It is only in the exceptional case, or rather what is regarded as the exceptional case, that a parental responsibility order is refused. Examples are *Re P (Parental Responsibility)*:[96] the father, who was old enough to be the mother's grandfather, was deeply confused over sexual boundaries and had little understanding of the difference between abusive and appropriate behaviour; the order was refused because it was found he intended to use it for improper or inappropriate ends to interfere with the mother's care of the child.[97] Note the order was not refused just because he had pornographic pictures of pre-pubescent girls in his possession and intended to bath with his daughter until she was 13 when he would be 85. A second example in *Re P (Parental Responsibility)*:[98] the father was serving long sentences of imprisonment for a succession of robberies; the order was refused because his criminal behaviour was an act of irresponsibility towards his children. The court said *obiter* that other "acts of such folly", for example, "for selfish and misguided reasons ... abandon[ing] ... family to pursue a career abroad, or ... break[ing] up the family by reckless acts of drunkenness"[99] could also lead to a refusal of an order. A third example is *M v M (Parental Responsibility)*:[100] the father was learning disabled and had now in addition sustained serious brain injuries in a motor cycle accident; the court, emphasising the motivation factor,[101] refused the order; this required him to be capable of reason, which he was not. He was also not capable of exercising rights, performing duties and wielding powers in relation to the child. A fourth example is *Re M (Contact: Parental Responsibility)*:[102] the child was a severely handicapped girl of 17 who functioned as a baby of 6 months; to give the father responsibility would place stress on the mother and undermine her ability to care for the child. So, despite his commitment to the child over a long period of time and a high degree of attachment, the order was not made. There was concern about the very real problem of the potential misuse of a parental responsibility order. A fifth example is *Re J (Parental Responsibility)*:[103] the order was refused because the child (who was 12) did not want contact with her father.[104] Orders have been refused where much younger children, in *Re G (A Child) (Domestic Violence: Direct Contact)*[105] one under four, did not want any contact with the father; in this case the child was fearful when he was mentioned.

The courts have stressed that a parental responsibility order is about status. Thus Ward L.J. in *Re S: Parental Responsibility* stated:

"It is wrong to place undue and therefore false emphasis on the rights and duties and the powers comprised in 'parental responsibility' and not to concentrate on the fact that what is at issue is conferring upon a committed father the status of parenthood for which nature has already ordained that he must bear responsibility".[106]

This was a case where the father had a conviction for possession of obscene "literature" (indecent photographs of children). Subsequently, the same judge reasoned that because it is desirable for a child's self-esteem to grow up wherever possible with a favourable and positive image of a parent, a court should, applying the paramountcy test, "wherever possible ... confer on a concerned father that stamp of approval because he has shown himself willing and anxious to pick up the responsibility of fatherhood and not to deny or avoid it".[107] But courts have been willing to give this stamp of approval to men who renege on the obligations of parenthood. Like the father who, though "in full employment", had not sent "a penny" to the mother for the maintenance of his two children;[108] further, he knew the mother was in financial difficulties. Of course, the Child Support Agency was chasing him[109]—and, as that was ten years ago, there is a little chance that by now it may have screwed some money out of him![110] Giving the stamp of approval to such men, who are now to be threatened with losing passports and driving licences[111] sends out strange and conflicting messages.[112]

Since parental responsibility orders are about status, they can be made even where the child is in local authority care[113] or has been placed for adoption.[114] A parental responsibility order may be granted, even when a contact order is denied.[115] This may be thought to be somewhat of an empty gesture. Can it really be for the child's benefit? Or is there inconsistency between seeing the order as a stamp of approval—which seems to emphasise the father's well-being—and tying it to the paramountcy principle, and thus endorsing the child's welfare?

An unmarried father who does not already have parental responsibility[116] may acquire it if the court makes a residence order[117] in his favour. If it does this it must also make a parental responsibility order.[118] If the residence order then comes to an end, he will retain parental responsibility by virtue of the parental responsibility order.

An unmarried father who does not have parental responsibility is nevertheless a "parent". He has a statutory duty to maintain the child. He has the right to apply to the court for a s.8 order (for example a specific issue order for a ruling on a matter of the child's upbringing). He is entitled to reasonable contact where his child is in the care of the local authority.[119]

STEP-PARENTS

Step-parents do not automatically have parental responsibility.[120] The Children Act 1989, as originally enacted, made no special provision for them to acquire it. The Adoption and Children Act 2002, in seeking an alternative to adoption, has done so. Section 112 of the 2002 Act, inserting s.4A into the Children Act (with effect from December 30, 2005) provides that a step-parent (by marriage or civil partnership) can acquire parental responsibility for a step-child by making a parental responsibility agreement or by obtaining a parental responsibility order. A step-parent can also acquire parental responsibility by obtaining a special guardianship order[121] or a residence order.[122]

The cohabiting partner of a parent cannot acquire parental responsibility by agreement or order. This seems anomalous given that the 2002 Act permits joint adoption by a couple whether or not they are married to each other.[123]

Where both birth parents have parental responsibility (they were married to each other or the father acquired parental responsibility by birth registration, agreement or order), the agreement must be made between both parents and the step-parent. If only the mother has parental responsibility, she and the step-parent may make the agreement, and would not have to bring this to the attention of the father. Whether this complies with the European Convention on Human Rights[124] may be doubted (and see Bainham 2001, p.236). It is likely that getting the agreement of the non-resident parent with parental responsibility will prove a stumbling-block, forcing step-parents to resort to court orders. As with parental agreements between the mother and unmarried father, there is no scrutiny of the agreement to determine whether it is in the child's best interests. The child has no say in the making of the agreement: s/he is an object of concern, not a subject. This has not been properly thought through because the child can apply to the court to bring the agreement to an end.[125]

Parental responsibility orders are governed by the paramountcy principle and the court must also be satisfied that making the order is better than making no order.[126] The "*Re H* guidelines"[127] may come to be applied as well. There is no requirement that account be taken of the child's wishes and feelings.[128]

Agreements and orders continue even if the parent and step parent separate or divorce.[129] There is nothing to prevent a parent then agreeing to share parental responsibility with a new partner or, indeed, a succession of partners. However, agreements and orders can be brought to an end by court order on application by any person with parental responsibility or, with the court's leave, by the child him or herself.[130]

Other persons can acquire parental responsibility. For example, grandparents[131] bringing up a child may seek a residence order and this will confer parental responsibility on them, giving them the competence to make decisions about the child, for example in relation to medical treatment.[132] Special guardians have parental responsibility: they have powers, which those with residence orders lack, to consent or withhold consent to the child's adoption and to appoint guardians.[133] Local authorities can also acquire parental responsibility when a care order is made in their favour; there are limits on what they can do (they cannot change the child's religion or surname, agree to adoption, appoint a guardian or remove him/her from the UK for more than a month).[134]

THE CONTENT OF PARENTAL RESPONSIBILITY

In what does parental responsibility consist? As we have already seen,[135] the legislation offers little or no guidance. What rights, duties, powers, responsibility and authority do those with parental responsibility have? Before we attempt a list and discuss the more important elements of parental responsibility in detail, three observations need to be made.

First, it should be stressed again that the absence of "parental responsibility" does not mean there is no obligation. Most obviously, the unmarried father has a duty to maintain his child whether he has parental responsibility or not.

Second, even where a parent lacks parental responsibility, there may be rights, for example to contact.[136] This is dependent on there being a relationship with the child which amounts to "family life" within the meaning of Art.8 of the European Convention on Human Rights.[137]

Third, parental responsibility must be seen within the context of increased understanding, and recognition in international law and domestic law, of children's rights.[138] Even before the "children's rights era", Lord Denning M.R. described custody as "a dwindling right which the court will hesitate to enforce against the wishes of the child, the older he is. It starts with the right of control and ends with little more than advice".[139]

The rights accruing with parental responsibility are now considered.

(i) The right to look after and bring up the child

It was common once to talk of a parent's right to possess his/her child,[140] but this language is redolent of property and is no longer used. Douglas (2004) defines the right in terms of freedom from arbitrary state interference. Seen in this way it is protected by Art.8 of the European Convention on Human Rights. It is also a right protected as against others by laws which criminalise child abduction.[141] Since it is also an offence to remove a child under 16 from the UK without the consent of everyone with parental responsibility, a parent could be criminally liable if s/he took a child out of the country without the consent of the other parent. There are defences to this.[142] There is also an important exception: a parent with a residence order can remove the child from the UK for up to a month without the consent of others with parental responsibility.[143] To prevent this happening, where, for example, there is concern that the child will not be brought back, a prohibited steps order may be sought.[144]

This right has been said to include a right to control the child's movements, but this must now be read subject to Lord Denning's cautionary note (quoted above) and to the *Gillick* principle, discussed in Chapter 13. A good contemporary illustration is the ruling that a local authority accommodating a child cannot place the child in accommodation against the wishes of a parent with parental responsibility.[145]

(ii) The right to contact

In *Re KD (A Minor) (Ward: Termination of Access)*, Lord Oliver said it would not be "inappropriate to describe such a claim as a 'right' ".[146] It is not an absolute right, but then few rights are. It certainly has to be seen in the context of the child's welfare. There is a statutory presumption of reasonable contact when a child is in local authority care[147] or under emergency protection.[148] But note the way this is expressed: the local authority must normally allow the child reasonable contact with his parents. This suggests, as case law has been stating since 1973,[149] that contact is a child's right. It is also expressed as such in the United Convention on the Rights of the Child. Article 9(3) provides:

"State Parties shall respect the right of the child who is separated from one or both parents to maintain personal relations and direct contact with both parents on a regular basis, except if it is contrary to the child's best interests".

The European Court of Human Rights has made it clear that the right to respect for family and private life under Art.8 of the European Convention on Human Rights includes the right of contact between parents and children.[150] English courts have been less willing, at least until recently, to use rights language. Thus, in *Re L (A Child) (Contact: Domestic Violence)*[151] Thorpe L.J. and Dame Elizabeth Butler-Sloss P. said such language was not appropriate. Thorpe L.J. thought there were "considerable difficulties with any return to the language of rights".[152] One he cited was "the creation of a right of the child does not lead to corresponding duties on parents. The errant or selfish parent cannot be ordered to spend time with his child against his will ...".[153] He preferred to talk instead of an "assumption" of the benefit of contact which was "the base of knowledge and experience from which the court embarks upon its application of the welfare principle in each disputed contact application".[154] Whether rights language is appropriate divides the commentators. Bainham (2005, pp.156–157) is strongly of the opinion that there is a right to contact: children have a right of contact with mothers and fathers, and mothers and fathers have rights of contact with their children. He points out that the question has now to be situated in the context of the European Convention and the Human Rights Act. "Whatever the domestic arguments about the concept of rights, contact is a *human right* or, put another way, a *Convention right* of both parent and child" (Bainham, 2005, p.157). There are few absolute rights, and the right to contact is certainly not one of them. The Convention recognises this: there are limitations to respect for family life in Art.8(2). These would, for example, justify denying a child-abusing father contact or refusing contact where a child has been badly affected by domestic violence. But short of such and similar cases, there is a mutual right to contact, and so states must take reasonable steps to uphold it. The jurisprudence of the European Court of Human Rights increasingly leans on states to enforce contact. Thus, in *H N v Poland* it held that the state had to take "all necessary steps to facilitate the [enforcement of contact] as can reasonably be demanded". Coercive sanctions against parents could be used: it was not, however, desirable to implement coercive measures against children.[155]

In *Zawadka v Poland*[156] the Court found the state to be in breach of its responsibilities under Art.8 in not taking steps to persuade the mother to allow the father to have contact with the child. The mother's reluctance was understandable: the father had previously abducted the child when he had contact. This trend has influenced the English courts, as, of course, it must. Thus, the Court of Appeal[157] has said that attempts to promote contact "should not be abandoned until it is clear that the child will not benefit from continuing the attempt". Dame Elizabeth Butler-Sloss P. conceded, however, that there is "a limit beyond which the court should not strive to promote contact". The welfare of the child had to be put "at the forefront and above the rights of either parent". And in *Re M (Contact: Long-Term Best Interests)*,[158] Scott Baker L.J. said:

"Where ... the court has the picture that a parent is seeking, without good reason, to eliminate the other parent from the child's, or children's, lives, the court should not stand by and take no positive action. Justice to the children and the deprived parent ... requires the court to leave no stone unturned that might resolve the situation and prevent long-term harm to the children".

In this case the mother had been unable to see the children for over eight years, and the children, now 15 and 13, did not want any contact with her. Although views of children as old as this ordinarily carry great weight, the court accepted that their perceptions had been corrupted by the malignancy of the views with which they had been force-fed over many years.

(iii) The duty to protect the child

Breach of this duty can lead both to criminal and civil liability. Thus, it is an offence[159] "wilfully" to assault, ill-treat, neglect, abandon or expose a child under 16 (or cause or procure any of these actions/omissions) in a manner likely to cause suffering or injury to health.[160] Failure to provide food, clothing, medical aid or accommodation or to procure these is deemed to be neglect.[161] Well-publicised prosecutions have taken place in recent years where parents have gone on holiday leaving a child behind to fend for him or herself. The offence is committed only if the act is "wilful": low intelligence parents who failed to procure medical aid for their child who died from malnutrition and hypothermia did not thus commit the offence.[162] There are other offences: causing the death of a child under three by overlying him or her in bed while drunk;[163] allowing a child under 16 to beg [164]are old examples. The main legislation is therefore three-quarters of a century old and reflects it. One new offence was created by the Domestic Violence, Crime and Victims Act 2004 s.5. It is a criminal offence to cause or allow the death of a child (or vulnerable adult) as a result of the unlawful act of a person who was a member of the same household as the child and had frequent contact with him/her.[165]

As far as civil actions are concerned, they lie in both assault[166] and negligence. There is a reluctance to impose too high a standard of care on those looking after children. This was explained by Browne-Wilkinson V.C. in public policy terms. The courts "should be slow to characterise as negligent the care which ordinary loving and careful mothers are able to give individual children, given the rough-and-tumble of home life".[167]

(iv) The liberty to punish the child

It is uncontroversial that parents may discipline a child. They may control the child's movements.[168] Courts can make a care order when a child is beyond parental control:[169] the implication is that parents have a duty to discipline their child. What is controversial is the power to inflict corporal punishment. At common law a person with parental responsibility could lawfully inflict moderate and reasonable corporal punishment.[170] And s/he could delegate this power to a person in loco parentis, such as a teacher. Section 1(7) of the Children and Young Persons Act 1933 gave teachers and other persons with lawful control or charge of a child an independent right to administer punishment.[171] The punishment had to be reasonable:[172] what was reasonable could not be predicted in advance, and gradually less and less was tolerated.

The move to reform started in the European Court of Human

Rights. This first held that judicial birching violated Art.3,[173] then that corporal punishment without parental consent was a breach of a parent's right to determine education[174]—not it be noted a breach of any right of the child[175]—and then that school punishments could amount to degrading treatment.[176] A campaign to outlaw corporal punishment in schools began in the early 1970s.[177] This bore fruit in 1986 in relation to state schools[178] and eventually in 1998 in the independent school sector.[179] Corporal punishment was removed from children's homes in 2001;[180] foster parents were banned from using it in 2002;[181] and nurseries and child-minders had the power taken away from them in 2003.[182] Discipline short of corporal punishment is still allowed: as far as schools are concerned, such force as is reasonable to prevent a pupil committing an offence, injuring or damaging the property of any person or engaging in behaviour prejudicial to the maintenance of good order and discipline.[183] The line between this and corporal punishment may not always be easy to draw (Hamilton, 1997).

The campaign to make it unlawful for parents to hit children started in the UK in the late 1980s (Freeman, 1988; Newell, 1989). It encountered resistance from those who wished to uphold parents' rights, from those who saw it as unwarranted interference into the private realm of the family, and those who wished to defend parents who responded to stress with force. Imagine that these arguments were raised to defend the husband's right to chastise his wife (Phillips and Alderson, 2003). In fact, they once were. Sweden legislated against the hitting of children as early as 1979,[184] since then there has been legislation in Finland (in 1983), in Norway in 1987, in Austria in 1998, in Cyprus in 1993, in Denmark in 1997, in Latvia in 1998, in Croatia in 1999, in Germany in 2000, Iceland in 2003, Romania and Ukraine in 2004, the Netherlands in 2007 and the highest courts in both Italy and Israel have ruled it to be unlawful.[185]

Yet when the UK Government issued a so-called consultation paper in 2000, it ruled out adopting the Swedish model:

"We have made it quite clear in that we do *not* consider that the right way forward is to make unlawful all smacking and other forms of physical rebuke and this paper explicitly rules out this possibility".[186]

It treated us to a series of questions like whether there were forms of physical punishment which should never be capable of being defended as "reasonable", for example physical punishment using implements. But if there is no case for physical punishment, these questions are at best otiose and at worst insulting.

And there is *no* case.[187] What is sometimes called the "safe smack" or the "loving smack" is an oxymoron.[188] Corporal punishment, however it is dressed up, is morally wrong. It is discriminatory: we do not justify assaults on anyone else: of course, we once did—husbands could chastise wives, masters punish servants, and corporal punishment was used on prisoners and members of the armed forces.[189] Imagine a consultation paper which asked if husbands should be allowed to smack their wives; imagine if it explicity ruled out the answer "no", and then asked where and with what they should be allowed to hit them. Imagine a consultation paper on domestic violence which countenanced "reasonable" domestic violence. The physical punishment of children undermines their fundamental rights to respect for human dignity and physical integrity. The consultation paper is contemporaneous with the Human Rights Act, and is totally at odds with its ideology and the commitments it makes. The legitimisation of hitting children is also inconsistent with other policies pursued by government today, for example and most obviously its zero tolerance towards domestic violence. We will come to recognise that the corporal punishment of children is a form of child abuse.[190] Much child abuse is anyway corporal punishment gone wrong.[191] Today's abuse is all too frequently yesterday's punishment. Some corporal punishment is also sexual abuse: much institutional corporal punishment certainly could be so categorised.

The argument that abolition would fly in the face of public sentiment is weak. Certainly, the Government found that there was considerable opposition to removing the parental privilege. But, first, it only sought to discover parents' views on smacking, not children's. Imagine eliciting opinion on domestic violence or marital rape and canvassing men's views only; second, in Sweden before the ban in 1979 only 35 per cent of parents thought that children should be bought up without corporal punishment. Three years after the ban, which was accompanied by a massive education campaign,[192] the figure was 71 per cent. By 2000 only 6 per cent of Swedes under 35 supported the use of corporal punishment; third, the Government may well be misreading public opinion, which may be concerned with parents being prosecuted for trivial smacks.[193] When a MORI poll asked whether parents would support a ban if reassured that there would not be prosecutions for trivial smacks, 76 per cent supported one for under two-year-olds, and only a slight majority (53 per cent) thought it should be lawful for children over two to be hit by parents;[194] fourth, governments should lead public opinion, not slavishly follow it. We would never have abolished capital punishment, legalised homosexual acts or passed race and gender equality laws had we had to rely on what popular sentiment wanted. Law can be used for social engineering, but not in isolation from other policies.[195] Law can change attitudes, as well as behaviour.[196] Those who are concerned about police intervention into the privacy of the home—a concern we used to hear, incidentally, in relation to domestic violence[197]—should look at the experience of countries which have made it unlawful to hit children, where the goal of the legislation has been to educate rather than to subject parents to penal sanctions.[198]

There is a concern that making it unlawful to hit children will lead to greater intervention into the family, more prosecutions of parents, more care proceedings (Thompson, 1993). But this is not the experience of countries which have passed such legislation.[199] Outlawing corporal punishment will more likely lead to fewer prosecutions, because there will be less abuse, to fewer care proceedings, and also to less delinquency and violent crime and thus a reduction in the prison population, because corporal punishment teaches violence and the victims of today became tomorrow's violent criminals.[200] Banning corporal punishment could thus be justified on utilitarian grounds. But even were it to be effective, even if it could be shown that it acted as a deterrent, it could not be justified on moral grounds.

In 1998 the European Court of Human Rights decided *A v United Kingdom*.[201] A step-father had repeatedly hit his nine-year-old step-son with a garden cane causing bruises which lasted up to a week. He was acquitted of causing actual bodily harm. The European Court ruled that the UK had failed to provide the child with sufficient protection against punishment which amounted to degrading treatment. English law thus violated Art.3 of the European Convention on Human Rights. As it did, it may be added, other international instruments including the UN Convention on the Rights of the Child.[202] The Consultation Paper,[203] already referred to, envisaged the need for reform—sadly, only because change was being forced by an international court. However, after it studied responses to the Consultation Paper,[204] the Government concluded that there was no need to alter the law since the Human Rights Act 1998 s.3 obligated the courts to take account of the European Court of Human Rights' "rulings". In 2003 the House of Commons Health Committee responded to the Laming report into the death of Victoria Climbié by urging the Government to remove the "increasingly anomalous reasonable chastisement defence".[205] And there was a Private Member's Bill to remove the defence of reasonable chastisement, but this failed.[206]

Again, and reluctantly, the Government gave some ground. It passed s.58 of the Children Act 2004.[207] This provides that reasonable punishment is no longer a defence to wounding and causing grievous bodily harm, assault occasioning actual bodily harm and to cruelty to persons under 16 (under the 1933 Act s.1). However, the defence remains available where the offence is common assault or where the battery does not occasion actual bodily harm (in common parlance does not leave a mark). Section 1(7) has also been repealed.[208] As far as civil law is concerned, s.58(3) removes the defence of reasonable punishment from tortious actions where the battery causes actual bodily harm: it would still be open to a child to sue a parent for battery where there is no actual bodily harm. Were this to happen it might prove a catalyst for further reform.

English law has thus stopped short of imposing an outright ban on the hitting of children by parents. It has reached a solution—that can only be temporary—which effects a compromise that satisfies no one. Those calling for an outright ban continue to do so, those who see the legislation as unnecessary meddling with parents' rights to rear children as they see fit are critical of bungling interference. The police are unhappy too: do they charge with actual bodily harm only to be told that it is only common assault? And what can parents be told? What message does s.58 convey? You may hit your children but not leave a mark! How are we to explain the current status of the reasonable chastisement defence: if your chastisement is reasonable, defined as no more than a common assault, you may raise the defence. But can we really tell parents in advance what is reasonable? Or is this something they will discover after the event, perhaps when magistrates reach a guilty verdict? The only safe advice to give parents is that there is no such thing as the safe smack.

We must be the laughing stock of countries which have had the courage to ban the hitting of children. The debate will continue. It will not be long before English law is challenged once again in the European Court of Human Rights. The reasonable chastisement defence remains. Of course, it can only be used if a child is assaulted. Can it be legitimate and proportionate to permit parents to use a defence which is not available were they to assault an adult? An action could be framed in terms of Art.3—it is degrading treatment—and Art.8—interference with private life—coupled with a claim that there is discrimination under Art.14. Since we only respond when caned by the European Court of Human Rights, this may be the best chance of further progress. But of one thing we can be certain: parents' liberty to hit their children will not survive another generation.

(v) Education: rights and duties

The true consumers of education are children and young persons. It might therefore be thought that it is they who would have rights in the education sphere. The UN Convention on the Rights of the Child,[209] the Universal Declaration of Human Rights[210] and the European Convention on Human Rights[211] also recognise the child's right to education. English law by contrast emphasises parental choice and imposes important duties on parents. But it is predicated on the assumption that there is an identity of interests between the parent and the child (and see Freeman, 1996b).

There is, surprisingly, no duty as such on children to attend school. The duty is imposed on parents. The Education Act 1996 requires the parent of every child of compulsory school age to "cause him to receive efficient full-time education suitable to his age, ability and aptitude and to any special educational needs he may have either by regular attendance at school or otherwise."[212] They are not obliged to send their children to school: they can if they wish educate them at home (but they must then comply with the National Curriculum[213]). Whether parents should be allowed this discretion is arguable: there is surely a case for children having a right to go to school.

Parents who do not choose the home schooling option, must both register the child at school[214] and secure the child's regular attendance thereafter.[215] Breaches of both of these duties are criminal offences. There are excuses for failure to comply with the second of these duties (absence with leave;[216] sickness or other unavoidable cause; days of religious observance;[217] the school not being within walking distance—two or three miles depending on the age of the child—and there being no suitable transport arrangements[218]). Children, it has been noted, do not have a duty to go to school; whether the unwillingness of a *Gillick*-competent child[219] to attend school would also be a defence for parents is debatable (see Grenville, 1988).

School attendance can be enforced in several ways. The LEA can prosecute, but this achieves little. Before the Children Act 1989 failure to attend school was a ground for care proceedings,[220] but it was accepted that taking children into care was no answer to truancy.[221] Care proceedings can still be brought under the Children Act 1989 if the harm suffered as a result of failure to attend school is significant enough to justify a care order.[222] But the standard response now is the education supervision order, introduced by the 1989 Act specifically to deal with school non-attendance.[223] An education supervision order can be made if the court is satisfied that the child is of compulsory school age and is not being properly educated.[224] Under such an order, the supervisor has the duty to advise, assist and befriend, and give directions to the supervised child and his parents so as to secure the child is properly educated.[225]

As will have been observed, parental duties in relation to education target principally truancy. The UN Convention on the Rights of the Child requires states to "take measures to encourage regular attendance at schools".[226] It does not question the legitimacy of compulsory education: of course some do (Jeffs, 2002). This is not the place to enter this debate. For us, of greater significance is whether the appropriate way of ensuring children attend school is to impose sanctions on parents, particularly since it has been held that ignorance of the child's truancy is no defence.[227]

Parents' rights in relation to education extend to be the type of education their children receive. Children are to be educated in accordance with the wishes of their parents.[228] There are limits. Thus, it has been held recently[229] that they cannot claim that the ban on corporal punishment in schools infringes their right to have their children educated according to their religious and philosophical convictions. Parents can withdraw their children from religious education and acts of collective worship.[230] They can also withdraw them from sex education classes.[231] It will be noted that in relation to all three of these questions, children have no rights in English law. The content of both religious and sex education is controversial: religious because the syllabus must reflect the dominance of Christianity[232] and because there must be "an act of collective worship on each school day";[233] sex education because it must emphasise the nature of marriage.[234]

Children cannot withdraw themselves from religious education. Nor can they insist on sex education if their parents wish to opt them out of this.[235] There is every reason for sex education; in particular, good sex education may cut our teenage pregnancy rates, which are higher than every other country in Western Europe.[236] It is difficult to see any reason for state schools teaching religion: in the USA, where religion is more dominant in society, religious education in state schools is prohibited. Why not here too (Hamilton, 1995)?

If parents disagree about a child's education the matter may be referred to the court for a specific issue order.[237] The matter is then determined according to the paramountcy test.[238] Thus, when a French father and English mother (who had primary care) disagreed over whether children should be educated at the Lycée Français in London, the court ruled in favour of the father.[239] It stressed the importance of preserving the children's bicultural identity.

(vi) The right to determine religion

Parents have no duty to instill religion into their child.[240] They have a right to determine the child's religious upbringing and education. For this reason, as we have seen, they can exclude their child from religious education in schools and from school assemblies. Freedom of religion is protected by the European Convention on Human Rights Art.9. However, where there are disputes about a child's upbringing, competing rights are balanced by an application of the welfare principle.[241] If a child is in local authority care, the authority cannot cause him/her to be brought up in any religious persuasion other than that in which s/he would have been brought up had the care order not been made.[242] Adoption agencies "must give due consideration" to the child's religious persuasion when placing for adoption:[243] they no longer have to have regard to parental wishes.[244] The courts no longer insist that carers, for example foster parents, bring up a child in that child's birth religion. Thus, in *Re P (Section 91(14) Guidelines) (Residence and Religious Heritage)*,[245] the Court of Appeal accepted that when foster parents, who were non-practising Catholics, obtained a residence order they were permitted to determine all questions of education and upbringing, and were no longer expected to maintain Jewish dietary laws for a child from an Orthodox Jewish background. The question of religion could only ever be one factor, albeit in a case such as this a weighty one, among a range of factors to be taken into account.

Parents who dispute a matter of the child's religious upbringing may seek a specific issue order. A good example is *Re J (Specific Issue Orders: Muslim Upbringing and Circumcision)*,[246] a dispute between an English mother (a non-practising Christian) and a Turkish Muslim father, also non-practising, over whether their five-year-old son should be circumcised, as is required by the Muslim religion, and brought up as a Muslim. On the latter question the court thought it inappropriate to require the mother to follow Muslim practices, and it did not make an order.[247] On the former question it decided that circumcision was not in this child's interest: he was not going to be brought up in a Muslim environment. In the Court of Appeal[248] a distinction was drawn between religious upbringing and religion. No matter what religion the child belonged to by birth—Muslim law says the child of a Muslim father is a Muslim[249]—the child's own perception of religion derived from involvement in worship and teaching within the family. Circumcision fell, so the court said, within those decisions which could not be taken by one parent-carer without the consent of another parent who had parental responsibility.[250]

(vii) The right to consent to medical treatment

A person who has parental responsibility can give valid consent to a child's medical treatment. There are exceptions: legislation does not permit female genital mutilation or circumcision;[251] the courts have taken the decision to consent to a non-therapeutic sterilisation away from parents with parental responsibility—such treatment can only be lawfully carried out with the leave of a High Court judge.[252] Second, the age of the child imposes some limits on the powers of those with parental responsibility. A child who is 16 or 17[253] or who is *Gillick*-competent[254] can validly consent to treatment. Such a child cannot—it has been held, controversially,[255]—refuse to consent to treatment. If s/he does so refuse, an adult with parental responsibility can give valid consent but, it has been said, treatment in such circumstances should not be given without court approval. Third, the High Court can override a decision by a parent to consent or to refuse to consent to a child's treatment. An example of overriding consent is *Re D (A Minor) (Wardship: Sterilisation)*:[256] the mother was prepared to consent to the sterilisation of her 11-year-old daughter who had Sotos Syndrome. The chance intervention of an educational psychologist financed by the National Council for Civil Liberties[257] led to this unnecessary operation being halted. Heilbron J. ruled that the girl could make up her own mind when she was older. An example of overriding refusal is *Re A (Children: Conjoined Twins: Surgical Operation)*:[258] the court sanctioned the separation of conjoined twins, contrary to the wishes of devout Roman Catholic parents from Gozo, and notwithstanding that the inevitable result of the operation would be the death of the weaker twin. Such cases are inevitably controversial. Equally controversial are cases—*Re T (A Minor) (Wardship: Medical Treatment)*[259] is an egregious example—where courts accept parental judgment to refuse medical treatment for their child, which is in the view of doctors in the best medical interests of the child. The case concerned a toddler who needed a liver transplant, without which his life expectancy was about two years. The parents, who were not married,[260] were health care professionals and the child had been taken to a "distant Commonwealth country"—both factors which assumed unacceptable weight in the court's reasoning. The parents' view, that the child had already suffered enough, was allowed to prevail, and the child, presumably, was allowed to die. The question, said the Court of Appeal, is not whether the parent is acting reasonably, but what is in the best interests of the child. It is clear law, most articulately expressed in an Australian judgment,[261] that

"...parental authority exists to authorise such surgery for the purpose, and only for the purpose, of advancing the welfare of the child. It does not extend to authorising surgery because of a perception that it is in the interests of those responsible for the care of the child or in the interests of society in general (e.g. for eugenic reasons). That which constitutes the welfare of the child ... falls to be determined by reference to general community standards, but making due allowance for the entitlement of parents, within the limits of what is permissible in accordance with those standards, to entertain divergent views about the moral and secular objectives to be pursued for their children".[262]

(viii) The right to name the child

The Births and Death Registration Act 1953 confers power to name a child to parents who have parental responsibility for the child immediately before he or she is born.[263] The unmarried father thus cannot register the child's birth,[264] but the separated father can. If either parent objects to the initial registration s/he can apply for a specific issue order that the child have his or her surname. It is only convention that dictates that a child takes his or her father's surname. A father cannot insist upon this. The surname must be registered within 42 days: there is no obligation to register a first name (if one is not given the registrar will enter only the surname, preceded by a horizontal line).[265]

Changing a child's surname has been said to be a "profound issue",[266] so much so that it is a decision that can only be taken by both parents who have parental responsibility.[267] Lord Jauncey said in *Dawson v Wearmouth* that a surname is "a biological label which tells the world at large that the blood of the name flows in its veins".[268] This, it may be thought, is somewhat extravagant language. It is doubtful whether surname is that important to children—for whom first name is more significant—or for most adults (we don't all sit in the House of Lords!) As Hale L.J. pointed out, in relation to a step-father who wanted the child's name changed to his, "it is a poor sort of parent whose interest in and commitment to his child depends upon that child bearing his name. After all, that is a privilege which is not enjoyed by many mothers, even if they are living with the child".[269]

Where a residence order is in force, the name of the child cannot be changed without the consent of all those with parental responsibility or the leave of the court.[270] It would seem that the consent of the child is not needed. Whether a child of sufficient legal competence can change his or her name was left open in *Re PC (Change of Surname)*.[271] So was the question whether a change of surname could be effected against the will of a competent child. Where there is no residence order in force, it should follow that since s.13 does not apply and in the light of s.2(7) of the Children Act, one person with parental responsibility could unilaterally change the name of the child. Of course, this might lead to more residence orders being sought, which would run counter to the Children Act philosophy. And it could lead to the chaotic situation of parents each changing their child's name.[272] Not surprisingly, it was therefore held in *Re PC* that where two or more persons had parental responsibility for a child, one of them could only lawfully effect a change of surname with the consent of the other or others with parental responsibility. Where only one person has parental responsibility, Holman J. in *Re PC* said that s/he could unilaterally change the child's surname. If the unmarried father disapproved he would need to seek (and obtain) a prohibited steps order.[273] However, the House of Lords in _Dawson v Wearmouth_[274] has ruled that any dispute over a child's surname should be referred to the court whether or not there is a residence order in force and whoever has or has not parental responsibility.

If a dispute about a child's name is referred to a court, the child's welfare is the paramount consideration.[275] The person wishing to change the child's name must show it is in the child's best interests.[276] The child's views are important, but not decisive.[277] In _Re S_,[278] they prevailed: the applicant child was _Gillick_ competent[279] and the change of name was requested to disassociate herself from an abusive father. Where the residential parent is seeking to change the child's name from that of the non-residential parent, the strength of the child's relationship with the absent parent is taken into account.[280] Cultural factors may also be relevant. Thus, in _Re S (Change of Names: Cultural Factors)_[281] the child had a Muslim mother and a Sikh father. The child had been given Sikh names. Following a divorce, the mother asked to change the child's name to a Muslim name. She argued that the Muslim community would not accept a child with Sikh names. The court held that the child should be known on a day-to-day basis by Muslim names. However, to preserve the reality of his parentage and Sikh heritage, nothing more than this should be done formally by deed poll.

The rules in relation to surnames do not apply to forenames.[282] Foster parents cannot unilaterally change the forename of a child in their care.[283] Adoptive parents, of course, acquire that right.[284]

(ix) Representing the child in legal proceedings

Subject to one important exception, a child can only bring or defend legal proceedings by his "litigation friend".[285] A person with parental responsibility is entitled to act in this capacity,[286] unless s/he has an interest adverse to the child. A "litigation friend" can be removed by the court if a proper case is made out: for example, parents who refused to accept the compromise of Thalidomide litigation were removed (through this was reversed on appeal).[287] The exception are proceedings under the Children Act 1989 and under the High Court's jurisdiction: children of sufficient age and understanding may act with the leave of the court and without a next friend or guardian.[288]

(x) Rights over child's property

These include the right to "receive or recover in his own name, for the benefit of the child, property of whatever description and whatever situated which the child is entitled to receive or recover".[289] They do not include a right of succession[290]—children cannot make wills—but in practice parents do have a right to inherit their children's property.[291] They do not have a right to their children's wages. The law on gifts given to children is uncertain: if, as is thought, the legal interest in gifts to young children vests in those with parental responsibility, it does so on trust for the children. Gifts to older children—whatever this means—belong to the children. Perhaps because these issues have provided, mercifully, no litigation, we search in vain for definite answers. Disputes are unlikely over train sets but they may well one day arise over a substantial gift of money, perhaps by a grandparent.

(xi) Some miscellaneous rights

Other rights may be briefly listed. They include:

the right to consent to a child's marriage;

the right to consent to a child's adoption;

the power to veto the issue of a passport to a child;

the duty to dispose of the child's corpse.[292]

EXERCISING PARENTAL RESPONSIBILITY

Parental responsibility may be held by more than one person, most obviously by two parents.[293] They may not agree, or one of them may not be available. The Law Commission thought that it was essential for those with parental responsibility to be able to make decisions independently. It saw a duty to consult as undesirable and unworkable: nor would it necessarily be in the child's interests if decision-making was delayed.[294] The Children Act 1989 accordingly provides that where more than one person has parental responsibility each of them may act alone, except where the consent of all is specifically required.[295] Whether the parent who does not have the care of the child should be able to interfere with day-to-day decisions taken by the caring parent is contentious (Bainham, 1990). The power to act independently is subject to the limitation that a person with a parental responsibility is not entitled to act in any way that is incompatible with a court order.[296]

There are certain decisions of such fundamental importance to the child that the consent of all those with parental responsibility is required. There is no definitive list of what these decisions are. Judicial authorities suggest long-term decisions relating to education,[297] circumcision of a male child,[298] the changing of a child's surname,[299] and controversial immunisations such as the MMR vaccine.[300] It is difficult to reconcile this development of the law with the clear statutory language of s.2(7).

A parent does not lose parental responsibility because someone else has acquired it through a court order. If, therefore, after a divorce, a step-parent acquires parental responsibility by agreement or a court order, the non-residential parent retains parental responsibility. Three persons will now have parental responsibility: none of them can act incompatibly with a court order[301] but each of them can, subject to what was said in the previous paragraph, act independently of the others. The same applies if anyone else acquires parental responsibility as, for example, grandparents, other relatives or foster parents may as a result of a residence order. Parents also do not lose parental responsibility when this is vested in a local authority by a care order or emergency protection order.[302]

A person with parental responsibility cannot surrender or transfer this to another person, but can "arrange for some or all of it to be met by one or more persons acting on his behalf."[303] Such delegation can be made to persons who already have parental responsibility, and to those like childminders and teachers who do not. Such agreements do not affect liability for failure to discharge parental responsibility.

Those who care for a child but do not have parental responsibility may, subject to the provisions of the 1989 Act, do what is "reasonable in all the circumstances for the purpose of safeguarding or promoting the child's welfare".[304] An obvious example would be consenting to the child's medical treatment after an accident. But it would not extend to acquiring a passport for a child or to changing the child's surname. Parents of a child accommodated by a local authority can remove the child from foster parents without notice:[305] it would clearly be reasonable to refuse to do so when the request was made, for example in the middle of the night or by a parent the worse for drink.[306]

Does the law give the non-residential parent—the parent who does not have day-to-day care—too much power? *Re P (A Minor) (Parental Responsibility Order)* suggests that "day-to-day" issues should be decided by the parent with whom the child lives.[307] According to Sumner J. this is in recognition of the "bond" that exists between the child and the principal carer, but it does not give that parent "greater rights".[308] Nevertheless, the non-residential parent can in most cases act independently.

Is this right? Is "caring about" as important as "caring for"? Smart and Neale (1999) do not think so. They point to dangers in letting the non-residential parent take decisions without the burden of performing the day-to-day care of the child. It gives the non-residential parent power, and can enable him to interfere in the life of the residential parent, even to the point of abusing her. This is particularly significant where there has been domestic violence (Hester and Radford, 1996). Allowing each parent to exercise parental responsibility may confuse the child, but this happens in intact families too. The best solution may be to let the residential parent take all the important decisions. But what is an important decision? Is diet? Religion? The reality is that few non-residential parents take part in major decision making. Maclean and Eekelaar (1997) believe joint decision making occurs in no more than "one in ten cases where contact is regularly exercised, and then only on a limited number of issues". Decisions for children are inevitably, it seems, taken by those who look after them. Fathers may have equal capacity with mothers for everyday caring, but mothers become more "expert" and fathers more distanced (Lupton and Barclay, 1997). This is inevitably accentuated when they do not live with their children (and see Lewis and Welsh, 2006). Fathers in Lewis and Welsh's study were principally involved in "macro-responsibility", responsibility for "earning, guiding, leading and steering the child, imposing a moral code and imparting values", that is more in "caring about" than "caring for". What are the implications of this for parental responsibility? The importance of contact, and of the child support obligation, rather than participation in everyday decision-making? Or can roles be so easily demarcated? Has English law created the right balance? Has s.2(7) been appropriately adjusted by the judges? There are no simple answers.

8

UNDERSTANDING DISPUTES ABOUT CHILDREN

This chapter looks at private law disputes about children. These may relate to more or less anything, but principally focus on where the child shall live, with whom s/he shall have contact and on questions relating to health care and education, including religious upbringing. These disputes are usually between parents (both of whom will normally have parental responsibility) but may also involve other relatives or others (foster parents, for example) caring for the child or wishing to do so.

THE PARAMOUNTCY PRINCIPLE

English law is unequivocal in stating that whenever a court considers a question relating to the upbringing of a child the paramount consideration is the welfare of the child.[1] There is no definition of "welfare" in the Children Act 1989, though there is a list of factors to guide decision-makers and indeed those who advise parties who are in dispute. The details of these are considered later in this chapter.[2]

What does "paramount" mean? Although it was formulated under previous legislation, when the test was "first and paramount", Lord MacDermott's explanation in *J v C* remains an authoritative starting point. That a child's welfare is paramount means

"... more than that the child's welfare is to be treated as the top item in a list of items relevant to the matter in question. [The words] denote a process whereby, when all the relevant facts, relationships, claims and wishes of parents, risks, choices and other circumstances are taken into account and weighed, the course to be followed will be that which is most in the interests of the child's welfare.... It is the paramount consideration because it rules upon or determines the course to be followed".[3]

This was stated in 1969, long before the Human Rights Act 1998 came into operation in 2000. The European Convention on Human Rights has no paramountcy principle; there is no reference in it to the best interests of the child.[4] There was thus some concern that the principle might be incompatible with the Convention or that at the very least Art.8, with its emphasis on the rights of parents, might dilute the force of the principle.[5] Was this concern justified? In *Hendricks v Netherlands*,[6] the European Commission had held that where there was a serious conflict between the interests of a child and one of his parents which could only be resolved to the detriment of one of them, the child's interests had to prevail under Art.8(2). This should have put concern at rest. And in several cases since English courts have affirmed the compatibility of the paramountcy principle with the Convention.[7] In one of these cases Thorpe L.J. rightly noted that "the acknowledgement of child welfare as paramount must be common to most if not all judicial systems within the Council of Europe".[8] Recently, the European Court of Human Rights has said that "in judicial decisions where rights under Article 8 of parents and those of a child are at stake, the child's rights must be the paramount consideration. If any balancing of interests is necessary, the interests of the child must prevail".[9] And Munby J., after referring to this decision, has described the welfare principle as a "core principle" of human rights law.[10] Thus those who feared the Convention jurisprudence would undermine the paramountcy principle have had their fears allayed.[11]

The enunciation of the paramountcy principle in the Children Act 1989 is contemporaneous with the UN Convention on the Rights of the Child.[12] Article 3(1) of this states:

"In all actions concerning children, whether undertaken by public or private social welfare institutions, courts of law, administrative authorities or legislative bodies, the best interests of the child shall be a primary consideration".[13]

It will be observed that this injunction is wider than the welfare principle in the Children Act: it applies to actions by public and private social welfare institutions, administrative authorities and legislative bodies, as well as to courts. The welfare principle applies only to courts. On the other hand, the best interests of the child are only a primary consideration, and not the paramount consideration. It could, of course, be argued that the UN

Convention's provision is easier to reconcile with the European Convention than is that in the Children Act.[14]

The paramountcy (or best interests) principle is easier to state than to apply. Robert Mnookin pointed out in 1975 that "deciding what is best for a child poses a question no less ultimate than the purposes and values of life itself".[15] And yet, as he concedes, the standard has come to be seen as "neutral".[16] But, as King and Piper point out, "the broad range of factors—genetic, financial, educational, environmental and relational—which science would recognise as capable of affecting the welfare of the child are narrowed by law to a small range of issues which fall directly under the influence of the judge, the social workers or the adult parties ...".[17]

The best interests principle is, of course, indeterminate.[18] One of the dangers of this is that, in upholding the standard, other principles and policies can exert an influence from behind the "smokescreen" of the principle. It can cloak prejudices: views about the place of women, anti-gay sentiments.[19] It can also be merely a reflection of "dominant meanings".[20] It has been argued (by Irène Thèry, 1989, p.82) that it is an "alibi for dominant ideology ... individual arbitrariness ... family and more general social policies for which the law serves as an instrument".

Different cultures will also, and inevitably, operate with different concepts of what is in a child's best interests.[21] A Christian parent and a Muslim parent may clash over whether their son should be circumcised. Both parents may have the boy's best interests at heart, but differ on their interpretation of what this requires. As discussed in the previous chapter,[22] the Court of Appeal thought it was not in a five-year-old's best interests to be circumcised against the wishes of his primary carer (the nominally Christian mother).[23] Was the court right? Did it allow the carer's wishes to prevail over the child's longer term interests? Do we know what these are? He may grow up to rediscover his Muslim roots and resent the decision to deny him a fundamental of his faith.

There is a distinction between, what has been called, "current interests" and "future-orientated interests".[24] And the two can come into conflict. Current interests tend to be formulated in relation to experiential considerations: future-orientated interests, by contrast, focus on developmental considerations. As Mnookin explained:

"The conditions that make a person happy at age seven to ten may have adverse consequences at age thirty. Should the judge ask himself what decision will make the child happiest in the next year? Or at thirty? Or at seventy? Should the judge decide by thinking about what decision the child as an adult looking back would have wanted made? ... How is the judge to compare 'happiness' at one age with 'happiness' at another age?"[25]

And what is "happiness"? When we refer to the child's best interests, are we stressing material welfare or spiritual? Is ultimate economic productivity an important consideration or are the more primary values, love, security and warmth in interpersonal relationships, of greater significance? The questions are endless, but where is the judge to turn for answers? There is no clear consensus within society either as to the best child-rearing strategies—take the debate about hitting children—or as to the appropriate hierarchy of values. Nobody may know *the* answer, and there may not be one, but the judge has to come to *an* answer. It is not surprising that when the Bible wished to teach "wisdom" (in the famous judgment of Solomon) it used a dispute over a child.[26]

Take a straightforward contest: a mother and father have separated and both want their child to live with them. The judge would need to compare the expected utility for the child of living with his mother with that of living with his father. To undertake this task the judge needs (i) information; (ii) predictive ability; (iii) some source for the values to inform his choice. All three of these requirements pose considerable problems.

Judges may get the information from various sources: the parties themselves, the child, welfare reports. But they rarely act possessed of full information. But even given that they had this, and were thus in a position to specify possible outcomes, how are they to predict what the probable results of alternative outcomes are? The problem is that "present-day knowledge about human behaviour provides no basis for the kind of individualised predictions required by the best-interests standard".[27] There are competing theories of human behaviour related to different conceptions of the nature of man, and no consensus as to which, if any, of these views is correct. And even if there were a right answer, it is difficult to see how it could be a totally reliable guide to predict what is likely to happen to a particular child. As Goldstein *et al.* point out: "no one can forecast just what experiences, what events, what changes a child, or for that matter his adult custodian, will actually encounter".[28] Anna Freud saw a number of reasons for believing that prediction was "difficult and hazardous". These include "environmental happenings in a child's life will always remain unpredictable since they are not governed by any known laws".[29]

The difficulty of making accurate predictions is attested to by the well-known Berkeley group study of 166 infants born in 1929. The aim of the study was to observe the emotional, mental and physical growth of "normal" adults. Arlene Skolnick, summarising the research, noted that the most surprising, and for us the most interesting, research finding was "the difficulty of predicting what thirty-year-old adults would be like even after the most sophisticated data had been gathered on them as children".[30]

Even if full information was to hand so that outcomes could be specified and their probability could be estimated, the judge would still have to decide which set of values to use to determine what is in a child's best interests. How is utility to be determined? Of course, an obvious method is to ask the person most affected—the child—what s/he wants. With older children this may indeed be appropriate.[31] Even if they cannot decide which parent, they may be able to offer guidance on the values they cherish. This is obviously not the case with younger children. The parents themselves could be asked to articulate the value system with which they are happiest: they might put the spiritual welfare of their children above material well-being. But, of course, they might differ. The US case of *Painter v Bannister*[32] (a dispute between the father and maternal grandparents over custody of a six-year-old boy) is a graphic illustration: the father prioritising intellectual stimulation, the grandparents security and stability.[33] And there are cases of mixed marriages where religious and cultural difference make parental consensus even on values impossible (we have already considered the conflict over circumcision between the Muslim father and Christian mother).[34] The judge's own values will inevitably play a part in his/her decision-making. Take a case like *May v May*:[35] the court preferred the father's approach to parenting, because he imposed discipline and stressed the importance of academic achievement, to the mother's more relaxed attitude to schooling and hence homework. In another case, the judge ruled against a mother (and her new partner) who were naturalists and took an uninhibited view of wandering around the house nude.[36] The Court of Appeal reversed the judge. The case of *Re P (Section*

91(14) Guidelines) (Residence and Religious Heritage)[37] has already been referred to: here the Court of Appeal upheld the decision to make a residence order in favour of local authority foster parents of a Down's Syndrome child. It also restricted further applications for residence by the natural parents. The parents were orthodox Jews (the father a rabbi), and the local authority had attempted without success to find an orthodox Jewish family to foster the child. She was now well-settled and well-cared for by non-practising Catholics. The court emphasised the importance of this and concluded the child's welfare was best served by remaining with them. In this case this was more important than the child's religious and cultural heritage, which, unhappily, she was now going to lose. But it was thought she had limited ability to appreciate this.[38]

English law offers guidance on the paramountcy principle. Section 1(3) of the Children Act is a checklist of factors that courts must take into account in deciding what is in the best interests of the child. It can also take into account other factors. Going through the list has been described as good discipline.[39] Recently, Baroness Hale has stressed in difficult or finely balanced cases, it is of great help to address each of the factors so as to ensure that "no particular feature of the case is given more weight than it should properly bear".[40] Certainly, if it can be shown that a judge has failed to take a factor into account which is relevant to the case, his decision is likely to be overturned on appeal. By contrast, the UN Convention's Art.3(1) leaves the determination of best interests at large: there is no checklist (Freeman, 2007, p.30–31). That a checklist is a good idea is indisputable. But it is no more than an important statement, and it does not "eliminate subjective value judgments about parenting and child care arrangements" (Dewar, 1992, p.366). The factors are merely listed. No indication is offered of the importance to be attached to the factors. The ascertainable wishes and feelings of the child is listed as the first item.[41] Does this mean it is the most important consideration? The right of children to express their views and to the heard in legal proceedings is regarded as central to the UN Convention on the Rights of the Child.[42]

THE WELFARE CHECKLIST

(i) The wishes and feelings of the child

Let us look then at the factors, beginning with the ascertainable wishes and feelings of the child, considered in the light of age and understanding.

First, how is a court to ascertain the child's wishes and feelings? The judge can interview the child in private.[43] There is a reluctance to do this: Wall L.J. explained why in the recent case of *Mabon v Mabon*:

"What is said in private by the child to the judge cannot be tested in evidence or in cross examination. As a consequence a judge ... cannot promise a child that any conversation with the child will be entirely confidential. That fact may inhibit children from expressing their true feelings to the judge."[44]

A child can also be made a party to proceedings (though not in the magistrates' court), and if this is done s/he will be separately represented. The Family Proceedings Rules r.9.5 provides that

"if in any proceedings it appears to the court that it is in the best interests of any child to be made a party to the proceedings, the court may appoint

(a) an officer of the Service[45] ...
(b) (if he consents) the Official Solicitor; or
(c) (if he consents) some other proper person

to be the guardian ad litem with authority to take part in the proceedings on the child's behalf".

The decision to make a child a party is only to be taken in cases of "significant difficulty" (including cases where the child's view is in conflict with the position of the adults).[46] This system of representation is "essentially paternalistic," the first priority of the guardian being to "advocate the welfare of the child he represents. His second priority is to put before the court the child's wishes and feelings".[47] Appointments under r.9.5 are unusual: a study in Leeds found that separate representation was ordered in 7.3 per cent of cases (Bellamy and Lord, 2003; see Douglas *et al.*, 2006 have similar findings). Whether denying a child automatic party status complies with the European

Convention on Human Rights may be doubted: Art.6 provides that "everyone is entitled to a fair and public hearing" (and see Fortin, 1999, p.244), and Art.14 outlaws discrimination, and children are undoubtedly discriminated against (Lyon, 2000, p.70). The Grand Chamber of the European Court of Human Rights did not think so, but the case involved a five-year-old.[48] One can only speculate as to what it would say were an older mature child denied the ability to present views to the court (but see Lowe and Douglas, 2006, p.503).

The main way of eliciting the child's views is through a welfare report.[49] The report is made by a child and family reporter (CFR) or by the local authority[50] "on such matters relating to the welfare of the child as are required to be dealt with". There is no power to order a residential assessment of one parent and child against the wishes of the other parent,[51] nor to order a local authority to instruct a child psychiatrist to prepare a report for the court.[52] It has been said that it is "through the CFR that the judge most evidently exercises that part of his function which is inquisitorial".[53] And that "judge and CFR are united sharing the same ultimate objective, namely, the protection of children and the advancement of their welfare."[54] There is no obligation to find out the children's wishes—protection seems a greater concern—and it may be that children are not seen alone or at all.[55] If children are not used to having their voices listened to, they may not find it easy to talk to professionals. Smart et al. (2001) found children wanted to talk to their parents about the separation, rather than express a view to social workers. And Smart and Neale (1999, p.33) thought professionals might be seen by children as "inflexible, intrusive, condescending, deceitful and reinforcing in a myriad of ways their superiority to the child". Nonetheless, the report will often record the child's wishes. Welfare reports guide, but do not control the courts.[56] But it is expected that the recommendations in a welfare report will be followed: a court departing from the recommendations is expected to give reasons for so doing.[57] There are reported cases where courts have not followed a recommendation, but such cases are rare.[58]

Where a child's wishes and/or feelings are known, what account should be taken of them? Should the wishes of young children be ignored? Should we regard those of older children as determinative?[59] How can we be sure that the views expressed by children are not the result of brainwashing or coaching?[60] Should we not be concerned about the child—a 14-year-old girl, for example—who is more concerned to safeguard her father's welfare than her own? Should the child have a right *not* to be asked to express any preference?[61] The child who expresses a preference risks hurting one parent and damaging their relationship, but failure to state one invites the judge to make an undesired decision.

The courts' response to these dilemmas has not been straightforward. The legislation does not require the child to be *Gillick*-competent[62] before his or her views are considered, and the courts have wisely not read this in. So account has been taken of the views of children who would not satisfy that test. An example is *Re M (Contact Welfare Test)*[63] in which the wishes of two children, aged seven and nine, determined a decision to refuse a mother contact. The children had lived with their father for over five years, contact with their mother had broken down and the children did not want to see her. Ordering contact against children's wishes, the court held, would be harmful to them.

The age of the child is an important consideration. It is rare for the views of children below the age of ten to be considered conclusive. Thus, in *Re R (A Minor) (Residence: Religion)*,[64] a nine-year-old's wishes were overridden. The case was a difficult one to decide. If the father was granted a residence order, the child would be excluded from the community in which he had grown up (the Exclusive Brethren). If, on the other hand, a residence order was granted to the aunt (a member of that community) he would no longer see his father. The court made a residence order in favour of the father though the boy himself favoured remaining within the society of the Exclusive Brethren. It should be stressed that the court was not passing judgment on the tenets of a religion.[65]

The views of children between 10 and 14 are sometimes acceded to. For example, those of an 11-year-old girl, said to be "mature beyond her years", who wrote a series of letters objecting to being returned to her alcoholic mother.[66] In *Re M, T, P, K and B (Care: Change of Name)*,[67] where the children were 15, 14, 12, 11 and 9 and their views were "the result of long deliberation, not been planted by others and [were] not transient or equivocal",[68] the court gave effect to them. The case centred on the worst abuse the judge had ever encountered, and the children, who had initiated the application to change their surnames,[69] were "absolutely terrified of their parents". One of the girls so much so that she wanted to change her face as well as her name. A further example is *Re S (Contact: Children's Wishes)*.[70] The judge was highly critical of the father's failure to respect the views of his children, aged 16, 14 and 12, that they didn't want to maintain contact with him. Children of such ages were entitled to have their views respected.[71] Certainly, courts are not bound by the wishes of children, whatever their age, and may well depart from them where, in the opinion of the court, welfare dictates a decision contrary to the child's wishes.[72]

(i) The child's needs

Second, the checklist refers to the child's physical, emotional and educational needs. What do children need? The evidence is that they need different things at different stages of their development: babies have very different needs from teenagers. Children whose parents separate or divorce have additional needs: thus the importance of maintaining a relationship with an absent parent, and the emphasis on reducing conflict. It is trite that divorce ends marriage, but not parenthood. And debates rage over whether children are better off extricated from their parents' unhappy marriage or whether this is preferable to a breakup. The truth is, as two early researchers put it, that "neither an unhappy marriage nor a divorce is especially congenial for children: each imposes its own set of stresses" (Wallerstein and Kelly, 1980, p.307).

It is important that needs are looked at objectively, and in the light of evidence. This item in the checklist can all-too-easily cloak judicial prejudices, about homosexuality,[73] nudity,[74] discipline,[75] etc. It can also become a hostage to particular theories: for example, John Bowlby's theory about maternal deprivation[76] led to a concern that courts were favouring mothers over fathers.[77] In two cases in the early 1990s the Court of Appeal emphasised that it was "natural" for young children to be with their mothers, but this was "a consideration not a presumption".[78] In *Brixey v Lynas*,[79] Lord Jauncey explained

"... the advantage to a very young child of being with its mother is a consideration which must be taken into account when deciding where lie its best interests.... It is neither a presumption nor a principle but rather recognition of a widely held belief based on practical experience and the workings of nature".[80]

He added that where a young child had been with his mother

since birth and there was no criticism of her ability to care "only the strongest competing arguments are likely to prevail".[81] There are rare reported cases where a residence order is granted to a father in respect of a young child: one is *Re K (Residence Order: Securing Contact)*,[82] where the child was only two. The parents were Indian and there was concern that the mother was untrustworthy and would take the child to India and frustrate any contact between the child and the father. The judge conceded the decision was "somewhat unusual": this is borne out by research (Priest and Whybrow, 1986) which has shown it is far more common for children to live with their mothers after separation. Orders—where one is sought—reflect this reality.[83]

The "natural parent" presumption must also be addressed. Lord Scott's remark, already quoted, that "mothers are special"[84] is in reality an affirmation of the importance of natural parents where there is a conflict between them and, for example, a foster parent.[85] The psychological evidence to support the presumption is very weak: children, as Goldstein *et al.* emphasised, respond to those who look after them and not necessarily to their progenitors.[86] But the courts continue to emphasise the presumption.[87] A dramatic example is *Re M (Child's Upbringing)*.[88] The Court of Appeal returned a Zulu boy to his parents in South Africa. He was ten, had lived with a white Afrikaner woman in London for four years and was so reluctant to go—his wishes and feelings were not consulted—that he had to be forcibly put on a plane. Thorpe J., at first instance, had argued that the Afrikaner woman was his natural parent, emphasising psychology rather than biology. The Court of Appeal saw it as in the interests of the boy that he should be brought up by his natural parents in South Africa. Ward L.J. (himself a South African by birth) said:

"I am under no illusions whatever about the harm that return to South Africa will cause. It is not just the uncertainty about the stability of his parents' marriage and their relationship nor about their housing conditions nor economic security nor personal safety. He will leave the comforts of Maida Vale for the comparative discomfort of Brakpan. I am sure he will cope with all of that.[89] The real harm is spelled out by [the consultant child psychiatrist] ... 'If you take him away now ... against his will, then the risk is that he will go downhill emotionally, he will go downhill psychologically, he will pine for [the foster mother] and [her girls], he will get grumpy, and disagreeable, he will not quickly grasp Ndelele and Afrikaans, he will be a bit of an outsider ... and everything may go horribly wrong.... To remove him in the middle of a turmoil of disagreement would be very profoundly damaging, to such an extent that the boy might never recover his poise and psychological well-being and confidence'."[90]

The postscript to this case is that he did not settle in South Africa, and his parents allowed him to return to London within a matter of months. The postscript I would like to write is about the boy now. He is 21. How has he developed? But we are not allowed to discover this.

Thorpe L.J. (as he now is) has not forgotten the "Zulu boy" case. In *Re H (A Child: Residence)*[91] he reiterated what he had said in that case: "the biological parent may not always be the natural parent in the eyes of the child".[92] This was a case in which a grandmother had been the child's sole carer, and Thorpe L.J. opined she was the psychological parent of the child. And, he added rightly, that "presumptions in favour of a natural parent are nowhere to be found" in the Children Act 1989.[93] Indeed, if they were, it is arguable that such a presumption would be incompatible with the European Convention on Human Rights. Smart *et al.*'s research (2001) demonstrates that children themselves value psychological ties over biological ones.[94]

Physical needs include material needs such as the need for adequate accommodation. Of course, a parent with a child who did not have adequate accommodation might well be a priority need for housing. But physical needs go beyond the purely material. The parent who can put time and energy into looking after a child may be able to cater better for a child's physical needs than one who has to devote time to employment. The workalcoholic father is less able to meet a child's needs than a full-time mother. On the other hand, courts have sometimes frowned on the father who devotes himself full-time to child care and lives on state benefits rather than seeking employment[95]—a clear example of the value system to which reference was made previously.[96]

Emotional needs include—apart from those already discussed[97]—sibling support.[98] "Brothers and sisters should, wherever possible, be brought up together, so that they are an emotional support to each other in the stormy waters of the destruction of their family".[99] Courts will accordingly try to make orders which do not split siblings. Sometimes, a split is inevitable: for example, where one child refuses to live with a parent, and it is in the interests of the other child to live with that parent nevertheless.[100] The further the siblings are apart in age, the weaker the presumption to keep them together is.[101] The presumption is also weaker where siblings are of different genders, the more so where there is also a wide age gap.[102]

Another emotional need is to keep contact with both parents. This is discussed elsewhere.[103]

Educational needs are also important but can usually be addressed by attaching conditions, for example as regards religious education, to an order, or by accepting undertakings. But cases do occasionally turn on different educational styles of respective parents. The US case of *Painter v Bannister*[104] stands out, as does the Court of Appeal's reasoning in *May v May*,[105] where the father's attitude to homework—the children were only eight and six—was critical. The mother and her new partner took a much more relaxed view.

There are, of course, other needs, for example medical needs such as that to know whether the child has HIV.[106] No exhaustive list can be provided.

(iii) The residential status quo

Third, the checklist refers to the likely effect on the child of any change in his/her circumstances. The courts have long emphasised the importance of maintaining the child's residential status quo. S/he will already been suffering stress as a result of parental separation: having to change schools and living arrangements will exacerbate this. Courts thus usually confirm the child's existing living arrangements.[107] As Ormrod L.J. said in *D v M (A Minor: Custody Appeal)*, "disruption of established bonds is to be avoided wherever it is possible to do so".[108] So if a child has a settled home with one parent, good reasons are required to justify a move to other parent. In *Re B (Residence Order: Status Quo)*[109] the judge was held to be wrong to disturb the status quo in the hope that different residence arrangements would make contact easier. The overwhelming factor for securing the child's future was the status quo. However, "the status quo is satisfactory or not. The more satisfactory the status quo, the stronger the argument for not interfering. The less satisfactory the status quo, the less one requires before deciding to change".[110]

Of course, what is "satisfactory" requires judgment and inevitably involves values. Thus, for example, Latey J. found Scientology so pernicious ("immoral and obnoxious") that he had no hesitation in moving children out of an environment in which it dominated, though this involved disturbing a lengthy status quo.[111] The Court of Appeal, on the other hand, was not prepared to disturb the status quo to return an eight-year-old girl with Down's Syndrome from an orthodox Jewish background to her parents where she had lived with a Catholic family for four years.[112] The status quo was satisfactory in that she had thrived, but was this to put her immediate welfare before her long-term interests?

Emphasising the status quo is not problem-free. It may encourage one of the parties to delay, and delay is "likely to prejudice the welfare of the child".[113] It may also encourage the abduction of a child: the courts have responded by insisting that the status quo is not relevant if achieved in this way.[114]

(iv) The child's age, sex, background

Fourth, the checklist draws attention to the child's age, sex, background and any characteristics of the child which the court considers relevant. Any characteristic could be considered relevant under this heading, for example a child's vegetarianism or a deaf child's membership of deaf culture. As far as age and sex are concerned, there were "rules" which provided that young children (indeed, girls of any age) were better off with their mothers,[115] and older boys were reared better by their fathers. If these were ever rules (or principles or presumptions), they no longer exist.[116] However, age is clearly linked to a child's needs—parental separation affects children differently according to their age—as well as their wishes and feelings.

"Background" embraces such matters as race, religion, culture and language. Of course, they may be related. In a case where contact by a father to a child of mixed race was an issue, "the significance of race"[117] was stressed. The courts recognise the special value of biological parents as providing links with the child's culture and heritage. The so-called "Zulu boy" case is a clear example of this.[118] Religious upbringing features less than it once did,[119] but cannot be overlooked. In *Re J (Specific Issue Orders: Muslim Upbringing*[120] (discussed in the previous chapter),[121] and in *Re S (Specific Issue Order: Religion: Circumcision)*,[122] in both of which cases neither parent strictly observed the tenets of their faith, application by Muslims to circumcise sons who had a non-Muslim parent were refused.[123] More interesting are cases where the child, as a result of upbringing, has a clear religious identity. *Re R (A Minor) (Residence: Religion)*,[124] discussed above,[125] gave the court an agonizing dilemma: the boy was firmly committed to the Exclusive Brethren faith but his father was no longer an adherent. The court decided the boy's long-term interests lay with the father, and not with the boy's religious identity.

The courts do not discriminate against a parent on grounds of religion. To do so would be to break Arts 9 and 14 of the European Convention on Human Rights.[126] In the past courts have ruled against parents whose religious practices were thought to harm a child, such as Scientology,[127] though it is dubious whether this is a religion. And against religions which caused the child to suffer social isolation[128] or indoctrination.[129] A child can always be protected against a harmful religious practice by a specific issue order or prohibited steps order: for example, a parent who was a Jehovah's Witness could be awarded a residence order and his refusal to consent to the child having a blood transfusion overruled.[130]

Culture is a broad concept. It embraces language.[131] It can include dress (important when placing a child who dresses traditionally in a family of the same ethnicity who may not do so); food (important where the child is a vegetarian or who eats only halal or kosher food); the celebration of festivals (which in a secularised society may be only marginally connected with religion). A heightened awareness of culture does not require toleration of harmful manifestations of that culture, such as female circumcision.[132] The importance of culture was stressed in *Re S (Change of Names: Cultural Factors)*:[133] a Muslim mother, divorced from the Sikh father, and now living in the Muslim community, was permitted to use Muslim names for the child—he had had his birth registered with recognisably Sikh names. But she was not given leave to change his name formally since that would contribute to his losing his Sikh identity. Maintaining the Sikh birth name would represent the reality of his parentage.

But it should be stressed that, however important culture and heritage are, they may be trumped by other welfare considerations. The case of the eight-year-old Jewish girl with Down's Syndrome, discussed above,[134] amply demonstrates this. The residential status quo prevailed, particularly since the girl herself had limited ability to appreciate the culture of which she was being deprived. The foster parents were clearly the girl's psychological parents.

(v) Harm suffered or at risk of being suffered

Fifth, account is to be taken of any harm which the child has suffered or is at risk of suffering. "Harm" is defined broadly: it means both ill-treatment and impairment of health and development.[135] It obviously includes sexual abuse: "the principle is clearly established that cases of sexual abuse which show a danger of repetition of that conduct if access [now contact] is afforded to a parent, or indeed show continuing or recent disturbance, may warrant ... a total withdrawal of access."[136] But courts have in the past allowed contact in circumstances where others (social workers, for example) might be more cautious.[137] They have also been rather more tolerant of domestic violence than they should.[138] But "harm" now includes "impairment suffered from seeing or hearing the ill-treatment of another",[139] so that violence perpetrated by one parent on another is to be taken account of.

Deciding whether a child is at risk of harm may be more difficult. In context of care proceedings it has been said that the court must reach a conclusion on facts, "not on suspicion or mere doubts".[140] Does this give too much benefit of the doubt to the parent who treads close to sexual boundaries[141] or to the alcoholic parent whose drink problem has not as yet harmed the child?[142] Again, values inevitably play a part in decision-making. Thus, a judge could find a naturalist lifestyle harmful to children,[143] and another judge could order supervised contact to a father with a history of psychiatric illness, alcohol and drug abuse who had Nazi sympathies and dressed his sons (aged five and eight) in Nazi uniforms.[144] Does exposing a child to racism not risk harming the child's development?

(vi) Parents' capability

Sixth, the checklist refers to how capable each of the child's parents, and any other person in relation to whom the court considers the question to be relevant, is of meeting his/her needs. All manner of questions arise here. A parent's capacity to bring up a child may be impaired by mental illness, by substance abuse, by having formed the wrong sort of relationship. In relation to the new partner, courts once frowned on mothers who formed lesbian relationships.[145] This is no longer so. They remain wary, as they should be, of new partners with records of sexual offences against children.[146] Adults can learn to parent: children, however, cannot wait.[147] Parents need not care for their children full-time but they must be able to make acceptable alternative arrangements: in one case,[148] which did not satisfy this criterion, the father proposed to use a rota of child minders, thus demonstrating that he did not understand the child's needs for continuity and consistency.

The court's powers

Finally, the checklist draws the decision maker's attention to the range of powers available to the court under the Children Act in the proceedings in question. The court is not restricted to making orders specifically sought. It has the power to make orders of its own volition.[149] The critical question is which order (if any) from the range of orders at the court's disposal would best promote the welfare of the child. Not every order is open to the court: most obviously, it cannot make a care order unless the conditions are satisfied.[150] Nor can it make an order in favour of someone who is not prepared to accept it. So, where a local authority applied for a care order in respect of two children with muscular dystrophy (it did so because one of them had been injured by a schizophrenic mother), it could not make a residence order in favour of grandparents who were willing to look after the children but who could only do so with the financial (and professional) support they would receive if a care order were made. The court made care orders against the wishes of the local authority.[151]

THE LIMITS OF THE PARAMOUNTCY PRINCIPLE

We have now looked at the checklist. It should be pointed out that courts are not limited to having regard to the factors in this. They can look at anything else they consider significant. The checklist certainly pours content into the paramountcy principle.[152] But it is not without further problems.

First, it should be noted that it does not apply to all disputes about children, only those about a child's "upbringing" and to questions about the administration of a child's property or income arising from it.

It does not apply outside the context of litigation: parents and local authorities are not bound by it.

It does not apply to Part III of the Children Act 1989, so does not govern the decision to place a child in secure accommodation.[153]

It only applies to questions which directly concern the child's upbringing.[154] A recent application of this was to hold that it had no application to the lawfulness of prison policy to separate children once they reached 18 months from their imprisoned mothers.[155]

(i) Freedom of publication

A question which has provoked much discussion and a lot of case law concerns the reconciliation of the paramounctcy principle with freedom to publish information which may not be in the best interests of a child. The answer to this dilemma is now to be found in the European Convention on Human Rights: in Arts 8 and 10. Since the two rights (private and family life and freedom of expression) must now be balanced, there is no room for the paramountcy principle. In *Re S (A Child) (Identification: Restrictions on Publication)*,[156] the House of Lords upheld the decision not to grant an injunction prohibiting the identification of a mother who was the defendant in a criminal trial charged with murdering her elder son in order to protect her younger son: the younger son's welfare was said not to be paramount. An injunction was however granted in *A Local Authority v W, L, T and R (By the Children's Guardian)*.[157] The children's mother had pleaded guilty to knowingly having infected the father with HIV. There was concern that there might be anger if news spread that the elder child (who was not HIV positive) was at a nursery school. The injunction restrained the publication of information about the parents' identities and details about the nursery. Although these two decisions do not turn on the paramountcy principle, but rather an application of the European Convention, they are consistent with paramountcy principle thinking. The first only indirectly concerned a child's upbringing and was in reality an attempt to protect the mother: the second directly related to the children's upbringing; if their parents' HIV status were known finding a foster parent placement might be difficult.

(ii) More than one child

Second, it seems to have occurred to no one when the Children Act was passed—and this includes commentators on the Act—that cases would arise where the upbringing of more than one child would be in issue and their interests would conflict. The courts first answered this by saying that it was the child who was the subject of the application whose interests were paramount.

Thus, where the mother is a teenager and there is an application for a care order in respect of her baby[158] or she is applying for contact with her baby,[159] the baby's welfare, not the teenager's, is paramount. But when they were confronted with the conjoined twins case in 2000[160] a different solution had to be found. Obviously, it was impossible to say that only one of them was the subject of the application. And it was difficult to say that it was in the interests of both twins to be separated since on separation the weaker twin would die (but see Freeman, 2001). The court resolved the problem by applying a test of "least detrimental alternative"[161] which, as we shall see, is thought by Goldstein *et al.* (1973) to a more realistic test than best interests.[162] This enabled it to declare surgery to separate the twins to be lawful, and to justify it as offering one child life in circumstances in which the death of the other was inevitable. It can be argued (and see Bainham, 2005, p.445) that the decision "maximise[d] the total welfare of all concerned". Is this an approach that might be adopted where the interests of children conflict with those of adults? Bainham thinks so: as does Eekelaar (2002).

CRITICISMS OF THE PARAMOUNTCY PRINCIPLE

There is considerable scepticism about the paramountcy principle (Elster, 1987; Mnookin, 1975; Reece, 1996).

It is said to be vague and unpredictable. This makes it difficult for parents (and others) to negotiate settlements about arrangements for children. More cases may, as a result, end up in court. One consequence of this is that money is expended on litigation which might be better spent on children.

It is also said to embody values, which may not be those of the parties or their community or, indeed, necessarily those of society. What counts as a child's best interests may be nothing more than professional prejudice—the values of "psy" professionals are engaged in social engineering (Masson, 1994): their views on race or homosexuality being geared to lead rather than to follow public sentiment.

The principle may also be culturally biased. The Act does not contain—though, of course, the Human Rights Act 1998 does—a non-discrimination principle.[163] It should not be forgotten that different cultures have different understandings of best interests, just as they have different understandings of childhood.[164] There are different views about child-rearing (and the state does not prescribe optimal standards), about the punishment of children, about education, dress, arranged marriages, etc. (and see Freeman, 2007, pp.33–40).

There is also concern, voiced strongly by Reece (1996), that the interests of adults are neglected in a reasoning process which sees children's best interests as determinative. Of course, there are other interests involved, and it is easy to overlook these when our vision is channeled to look only at children. But are children's interests not the most important? The disputes are about them, and they are not usually instigated by them. Children constitute the future: we should want to make this the best we can. Of course, there are limits to what we can do. If the only consideration were the best interests of children, we would spend much more than we currently do. All policies would be subjected to a child impact analysis.[165] No expense would be spared. Children would get the best education, the best medical treatment, etc. whatever it cost. But we have to be realistic. This is one reason why it has been suggested[166] that the test should not be paramountcy or best interests, but rather "the least detrimental alternative". It is not in the best interests of a child to be the subject of the sort of dispute which leads to court intervention.

Debates also range on the relationship between best interests and children's rights. The UN Convention on the Rights of the Child contains both a best interests principle (though this is a lower standard than that in the Children Act 1989),[167] and many rights, including a range of important participatory ones.[168] Can a proposed outcome for a child be in his or her best interests where it conflicts with his/her rights? What if a child's views (his/her "wishes and feelings") conflict with what adults/professionals think is in his/her best interests? These important questions will be examined in Chapter 13 after we have looked at children's rights.[169]

THE ORDERS

But we must now look at the orders a court can make when a dispute about children is taken to it.

(i) No order

First, it can make no order. Section 1(5) of the Children Act 1989 lays down that a court "shall not make the order or any of the orders unless it considers that doing so would be better for the children than making no order at all." This "no order" or minimal intervention principle is key to understanding the legislation (but see Fox-Harding, 1991; Freeman, 1992). The Law Commission was concerned that orders (then for custody and access) were routinely made without considering whether there was any benefit in such orders for children.[170] It thought similarly about public orders (the care order notably) and wanted local authorities (and courts, if authorities failed to do so) to consider other ways than compulsory action of addressing families having difficulties bringing up their children.

The "no order" principle complements the welfare principle: it is clearly not in the best interests of a child to be the subject of orders which are unnecessary. It encapsulates "deregulation" (Douglas); it symbolises the "privatisation" of the family (Bainham, 1990; Cretney, 1990). It reflects the philosophy of Goldstein *et al.* (1979) who argued that a policy of minimum coercive intervention by the state accorded with their "firm belief as citizens in individual freedom and human dignity" (1979, p.12). *Whose* freedom and *what* dignity this philosophy upholds has been questioned (Freeman, 1997). It has to be said also that the philosophy is consonant with Art.8 of the European Convention on Human Rights, which protects family privacy.[171]

Opinions differ on what s.1(5) means. Does it say that the best solution is no order? Or is it, as Bainham (1990, p.221) suggests, neutral as to whether intervention is desirable? Not suprisingly it has been found (Bailey-Harris *et al.*, 1999) that practitioners and district judges are not consistent in the ways they approach s.1(5). The research found "no order" in about 5 per cent of cases. There are other indications that the number of such orders is declining.[172]

One issue to have exercised the courts is whether s.1(5) creates a burden of proof to show that a proposed order is for the child's benefit. According to Munby J.[173] it does: he ruled that the party applying for the order had to make out "a positive case that on a balance of probabilities it is in the interests of the child that that order should be made."[174] Thorpe L.J. has, on several occasions,[175] expressed a different view. In one case he said that he didn't think "such concepts of presumption and burden of proof had any place in Children Act litigation because the judge exercised a function that is 'partly inquisitorial'".[176] Ward L.J. has since agreed: s.1(5) does not "create a presumption one way or another. All it demands is that before the court makes any order it must ask the question: Will it be better for the child to make the order than making no order at all?"[177]

A good example of the case for an order is *B v B (A Minor) (Residence Order)*.[178] This was an unopposed application for a residence order by a grandmother who had been looking after her grandchild for ten years. She needed parental reponsibility in order to make decisions about the child: for example, to authorise various school activities. A residence order was made. On balance it was better that the order was made than not made. Another is *Re S (Contact: Grandparents)*,[179] an application by grandparents for a contact order. By the time of the hearing the mother was prepared to allow contact. For this reason, the judge made no order. The Court of Appeal held that, given the antagonism between the parties, a contact order should be made: this would obviate the need to return to court should the mother frustrate contact again.

There are four orders in s.8 of the Children Act 1989 (known as "Section 8 orders"). They are: the residence order; the contact order; the specific issue order; and the prohibited steps order.

(ii) The residence order

Each of these orders must be examined in turn. The residence order is an order "settling the arrangments to be made as to the person with whom the child is to live".[180] In the case of married parents,[181] who already possess parental responsibility, this is all it does. The parent with whom the child does not live after separation on divorce (whom we will call the non-residential parent) continues to have parental responsibility and is able to exercise it to the full, except only that he will lose his right to look after the child where there is a residence order in favour of the other parent. He cannot act incompatibly with the residence order:[182] it is far from clear what this means. By contrast, if a step-parent is granted a residence order he acquires parental responsibility and retains it so long as the order is in force. The most common recipient of a residence order is a parent but it can be a grandparent, an aunt or anyone. It has been said that it cannot be made in favour of a child,[183] but there is no reason why, in appropriate circumstances, it could not be (for example where a mature sibling was looking after a younger child).

A residence order can be made in favour of two people, even if they do not live together.[184] So what is usually called a "shared" or "joint" residence order can be made, facilitating joint or co-parenting. American writers have argued that it "appears more fully to satisfy the needs of both parents", and that it does not, contrary to fears, make the child "a 'yo-yo' whose loyalties are divided and whose stability is undermined by shifting living arrangements" (Roman and Haddad, 1979, pp.117 and 118). English judges were reluctant to make shared residence orders.[185] In cases in 1994, the Court of Appeal held they should only be made in exceptional circumstances,[186] and subsequently, only where it could be shown that it would provide a positive benefit for the child and there were no concrete issues between the parties which still needed to be resolved.[187] But judges are now more willing to make shared residence orders and no longer insist on finding exceptional circumstances or a positive benefit. In *D v D (Shared Residence Order)*[188] Hale L.J. said she would not "add any gloss on the legislative provisions, which are always subject to the paramount consideration of what is best for the children concerned".[189] A shared residence order was made in favour of parents who still displayed animosity towards each other. By contrast, the children, who were in effect living with both parents, were coping remarkably well. A similar case is *A v A (Shared Residence)*:[190] a shared residence order was made, even though the parents were unable to co-operate. The children were anyway spending 50 per cent of their time with each parent. The order was made to "reflect the fact that the parents are equal in the eyes of the law, and have equal duties and responsibilities towards their children."[191] The court saw a risk that a sole residence order could be misinterpreted as enabling control by one parent when what the family needed was co-operation, which a shared residence order would recognise. A shared residence order was made also in *Re F (Shared Residence Order)*[192] even though the parents' homes were separated by a considerable distance (Hampshire and Edinburgh). It was stressed that such an order could be made even where the amount of time spent in the two homes was uneven (in this case school terms were to be spent with the mother, and holidays with the father). That children want a shared residence order is also an important consideration.[193]

A court can attach a condition to a residence order.[194] In *B v B (Residence: Condition Limiting Geographic Area)*[195] a condition was attached that the mother and child should reside within an area bounded by the A4 to the north, the M25 to the west and the A3 to the south and east. This was justified because of the exceptional circumstances: the mother had made two applications to relocate to Australia and her reason for wanting to move from the south of England to the north was to get away from the father. The condition must not be incompatible with the residence order itself: thus a judge refused to attach a condition that a mother resided at a particular unit and complied with the instructions of its staff to the point of possibly handing over the child to the care of the staff.[196] The Court of Appeal has said courts are "not in a position ... to override [a mother's] right to live her life as she chose."[197] A condition that her partner should not reside with her and her children was rejected.[198]

Applications for residence orders can be made *ex parte*.[199] But they are only granted exceptionally, for example on cases of child abduction.[200] An allegation that the mother was a cannabis user was not, it was held, sufficient to justify making an *ex parte* order in favour of the father.[201] *Ex parte* orders should be short: a norm of seven days has been suggested.[202]

(ii) The contact order

The contact order is the most commonly sought of the s.8 orders,[203] and has proved the most troublesome. The Children Act Sub Committee's Report *Making Contact Work* noted the "widespread perception that [contact] disputes are better addressed outside the court system. There is a widespread feeling that an application to the court should be the last resort."[204]

To address contact problems, particularly enforcement issues, the law on contact has been augumented since the Children Act 1989. The order itself is first discussed: the new powers added since 1989 follow after.

A contact order is "an order requiring the person with whom a child lives, or is to live, to allow the child to visit or stay with the person named in the order, or for that person and the child otherwise to have contact with each other".[205] The construction is significant: reflecting contact as the right of the child, the emphasis is on the child.

A contact order can provide for the child to have contact with any person, for example a sibling. A child may apply for leave to seek a contact order.[206] The question has therefore arisen as to whether a child could use this mechanism to force a recalcitrant parent to see him/her. A case was reported in 1993 but it seems it was settled and no ruling given.[207] A boy of 15 sought to force his mother to spend more time with him. The *Guardian* thought the issue serious enough to devote a leading article to urging that the application be resisted.[208] The question resurfaced in the debates which led to Children and the Adoption Act 2006. The Joint Committee on the Draft Children (Contact) and Adoption Bill favoured introducing a power to compel an unwilling parent to have contact with a child.[209] The Government rejected this, citing "potential distress, or even harm, such contact could cause to the child."[210]

Contact may be direct (staying or visiting contact). It can also be indirect (by letter, birthday or Christmas cards/presents, telephone conversations). Examples of indirect contact are *Re P (Contact: Indirect Contact)*,[211] where the father was a former drug addict, just released from prison; and *Re L (Contact: Genuine Fear)*,[212] where the mother's phobia of the father was such that the emotional effect on her of direct contact would be "profound and possibly destabilising". Supervised contact may also be ordered. There is increased use also of contact centres, where contact can be supervised by a social worker (or a volunteer) and a safe environment created for the child. Whether supervision is adequate has been questioned (Aris *et al.*, 2002). In a rare case a court may refuse even indirect—and supervised—contact between a parent and a child.[213]

Rather more puzzling is whether a contact order includes an order that there shall be "no contact". In *Nottingham County Council v P*[214] it was held that it did. However, the better view is that if this is what is required a prohibited steps order should be applied for. And so the court held in *Re H (Minors) (Prohibited Steps Order)*,[215] when it made such an order against the mother's former cohabitant preventing him from having or seeking contact with her children. An order for "no contact" would have required the mother to prevent contact—and she was not in favour of his having contact, since he posed a risk to her children.

Whenever a court makes or varies a contact order, it must attach a notice warning of the consequences of failing to comply with it.[216]

The residential parent may be hostile to contact taking place. Since contact is considered a child's right and beneficial to his/her well-being, courts guard against contact being thwarted by parental opposition. Parents should not be allowed to think that the "more intransigent, the more unreasonable, the more obdurate and the more uncooperative they are, the more likely they are to get their own way".[217] Two types of case must be distinguished. Opposition to contact may be justified if the parent's fears are "genuine and rationally held",[218] for example where there is a risk of violence to the child,[219] or of the child being abducted (particularly where this is out of the jurisdiction). It may not be justified if it is not rational. But it is very easy to stigmatise the residential parent as emotional, rather than rational. Those who oppose contact are usually mothers. The law finds it difficult to resist labelling reluctant mothers as deviant (Boyd, 1996), even as it perceives fathers who want contact as "good". A parent who makes malicious allegations of abuse risks her own contact with the child being seen as potentially damaging.[220]

The relationship between contact decisions and the provision of financial support has been questioned (Kitch, 1991). There are many problems with making this link. Children subject to an order which conditioned contact on the fulfilment of maintenance obligations could be financially disadvantaged. More families would become dependent on the welfare system. It would also reinforce the law's gender bias. As Czpanskij explains:

"The central metaphor is that contact with a child is a commodity to be bought and sold. But unlike normal commodity contracts, the buyer and seller are not equals. Here, only the buyer has legal control. If he elects to purchase contact with the child by paying support, he has the right to so so; the seller cannot refuse to sell. If the buyer elects not to pick up his purchase, the seller cannot require him to do so. Since nearly all residential parents are women and non-residential parents are men, the buyers are nearly always fathers" (1989, p.650).

The danger is that "the father's desire for contact with his children is given a preference over the mother's need for regular financial support for the children" (*ibid.*, p.646). Contact decisions should not become entangled with the provision of financial support.[221] Nevertheless, it is not suprising that parents who see their children are more likely to support them (Maclean and Eekelaar, 1997, p.127).

There is increasing concern about domestic violence in contact disputes. There is evidence that men who are violent to their partners may be violent also to their children (Hester and Radford, 1996). Abuse in the course of a contact visits is not uncommon. Contact visits may be used to harass or to perpetuate violence. Yet professionals were found (*ibid.*, p.23) to have "a strong commitment to the idea of maintaining contact for children with non-resident fathers, even where there had been child abuse and the children were afraid". Even so, most mothers did their best to assist their ex-partners to have contact with their children where they believed it would benefit the children. But, unsurprisingly, when they opposed contact the problem was seen, by professionals and courts, as mothers' intransigence rather than fathers' violence.

The courts, belatedly, have begun to react to domestic violence. Wall J. commented in one case that "too little weight ... is given to the need for the father to change" so as to "demonstrate that he is a fit person to exercise contact, that he is not going to destabilise the family, that he is not going to upset the children and harm them emotionally".[222] So "violent fathers are now expected to deal with drink and drug problems and to confront their violence in counselling or therapy" (Kaganas and Day Sclater, 2000, p.633). Where direct contact is not appropriate, indirect contact may be allowed.[223] The leading case is *Re L (A Child), Re V (A Child), Re M (A Child), Re H (A Child) (Contact: Domestic Violence)*.[224] The Court of Appeal dismissed appeals by four fathers against orders allowing them indirect contact, but refusing them direct contact: in each of the cases there was violence, some of it extreme. It held there was no presumption against contact with a violent parent; the only principle applicable was the paramountcy of the child's welfare. The court drew on an expert report (written from a child and adolescent psychiatry perspective),[225] but rejected its recommendation that, where a parent is or has previously been violent, there should be a presumption against contact. The court accepted that violence to a partner involves "a significant failure in parenting—failure to protect the child's carer and failure to protect the child emotionally".[226] In cases since, direct contact has been refused to a violent father who had killed his wife.[227] And no contact at all was allowed in a case where the levels of violence had been "unusually high".[228]

New Zealand has a presumption against unsupervised contact in cases of violence (Perry, 2006). The Government is opposed to introducing one in England. There are, however, *Guidelines* prepared by the Children Act Sub-Committee of the Lord Chancellor's Advisory Board on Family Law.[229] These include that the court should:

"... only make an order for contact if it can be satisfied that the safety of its residential parent and the child can be secured before, during and after contact."[230]

This is, in effect, a presumption against contact: as a *Guideline* it is not, however, binding. If domestic violence is found and direct contact is to be ordered, after applying the welfare checklist,[231] courts are required to consider, inter alia, whether contact should be supervised, whether any conditions should be attached (for example, seeking treatment), whether a non-molestation order[232] should be made.[233]

There is thus greater sensitivity to the problem of domestic violence. But in *Re L*, the President did warn of the danger of the "pendulum swinging too far against contact where domestic violence has been proved".[234] A vocal men's movement will do its best to stop this happening (Kaganas, 2006). Research by the Woman's Aid Federation of England (see Saunders, 2001) revealed courts still failing to protect victims of domestic violence. Nearly 50 per cent of refuges contacted reported that, if contact was ordered in the face of alleged abuse, adequate measures were not being taken to ensure the safety of the child and the residential parent. Local contact centres provided only "low vigilance" contact, not supervised contact. Nearly half the refuges were aware of cases where men used contact to find former partners; 23 per cent were aware of women, who were victims of domestic violence and whose children were on the Child Protection Register, being ordered to hand over their children for contact visits. Many of the refuges reported that children had been harmed during contact. Two years later Women's Aid produced similar findings (Saunders and Barron, 2003). Additionally, this survey revealed that only 6 per cent of refuges and domestic violence services thought children who said they did not want contact with a violent parent were being listened to and taken seriously. More recently, Smart and May (2004) concluded that courts were still operating under an assumption in favour of contact, and that courts would not deny contact in the absence of "substantial" proof of harm, or risk of harm, in the course of contact.

Contact centres are designed as a resource to assist fathers who might otherwise lose contact with their children.[235] Whether they are being used appropriately where there has been violence or abuse has been doubted (Humphreys and Harrison, 2003a). It may be that the existence of contact centres is encouraging courts to make orders for supervised contact where indirect contact might be more appropriate. Humphreys and Harrison also believe (2003b) that centre coordinators do not always know about the violence involved: men deny or minimise this. Risks are thus not always properly investigated, and may be under-estimated because the ideal upheld by the centres is pro-contact.

Contact orders are one of the most difficult orders to enforce. When mothers refuse to comply with an order, fathers suffer an injustice; courts may be in breach of the European Convention on Human Rights if they do not take effective steps to enforce contact. Courts have a number of options. First, breach of a contact order is a contempt of court, punishable by fine or imprisonment.[236] Fines reduce the money available to the child. Committing the parent to prison is equally blunt a remedy. It

"may well not achieve the object of reinstating contact; the child may blame the parent who applied to commit the carer to prison; the child's life may be disrupted if there is no-one capable of or willing to care for the child … it cannot be anything other than emotionally damaging for a child to be suddenly removed into foster care … from … a mother, who in all respects except contact is a good parent".[237]

While acknowledging these problems, the courts have been increasingly willing to impose fines and custodial sentences for breaches of contact orders. Seven days' prison is a common sentence.[238] Prison should not be used, however, where a fine is more appropriate, even if the contemnor cannot afford to pay the fine.[239] Contempt proceedings must, of course, comply with Arts 6 and 8 of the European Convention on Human Rights: the contemnor should thus be represented.[240]

Second, the court can transfer the child to the parent whose contact is being obstructed, or threaten to do so.[241] A recent example of this is *V v V (Contact: Implacable Hostility)*:[242] residence was transferred from the mother to the father. The mother not only resisted contact but made unsubstantiated allegations that the father had abused the children. Moving the child in this way is a last resort.

Third, the court can make a family assistance order[243] where it thinks this may assist with contact arrangements.[244] These have not been used very often, perhaps because of the cost involved. But the Children and Adoption Act 2006 encourages their use and the order may become more common in difficult contact

cases. It provides that where a contact order is in force, the
family assistance order "may direct the officer concerned to give
advice and assistance as regards establishing, improving and
maintaining contact...".[245]

Fourth, the court may direct a psychiatric assessment. In *Re S
(Contact: Promoting Relationship with Absent Parent)*,[246] the Court of
Appeal directed that a psychiatrist should assess the family, and
report on the propects for contact.

Fifth, although a s.37 direction[247] is not usually appropriate in a
private law dispute, it may be used in an intractable contact case
if there is a coherent care plan which might involve the removal
of children from parents.[248]

There are now new initiatives to tackle the problem of the
difficult contact dispute.[249] Some proposals, for example curfews
and tagging, were, mercifully, dropped. The Children and
Adoption Act 2006 does, however, add a new battery of enforcement powers. First, where the court is satisfied beyond all
reasonable doubt and without reasonable excuse that a person
has failed to comply with a contact order, it can make an
enforcement order. This imposes a requirement to do up to a
maximum of 200 hours unpaid work on a person who has broken the order.[250] Before the court can make the order it must be
satisfied that making it is necessary to secure compliance with
the contact order, and that "the likely effect on the person of the
enforcement order proposed ... is proportionate to the seriousness of the breach".[251] The child's welfare is not the paramount
consideration, though it must be taken into account. One must
wonder whether it has been taken account of by the government:
if the mother is doing unpaid work at weekends this is unlikely
to redound to a child's benefit. It should not be overlooked that
nearly all mothers do a considerable amount of unpaid work all
the time—perhaps the government hasn't noticed! The order can
only be made on the application of (i) the residential parent (does
this mean it can be used to make an unwilling parent have
contact? As previously noted,[252] this innovation was explicitly
rejected); (ii) the person in whose favour a contact order with the
child was made; (iii) an individual subject to a condition under
s.11(7)(b) or a contact activity[253] condition imposed by the contact
order; or (iv) the child concerned (with the leave of the court,
which may only be given where the court is satisfied that the
child has sufficient understanding to make the application). It
follows that if a mother obstructs a child's contact with his/her
father, the child can initiate a procedure which may lead to the

mother being compelled to do unpaid work. It is too early to say whether enforcement orders are being used (and if so before or after other sanctions). But many of the reservations expressed by courts [254] are equally pertinent.

Second, compensation can be ordered for financial loss caused by the breach of a contact order.[255] For example, reimbursement of travel costs and lost holidays. The court must take into account the financial circumstances of the individual in breach and the child's welfare, though again this is not the paramount consideration. It is not expected that compensation orders will be much used. Often loss will not justify a court's resources.

Third, there are new powers to make contact activity directions and conditions.[256] Directions can only be made where a court is considering whether to make a contact order (or vary or discharge one). They cannot be made on a final contact order. Conditions can only be made upon the making of a contact order (or its variation). Conditions are enforceable though contempt, an enforcement order or by a financial compensation order. There are no sanctions for non-compliance with directions.

A direction is one "requiring a party to the proceedings to take part in an activity that promotes contact with the child concerned".[257] Types of contact activity include classes and counselling or guidance sessions of a kind that may assist a person to establish, maintain or improve contact with a child.[258] They may, by addressing a person's violent behaviour, enable or facilitate contact. They may also include sessions in which information or advice is given regarding making or operating arrangements for contact with a child including making arrangments by means of mediation. A direction, however, cannot direct mediation (or medical or psychiatric examinations). Directions can only be made where there is a dispute over contact, a strange limitation. Children can only be made to participate in any activity if they are the child of the parent concerned. In deciding whether to make a direction, the paramount consideration is the welfare of the child.

A contact activity condition "requires an individual to take part in an activity that promotes contact with the child concerned".[259] It must specify the activity. Conditions can only be imposed on a child if s/he is a child of the parent concerned. In deciding whether to make a condition, the court must be satisfied that the activity is appropriate in the circumstances of the case. There is no requirement to regard the child's welfare as the paramount consideration.[260]

Financial assistance may be available to assist persons who are required to undertake a contact activity. A CAFCASS officer may be asked to monitor a person's compliance with a contact activity or condition, and report to the court on any failure to comply.

Fourth, CAFCASS officers can be asked to monitor compliance with a contact order (or an order varying contact) and to report to the court on such matters relating to compliance as the court may specify. The court can make this request on making or varying the contact order or at any time in subsequent contact proceedings. Monitoring can last for a maximum of 12 months. Those who can be monitored are a person required to allow contact with a child, a person whose contact with the child is provided for, and a person who is subject to a condition under s.11(7)(b) of the Children Act 1989.[261]

None of these additions will solve the problem. There will remain parents who will not allow contact and parents, who are less censured, who are not interested in maintaining a relationship with their children. It has been doubted (Herring, 2003) whether contact which is coerced by threat or pressure is effective contact conducive to a child's best interests. One recent study (Trinder *et al.*, 2002) concluded that couples who rely on the law to resolve contact disputes aggravate the problem. They argued that it would be better to focus on services to improve relationships between parents and parents and children: to some extent the 2006 Act has taken note of this. The concern will remain that, as Smart and Neale (1999, p.336) put it, that "in its current form the law is beginning to look like a lever for the powerful to use against the vulnerable, rather than a measure to safeguard the welfare of children."

(iii) The specific issue order

The specific issue order is "an order giving directions for the purpose of determining a specific question which has arisen, or which may arise, in connection with any aspect of parental responsibility".[262] This order can be made to resolve any dispute relating to the exercise of parental responsibility: for example, about a child's education,[263] medical treatment,[264] a decision to move a child abroad[265] or change a child's surname,[266] require that a child is told of his father's identity[267] or authorise the interview of a child for legal proceedings.[268] There does not have to be a dispute: it is sufficient that there is a question which must be answered. In *Re HG (Specific Issue Order: Sterilisation)*,[269] parents sought the court's permission to have their 17-year-old learning disabled daughter sterilised.[270] Disputes must relate to something of importance,[271] otherwise courts would be faced with disputes about food or clothing. Of course, where there is cultural conflict these may be matters of importance (kosher meat[272] or a Muslim veil).

The number of orders is going up. We are not told how many applications there are. There were over 3000 orders in 2003, less than 2500 in 2000.[273] They are mainly used by non-residential parents (and therefore fathers) to challenge decisions taken by residential parents (usually mothers). The significance of this is rarely commented upon (Gilmore, 2004). Does it enable absent fathers to meddle, even to harass, or should we just see it as legitimate input by men exercising equal parental responsibility?

(iv) The prohibited steps order

The prohibited steps order is "an order that no step which could be taken by a parent in meeting his parental responsibility for a child, and which is of a kind specified in the order, shall be taken by any person without the consent of the court."[274] When a court makes a prohibited steps order it makes a specific ban upon the exercise of an aspect of parental responsibilty. It can be used to prohibit contact with a parent or someone else (for example, the parent's partner),[275] to prevent a child's school,[276] religion or surname[277] being changed, to stop a child being removed from the country, particularly where there is a fear that s/he might not be brought back.[278]

The number of orders has been increasing. There were 7343 orders in 2001: in 2003 there were 9487.[279] There is no information on the number of applications, so we have no insight into success rates. Nor do we know who brings them and why they are brought.

RESTRICTIONS ON ORDERS

There are restrictions on the use of s.8 orders. In the main, these relate to specific issue and prohibited steps orders.

The order must relate to an aspect of parental responsibility. So, a prohibited steps order cannot be made prohibiting a father from having any contact with the mother.[280] Whether a question relates to parental responsibility is not always easy to determine: waiving a child's confidentiality—she had a notorious father—

was held[281] to be an aspect of parental responsibility, so that a prohibited steps order could be made. The person against whom the order is directed need not have parental responsibility (the mother's partner, for example).[282] A neighbour could be stopped from speaking to a child, though clearly s/he has no parental responsibility (Herring, 2004, p.427).

There is no power to make an occupation or non-molesatation order through a s.8 order. Resort must be had to the Family Law Act 1996.[283] However, if the order sought is not identical to one available under the 1996 Act—it seeks to prohibit contact and not merely molestation—an order may be made.[284]

There is no power to make a disguised residence or contact order using a prohibited steps or specific issue order.[285] Since local authorities cannot apply for residence or contact orders, it is they who are most affected by this limitation. So, in *Nottingham County Council v P*,[286] it was held to be contrary to s.9(5)(a) to order, on a local authority's application under s.8, a father to leave the home and have no contact with the child: the application was clearly designed to determine the residence of the child and whom she had contact with. It has an impact also ouside the local authority context: for example, it has been held that a specific issue order cannot be sought to return a child to a parent where there has been a snatch, since this could be achieved by a residence order with conditions attached.[287]

There is no power to make a s.8 order if the High Court would not be able to make the order using its inherent jurisdiction.[288] The effect of this is that local authorities cannot obtain care or supervision of a child through a specific issue or prohibited steps order. In other words, they must satisfy the threshold condition in s.31(2) of the Children Act 1989,[289] and not merely convince a court that care or supervision is in the child's best interests.[290]

There are also restrictions which apply to s.8 orders more generally.

A s.8 order is not to be made in respect of a child who has attained the age of 16, nor should any order be expressed to have effect beyond a child's 16th birthday, unless the court is satisfied that the "circumstances of the case are exceptional".[291] If it does so direct, the order ceases to have effect on the child's 18th birthday.[292] What constitutes "exceptional circumstances" is not clear. And it may never be clarified because it is likely that most applicants who want an order to last until the child's majority will seek an enhanced residence order, which continues until the child is 18 and does not require exceptional circumstances to be established.[293] A parent with a physically handicapped or learning disabled child might still seek an "enhanced" residence order: presumably these are the sort of situations in which "exceptional circumstances" may be readily accepted.

Only residence orders are available if the child is in local authority care. So, a parent cannot challenge local authority decision-making by seeking a contact order or a specific issue or prohibited steps order. If a residence order is made, the care order is discharged.[294]

Local authorities cannot apply for—and they cannot be granted—residence or contact orders.[295]

It has been said that a residence order cannot be made in favour of a child.[296] But a parent may be a child and there can surely be no objection making a residence order in favour of a 16-year-old mother. Similarly, circumstances can be envisaged where it is in a child's best interests that his 16-year-old sister be granted a residence order in respect of him.

FAMILY PROCEEDINGS

The court has the power to make s.8 orders in "family proceedings" in which a question arises with respect to the welfare of any child.[297] "Family proceedings" are defined[298] as any proceeding under:

the inherent jurisdiction of the High Court;[299]

Pts I, II and IV of the 1989 Act;

Matrimonial Causes Act 1973;

Domestic Proceedings and Magistrates' Courts Act 1978;

Pt III of the Matrimonial and Family Proceedings Act 1984;

Human Fertilisation and Embryology Act 1990 s.30;

Family Law Act 1996;

Crime and Disorder Act 1998, ss.11 and 12;

Adoption and Children Act 2002;

Civil Partnership Act 2004 Schs 5 and 6;

Children Act 2004.

Thus, s.8 orders can be made in a wide range of proceedings including divorce, adoption and domestic violence (occupation and non-molestation orders). But even so, Pt V of the Children Act is excluded, so that a residence order cannot be made on an application for an emergency protection order or child assessment order.[300] There is also no power to make s.8 orders in proceedings brought under the Child Abduction and Custody Act 1985.[301] If a court therefore does not return a child under this Act, a separate application would be required if a residence or contact order were sought to regularise relationships.

WHO CAN SEEK SECTION 8 ORDERS?

Section 8 orders can be made either upon application or, once proceedings have commenced, by the court itself upon its own motion, wherever it "considers that the order should be made even though no such application has been made".[302] It has been said that a court can make an order—in this case in favour of foster parents—when the parties themselves were not permitted to seek leave to apply for the order.[303]

The following persons are entitled to apply for any section 8 without leave: a parent; a guardian; a special guardian; a stepparent who has parental responsibility for the child; a person in whose favour a residence order is in force with respect to the child.[304]

The following persons are entitled to apply for a residence or contact order without leave: a party to a marriage or civil partnership in relation to whom the child is a child of family; a person with whom the child has lived for at least three years; a person who has the consent of each person in whose favour a residence order was made; a person who has the consent of the local authority when a child is in care; any other person who has the consent of each person, if any, with parental responsibility for the child.[305]

Other persons can apply for s.8 orders with the leave of the court. Children themselves can apply.[306] This provoked headlines and criticisms that the law was allowing children to "divorce" their parents (Freeman, 1996a). Needless to say, the moral panic was far wide of the mark. There were, however, a cluster of cases in which adolescents sought court orders to confirm their living arrangements with people other than their parents.[307]

To apply for a s.8 order a child needs leave. The court may only grant this if it is satisfied that the child has "sufficient understanding" to make the proposed application.[308] In *Re CT (A Minor) (Wardship: Representation)* Waite L.J. approved remarks of Sir Thomas Bingham M.R. that

"where any sound judgment on these issues calls for insight and imagination which only maturity and experience can bring, both the court and the solicitor will be slow to conclude that the child's understanding is sufficient".[309]

Netherthless, children have the right to initiate the process, a right which should not be "impeded".[310] The argument has been put that the person in whom parental responsibility should vest under the residence order should make the application, not the child.[311] Booth J. dismissed this argument: it was wrong to "fetter the statutory ability of the child to seek any s.8 order ... if it is appropriate for such an application to be made".[312] The court can take into account the likelihood of the proposed application succeeding, and can refuse leave even when the child satisfies the "understanding" test.[313] Different views have been expressed as to whether the decision to grant leave should be governed by the paramountcy principle:[314] that it should be an important, but not the paramount, consideration is the conclusion which has prevailed.[315]

In leave applications by persons other than children, the court must have particular regard to the nature of the proposed application, the applicant's connection with the child, any risk that the proposed application might disrupt the child's life by harming him or her, and, where the child is being looked after by a local authority, the authority's plans for the child's future and the wishes and feelings of the child's parents.[316] Since a leave application is not a question with respect to the upbringing of the child,[317] the child's welfare is not the paramount consideration when the court comes to exercise its discretion.[318] There is no reason why the child's views should not be considered.

It was the view that leave should not be granted unless the substantive application had a reasonable prospect of success.[319] Subsequently, it was said that the proper approach was to enquire whether there was a "good arguable case".[320] Concern has been expressed that, in substituting such a test for that in the legislation—or rather superimposing it on the s.10(9) test— applicants may not be getting the fair trial to which they are entitled under Art.6 of the European Convention on Human Rights.[321] That leave has been granted does not mean the application will succeed. Obviously, those with a close connection to the child are more likely to be granted leave. Grandparents, for example, will often have such a strong case that it is difficult to envisage leave being refused.[322] Indeed, there is a case for treating grandparents as a special category, able to apply for s.8 orders as of right (but *cf.* Douglas and Ferguson, 2003). Thorpe L.J. has stressed the "value of what grandparents have to offer, particularly to children of disabled parents"[323]—even more so, I would add, where the children themselves have special needs.

THE FAMILY ASSISTANCE ORDER

Until the 1989 Children Act it was possible to make supervision orders in private law proceedings. The 1989 replaced this with the family assistance order.[324] This requires a CAFCASS officer to be made available or the local authority to make an officer of the authority available "to advise, assist and (where appropriate) befriend any person named in the order".[325] The order may name any parent, guardian or special guardian of the child, any person with whom the child is living or in whose favour a contact order is in force with respect to the child, and the child him or herself. The family assistance order aims "to provide short-term help to a family, to overcome the problems and conflicts associated with their separation or divorce. Help may well be focused more on the adult than the child".[326]

A family assistance order may be made by the court in any "family proceedings". No other order has to be made. Orders are made by courts acting of their motion. Parties may request one; they cannot apply for one. The requirement (in the Children Act 1989) that the circumstances of the case have to be "exceptional"[327] has been removed by the Children and Adoption Act 2006,[328] and it is expected that there will be greater use of the order to facilitate contact arrangements. Orders require the consent of everyone named in the order, with the exception of the child: in the case of older children this seems wrong, but there is nothing to prevent a court eliciting a child's views.

The 2006 Act provides that where a s.8 order is in force the family assistance order "may direct the officer concerned to report to the court on such matters relating to the section 8 order as the court may require ...".[329] Where a contact order is in force, the family assistance order "may direct the officer. ... To give advice and assistance as regards establishing, improving and maintaining contact."[330]

Under the 1989 Act family assistance orders were limited to six months. The 2006 Act has extended this to 12 months. Nevertheless, it is designed as a short-term remedy. Since it has been mainly used in relation to contact disputes, it is envisaged that greater use will now be made of it.

DIRECTING AN INVESTIGATION

If in the course of a private law dispute a court becomes concerned that there might be something seriously amiss—a suspicion, for example, that the child is being abused or neglected—there is power to direct the appropriate local authority to undertake an investigation of the child's circumstances.[331] Where a direction is made, the authority must investigate and consider whether any action is required and, if so, what this should be. It must report back to the court within eight weeks. Where it decides to take no action, that is the end of the matter: it is not open to the court to make a care or supervision order, though it might still make a family assistance order.[332] Does this give local authorities too much power? Should courts be able to require local authorities to apply for a care order? The balance of power between courts and local authorities has generally tilted towards the courts, but not so here. A question may be raised (see also Herring, 2004, p.525) as to whether there is a breach of the European Convention on Human Rights when a court fails to protect a child from what it supposes is abuse. This has not been tested, but it surely will.[333]

This procedure is reserved for the exceptional case. It has been invoked to deal with an intractable contact dispute, where the judge had concluded that the children were suffering significant harm in their mother's care. She was seeking to instill in them the false belief that their father had sexually abused them. The result was that residence was transferred to the father with a two-year supervision order made in favor of the local authority.[334] It has also been invoked where, although there was no criticism of the care offered by two lesbians, the court thought there were long-term concerns.[335] Whether these were justified or an example of a judge's values—common at that time[336]—is debatable. A direction should not, it has been held, be made where evidence that public law intervention might be required was no more than speculative.[337]

BARRING FURTHER APPLICATIONS

Because some litigants, perhaps especially in cases where issues about children are contested, will not take no for an answer and wish to make repeated applications to the court, the court can, under s.91(14) of the Children Act 1989, require a party to obtain the leave of the court before applying for any further orders. The Court of Appeal has said this is not a breach of the right to a fair trial under the European Convention on Human Rights.[338] But it is clearly a substantial interference with the right of access to the courts and can only be justified if there is evidence that future applications are likely to be unreasonable, vexatious or frivolous.[339] A number of guidelines have been laid down.[340] Section 91(14) is to be read in conjunction with the paramountcy principle. The power is "draconian" and is only to be used "sparingly". It is a "useful weapon of last resort in cases of repeated unreasonable applications". Further, the degree of restriction should be proportionate to the harm it is intended to avoid. Accordingly, the court imposing the restriction should carefully consider the extent of the restriction to be imposed and specify, where appropriate, the type of the application to be restrained and the duration of the order.

Two new orders may be briefly considered here. Both are designed as alternatives to adoption. There is fuller discussion of one of them—special guardianship—in Chapter 11.

THE ENHANCED RESIDENCE ORDER

First, there is the enhanced residence order.

The Adoption and Children Act 2006[341] has inserted s.12(5) into the Children Act 1989. This empowers the court when making a residence order in favour of a person who is not a parent or guardian of the child to direct, at the request of that person, that the order continue in force until the child reaches the age of 18. Where a residence order includes such a direction, an application to vary or discharge the order may only be made with the leave of the court.[342] It was possible to do this under the 1989 Act but the circumstances had to be "exceptional".[343] This is no longer so. It is anticipated that enhanced residence orders will become the norm where non-parents, grandparents for example, are bringing up children. The value of the new order is that it gives the carer and the child security, while preserving the parent–child relationship, which adoption would terminate. The main drawback of the order—which might inhibit applications— is that it may be easier to get financial assistance with a special guardianship order.[344]

THE SPECIAL GUARDIANSHIP ORDER

Second, there is special guardianship.[345]

Special guardianship is designed to meet the needs of a carer and a child where adoption is not suitable and where a residence order, even an enhanced residence order, does not offer sufficient security. Special guardianship may be suitable where it is not in a child's best interests to have his relationship with his/ her parents severed by adoption but where his or her carers are doing so on a permanent basis. It might also be an attractive option for an older child who does not want to be adopted, and possibly offer an alternative to adoption where the parties do not accept the institution of adoption.[346] Special guardians have more powers than those with enhanced residence orders: for example, they can appoint a guardian to act in their stead after their death. Also, it is more difficult for parents to apply to vary or discharge a special guardianship order. Special guardians are also entitled to support from the local authority.[347]

The following persons can apply for a special guardianship order:[348] a guardian of the child; a person with a residence order; a person who has the consent of all those with a residence order; any person with whom the child has lived for three of the previous five years, provided the person with parental responsibility consents (including the local authority if the child is in care); any other person who has the consent of all persons with parental responsibility; a local authority foster parent with whom the child has lived for at least one year immediately preceding the application.

Other persons can apply with the leave of the court.[349] The court will consider the same matters as it does when considering leave applications for s.8 orders.[350] A child can apply with leave, but once again the court must be satisfied s/he has sufficient understanding to make the proposed application.[351] The court can also make a special guardianship order of its own motion in any family proceedings (including adoption proceedings).[352]

The decision to make a special guardianship order is governed by the paramountcy principle and the other principles in s.1 of the Children Act 1989.[353] Before making an order, the court must consider whether a contact order should be made between the child and his birth family.

A special guardian acquires parental responsibility for the child. This can be exercised to the exclusion of any other persons with parental responsibility (apart from any other special guardian).[354]

A special guardianship order discharges any existing care order or related contact order.[355]

While it is in force, no one may cause the child to be known by a new surname, or remove the child from the UK (except for up to three months) without the written consent of every person with parental responsibility for the child or the leave of the court.[356]

Those with a good memory will recall custodianship (Freeman, 1986). Special guardianship resembles this. Custodianship lasted but four years (1985–1989). It was not popular—the name did not help. But it was used in the main by grandparents (Bullard *et al.*, 1991). It is to be expected that grandparents and other relatives, as well as foster parents, will find attractions in special guardianship. Some may be deterred by the need for a local authority investigation: they may opt for the enhanced residence order instead.[357]

9

UNDERSTANDING CHILD
PROTECTION

DISCOVERING CHILD ABUSE

We have not always protected children from abuse or neglect. Or
wanted to do so. And even when we have tried we have often
failed. We first passed legislation to target child cruelty in 1889,[1]
66 years after legislation was passed to protect animals from
cruelty. The Attorney General counselled against interfering
with the "legitimate conduct of parents and guardians with
regard to children".[2] The sponsor of the Bill retorted that he was
"anxious that we should give [children] almost the same protection that we give ... domestic animals."[3]

We discovered what we called child cruelty in the latter half of
the nineteenth century. But, what we now call child abuse was
only recognised as a social problem in the 1960s (Radbill, 1974;
Pinchbeck and Hewitt, 1973). As far as sexual abuse was concerned, a discrete veil had been drawn. A report of the London
Society for the Prevention of Cruelty to Children in 1884 referred
to 12 cases which concerned "an evil which is altogether too
unmentionable".[4] The public was, however, sensitised to the
problem of child prostitution by William Stead in 1885, and the
age of lawful consent to sexual intercourse for girls was raised
from 13 to 16.[5] Child sexual abuse within the family was not
discussed publicly: it was thought to be exclusively a vice of the
poor, linked to low intelligence and the product of overcrowded
sleeping conditions. Incest did not become a crime until 1908.[6] A
Royal Commission on Venereal Diseases in 1916 took childhood
infections for granted.[7] When gonorrhea was observed to be
prevalent among girls in institutions, a *Lancet* editorial offered a
simplistic explanation and simple advice: "No towels, baths, or
bedroom chambers should ever be shared by girl children in
institutions".[8] There was not even a hint of suspicion that these
girls might have been sexually abused. But, as Carol Smart (1999)
has shown, though the orthodoxy may have been innocent

transmission, "there were counter-discourses available from within the medical profession itself", mainly from prominent female doctors. Smart draws attention too to the belief, "reported as 'fact'" in the Report of the Royal Commission, that sex with a virgin would cure a man of venereal disease. And so it was, neither abuse nor rape, but "misdirected medical effort" (Smart, 1999, pp.397–398). The legal response at the time, and for decades after, was to blame the victim (Ryan, 1976). A report in 1925 recommended radical reforms, but these met with legal resistance.[9] The legal establishment's view rested upon

"a specific understanding of childhood as a phase both of resilience and insignificance. Children did not matter in this scheme of things, at least the working class girls they were likely to see did not matter. On the other hand men ... did matter; they were recognised as legal subjects" (Smart, 1999, p.403).

When, more than 60 years later, the Butler-Sloss report[10] looked forward to a time when children would be persons in their own right, not merely objects of concern, what may have been overlooked was that in relation to sexual abuse they had hardly even become objects of concern.

For a social problem to exist it must be recognised as such. A whistle must be blown: it must also be heard by those with the power to do something about it. As Howard Becker explained (1963, p.162): "Even though a practice may be harmful in an objective sense ... the harm needs to be discovered and pointed out."[11] The recognition of physical abuse as a social problem has come slowly. In the past doctors were unaware of the possibility of abuse as a diagnosis. In the twentieth century, the mechanics of diagnosis were improved by the development of techniques such as the X-ray.[12] But the decision to X-ray depends on the doctor's definition of the situation: unless the parent's word is doubted, the next step will not be taken. The medical profession was for too long reluctant to believe that parents could inflict injuries on their children. Doctors were also reluctant to become involved in a criminal process over which they had no control and which they saw as of no value. It was the radiologists who "discovered" child abuse.[13] Pfohl explains (1977, p.319):

"...the discovery of child abuse as a new 'illness' reduced drastically the intra-organizational constraints on doctors 'seeing' abuse. ... Problems associated with perceiving parents as patients whose confidentiality must be protected were reconstructed by typifying them as patients who needed help. ... The maintenance of professional autonomy was assured by pairing deviance with sickness."

The fact that child abuse was "discovered" by the medical profession has left an important legacy. As Eliot Freidson observed (1970, p.328): "medical definitions of deviance have come to be adopted even where there is no reliable evidence that biophysical variables 'cause' the deviance or that medical treatment is any more efficacious than any other kind of management".[14] The medical model assumes the problem is an individual one: treatment of the parent is thus to be the most reasonable intervention, through this does not stop the system meting out "punishment in the guise of help".[15] Legal responses to child abuse have been triggered by medicalisation of the problem.[16]

The radiologists "discovered" child abuse, but it was other medical men who brought it to the attention of the general public. Paediatricians were the "moral entrepreneurs".[17] In doing so they put limits on the phenomenon which were clearer than perhaps was indicated by commonsense experience.[18] Paediatricians, unlike radiologists, had attained "valued organizational status prior to the discovery", but were again "sliding toward the margins of the profession" (Pfohl, 1977, p.314). The discovery of what they called "the battered baby syndrome" provided them with a justification for attracting more resources and an enhanced status. The concept remained in currency for more than a decade.[19] Henry Kempe's article revealing the syndrome was published in 1962. He attributed parental violence towards young children to psychiatric factors. The parents, he noted, were often of low intelligence: they were "immature, impulsive, self-centered, hyper-sensitive and quick to react with poorly controlled aggression."[20] By emphasising the "battered baby", as opposed to "physical abuse", Kempe was targeting as wide an audience as possible.

In Britain, the problem was first "discovered" by two orthopaedic surgeons, Griffiths and Moynihan in 1963, who adopted Kempe's interpretation and language (Griffiths and Moynihan, 1963). But it was paediatricians and forensic pathologists who were largely responsible for bringing the "battered baby" to public attention. The Kempe understanding had a considerable influence on the NSPCC in the late 1960s and also on official government guidance in the early 1970s (Freeman, 1983, ch.4). The public inquiry into the death of Maria Colwell "catapulted" (Parton, 2006, p.30) child abuse into the centre of public, political and media attention.

Maria died aged seven, having been returned to her mother and step-father after spending five years in local authority care. They had wanted her back and the policy then (the early 1970s) was to comply with parental wishes where this was possible. She was killed by her step-father,[21] but it came to be accepted failed by the "system" (*Colwell Report*, 1974, p.86). Child abuse was now firmly on the agenda. Indeed, so much so that many of the other evils perpetrated against children were, and often continue to be, overlooked. More children are injured and killed as a result of accidents, many of them preventable, than acts of violence. And little attention was given to child poverty, which rose steeply in the 1980s and 1990s, or racial discrimination, or inadequate education, or lead paint poisoning or pollution.[22] Why then the focus on child abuse? Could it be that the pinpointing of parental violence enables us to concentrate on "them", rather than us? It results in an excessive concentration on one group of families. It is comforting for us to view the child abusers as a race apart, perhaps even more so when, as in the Victoria Climbié case (Laming, 2003), they are truly outsiders.[23]

The medical model reinforces the separation for it requires that abusing parents be studied in terms of what is "wrong" with them. And it requires exceptionalist solutions, for their "problems are unusual, even unique, they are exceptions to the rule, they occur as a result of individual defect. ... And must be remedied by means that are ... tailored to the individual case" (Ryan, 1976, p.17). There may be something erroneous with a classification system that divides parents into two groups, those who abuse their children, and those who do not. Zigler (1980, p.176) suggests we conceptualise child abuse as "a continuum on which everyone can be placed". Of course, such an approach is "threatening because within it the child abuser is viewed as very much like the majority of parents who have never been reported for child abuse" (Zigler, 1980, p.177). Most parents—some, for example, Zigler (1980, p.9) would say "all", parents are capable of abusing their children. Of course, much depends upon how child abuse is defined.[24]

Nearly 25 years separates the recognition of physical abuse as a social problem from the emergence of child sexual abuse in this way. As already indicated,[25] there were opportunities missed particularly in the 1920s. It is astonishing today to think that there was no discussion of child sexual abuse in the 1960s, the 1970s or for most of the 1980s.[26] Again, the moral entrepreneurs were paediatricians, Marietta Higgs and Geoffrey Wyatt. Their diagnosis in five months in 1987 of 121 children as sexually abused in one area (Cleveland) caused a "moral panic" and led to their being labelled as "folk devils".[27] Many of these children were sexually abused, but many were not, and it was easy for misdiagnosis and error to deflect attention away from the revelation that child sexual abuse was rampant. On the other hand, parents' rights were ignored, and many children were unnecessarily damaged.[28] The physical abuse of children might not have emerged had it not been for paediatricians. Child sexual abuse would have surfaced without them. The efforts of rape crisis groups and incest survivor groups were pointing to the problem before Cleveland, and Childline, a national freephone call line, had been established in 1986. Nevertheless, Cleveland was the trigger: only seven years earlier in 1980, when the term "child abuse" was first officially used (DHSS, 1980), four categories were specified, and sexual abuse was not one of them.[29]

WHAT IS CHILD ABUSE?

What is child abuse? What constitutes abuse is "not self-evident" (Diduck and Kaganas, 2006, p.345). It is a social construction. To take one example, in the eyes of some (a minority) hitting a child is a form of child abuse; most do not so categorise it. Some, for example David Gil (as we will see shortly), define abuse very broadly: others, David Archard, for example, are concerned that what is abuse should be confined to "something serious enough to warrant [state] intervention" (Archard, 1993, p.149). Gil, by contrast, defines abuse as anything which interferes with the optimal development of a child (Gil, 1970). The National Commission of Inquiry into the Prevention of Child Abuse (1996) similarly adopts a broad definition, clearly derived from Gil. It says:

"Child abuse consists of anything which individuals, institutions or processes do or fail to do which directly or indirectly harms children or damages their prospects of safe and healthy development into adulthood".

Arguments surrounding definitions of child abuse reflect ideological differences, including different understandings of childhood and of appropriate child development (Ashenden, 2004,
p.55), and may prove intractable (Stoll, 1968). The National
Commission's definitions got a hostile response: a Government
minister responding that "child care workers need clear advice
on the signs of abuse, not vague definitions which are in danger
of being misinterpreted".[30]

Much depends on who is doing the defining, and for what
purpose. A definition for a reporting law[31] or for management
guidance has very different functions from one developed to
research how much abuse there is or how the courts operate. The
definition selected may have important implications for civil
liberties, as it may for deciding how resources are to be dis-
tributed or who is entitled to services. Lawyers are likely to
define abuse rather differently from doctors or social workers
(Freeman, 1983, p.109). Accidents pose a problem: it is not
always easy to distinguish intentional behaviour from that which
is accidental. Children can suffer injuries when placed in situations in which an "accidental" injury occurs (Bourne and Newberger, 1977, 701). "Accident", like "child abuse", as indeed
"sexual"[32] are social constructions: they are not distinct categories. They are labels created by doctors, hospital staff, the
police, social workers, coroners, judges—people who have the
authority to decide whether a specific act or omission is to be
designated as deviant. The agent's moral beliefs and stereotypic
understandings influence his/her definitions (do men and
women define abuse differently?), and reactions to people's
behaviour. And certain individuals are more likely to be defined
as abusers than others (see Rubington and Weinberg, 1981).

A simple example of this conflict of interpretation can be seen
by examining the UK Government's First Report to the UN
Committee on the Rights of the Child in 1994.[33] This claimed the
UK complied with Art.19 of the UN Convention on the Rights of
the Child. But then—less so now[34]—UK law allowed reasonable
corporal punishment of children, and Art.19 requires States
Parties to take all appropriate measures to protect the child
against all forms of physical or mental violence, injury or abuse,
neglect or negligent treatment, maltreatment or exploitation,
including sexual abuse, while in the care of parents, legal guardians or any other person who has care of the child.

English law does not define abuse as such. For the purposes of
coercive intervention into the family to protect children from

abuse, the threshold is "significant harm".[35] A care order which may remove a child from his/her family can be made if the child is suffering significant harm or is at risk of so doing. This must be attributable to a lack of reasonable parental care (or the child being beyond parental control). "Significant" is defined by reference to a comparison of a child's health and development with that of a "similar" child. "Harm" includes ill-treatment or the impairment of health and development. "Health" encompasses physical and mental health, and ill-treatment includes "sexual abuse and forms of ill-treatment which are not physical". The details will be discussed later in this chapter.[36] These definitions are given here for us to pause to observe that

"the definition of 'significant' can scarcely be said to give any sort of guidance to parents, in that the characteristics of a 'similar child' are not given and, more critically, 'reasonable', 'abuse', 'ill-treatment', 'impairment' and 'development' are not further defined and thus fail to give clear legislative guidance either to parents or carers or to those who may have to intervene in families in order to protect children" (Lyon, 2000, pp.100–101).

Rather more helpful—though not, it may be added, to parents who are unlikely to have access to it—is the government document, *Working Together To Safeguard Children* (Department of Health *et al.*, 2006).[37] This lists the categories of abuse for the purposes of registration on the child protection register, and for statistical purposes. They are physical abuse, emotional abuse, sexual abuse and neglect. Each category is explained. Thus, physical abuse is said to include hitting, shaking, throwing, poisoning, burning or scalding, drowning, suffocating (including Munchausen's syndrome by proxy).[38] Emotional abuse may involve "conveying to children that they are worthless or unloved, inadequate, or valued only insofar as they meet the needs of another person".[39] Sexual abuse includes penetrative and non-penetrative acts and non-contact activities, for example involving children in looking at or in the production of pornographic material.[40] Neglect is "the persistent failure to meet a child's basic physical and/or psychological needs", for example for adequate food, shelter and clothing or appropriate medical care. It may also include "neglect of, or unresponsiveness to, a child's emotional needs".

This list is wider than its earliest formulation in 1980, from which sexual abuse was missing. The scope for state intervention in the family was thought, in 1995, to have widened: "the threshold beyond which child abuse is considered to occur is gradually being lowered".[41] This was attributed to "an emphasis on the rights of children as individuals, ease of disclosures, the influence of feminist social theories about victimisation and public expectation that the state should intervene in the privacy of family life".[42] Whether this is still the case may be disputed.

CAN IT BE EXPLAINED?

Why does abuse happen? Three explanations have been posited. The dominant model emphasises psychopathological factors. In the words of one of its critics, Richard Gelles, "anyone who would abuse or kill his child is sick".[43] The psychopathological model of child abuse represents what ordinary people think about the parents of abused children. That we should want to think of abusive parents as "sick" may tell as something about ourselves, Gil (1970, p.17) explains:

"parents ... may derive gratification from the sickness-as-cause interpretation, since it may fill them with a sense of security. For if abusive behaviour were a function of sickness most parents could view themselves as free from the dangers of falling prey to it, since they do not consider themselves sick".[44]

This model is found in suggested explanations of both physical and sexual abuse of children. Thus, it is often suggested that children who are abused, physically or sexually, repeat this behaviour towards their own children.[45] There are many problems with the psychopathological model. Thus, there is little agreement as to the make-up of the alleged psychopathy. Rarely does the literature which hypothesises individual pathology use control groups.[46]

The second posited explanation is socio-environmental. It sees the causes of abuse in the stress and frustration which result from "multi-faceted deprivations of poverty and its correlates, high density in overcrowded, dilapidated, inadequately served neighbourhoods, large numbers of children, especially in one-parent, mainly female-headed households, and the absence of child care alternatives", as well as poor education and "alienating circumstances in most work places" (Gil, 1975, p.352). Gil does not suggest, though others (for example, Pelton (1978) do) that poverty is a direct cause of child abuse. Rather, he claims it operates through an intervening variable, namely, "concrete and psychological stress and frustration experienced by individuals in the context of culturally sanctioned use of physical force in child rearing" (Gil, 1975, p.352). It was common once to believe that sexual abuse could also be explained in socio-environmental terms: it was thought to be an activity of the lowest socio-economic classes.[47] Social isolation was a commonly-cited supposed cause (Kempe and Kempe, 1984, p.51). There is evidence of social deprivation among known child abusers, but this does not explain why poverty should cause abuse.[48] The majority of those who live in a poor environment do not abuse their children. And abuse, physical and sexual, does exist in middle-class families. Straus *et al.* (1980) found that stress is more likely to lead to abuse in poor-to-middle income families than it is in very poor or very wealthy families. According to Gelles (1980, pp.98–99)

"the reason why stress does not increase the risk of child abuse among the poor and well-do-do seems to be their ability and likelihood of reacting to stress. The poor . . . encounter stress as a normal part of their lives. . . . The well-to-do adapt to stress by using their financial resources to help alleviate problems".

A third explantation situates child abuse within culture. As far as sexual abuse is concerned, this interpretation draws upon feminism.[49] For feminists child sexual abuse is an example of the inequality between men and women within patriarchy. Wattenberg (1985, p.206) comments: "the father rapes, abuses, brutalizes, and assaults the children and the mother, but somehow it is the mother's or child's fault". An understanding of abuse requires an understanding of power. Most perpetrators of sexual abuse are men, and most victims are female.[50] Many of the early studies included women in the number of perpetrators but this was because they had "allowed" sexual abuse to occur (Russell, 1984, p.219). It is common to find "mother blaming" in the orthodox literature on sexual abuse (Justice and Justice, 1980; Forward and Buck, 1981). Nelson asks (1987, p.108): "could it be because it is such a powerful defence against admitting the male abuse of power? And because without it family therapists might be like emperors without clothes?" Feminism finds the explanation of child sexual abuse in the way in which male sexuality is constructed. Frosh (1987, p.334) explains:

"The characteristic patterns of masculinity, focusing on independence and 'hardness' and turning away from intimacy and nurture follows from this. In particular it produces a severely narrowed rendering of sexuality, operating primarily in two divergent ways. First, sex is one of the few means by which men aspire to closeness with others, and as such it becomes the carrier of all the unexpressed desires that men's emotional illiteracy produces. However, this same process makes sex dangerous to men whose identity is built on the denial of emotion; sex then becomes split off, limited to the activity of the penis, an act rather than an encounter. At the same time, sex becomes tied up with competition, separation and power—something other than to create a bond with another. The link between such a form of masculinity and sexual abuse is apparent: it is not just present, but *inherent* in a mode of personality organisation that rejects intimacy. Sex as defence and as triumph slides natually into sex as rejection and degradation of the other".

As Diduck and Kaganas note (2006, p.351), the feminist understanding of sexual abuse has "to some extent, prevailed". They point to new offences in the Sexual Offences Act 2003 based on thinking that these occur as a result of an abuse of power.[51]

The physical abuse of children can also be explained in terms of power and our definitions of children as objects rather than rights-holding persons.[52] Gil sought the aetiology of child abuse in "society's basic social philosophy, its dominant value premises, its concept of humans, the nature of its social, economic and political institutions".[53] Violence is, of course, common in asymmetric relationships (master and slave, male–female relationships). And physical force has been used for disciplinary purposes in all such contexts.[54] But nowhere is this clearer than in the relationship of adults to children: and we do not need to limit ourselves to the rather obvious fact that the physical punishment of children is culturally acceptable.[55] To understand violence against children, or child abuse more generally, it is important to examine our concept of childhood, to look at social policies which sustain different levels of rights for children. We no longer subscribe to notions of children as property, but the legacies of such an ideology remain firmly implanted within our consciousness. As already indicated, it was never doubted that Maria Colwell should be returned to her mother: her mother wanted her back.[56] Or that the "Zulu boy" would be returned to his parents in South Africa, even though he did not want to go—

and, of course, was not asked to express an opinion one way or the other.[57] Or that litigation can be pursued about children—the *Williamson* case[58] is a striking illustration—without their participation or anyone to speak on their behalf.

If the cultural explantation is accepted and it is, I would argue, far the most convincing, a cultural revolution is required before we see an end to child abuse.[59] Only the most tentative steps have been taken to achieve this.

THE CRIMINAL LAW'S RESPONSE

How can the law protect children from abuse?

We must first consider the criminal law, and its limits. There is no criminal offence as such of child abuse, but children may be victims of the whole range of assaults in the Offences Against the Person Act 1861. In addition, children are protected by the specific offences listed in the Children and Young Persons Act 1933 s.1(1), discussed in an earlier chapter.[60] As we have seen, it remains lawful for a parent to inflict common assault on a child in the name of punishment: children thus have less protection from violence than adults.[61] There are also sexual offences against children. The Sexual Offences Act 2003 created new offences including sexual activity with a child family member,[62] and "inciting a child family member to engage in sexual activity".[63]

It is now possible for children to give evidence in criminal trials by means of a video link.[64] But the conviction rates remain low, making one ask whether it is worth putting a child through the pain of a criminal trial.[65] There is the danger that if a parent fears prosecution s/he may neglect or delay seeking medical treatment for an injured child because of a fear of the consequences. If a parent is acquitted, and most are, s/he may see the verdict as a vindication of the legitimacy of his/her behaviour—this may be especially so where the abuse is punishment that has gone wrong—it may make working with him/her to improve parenting skills more difficult to accomplish. If there is a conviction, the child may also suffer. Indeed, the child may also suffer because there will have to be a delay in offering therapy because of a concern that it might colour the evidence the child would give at a criminal trial.[66]

A criminal prosecution is important nevertheless because of the message it communicates. Were it not for this, it might be necessary to endorse Fortin's comment (2003, p.433) that "a child's rights to protection would be better served by child law alone, without involving the criminal justice system".

PROTECTING CHILDREN THROUGH CHILD LAW

As just implied, the main vehicle for protecting children is child law. The law is contained in the Children Act 1989, as expanded by the Children Act 2004, which itself has been amended by the Childcare Act 2006.

(i) Partnership

A key principle is partnership. The concept is not specifically found in the Children Act 1989.[67] Fisher *et al.* (1986, p.125) explained the importance of "partnership with clients, in which the primary caring role of the family is reasserted but effectively *supplemented* by public services", because the " 'good society' must ... treat those in need of child care services as fellow citizens rather than as 'inadequate' parents or children". The Department of Health went on to explain that "measures which antagonise, alienate, undermine or marginalise parents are counter-productive".[68] The Act reflects partnership in many ways. Two of the most significant are the retention of parental responsibility by parents, even when a child is in care;[69] and the non-intervention principle in s.1(5), so that intervention in the family should be limited to cases of "significant harm" (or risk of it),[70] and no order should be made unless it is better for the child than not making it. Even where the court thinks it appropriate to make an order it may consider making an order such as a residence order[71] which is less restrictive of a parent's freedom to act. This philosophy is also encoded in the policy advocated by the Department of Health that placements with relatives or friends should be explored before other forms of placement are considered.[72] The Act also stresses that local authorities are under a general duty when safeguarding the welfare of children in need to promote the upbringing of children by their families.[73] Where a local authority is looking after a child, it is to endeavour to promote contact between the child and his/her parents.[74]

(ii) Prevention

Minimal intervention is exemplified by Pt III of the Children Act 1989 which emphasises prevention and family support.[75] This has been extended by the 2004 Act which requires local authorities to make arrangments to promote co-operation between themselves and "key partner agencies"[76] and other relevant bodies to improve the well-being of children in their area. The importance of parents and others caring for children in improving the well-being of children is also stressed.[77] The provision of family support may obviate the need to take then, or subsequently, coercive action. Its importance must therefore not be overlooked.

Local authorities have a general[78] duty to safeguard and promote the welfare of children in their area who are in need and so far as is consistent with that duty to promote the upbringing of such children by their families, by providing a range and level of services appropriate to those children's needs.[79] A child is "in need" if:

"(a) he is unlikely to achieve or maintain, or to have the opportunity of achieving or maintaining a reasonable standard of health or development without the provision for him of services by a local authority under this part;

(b) his health or development is likely to be significantly impaired or further impaired, without the provision for him of such services; or

(c) he is disabled".[80]

A child is disabled if blind, deaf or mute or suffering from mental disorder or is substantially and permanently handicapped by illness, injury or congenital deformity or such other disability as may be prescribed.[81]

The definition of need is wide: a clear indication of the emphasis on preventive support and services for families. On the other hand, the duty is owed to a restricted group of children (Hardiker *et al.*, 1991). It would be tempting for local authorities to equate "in need" with "at risk" but this is not permitted.[82] It is provided that "any service provided by an authority in the exercise of [s.17] functions ... may be provided for the family of a particular child in need or for any member of his family, if it is provided with a view to safeguarding or promoting the child's welfare".[83] This is designed to promote the upbringing of children by their families. It does not mean, so the House of Lords held, that the authority has a duty to provide accommodation for a child's parent so that the child can live with the parent. If there were such an obligation, this would turn social services departments into housing authorities, and subvert the powers and duties of housing authorities as laid down in housing legislation.[84]

Before deciding what services, if any, to provide for a child, the local authority is required, so far as is reasonably practical and consistent with the child's welfare, to ascertain the child's wishes and feelings regarding the provision of those services and, having regard to his/her age and understanding, give due consideration to such wishes and feelings as they have been able to ascertain.[85]

The services provided (under Pt III) may include giving assistance in kind or in exceptional circumstances in cash.[86] Direct payments may be made to a person with parental responsibility for a disabled child of 16 or 17 to purchase a service which would otherwise have been provided by the authority itself.[87] Where a relative or a foster parent, but not a parent or step-parent, is looking after a child under a residence order, the authority may make a contribution to the cost of this.[88]

In addition to the general duty, local authorities have a number of specific duties. The most important of these are

(i) to identify children in need;[89]

(ii) to promote the upbringing of children by their families;[90]

(iii) to prevent children suffering ill-treatment and neglect (including the duty to use Pt III services to reduce the need to bring care or supervision proceedings or criminal proceedings in respect of children);[91]

(iv) to provide day care for under-fives not attending school.[92]

(iii) Providing accommodation

Although assistance in kind may now include accommodation,[93] there is a separate provision (in s.20) dealing with this. This provides that a local authority must provide accommodation for any child in need aged under 18 within its area who appears to require accomodation as a result of (i) there being no person with parental responsibility for him/her (e.g. the orphan);[94] (ii) his being lost or abandoned; or (iii) the person who has been caring for him/her being prevented, whether or not permanently and for whatever reason, from providing him/her with suitable accommodation or care. Before the Children Act 1989 accommodation was "voluntary care".[95] It is now seen as a service which parents with a child in need may seek to take up so long as it is in the best interests of the child. It is intended as a voluntary arrangement. However, parents may be offered it as an alternative to an authority seeking a care order, where it considers that the child is at risk, and, since it is less intrusive, most parents would take the option (Packman *et al.*, 1986). Local authorities have a discretion to provide accommodation for a child even if the child is not in need, if it considers that to do so would safeguard or promote the child's welfare.[96] This enables "respite care" to be provided.

Accommodation cannot be provided when anyone with parental responsibility who is willing and able to provide, or arrange for, accommodation objects.[97] There is no requirement that the accommodation is suitable or even safe: if it isn't, the authority must consider coercive measures. Since the criterion is parental responsibility, if a divorced mother asks for her child to be accommodated, the father can object. An unmarried father cannot, unless he has required parental responsibility. If the mother has a residence order and the father does not (or vice versa), her decision to ask the local authority to accommodate her child is effective whatever his objections.[98]

Under the system of voluntary care before the 1989 Act, where a child had been in voluntary care for six months, 28 days' notice was required before a parent could remove the child. Although on paper this looked inflexible, it worked, and it did prevent leaving children vulnerable to sudden removal from foster parents. But now "any person with parental responsibility" may "at any time" remove the child from accommodation.[99] This could be a parent with whom the child has no contact. It was said that a period of notice was "inappropriate".[100] But it is equally inappropriate that a parent should be able to insist upon immediate return—in the middle of the night, to take an extreme example. In debates on the Bill much was made of the "inebriated" parent demanding a child's return when not (clearly) in a fit state to take the child away.[101] It has to be said that such concerns have not materialised. In practice, providing a breathing space before removal can be stipulated for in an accommodation agreement. And there are ways of preventing a removal (Freeman, 1992, pp.66–69), most obviously by securing an emergency protection order[102] or, in an extreme case such as the drunk parent turning up in the middle of the night, by invoking police protection.[103] It was thought that s.3(5) of the 1989 Act could be used, but it has been held that it cannot.[104]

Can a child ask to be accommodated? The law distinguishes children of 16 and 17 from those who are younger than 16. A child of 16 or over must be accommodated by the local authority if "in need", where it considers the child is likely to be "seriously prejudiced" if accommodation is not provided. There is no need for parental approval.[105] The homeless child, the child escaping an abusive environment can thus, at least in theory, be accommodated. If the child is under 16, and is *Gillick*-competent, there is a case for arguing that s/he should be able to decide whether to be accommodated. Section 20(6) indicates that a child's wishes should be ascertained and due consideration given to them. This does not suggest that children have the right to be accommodated. As we have seen,[106] a child could seek leave to apply for a residence order, but not one in favour of a local authority.[107] An application, or a request to a local authority to be accommodated, may suggest that the child is beyond parental control and thus care proceedings are appropriate. Questions may also arise if a child in accommodation wishes to stay there and a parent seeks his/her return. If the child is 16 or over, s/he can so insist.[108] But what of the *Gillick*-competent child who is under 16? Again, it would seem that the only remedy available is a care order, if the child is beyond parental control or is likely to suffer significant harm if returned to parental care. An example might be the girl of 14 or 15 for whom a marriage has been arranged.[109] This could also be the rare situation where inherent jurisdiction could be invoked.[110]

A refusal to accommodate may be challenged by judicial review. This was attempted unsuccessfully in *R v Royal Borough of Kingston-Upon-Thames Ex p. T*,[111] where the mother wanted accommodation to be offered different from that the authority was prepared to make available. The authority was not exercising its discretion perversely or unreasonably, even though the child's sister was already accommodated where the mother was asking for this child to be accommodated. A refusal cannot be challenged by means of a specific issue order under s.8.[112] The question as to whether or not a child is in need does not raise a question in connection with any aspect of parental responsibility. If no other method of challenge is available, the aggrieved parent may use the local authority's complaints procedure.[113]

Accommodation is not "care". The local authority thus does not acquire parental responsibility. The significance of this is apparent from the *Tameside* case, which held that a local authority cannot place a child in accommodation of which the parents do not approve. In this case it wished to transfer an accommodated child from residential care to foster care: the court accepted that it could not do so without the parents' permission.[114] Accommodated children are, however, "looked after" children and this has legal consequences: for example, the mother of such a child cannot claim child benefit.[115]

Two-thirds of children who are looked after by local authorities are accommodated (usually for short periods of time).[116] *Guidance* stresses that although accommodation is valuable but nevertheless where the child's welfare demands it "compulsory intervention ... will always be the appropriate remedy".[117]

(iv) The duty to investigate

Where there is a suspicion of abuse, the local authority has a duty to investigate.[118] The duty arises when the authority is informed that a child in its area is subject to an emergency protection order,[119] is in police protection,[120] has contravened a curfew order,[121] or when the authority has "reasonable cause to suspect that a child is suffering, or is likely to suffer, significant harm".[122] The information, which can come from a variety of sources including the child,[123] need only lead to a suspicion to justify the launching of an investigation.[124] As Lord Nicholls has explained, "local authorities would be prevented from carrying out effective and timely risk assessments if they could only act on the basis of proven facts".[125] Where there is a suspicion, the local authority must make "such enquiries as they consider necessary to enable them to decide whether they should take any action to safeguard or promote the child's welfare".[126] But there is no power to enter the home where a child is living if the parents refuse entry. It is all too easy for social workers to be fobbed off by parents who say the child is not there.[127] Where entry is refused and a child cannot be seen, the local authority must apply for an emergency protection order, a child assessment order, a care order or a supervision order unless satisfied that the child's welfare can be satisfactorily safeguarded without doing so.[128] But, having seen the child, the authority is not under a duty to apply for an order, even if, in its opinion, the child would be best protected by applying for an order. As Eekelaar

(1990) points out, there is a duty to investigate with a view to deciding what it should do, but no duty to do anything as a result of the investigation. A court has no jurisdiction to prevent a local authority undertaking a s.47 investigation.[129] It may restrain a parent from co-operating with the investigation by issuing a prohibited steps order[130] to the parent.

Inter-agency co-operation is expected. So it is the duty of other local authorities, any local education authority, any local housing authority, any health authority,[131] and any other person authorised by the Secretary of State to assist the local authority with its enquiries, in particular by providing relevant information and advice if called upon by the authority to do so.[132] The list omits the police, but "police refusal to co-operate ... would be indefensible".[133] There is no obligation to assist a local authority where doing so would be "unreasonable in all the circumstances of the case".[134] The public interests may be in conflict, particularly where the medical profession is concerned: the public interest in preserving confidentiality and the public interest in protecting children from abuse and in detecting criminal offences.[135] Although there is a danger that less abuse may be disclosed to medical practitioners if it is known that confidentiality may be breached, on balance it is "reasonable" that suspicions of abuse should be communicated to protective agencies.[136] The first *Working Together* was in no doubt that "ethical and statutory codes concerned with confidentiality and data protection are not intended to prevent the exchange of information between different professional staff who have a professional responsibility for it ensuring the protection of children".[137] And the General Medical Council in November 1987 expressed the view that the interests of the child are "paramount", and override the general rule of professional confidence. It continued: "not only is it permissible for the doctor to disclose information to a third party but it is the duty of the doctor to do so".[138]

In a number of countries there is mandatory reporting of child abuse (Maidment, 1978; Christoferson, 1989). The Review of Child Care Law (1985, para.12.4) decided against introducing this in England. There is therefore no legal duty on the public to report suspicions or knowledge of incidents of child abuse. If they do, their anonymity can be protected.[139] Whether more incidents of child abuse would be reported if a mandatory reporting law were introduced may be doubted.[140]

(v) The child protection conference

The child protection conference is "central" to child protection procedures. As *Working Together* explains: "it brings together the family and the professionals concerned with child protection and provides them with an opportunity to exchange information and plan together. The conference symbolises the inter-agency nature of assessment, treatment and management of child protection".[141] The initial child protection conference decides whether the child should be placed on the Child Protection Register, and appoints a "key worker".[142] *Working Together* stresses the "need to ensure that the welfare of the child is the overriding factor guiding child protection work".[143] The importance of professionals working in partnership with parents and the concept of parental responsibility are also emphasised.

There is also a child protection review designed to review the plan, evaluate the risk and ensure that the child continues to be adequately protected. It also considers whether the child's name should remain on the register.

There is no right for parents to attend the child protection conference. It is not a breach of natural justice not to invite them.[144] *Working Together* sees their exclusion as "exceptional", so that it needs to be "especially justified",[145] for example where there is a strong risk of violence by the parents (towards the child or the professionals). If they are excluded, other methods of communicating their views to the conference should be found (Savas, 1996). Children are to be encouraged to attend child protection conferences whenever they have sufficient understanding and are able to express their wishes and feelings, and participate in the process of investigation and assessment, planning and review.[146] If the child's attendance is inappropriate (or s/he does not wish to attend), a "clear and up-to-date account of the child's views by professionals who are working with the child" is to be provided. If the interests of parents and children conflict, the child's interests should take "priority".[147]

The Child Protection Register is "not a register of children who have been abused but of children for whom there are currently unresolved child protection issues and for whom there is an inter-agency protection plan".[148] Registration is not to be used for the ulterior purpose of obtaining resources for a family which might "otherwise not be available".[149] The purpose is to provide a record and ensure that plans are formally reviewed every six months.[150] Only a child protection conference can place a child's name on a register. The consequences of registration are sufficiently serious to impose a legal duty on the child protection conference to act fairly. Not to do so is to risk successful challenge by judicial review.[151] *Working Together* advises that where there is information about an abuser, s/he must be informed and told of the possibility of "questioning the details or making representations about the entry".[152]

When a question of child protection arises, action under s.47 should be seen as the "usual first step".[153] Most cases get no further. The parents co-operate and no further formal action is required. Where further action is required there may be urgency and, to achieve what may be short-term protection or evidence gathering for longer-term coercive intervention, two orders exist (and there is also police protection).

(vi) The emergency protection order

The first of these orders is the emergency protection order (see Masson, 2005). The purpose of the order is to enable the child in a genuine emergency to be removed from the place were s/he is, or retained where s/he is (for example, a hospital), if and only if this is what is necessary to provide immediate short-term protection.[154] An application for an EPO is "an extremely serious step" and is not regarded as a "routine response to allegations of child abuse or a routine first step to initiating care proceedings".[155] On the other hand, as we have seen,[156] a local authority must apply for an EPO (or child assessment order, care order or supervision order) if, while investigating, they are denied access to the child or information as to whereabouts, unless satisfied that the child's welfare can be satisfactorily safeguarded without their doing so.[157]

To comply with Art.8 of the European Convention on Human Rights, intervention must be proportionate to the risk involved. The EPO has been described as "draconian", requiring "exceptional justification" and "extraordinarily compelling reasons". "Separation is only to be contemplated if immediate separation is essential to secure the child's safety: 'imminent danger' must be 'actually established'". Both local authority and court should approach every application "with an anxious awareness of the extreme gravity of the relief being sought".[158] It will thus be the very rare case in which a so-called "dawn raid" can be justified.[159]

The local authority should always explore alternatives to

seeking an EPO: one solution is to remove the alleged abuser from the home. It is possible to use Sch.2 para.5 of the 1989 Act to provide housing or cash assistance to an abuser to enable him to leave. If it gets an EPO, it can request an exclusion requirement be attached to the order.[160] A power of arrest can also be attached to the requirement.[161]

There are three grounds upon which an EPO can be made. On the application of any person, if the court is satisfied that there is reasonable cause to believe that the child is likely to suffer significant harm if s/he:

(i) is not removed to accommodation provided by or on behalf of the applicant; or

(ii) does not remain in the place in which s/he is then being accommodated.[162]

The court—not the applicant—must be satisfied about the likelihood of significant harm.

Second, an order can be made on the application of a local authority or the NSPCC,[163] where it has reasonable cause to suspect that a child is suffering, or is likely to suffer, significant harm and its enquiries are being frustrated by access to the child being unreasonably refused, and the applicant has reasonable cause to believe that access to the child is required as a matter of urgency.[164]

Third, in the case of an application by the NSPCC, the applicant has reasonable cause to suspect that a child is suffering, or is likely to suffer significant harm, the applicant is making enquiries with respect to the child's welfare and the enquiries are being frustrated by access to the child being unreasonably refused to a person authorised to seek access, and the applicant has reasonable cause to believe that access to the child is required as a matter of urgency.[165]

Even if the conditions for an EPO are satisfied, one should not be made unless the welfare principle is satisfied, and should only be made if an order is better for the child than not making the order.[166] An application for an EPO is not a family proceeding; accordingly a s.8 order, such as a residence order, cannot be made instead.

An EPO gives the applicant parental responsibility for the child, but this is limited: the power to remove or prevent removal of the child can only be exercised to safeguard and promote the child's welfare. And the applicant can only take such decisions about the child's upbringing as are reasonably required to safeguard or promote the child's welfare.[167] Bearing in mind the fact that the order only lasts for eight days[168] (an extension for seven further days and once only is only permitted to the local authority or NSPCC applicant).[169] No order should be made for "any longer than is absolutely necessary to protect the child".[170] Where an application is made *ex parte* careful consideration should be given to making the order for the "shortest possible period commensurate with the preservation of the child's immediate safety".[171]

There is no appeal against the making or refusal to make a emergency protection order.[172]

There are surprisingly few EPOs, less than half the number of place of safety orders made before the 1989 Act.[173] This suggests local authorities are being less interventionist, perhaps seeking to accommodate children pending further investigations, before applying if necessary for a care order.

(vii) The child assessment order

The second order is the child assessment order. This is designed for the situation where there is fear for a child's health, development or safety but no hard evidence: for example, a child has been failing to attend a nursery or family centre, or a neighbour has heard a child's screams, or a child has not been seen for some time and there are suspicious circumstances. According to the *Guidance*, a CAO will usually be most appropriate where the harm is "long-term and cumulative rather than sudden and severe" or there may be "nagging concern about a child who appears to be failing to thrive".[174]

Only the local authority and the NSPCC may apply for a CAO.[175] An application by a local authority should always be preceded by an investigation under s.47. An order can be made only if three conditions are satisfied:

(i) the applicant has reasonable cause to suspect that the child is suffering, or is likely to suffer, significant harm;

(ii) an assessment of the state of the child's health or development, or of the way in which s/he has been treated, is required to enable the applicant to determine whether or not the child is suffering, or is likely to suffer significant harm; and

(iii) it is unlikely that such an assessment will be made, or be satisfactory, in the absence of a CAO.[176]

An application is not a "family proceeding": so, with one exception, the court must either make the order or refuse so to do: it cannot make any other kind of order.[177] The exception is that it can make an EPO instead of a CAO.[178] Applications are governed by the paramountcy principle, and the presumption of no order in s.1(5).[179]

The CAO is not intended as a substitute for an EPO. However, if the real purpose of an application is to have the child assessed, consideration should be given as to whether that objective "cannot equally effectively, and more proportionately" be achieved by a CAO rather than an EPO.[180]

Child assessment applications must be heard by a full court conducting a hearing on notice, and not, as one concerned MP put it, by "a magistrate sitting at home in his pyjamas".[181] The applicant must take such steps as are reasonably practicable to ensure that prior notice of the application is given to the parents, anyone else with parental responsibility or who is caring for the child, any person allowed to have contact with the child by virtue of an order under s.34, and the child.[182] The child will be usually be represented by a guardian ad litem. The application may be challenged. There is a right of appeal against the making of, or the court's refusal to make a CAO. The court may prevent a further application being made by particular persons including the local authority without the court's leave, or refuse to allow a further application for a CAO within six months, without leave.[183]

The court can allow up to seven days for the assessment.[184] When being debated in Parliament, concern was expressed as to how an assessment could be done in this short time span.[185] The *Guidance* is alert to this problem and recommends the applicant "should make the necessary arrangement in advance of the application, so that it would usually be possible to complete within such a period an initial multi-disciplinary assessment of the child's medical, intellectual, emotional, social and behavioural needs".[186] This, it adds, "should be sufficient to establish whether the child is suffering, or likely to suffer, significant harm and, if so, what further action is required".[187] It was anticipated that CAOs would not be sought much. This has proved to be the case. One reason why orders are not sought may well be the short time-limit (Dickens, 1993, p.97). Another is that the threat to seek the order may be sufficient to persuade parents to agree to an assessment of the child.

A CAO does not confer parental responsibility on the applicant. But it has two effects. First, there is a requirement that any person who is in a position to do so produces the child.[188] Second, it authorises the carrying out of the assessment in accordance with the terms of the order.[189] If the child is not produced, grounds for seeking an EPO will be made out.[190] As with EPOs, a child of sufficient understanding to make an informed decision may refuse to submit to a medical or psychiatric examination or other assessment.[191] The child can be kept away from home for the purpose of the assessment,[192] but the *Guidance* cautions against overnight stays: "the assessment should be conducted with as little trauma for the child and parents as possible".[193] If the court directs that the child may be kept away from home, it must also give directions about the contact the child is to have with other persons during this period.[194] Although the Act does not prescribe reasonable contact, such a presumption can be implied. The question of contact is governed by the paramountcy principle but, since it is a direction, not an order, it is not subject to the presumption of "no order" in s.1(5). The child's wishes and feelings are not matters to which the Act directs attention in this context, but it is clear that they ought to be considered.[195]

It is easy to be sceptical about CAOs. They are not much used:[196] it is impossible to estimate how often they are threatened. Since they require an inter-parties hearing, they cannot be obtained very speedily and, seven days may be insufficient where the examination is not merely medically related. But it does have advantages (Harding, 1989; Wilson, 1989): notably, the child can be seen by the family doctor in a familiar environment, thus protecting the child from stress and worry; the parents are likely to co-operate so that the social work relationship with the family is not damaged; and the child is protected in serious situations, short of emergencies.

(viii) The role of the police

The police also have an important role in child protection, (Cobley, 1992; Borkowski, 1995). This may be especially valuable where a child is abandoned or is left at home while parents go away on holiday or in serious cases of domestic violence where a child might be exposed to serious violence as well. The power the police have may also be useful with homeless or runaway children.

Where a police officer has reasonable cause to believe that a child would be otherwise likely to suffer significant harm, s/he may remove the child to "suitable accommodation".[197] Alternatively, s/he may take such steps as are reasonable to ensure that the child's removal from hospital, or other place in which s/he is being accommodated, is prevented.[198] When these powers are exercised, the child is said to be in police protection.[199] No child can be kept in police protection for more than 72 hours.[200]

There is no power of search attached to this provision in the Act.[201] A child can therefore only be taken into police protection once the officer has found the child.

As soon as reasonably practicable after taking a child into police protection, the officer must inform relevant local authorities, the child (and take such steps as reasonably practicable to discover the child's wishes and feelings), his/her parents and other persons with parental responsibility and any other person with whom the child was living before being taken into police protection about the steps that have been taken in relation to the child.[202] The case must be inquired into by a "designated officer".[203] The designated officer may apply on behalf of the local authority for an EPO to be made in respect of the child.[204] The duration of police protection and the EPO cannot in total exceed eight days, and the police cannot apply for an extension, nor can they commence care proceedings. When inquiries have been completed, the child must be released, unless the designated officer considers that there will be reasonable cause for believing that the child will suffer significant harm if released.[205]

The police do not acquire parental responsibility, but must do what is reasonable in all the circumstances of the case to safeguard or promote the child's welfare, bearing in mind the short period of time that police protection lasts.[206] This will include emergency treatment. If assessment is required, perhaps to investigate whether sexual abuse has taken place, it will be necessary to seek an EPO (the police cannot apply for a CAO). Whether a *Gillick*-competent child[207] can refuse to submit to treatment is not addressed in the legislation. The question is left open as to whether common law principles or similar statutory provisions should be applied. The *South Glamorgan* decision would suggest the same result, *viz.* the child cannot refuse treatment whichever set of principles is applied.[208]

(ix) The Human Rights Act and child protection

If longer-term protection is thought to be needed, a care order (or a supervision order) may be sought. When a child dies or is severely injured local authorities are blamed for their failure to take action, but over-zealous intervention as in the Cleveland crisis is also criticised (Freeman, 1989). Debates have raged at various times over whether local authorities are overly inter-ventionist (Geach and Szwed, 1983), or whether a "rule of opti-mism" prevails, as Dingwall and Eekelaar (1983) found in their study of the policies of a number of local authorities. But it must never be forgotten that local authority decision-making takes place in the shadow of court rulings. If courts emphasise the rights of parents, if they stress rehabilitation of children with families, if they refuse to make care orders, the hands of social workers are tied. Nor can we understand the limits of coercive intervention into families without appreciating the impact of the Human Rights Act 1998 and the norms in the European Con-vention on Human Rights, particularly Arts 8 and 6. At the same time, it should not be forgotten that the UN Convention on the Rights of the Child, which mandates the UK to take

"all appropriate legislative, administrative, social and educa-tional measures to protect the child from all forms of physical or mental violence, injury or abuse, neglect or negligent treatment, maltreatment or exploitation, including sexual abuse, while in the care of parent(s), legal guardians(s) or any other person who has care of the child".[209]

The European Convention on Human Rights must now be seen as a framework within which child protection decisions are taken. Since local authorities and courts are public authorities, they must exercise their powers and duties in compliance with the European Convention.[210] The case law of the European Court of Human Rights must be taken account of by English courts,[211] and social work practice is also constrained by it. A local authority in breach of the Convention may have an award of damages made against it.[212]

Article 8(1) of the European Convention recognises the right to respect for private and family life. In *Haase v Germany*,[213] the European Court of Human Rights held that authorities should make a careful assessment of the impact of proposed care mea-sures on parents and children, and of the alternatives to taking children into public care. Further, that following a removal into care, a stricter scrutiny is called for in respect of any further limitations by the authorities, for example in respect of restrictions on parental rights and contact. It also ruled that taking a child into care should normally be regarded as a temporary measure to be discontinued as soon as circumstances permit; the ultimate aim should be to reunite the child with the natural family. In *Hokkanen v Finland*, the European Court of Human Rights held that a "fair balance has to be struck between the interests of the child in remaining in public care and those of the parent in being reunited with the child". However, in carrying out that balancing exercise, "the best interests of the child … may override those of the parent".[214]

It is important to recognise the emphasis in European jurisprudence on proportionality. Thus, the level of state intervention must be proportionate to the risk the child is suffering.[215] Thus, in *K and T v Finland*[216] a baby was removed at birth from a mother with schizophrenia. The parents were given no chance to work out their problems with the help of relatives or to take advantage of support measures provided by social and health care authorities. At the time of the birth the mother was in a relatively good mental condition. The court found "the reasons to justify the care orders were not sufficient and the methods used in implementing those decisions were excessive".[217] States have a margin of appreciation, a space to exercise discretion. Thus, only where a state's response is clearly disproportionate, as in *K and T v Finland*, will a breach of the Convention be found.[218]

The margin of appreciation doctrine is premised on the need for the European Court of Human Rights to take account of social and cultural conditions which differ from state to state. Does this mean an English court should not invoke it? In *Re N (Leave to Withdraw Care Proceedings)*,[219] this was Bracewell J.'s view. She said that when considering whether a child should be removed from parents the test was is there "a pressing social need for intervention by the State at this stage in family life and is the response proportionate to the need?"[220] If the response is not proportionate, why should there be deference to the decision-makers?[221] This is not an easy dilemma to resolve, and one which will continue to be debated.

The question also arises as to the extent to which parents of a child should be involved in the decision-making processes instigated by a local authority. In addition to Art.8, there is also

Art.6 (the right to a fair trial) to consider. It has been held recently that actions taken by a local authority before the birth of a child cannot constitute an interference with a parent's procedural rights under Art.6.[222] But in relation to children it is clear that Arts 6 and 8 have a role to play in the decision-making process, court hearings and child protection process generally. So, reports which a local authority intends to use in a court hearing should be disclosed to parents, unless there is a compelling reason for not so doing.[223] It is essential that parents whose child is the subject of care proceedings should have access to a lawyer.[224] And parents are entitled to be kept informed of the local authority's plans in relation to their children.[225]

But the courts are reluctant to find there has been an interference with parents' procedural rights. In *Re L (Care Proceedings: Human Rights Claims)*[226] Munby J. emphasised that children also have rights under the Convention that have to be protected. He commented: "Too many care cases already take far too long ... it would be a terrible irony if the necessary pursuit of European Convention rights by unnecessary and inappropriate procedures were itself to add to the scourge of the delay...".[227]

Local authorities are thus faced with a real dilemma. How do they protect children—and this is their rationale—while at the same time ensuring that the rights of parents are upheld? The protection of children has to be the primary concern. Thus, courts which have stressed that there needs to be a substantial departure from good practice before parents' human rights can be said to be infringed[228] must be right.

(x) Applying for a care order

Only the local authority and the NSPCC may apply for a care order or supervision order. The police, the local education authority and parents can no longer bring (or in the case of parents since 1963 initiate) care proceedings.[229] The police were formerly able to commence proceedings where the commission of a criminal offence by the child was the basis of the application. The abolition of the offence condition removed the rationale for police applications. Similarly, the removal of the "school refusal" ground takes away the basis for LEA applications.[230] The status and position of the parent is discussed in the section on "beyond parental control" (see below).

Where the NSPCC (or other "authorised person") proposes to make an application, it is required, where reasonably practicable and before it makes an application, to consult the local authority in whose area the child is ordinarily resident.[231]

No care or supervision orders may be made with respect to a child who has reached the age of 17 (or 16 if the child is married).[232] Until the 1989 Act was implemented, wardship would have been used where the child was under 18: this option is no longer open.[233]

Until after the Maria Colwell case the child was not a party to care proceedings. Now the child and anyone with parental responsibility are parties.[234] Fathers without parental responsibility are not automatically parties, but they should be served with notice of the proceedings and be permitted to participate in them, unless there is some justifiable reason for not joining the father as a party.[235] It is open to any other person to apply to be joined as the party: the court can so direct.

THE GROUND

Until 1989 there were seven conditions upon the proof of one of which, plus the overriding condition that the child was "in need of care and control," which s/he was unlikely to receive unless the court made a care order, the court could make such an order.[236] These conditions were swept away by the Children Act 1989, and there is now just one ground, usually referred to as the "threshold criteria". This is the only trigger for local state intervention into the family. Without proof of these minimum conditions, no compulsory or coercive measures can be taken against the parents of children.[237] The Lord Chancellor, in 1989, explained that "the integrity and independence of the family are the basic building blocks of a free and democratic society".[238] Accordingly, he argued that "unless there is evidence that a child is being or is likely to be positively harmed because of a failure in the family, the state, whether in the guise of a local authority or the court, should not interfere".[239] More recently, Lord Nicholls in *Re O and Another (Minors) (Care: Preliminary Hearing); Re B (A Minor)* explained: "the purpose of this threshold requirement is to protect families, both adults and children, from inappropriate interference in their lives by public authorities through the making of care and supervision orders".[240] Before the 1989 Act it was possible, using wardship, to intervene on welfare considerations alone. This is no longer so: if it were, it is doubtful whether it would be European Convention compliant.[241]

However, the triggering provision in s.31(2) must read together with the central principles in s.1 of the Act, so that there is a "welfare" stage[242] and furthermore a care (or supervision) order is only to be made if it is better for the child than not making the order.[243] But in determining whether the threshold criteria are met the child's welfare is not the court's paramount consideration.

The threshold criteria provide that a court may only make a care or supervision order (hereafter reference will be to care but, unless otherwise stated, this includes supervision) if it is satisfied:

"(a) the child concerned is suffering significant harm, or is likely to suffer significant harm; and

(b) the harm or likelihood of harm is attributable to—

(i) the care given to the child, or likely to be given to him if the order were not made, not being what it would be reasonable to expect a parent to give him; or

(ii) the child's being beyond parental control".[244]

These minimum conditions are the same for a care order and a supervision order. A supervision order cannot be upgraded to a care order without proof again of the threshold criteria.

The threshold criteria, it will be observed, are in two limbs: one focuses on significant harm, the other, "the attributable condition", on parenting (or rather the lack of reasonable parenting). The then President of the Family Division warned, shortly after the Act was implemented, against a "strict legalistic analysis of s.31". He did not believe that Parliament intended the words of s.31(2) to be "unduly restrictive when the evidence clearly indicates that a certain course of action should be taken in order to protect the child".[245] Of course, there has been a careful reading of the text by commentators (Freeman, 1990; Cretney, 1990; more broadly see Adcock and White, 1998) and courts. This is both inevitable and desirable. As Lowe and Douglas (2006, p.737) point out, "s.31 is the benchmark against which State intervention into the family is or is not justified".

An analysis accordingly follows.

(i) Harm

First, we must look at "significant harm" and, therefore, initially at "harm". This is defined in s.31(9) as amended, as "ill-treatment or the impairment of health or development including, for example, impairment suffered from seeing or hearing the ill-treatment of another".[246] "Ill-treatment" is defined in s.31(9) as including "sexual abuse and forms of ill-treatment which are not physical". Sexual abuse is not as such defined. There is no universally accepted definition of what constitutes sexual abuse (Finkelhor, 1984; Haugaard and Reppucci, 1988; Faller, 1998; see also Freeman, 1997). Where is the line to be drawn? One court thought that a father's "vulgar and inappropriate horseplay" with his daughter was not sexual abuse.[247] How important is the intention of the abuser? It may be argued that anything that gives him sexual gratification is abuse. A useful working definition is

"Any child below the age of consent may be deemed to have been sexually abused when a sexually mature person has by design or neglect of their usual societal or specific responsibilities in relation to the child engaged or permitted the engagement of that child in any activity of a sexual nature which is intended to lead to the sexual gratification of the sexually mature person".[248]

Physical abuse is obviously ill-treatment, though reasonable corporal punishment by a parent is not so regarded.[249] Emotional abuse,[250] although not specifically mentioned, is clearly an example of non-physical ill-treatment (Freeman, 1992, p.104). Fabricated or induced illness (previously called Munchausen's syndrome by proxy) may well constitute emotional abuse.[251] "Neglect" is also not specifically mentioned, but is clearly either "ill-treatment" or the impairment of health or development, depending on what form the neglect takes. Failure to obtain medical treatment is also ill-treatment, and impairment of health. Domestic violence in a child's presence is also, since the Adoption and Children Act 2002,[252] harm within the meaning of s.31(2).

"Development" is defined as "physical, intellectual, emotional, social or behavioural development", and "health" as "physical or mental health".[253] Not attending school can impair both intellectual and social development.[254] Poor nutrition and low standards of hygiene can impair both health and development. "Harm" is wide enough to embrace "moral danger"—itself a ground for a care order under previous legislation (Freeman, 1990, pp.154–155).[255] So involving children in prostitution and other forms of commercial sexual exploitation is

"harm". So is forced marriage.[256] Ceremonies of exorcism per-
formed to drive the devil out of children are also abuse—they
will often anyway include physical ill-treatment.[257] The latest
Working Together To Safeguard Children, while accepting the need
to be sensitive to culture, warns that "child abuse cannot be
condoned for religious or cultural reasons".[258] Female genital
mutilation remains endemic, despite legislation outlawing it.[259] It
is not intended as an act of abuse—of course, a lot of abuse
isn't—so *Working Together To Safeguard Children* advises that "it
may not be appropriate to consider removing the child from an
otherwise loving family environment".[260] Much depends upon
how "significant" is interpreted (this is discussed below).

(ii) Significant harm

"Harm" by itself does not trigger coercive intervention. It must
be "significant". The DHSS *Review of Child Care Law* (1985,
para.15(15)) stresses the importance of this.

"Having set an acceptable standard of upbringing for the child,
it should be necessary to show some substantial deficit in that
standard. Minor shortcomings in the health or care provided or
minor defects in physical, psychological or social development
should not give rise to any compulsory intervention unless they
are having, or are likely to have, serious and lasting effects upon
the child".

The Act does not define "significant": case law following the
Guidance has adopted a dictionary definition of "considerable,
noteworthy or important",[261] but this does not assist overmuch.
It is a lesser standard than would have been imposed by the
adjective "serious" (the test in Goldstein *et al.*, 1979, p.72). It is
also a lesser standard than "severe". Harm may be significant in
a number of ways: in amount, in effect, in importance. It can exist
in the seriousness of the harm or in the implications of it.[262]
Stubbing a cigarette out on a baby's bottom is significant because
of what it portends. What is significant may depend on the age of
the child: shaking a baby is significant, doing this to a 13-year-
old of much less significance.

What is significant must be put into context. An excellent
illustration is the case of *Re B*[263] decided before the Act came into
operation. The court referred to a "spectrum of abuse" and an
"index of harm". The case concerned a four-year-old boy who

had been sexually abused by his father. However, it was a loving, stable home and there was an excellent relationship between the mother and the boy, both of whom were devastated by the rupture caused by the abuse. The judge felt able to conclude that the boy could be safely reintegrated into the family.

"Significant" has to be situated, then, within relationships. It is necessary to look at *this* child in the context of *this* family: abuse in one context is not necessarily abuse in another. And context must also include culture. Clearly, there are limits to this: we cannot exculpate practices such as female genital mutilation because they are common among a particular group (Freeman, 1995). But what is "significant" must depend in part upon what is expected, and different cultures have different expectations of acceptable child-rearing behaviour.

The Act uses "significant harm" as the trigger. But it should not be forgotten that insignificant harm may betoken risk of significant harm, and so cannot be overlooked. For example, parents who use physical punishment excessively—even if they do not infringe the new norm in s.58 of the Children Act 2004—should sound warning bells to those deputed to protect children. Too many child death cases are exercises of discipline which have gone badly wrong.

(iii) The similar child

Where the harm is the result of ill-treatment no further guidance is offered. Where it is impairment of health or development, the Act uses the comparator of "similar child".

"Where the question of whether the harm suffered by a child is significant turns on the child's health or development, his health or development shall be compared with that which could reasonably be expected of a similar child".[264]

The reference is to a "similar child", not a child of similar parents. According to the Lord Chancellor in 1989, it is a child with the same physical attributes as the child concerned, not a child of the same background.[265] On this test, the development of a two-year-old has to be compared with that of other two-year-olds, not with other two-year-olds from similar backgrounds. Does this mean the child from a poor environment, perhaps with a mother only, is to be compared with children from materially comfortable and stimulating environments? The *Guidance* thinks not:

this advises that we "may" need to "take account of environmental, social and cultural characteristics of the child".[266] This
must be the better view: any other one would be unfair and
would lead needlessly to large numbers of children of the poor
finding their way into public care. It is clearly also important that
children with special needs (those for example with Down's
Syndrome) are not compared with children not so handicapped.
It may look relatively easy to compare, for example, a deaf four-
year-old with other deaf four-year-olds, but the value of this may
be more apparent than real. For example, is a child of deaf
parents a "similar child" to a deaf child of hearing parents? If we
take account only of the characteristics of the child, as the Act
requires, a deaf child of deaf parents is like a deaf child of
hearing parents. But there are significant differences; the environment is different, the experiences of parents are different, the
attitudes to deafness and education of the deaf may be different
(see further Freeman, 1992, p.107).

The courts have offered little guidance. Of interest is *Re D
(Care: Threshold Criteria: Significant Harm).*[267] A care order was
made in respect of a child of a Jamaican mother. There were a
number of abusive incidents, including holding the child out of
the window, beating her with a belt and threatening her with
eviction from the home. Wilson J. said we were "one society
governed by one set of laws. It would concern me if the same
event could give rise in one case to a finding of significant harm
and in another to a finding to the contrary". However, the judge
conceded that

"if a child can say to himself or herself 'my brothers, sisters and
friends are all treated in this way from time to time: it seems to
be part of life' that child may suffer less emotional harm than a
child who perceived himself or herself to be a unique victim".

It has been argued (Freeman, 1990; Brophy, 2000, 2003; Brophy *et
al.*, 2003) that the ethnic background of the child is relevant:
"Muslim children, Rastafarian children, the children of Hasidic
Jews may be different, and have different needs from children
brought up in the indigenous, white, nominally Christian culture" (Freeman, 1990, p.153). Against this it has been said
(Bainham, 1993, p.103) that allowances for cultural background
ought not to be made, except at the welfare stage. *Re D* (above)
supports Bainham's view, though on the facts it is not a decision
from which I would dissent.

(iv) The temporal dimension

The child must be suffering significant harm or likely to suffer significant harm. The original Bill used the words "has suffered" rather than "is suffering". Past harm does not meet the criterion unless it points to present or future harm.[268] That the present tense is used should not be taken too literally: by the time of the hearing, the child will have been removed from the abusive environment and will no longer necessarily be suffering significant harm. A care order, obviously, can be made. The leading case is *Re M (A Minor) (Care Order: Threshold Conditions)*.[269] The father had murdered the mother in front of the four children. He was sentenced to life imprisonment with a recommendation for deportation (he was Nigerian). Three of the four children were placed with Mrs W, the mother's cousin, but she did not feel able to cope with M, who was then less than 4 months old. In due course, Mrs W wanted to offer M a home as well. The father had parental responsibility: fathers who murder their wives retain this, of course (*cf.* Bainham, 2005, p.487 n.1). The local authority, M's guardian ad litem and the father all wanted a care order to be made and for M to be placed for adoption outside the extended family. Bracewell J. made the care order. The Court of Appeal allowed Mrs W's appeal, and substituted a residence order in her favour. The House of Lords restored the care order, through it was accepted that Mrs W was looking after M well. The Lords were of the view that they expected the child to continue to live with Mrs W, but "having regard to the history and circumstances it was highly desirable that the local authority should exercise a watching brief...".[270] The House of Lords construed "is suffering" to refer to the circumstances at the point of local authority intervention. Lord Mackay L.C. said:

"...where, at the time the application is to be disposed of, there are in place arrangements for the protection of the child by the local authority on an interim basis which protection has been continuously in place for some time, the relevant date with respect to which the court must be satisfied is the date at which the local authority initiated the procedure for protection under the Act from which these arrangements followed".[271]

This reasoning must be right, even if a care order seems the wrong conclusion: Mrs W should have been granted a residence order (Masson, 1994). But interpretational problems remain. For example, what is meant by "arrangement". Clearly, this must include emergency protection orders, interim care orders and police protection (into which the children were initially taken in this case). But does it include s.20 accommodation? The cases now conclude it does.[272] Again, this looks convincing, but it too leaves open questions: for example, whether the child can be said to be suffering significant harm if accommodated for a lengthy period of time. Masson (1994) also raises the question of whether an adjourned child protection conference can be characterised as a protective arrangement. Much will depend upon whether a narrow or wide interpretation of s.31(2) is called for: if the threshold criteria are to protect families from undue interference a narrow construction is called for, and less formal interventions will not be considered "arrangements". If it is to be interpreted as a child protection measure, a wider construction may be appropriate. There is a strong case for adopting an interpretation which supports the child's welfare.

A care order may also be made if the child is likely to suffer significant harm. Most cases where harm is anticipated will occur where the child has suffered significant harm at some time in the past and, it is thought, is likely to do so again.[273] The *Guidance* gives examples:

"Where physical abuse of a child is associated with bouts of parental depression ... where a newly-born baby, because of the family history, would be at risk if taken home. ... Where the welfare of a child looked after ... under voluntary accommodation arrangements ... would be at risk if the parents went ahead with plans to return him to an unsuitable home environment".[274]

But "the conditions are intended to place a sufficiently difficult burden upon the applicant as to prevent unwarranted intervention in cases where the child is not genuinely at risk".[275] In addition, there are human rights constraints: any action must be proportionate.

What does "is likely" mean? The leading case is *Re H (Minors) (Sexual Abuse: Standard of Proof)*[276] (Hayes, 1997). The mother had four daughters, two by her husband and two by her subsequent partner. The eldest girl, aged 15, alleged sexual abuse over a long period by the mother's partner. He was tried for rape and acquitted. The local authority nevertheless sought care orders in respect of the three younger girls. The authority argued that he had indeed abused the eldest girl or that there was a substantial risk that he had done so, and that accordingly the younger girls were likely to suffer significant harm if care orders were not made. There is a lower standard of proof in civil cases. The judge recognised the real possibility that sexual abuse had taken place, but could not be sure to the "requisite high standard of proof". The local authority's appeal was dismissed both by the Court of Appeal and the House of Lords.

The House of Lords addressed a number of questions. First, the meaning of "likely". They said this meant that the occurrence of significant harm was a real possibility, "a possibility that cannot sensibly be ignored".[277] Second, they looked at the burden of proof. This, they held, was for the local authority to prove its case. The standard of proof was the ordinary civil standard (and see Cobley, 2006). There was some difference here between the judges. The majority was of the view that "the more serious the allegation, the more cogent is the evidence required to overcome the unlikelihood of what is alleged, and thus to prove it".[278] The minority preferred a simple balance of probabilities test. Lord Lloyd, it is submitted correctly (Freeman, 2000b, 550), pointed out that the test which the majority favoured would have the "bizarre" result that the more serious the anticipated injury, the more difficult it would be for the local authority to satisfy the standard of proof (Spencer, 1994). The majority may have believed that the sexual abuse of step-daughters was a rare event—in which case they are wrong. But the question in issue was not the probability of any step-daughter being abused, but the ones in this case. A better comparator population than step-daughters as a whole would be step-daughters in cases where other girls in the family have complained.

It was on the question of upon what evidence a risk of harm can be based where the Lords were particularly divided. The majority thought there was a two-stage test: to make a finding on the primary facts and then based on that to assess whether the risk of future harm was a real possibility. Since it has been found that sexual abuse had not been proved, there was nothing from which a risk of harm could be inferred. A finding of risk of harm could not be made on mere suspicions. The minority did not agree. For Lord Lloyd the question was: "Is the court satisfied that there is a serious risk of harm in the future?"[279] For Lord Browne-Wilkinson "to be satisfied of the existence of risk does not require proof of the occurrence of past historical events but proof of facts which are relevant to the making of a prognosis".[280]

A balance has to be struck between the rights of parents not to be at risk of having their children taken from them on the basis of false allegations of child abuse and the rights of children to be protected. Has *Re H* tilted the balance too far in the parents' favour? It is my view that it has. It may be that the decision exposes children to inhuman and degrading treatment—in which case the government may find itself exposed to an Art.3 challenge.

(v) Attribution

The second limb requires the court to be satisfied that the significant harm is attributable to the care given, or likely to be given to the child not being what a reasonable parent would give to the child (or, as discussed below, to the child's being beyond parental control). The *Guidance* states that "harm caused solely by a third party is excluded (unless the parent has failed to prevent it)".[281] The main problem has arisen where it cannot be proved who is responsible for the child's injuries: it could be either parent or a baby-sitter or a childminder. The leading case is *Lancashire CC v B*.[282] A young baby was looked after partly by her parents and partly by a childminder, who also had a child. The baby suffered serious non-accidental head injuries as a result of being violently shaken. It was impossible to establish whether the parents or the childminder were responsible. The local authority sought care orders in respect both of the baby and the childminder's child. Both applications were refused but the Court of Appeal allowed the authority's appeal in respect of the baby. The parents of the baby appealed to the House of Lords, arguing that the harm suffered by their child had to be attributable to their care, and that the continuation of the care proceedings infringed their right to family life under Art.8 of the European Convention. The House of Lords held that where there is significant harm or risk of such harm, then in the case of so-called "shared care arrangements" provided it can be shown to have been inflicted by one of the carers there is no need to identify the actual perpetrator to satisfy the attribution condition. There was furthermore no breach of Art.8: the steps taken by the local authority were "no more than those reasonably necessary to pursue the legitimate aim of protecting [the baby] from further injury".[283] Of course, if the childminder were the perpetrator, the dropping of care proceedings in respect of her child may well have exposed him to abuse. But since there was no injury to that child, and the identity of the person who injured the baby could not be established, it was impossible to conclude that he was at risk of significant harm.

The *Lancashire* decision only applies where there is a shared care arrangement. If it applies where there is a child minder it must also apply where there is a baby-sitter. It presumably must also apply where a relative, such as a grandparent, shares care with the parent, perhaps looking after the child while the parents are at work. It seems that it does not apply where a person only has "fleeting contact" with the child.[284]

(vi) The quality of care

The quality of care must fall below what it is reasonable to expect of a parent. "Care" is not defined, but must include catering for the child's total needs (physical, emotional, intellectual, behavioural, social), and not just having physical charge.[285] The care given to the child is not what it would be reasonable for *this* parent to give (perhaps living in a high-rise flat on income support, with three children under five and a partner in prison), but what it would be reasonable to expect *a* parent to give. The standard is objective. It concentrates on the "needs of the child ... rather than on some hypothetical child and the hypothesis is transferred to the parent".[286] The emphasis is on this child, given this child's needs. If he has asthma or brittle bones, he may need more care or a different type of care from a "normal" child. If a parent could provide this, then this parent is failing if s/he cannot. The *Guidance* emphasises that

"the court will almost certainly expect to see professional evidence on the standard of care which could reasonably be expected of reasonable parents with support from community-wide services as appropriate where the child's needs are complex or demanding, or the lack of reasonable care is not immediately obvious".[287]

(vii) Beyond parental control

The child's being beyond parental control was in the pre-1989 legislation but was not then linked with harm to the child.[288] Being beyond parental control thus survives as a "ground" only where there is significant harm to the child (or this is likely). Children who are beyond parental control may cause significant harm, but this is not the test. Proving that the sexually promiscuous teenager or the glue-sniffing child is likely to suffer significant harm may not be difficult, but attributing it to their being beyond parental control may not be so easy. It is not entirely clear whether control is an objective standard (is the child beyond the control of a reasonable parent? In other words, it is the child's fault). Or a subjective one (is s/he beyond the control of parents who are in some way at fault?). Since this limb of the sub-section makes no reference to reasonableness, it has to be assumed that the subjective test applies—s/he is beyond the control of his/her parents. That would be consistent with the threshold conditions as a whole, which are about limiting state interference with parental autonomy. It would be right to interfere when *these* parents cannot control their child. But the *Guidance* says it is immaterial whether it is the fault of the parents or the child, suggesting, somewhat equivocally, that "beyond parental control" can be looked at both ways.[289]

What is meant by "parental" has been left open. It presumably includes all those who are exercising parental functions and responsibilities. A child being looked after by grandparents can, on this interpretation, be beyond their control. This is supported by *M v Birmingham City Council*[290] holding that parental control can refer to the control exercised by a parent and her partner who is not a parent of the child.

According to *M v Birmingham City Council* the phrase "beyond parental control" is "capable of describing a state of affairs in the past, in the present or in the future".[291]

(viii) The welfare stage

If the court finds the threshold criteria are met, it must proceed to consider what kind of order, if any, is in the best interests of child. It must remember also that the human rights constraints which require that the action taken should be proportionate and no more than is necessary to protect the welfare of the child.[292]

There are two distinct stages, the threshold criteria stage and the welfare stage. Only the latter is governed by the paramountcy principle. The court is also bound at this stage to have regard to the checklist in s.1(3), and to consider whether it is better for the child to make any order than to make no order at all. Applying the welfare principle involves both looking at the past and into the future.[293] At the welfare stage the court is adopting an inquisitorial role.[294] The welfare stage is the point at which the court will consider whether it is more appropriate to make a supervision order than a care order (or vice versa).

As far as looking at the past is concerned, a particularly difficult problem arises where, as in the *Lancashire* case, it is not clear who injured the child. The House of Lords has since addressed this "uncertain perpetrator" problem in *Re O and Another (Care: Preliminary Hearing); Re B (A Minor)*.[295] This involved two appeals. In the first case (*Re B*) it was probable that the father had caused the harm, though the mother could not be ruled out. In the second case (*Re O*), one of the parents was the perpetrator, but it was unclear which. In both cases the threshold criteria were satisfied. In *Re B* the Court of Appeal held that since it had not been proved that the mother had been responsible for the child's injuries, the court should proceed at the welfare stage on the basis that she did not pose a risk to the child. In *Re O*, however, it held that the mother could not be disregarded as a risk to the sibling—the injured child having died. The House of Lords ruled that the court should proceed at the welfare stage "on the footing that each of the possible perpetrators is indeed, just that: a possible perpetrator".[296] Lord Nicholls thought it would be "grotesque" if, because it could not be shown which parent had harmed the child, the child had to be treated as not at risk from either of them.[297]

If this amounts to removing children on "suspicions", it may concern us. Both Bainham (2005) and Herring (2004, p.543) are of the view that suspicion calls for supervision orders rather than care orders. And certainly Lord Nicholls is not adhering to the reasoning he adopted in *Re H*, discussed above.[298] But in *Re H* there was no harm proved, and in *Re O* there clearly was. Subsequently, the Court of Appeal ruled that possible perpetrators could be excluded—in this case a grandmother and a night nanny—if there was no real possibility that they were implicated, thus reducing the number of possible perpetrators.[299]

Another question which has arisen is whether unproven allegations of harm can be taken into account at the welfare stage. In *Re M and R (Child Abuse: Evidence)*[300] there was "a real possibility that [sexual] abuse" had been committed. But the judge held, following *Re H*, that "such a possibility cannot justify a conclusion that the threshold criteria are satisfied". On appeal, it was argued that the judge, having found there was a real possibility of sexual abuse, had erred not taking into account the allegations of sexual abuse in his assessment of the children's welfare at the welfare stage. This was despite the balance of psychiatric evidence being unanimously to the effect that sexual abuse had probably occurred. It was argued that s.1 should be approached differently from s.31 because under s.1 the child's welfare was paramount and this "justified and indeed required the court to act on possibilities rather than on proof or preponderance of probability". These arguments were rejected: "They amount to the assertion that under s.1 the welfare of the child dictates the court should act on suspicion or doubts, rather than facts. To our minds the welfare of the child dictates the exact opposite".[301] *Re H* was followed (see Freeman, 2000b, p.551 for a critical comment). Lord Nicholls in *Re O* follows the Court of Appeal's reasoning in *Re M and R*: at the welfare stage "the court should proceed on the footing that the unproven allegations are no more than that".[302]

(ix) The care plan

As far as the future is concerned, the court must consider whether it is better for the child to make any order than to make no order at all.[303] To this end it must consider the local authority's care plans. Through not in the original Children Act[304] it is long-established practice that a local authority applying for a care order must submit a care plan.[305] This is now a statutory obligation. The care plan will suggest where the child should live and what contact there should be with family. The court can suggest alterations to the care plan, but it cannot attach conditions to a care order.[306] If the court is not satisfied that the plan is in the child's best interests, and it suggests changes which the local authority rejects, it can refuse to make an order.

But what if the local authority subsequently deviates from the care plan submitted to the court? Concern has been expressed over the lack of control regarding the implementation of a care plan once a care order has been made. Children, particularly those without parents actively interested in them, might be vulnerable and allowed to drift in care. In *Re S (Minors) (Care Order: Implementation of Care Plan); Re W (Minors) (Care Order: Adequacy of Care Plan); Re W (Minors) (Care Order: Adequacy of Care Plan)*,[307] two local authorities had failed to implement the care plans. The Court of Appeal identified gaps in the Children Act 1989 in respect of care plans and proposed ways in which these gaps could be filled, including starring essential milestones in the care plan, which if not met would enable the child's guardian or the local authority to apply to the court for directions. The House of Lords allowed the appeals. Lord Nicholls said:

"Where a care order is made the responsibility for the child's care is with the authority rather than the court. The court retains no supervisory role, monitoring the discharge of its responsibilities. That was the intention of Parliament".[308]

The judicial innovation of "starred milestones"—allegedly to make the 1989 Act compatible with human rights and therefore justified by s.3 of the Human Rights Act 1998—went well beyond the bounds of interpretation required by s.3, and was tantamount to legislation. But the Lords agreed problems had been identified and, as a result, s.118 of the Adoption and Children Act 2002 was passed. This requires local authorities to keep care plans under review or make a new one where necessary, and to appoint a person whose task it is to participate in the review, monitor the authority's functions and, where appropriate, refer the care plan to a CAFCASS officer who has the power to refer the matter back to the court. The success of this provision is dependent on the willingness of the local authority to refer the matter to CAFCASS and also upon what CAFCASS then does, and how expeditiously. The question of whether courts should have more power remains.

THE ORDERS

The court can make a number of orders. It can make no order at all. It can make a s.8 order, a supervision order or a care order. If the threshold criteria have not been satisfied, it can still make a s.8 order: consequently, it is possible for the child not to be returned to parents but for a residence order to be made in favour of grandparents, for example. Nor should the duties in Pt III of the Act be overlooked. The essential question revolves around the amount of control required to protect the child. A care order gives the local authority more control than a supervision order, and this gives it more control than a residence order (though this can be made with a supervision order).[309] If the court is not in a position to make a final order, it can make an interim order.[310]

(i) The care order

A care order places the child in the care of a designated local authority.[311] It then becomes the duty of the local authority to receive the child into their care and keep him in care while the order remains in force.[312] The order vests parental responsibility in the authority.[313] Parents do not lose their parental responsibility upon the making of a care order,[314] but the authority has the power to determine the extent to which a parent (or guardian, special guardian, step-parent with parental responsibility) may meet his/her parental responsibility, insofar as it is necessary to do so) to safeguard or promote the child's welfare.[315] The parental responsibility acquired by a local authority is subject to limitations: they cannot cause a child to be brought up in any religious persuasion other than that s/he would have been brought up in if no order had made; they cannot agree or refuse to agree to an adoption order or appoint a guardian; they cannot cause the child to be known by a new surname without the written consent of every person with parental responsibility or the leave of the court. The child cannot be removed fron the UK without the written consent of persons with parental responsibility or the court's leave.[316]

A care order lasts until a child is 18[317]—this may soon be extended to 21—unless it is brought to an end earlier. An application to discharge the order can be made by any person with parental responsibility, the child himself or the designated authority.[318] A person who does not have parental responsibility—a grandparent for example—can, with the leave of the court, apply for a residence order and, if this is granted, the care order is discharged.[319] The making of an adoption order (or placement for an adoption order) also ends any order made under the Children Act 1989.[320]

(ii) The supervision order

A supervision order puts the child under the supervision of a designated local authority or a probation officer.[321] It does not vest parental responsibility in the local authority. It is the duty of the supervisor to advise, assist and befriend the supervised child (and not the parent); to take such steps as are reasonably necessary to give effect to the order; and, where the order is not wholly compiled with or the supervisor considers it is no longer necessary to consider whether or not to apply to the court for its variation or discharge.[322]

The supervision order lasts for one year (though it can be less).[323] It can be extended on application of the supervisor to a maximum of three years.[324] It cannot be converted into a care order: if that is what is required it needs to be applied for, and the threshold criteria need to be satisfied again.

A supervision order subjects the supervised child to directions by the supervisor: s/he can be required to live at a specific place, to present him or herself to a specified person and to participate in specified activities, such as education and training.[325] A supervision order may also include a requirement that a "responsible person" take all reasonable steps to ensure the child complies with any direction given by the supervisor.[326] The responsible person must consent to this. The supervisor cannot give directions about the child's medical or psychiatric examination or treatment,[327] but the court can make directions regarding this.[328] But a child of sufficient understanding to make an informed decision may refuse to consent to this.[329]

(iii) Choosing between them

The threshold criteria for care and supervision orders are the same. But the orders are very different. In particular, the care order, but not the supervision order, vests parental responsibility in the local authority. And, second, where there is a care order the local authority has a duty to look after and safeguard and promote the child's welfare.[330] This is not the case with supervision orders. Supervision, it has been said, is not a "watered down version of care".[331] Since a care order is the more "draconian" order, there must be strong and cogent reasons to make a care order rather than a supervision order.

If the local authority wishes to remove the child from parents this can only be effected by a care order.[332] Where there has been serious harm or sexual abuse, it has been said that a care order is the appropriate order to make.[333] Since a supervision order requires co-operation between parents and the local authority, one is appropriate only where there is at least a reasonable relationship between parents and the authority.[334] Clearly, where the authority wishes to make decisions about the child, for example about his education, a care order which gives it parental responsibility is the route to pursue. A good example of this is *Re V (Care or Supervision Order)*:[335] the child, a boy nearing his 17th birthday, suffered from cerebral palsy. His mother wished to keep him away from the special school at which he was a weekly boarder. The advantages of the school were such he was likely to suffer significant harm if deprived of the opportunities the school could give him during the crucial last 12 months of his minority. The Court of Appeal substituted a care order for the order made by the judge (a supervision order with conditions, which could not anyway be made). It should be stressed that a care order was thought appropriate here even though there was no intention to remove the boy from his parents' care. The case is also instructive for the sensitive handling of a learning disabled child's wishes and feelings.

Courts make supervision orders less frequently than care orders: in 2004 there were 3,012 supervision orders and 7,796 care orders.[336] This may reflect local authorities reluctance to secure what they consider to be a weak order. But it may be that a result of human rights legislation will be to encourage courts to make supervision orders since they are less intrusive into family life.[337]

(iv) Interim orders

If the court is not in a position to make a final order it may make an interim care or interim supervision order. An interim order cannot be made unless the court "is satisfied that there are reasonable grounds for believing that the circumstances with respect to the child are as mentioned in section 31(2)".[338] The court does not have to be satisfied that the threshold conditions exist, only that there are reasonable grounds for believing that they do. The purpose of an interim care order is "to enable the court to safeguard the welfare of a child until such time as the court is in a position to decide whether or not it is in the best interests of the child to make a care order".[339] An interim care order is "an essentially impartial step, favouring neither one side nor the other, and affording no one, least of all the local authority … an opportunity for tactical or adventitious advantage".[340] The interim order is "a holding position".[341] Courts must bear in mind that not making a final decision causes delay, and this in itself may prejudice the welfare of the child. They must also recognise that even temporary removal of a child may breach the parents' human rights. It is also now clear that, as Lord Nicholls put it, "an interim care order is not intended to be used as a means by which the court may continue to exercise a supervisory role over the local authority in cases where it is in the best interests of a child that a care order should be made".[342]

Where the court makes an interim order it can give certain directions:[343] this is not so with a full order. The directions are limited to "medical or psychiatric examination or other assessment of the child". In *Berkshire CC v C*[344] this was held to include that the child be assessed by a suitable qualified social worker, a direction that it might be thought interferes with local authority decision-making. Even more controversially, the House of Lords has held that assessments did not have to be of the same type as medical or psychiatric, and that the assessments could include the parents. It held that a condition for residential assessment could be attached to an interim care order.[345] As Lord Browne-Wilkinson sensibly recognised, it is impossible to assess a young child without seeing him with his parents.[346] Of course, the effect of the decision was to compel an authority to spend money (estimated at between £18,000 and £24,000) on a programme which it thought had little prospect of success and might even put the child at risk. It was said that the purpose of s.38(6) is "to enable the court to obtain the information necessary for its own decision, notwithstanding the control over the child which in all other respects rests with the local authority".[347] The balance is a difficult one to achieve. "Assessment", it has subsequently been held, cannot include therapeutic treatment. In this case the judge had made an interim care order and directed residential assessment of the mother at a hospital, despite the local authority's objections. The hospital recommended that the mother be offered intensive psychotherapy. The House of Lords, agreeing with the first instance judge and reversing the Court of Appeal, held that the purpose of s.38(6) was to provide the court with information.[348] Baroness Hale explained:

"What is directed under s.38(6) must clearly be an examination or assessment of the child, including where appropriate her relationship with her parents, the risk that her parents may present to her, and the ways in which those risks may be avoided or managed, all with a view to enabling the court to make the decisions which it has to make under the 1989 Act with the minimum of delay. Any services which are provided for the child and the family must be ancillary to that end. They must not be an end in themselves".[349]

An intriguing argument is that parents have rights under Art.8 of the European Convention for state assistance to enable them to become better parents. The House of Lords firmly rejected any such suggestion.[350] Big questions remain, including who should pay for an assessment. This is not, it is submitted, for the courts to decide, but is a matter for Parliament.

Section 38(6) says a child of sufficient understanding to make an informed decision may refuse to submit to an examination or assessment. This may be a real problem where a young girl is thought to have been sexually abused but is refusing to be examined, perhaps to protect her father. Her best interests may be in conflict with her rights. The courts have not as yet had to resolve this. But it has been held that there is inherent power to override a competent child's refusal to submit to an examination.[351] This is plainly wrong, and should not be followed.

The court may make any number of interim orders: an initial order may last for up to eight weeks, and subsequent orders for a maximum of four weeks.[352]

(v) Exclusion requirements

There is power to attach an exclusion requirement to an interim care (but not interim supervision) order. This power was added to the 1989 Act in 1996.[353] Courts can thus exclude a suspected abuser from the family and thus protect the child without the need to remove him or her. There are three conditions of which the court must be satisfied before it can attach an exclusion requirement:

(i) there is reasonable cause to believe that if a relevant person is excluded from the child's home s/he will cease to suffer (or cease to be likely to suffer) significant harm;

(ii) there is another person (a parent or some other person) living in the home able and willing to give the child the care which it would be reasonable to expect a parent to give; and

(iii) that person consents to the inclusion of the exclusion requirement.

A power of arrest can be attached to an exclusion requirement.[354] As an alternative to attaching an exclusion requirement, the court may accept an undertaking:[355] a power of arrest cannot be attached to this.[356]

There is no evidence of how much use is made of exclusion requirements. Much depends upon local authorities' willingness to request them and of the attitudes of the other person (in practice invariably the mother) who have to choose between her partner and her child.[357]

(vi) Discharge of orders

Care orders may be discharged. An application may be made by any person with parental responsibility, the child him or herself or the local authority.[358] Most are made by local authorities: they are required at every statutory review of a child in their care to consider whether to apply for a discharge. The court may, instead of discharging the care order, make a supervision order.[359] The threshold conditions need not be proved again.[360] The paramountcy principle governs.[361]

There is no provision in the legislation which could enable a court to postpone the discharge of a care order to enable a phased return of the child to his family (Lowe and Douglas, 2006, p.789).

Applications for the discharge or variation of a supervision order may be made by any person with parental responsibility, the child him or herself or the supervisor.[362] A person with whom the child is living can apply to vary a requirement which affects him/her made under the supervision order.[363] Again, the paramountcy principle governs. The court cannot substitute a care order unless the threshold conditions are satisfied.

LOCAL AUTHORITIES AND WARDSHIP

Until the Children Act 1989 local authorities were able to use wardship to get children into care and to keep them there (Masson and Morton, 1989). Indeed, in 1989 two-thirds of wardship applications were by local authorities. The Children Act 1989 restricts the local authority's recourse to wardship in four ways.

First, the High Court's powers to commit a child to care are abolished.[364]

Second, the inherent jurisdiction of the High Court cannot be exercised to require a child to be placed in care, supervised by a local authority or accommodated by or on behalf of a local authority.[365]

Third, if the local authority wishes to apply to the court for an order under inherent jurisdiction, it must obtain leave and satisfy conditions.[366] The court must be satisfied that the result could not be achieved by the local authority applying for an order other than by exercise of the court's inherent jurisdiction, and there is "reasonable cause" to believe that the child will suffer significant harm if the jurisdiction is not exercised. It seems that the authority has to satisfy the same test as for a care order, even though it does not wish to acquire parental responsibility. Would not a lower standard have served the interests of the inherent jurisdiction where sensitive medical issues have been involved: sterilisation of the learning disabled,[367] overruling a 16-year-old anorexic's refusal to be treated,[368] emergency medical treatment of a child in care including life-saving treatment.[369] Another example is an injunction to prevent a violent father discovering his child's whereabouts.[370]

Fourth, the High Court cannot exercise inherent jurisdiction "for the purpose of conferring on any local authority power to determine any question ... in connection with any aspect of parental responsibility for a child".[371] It cannot therefore confer on a local authority parental responsibility that it does not already have. Is there a distinction between asking the court for powers and asking the court to exercise its own powers? In *Devon CC v S*[372] Thorpe J. seemed to accept this distinction. He held it to be proper for a local authority to invite the court to exercise its inherent jurisdiction to protect children, in this case by restricting a non-family member, a paedophile, from contacting or communicating with the child.[373]

These restrictions are consistent with the ideology of the legislation. It is right that state intervention into the lives of families should be circumscribed, and not left to depend on a judge's interpretation of welfare. But some cases of abuse may slip through the net. This, at least, was the concern (Freeman, 1992, pp.111–112); but it is doubtful whether it has happened.

10

UNDERSTANDING CHILDREN IN CARE

CHILDREN IN CARE

Children in care, "children of the state" as they have been called (Stein, 1988; Freeman, 1983, p.147), are a vulnerable minority. Many of them are "born to fail" (Wedge and Prosser, 1973), and they tend to come from families who have "failed". "Being in care", one child in the *Who Cares?* Project, 30 years ago, said, "you've got a cross on your back. You feel marked" (Page and Clark, 1977, p.17).

In 2003 there were 376, 000 children in need;

there were 26,600 on child protection registers;

there were 61,000 who were "looked after" at 31 March 2003;

of these 41,100 were in foster care;

and 5,900 in residential care, including secure units;

3,400 children in care were placed for adoption.[1]

Over several decades there have been continuing concerns about children growing up in care (Kahan 1979, 1994; Parker *et al.*, 1980; Sinclair and Gibbs, 1998). It is estimated that 27 per cent of looked after children of school age during 2001–2002 held statements of special educational needs: compared with national figures for all children in England, looked after children are almost nine times more likely to have such a statement. Looked after children of the age of criminal responsibility (ten) are three times more likely to be cautioned or convicted of an offence than others: almost 10 per cent of children looked after for a year or more who are ten or over had been convicted or subject to a final warning or reprimand during the year. This compares with 3.6 per cent for all children (quoted in Rose *et al.*, 2006, p.25).

Since 1997, government policy has specifically aimed at improving outcomes for these vulnerable children through such initiatives and programmes as *Quality Protects, Choice Protects* and *Every Child Matters,* some reference to which has been made in Chapter 6.[2]

THE LOCAL AUTHORITY'S DUTIES

The Children Act 1989 provides the legal framework for working with children in need and their families.[3] The Act imposes a number of duties on the local authority in respect of children "looked after" by them. The duties to children being "looked after" apply to children accommodated and to children subject to care orders.[4] The duties are the same whether or not the children are subject to care orders though, as we have seen, where there is a care order the local authority has parental responsibility and thus greater control.[5]

It is the duty of a local authority looking after a child to "safeguard and promote" the child's welfare and to make such use of services available for children cared for by their own parents "as appears to the authority reasonable".[6] These need not be services provided by the local authority itself. Before making any decision about a child they are looking after, or proposing to look after, a local authority is, so far as is reasonably practicable, to ascertain the wishes and feelings of the child, his/her parents, persons with parental responsibility and any other person whose wishes and feelings the authority considers relevant regarding the matter to be decided.[7] "Child" is not qualified by a test as to understanding, so that any child who can communicate wishes and feelings should be listened to. "Parent" includes the unmarried father. They also include all the relevant statutory agencies which have been involved with the child. The child's GP and school may be consulted.[8]

In making decisions "due consideration" is to be given to the wishes and feelings of the child, such as have been ascertained (having regard to age and understanding), to such wishes and feelings of parents, persons with parental responsibility and others the authority considers relevant, and "to the child's religious persuasion, racial origin and cultural and linguistic background".[9]

The 2004 Children Act has added the duty to safeguard and promote the welfare of a child looked after by promoting the child's educational achievement.[10]

(i) Race matters

The emphasis on race, religion, culture and language is underscored by provisions in Sch.2 of the 1989 Act regarding race.[11] Every local authority in making arrangements about day care or encouraging people to act as foster parents is to have regard to "the different racial groups to which children within their area who are in need belong".[12] And *Principles and Practice in Regulations and Guidance* also emphasises this: "since discrimination of all kinds is an everyday reality in many children's lives, every effort must be made to ensure that agency services and practices do not reflect or reinforce it".[13] The *Guidance* regards ethnic origin, cultural background and religion as "important factors for consideration".[14] It stresses that where reuniting the child with his or her family is the goal, there is greater chance of success if the foster parents are of similar ethnic origin. But it acknowledges that "there may be circumstances in which placement with a family of different ethnic origin is the best choice for a particular child".[15] Examples are where there are strong links with prospective foster parents; a child's preference and need to remain close to school, friends and family where ethnic appropriate foster parents cannot be found in the locality; and children with special needs. In addition, siblings or step-siblings who are not of the same ethnic origin may need placement together.[16]

In relation to children of mixed ethnic origins, the *Guidance* advocates "placement in a family which reflects as nearly as possible the child's ethnic origins".[17] It adds that the choice should be influenced by the child's previous family experience.[18]

(ii) Rehabilitation with family

There is a duty to encourage rehabilitation with the family. To this end, it is provided that, unless to do so would not be reasonably practicable or consistent with the child's welfare, the authority should make arrangements for the child to live with his family.[19] Accommodation should be near the child's home,[20] and siblings should be accommodated together.[21]

(iii) Protecting the public

The local authority is allowed to derogate from its duties to protect the public from "serious injury".[22]

A local authority can keep a child who is "looked after" by it in secure accomodation for up to 72 hours in any period of 28 days without a court order. To do so for a longer period of time requires a court order. The child must have a history of absconding, be likely to abscond and if he does so to suffer significant harm or be likely to injure himself or other persons. A child's liberty cannot be restricted unless one of the criteria is met. The paramountcy principle does not apply to court decisions; nor does s.1(5) have any application.[23]

(iv) Providing accomodation

The local authority must provide accommodation and maintain children they are looking after.[24] Accommodation may be with a family, a relative, any other suitable person (a foster parent) "on such terms as to payment by the authority and otherwise as the authority may determine".[25]

It may also be in an appropriate children's home, community home, voluntary home, registered children's home, home with special facilities. An important option is to allow the child to stay at home, subject or not to supervision. In making such a decision there is a need to balance the rehabilitative goal with the need to protect the child's welfare. There are regulations providing safeguards where the child is allowed "home on trial" (Freeman, 1992, pp.122–123).

(v) The Human Rights Act 1998

When the Children Act was passed in 1989 few, if any, gave any thought to the European Convention on Human Rights. But, of course, removing a child from parents is a breach of the rights of both parents and children under Art.8(1). It must therefore be justified under Art.8(2). This has already been discussed.[26] But the obligation to respect family life is a continuing one and remains while the child is in care. The European Court of Human Rights observed in *L v Finland*:

"... taking a child into care should normally be regarded as a temporary measure to be discontinued as soon as circumstances permit ... any measures of implementation of temporary care should be consistent with the ultimate aim of reuniting the natural parent and child. ... A fair balance has to be struck between the interests of the child in remaining in public care and those of the parent in being reunited with the child ... in carrying out this balancing exercise, the Court will attach particular importance to the best interests of the child, which, depending on their nature and seriousness, may override those of the parent. In particular, the parent cannot be entitled under Art.8 of the Convention to have such measure taken as would harm the child's health and development".[27]

It follows that care measures should be seen as temporary, and rehabilitation should be the goal. Even so, circumstances may dictate that the child's interests in remaining in care override those of the parents in being reunited with her/him.[28] It also follows that contact between parents and children should be valued, and that where it is restricted limits which are put on it must be justified as necessary and proportionate under Art.8(2).[29] The burden of justifying restrictions on contact is on the local authority.

CONTACT WITH PARENTS

Contact between parents (and others) and children in care is a most significant area of contention. In 1983 parents were given the right to apply for an "access order" where access was "terminated", or the local authority refused to make arrangements for it.[30] But "terminate" did not preclude an authority regulating it "restrictively".[31] The Review of Child Care Law in 1985 expressed concern that "family links [were] seldom given much consideration",[32] and that there was little practical help offered to encourage parents' visits. Research at this time found that 40 per cent of children in care for three years or more had lost contact with their parents by the time two years had elapsed, and yet there were no social work reasons for the exclusion of the family in two-thirds of the cases (Millham *et al.*, 1986).

There is now a presumption of reasonable contact.[33] The authority has a duty to allow the child reasonable contact with:

(a) his parents;

(b) any guardian of his;

(c) any person, who before the care order was made, has a residence order;

(d) any person who had care of the child under the inherent jurisdiction of the High Court before the care order was made.[34]

The parents include the unmarried father.

Re E (A Minor) (Care Order: Contact) confirms that there is a presumption of reasonable contact.[35] Simon Brown L.J. gave four reasons for the presumption. First, it gives the child the security of knowing that his parents love him and are interested in his welfare. Second, it reassures the child that he hasn't been abandoned. Third, it enables the child to commit him or herself to the substitute family with the "seal of approval" of birth parents. Fourth, it gives the child the "necessary sense of family and personal identity". And, while it might be thought to undermine the chances of a permanent placement, the judge explained, correctly, that it could increase the chances of such a placement, whether on a long-term fostering basis or by adoption.[36]

Subject to any court order, it is for the authority to decide what is reasonable contact in the circumstances.[37] The authority's view of what is reasonable must safeguard and promote the child's welfare because of the duty in s.22(3), which has already been discussed.[38] The *Guidance* advises that the degree of contact should not necessarily remain static: the authority may "plan for the frequency or duration of contact to increase or decrease over time".[39] The local authority should indicate its intentions in the plan[40] which is submitted to the court before the care order is made and, where possible, should have discussed this with the child and the parents. If there are disagreements these can be resolved by the court making an order as to the degree of contact: this may improve such conditions, for example, as to time, place, amount and supervision, as the court considers appropriate.[41]

The court can make an order of its own motion if it considers that the order should be made.[42] It is specifically empowered to make a contact order when it makes a care order.[43] The court may also make an order "as it considers appropriate" on an application made by the authority or the child,[44] or by parents (including the unmarried father), a guardian, any person who had a residence order or care and control under the High Court's inherent jurisdiction before the care order was made, or by any person who has obtained the leave of the court (the most likely applicants for leave being grandparents).[45]

Only the local authority and the child may apply for an order for contact to be refused.[46] Since there is no duty on the child to maintain contact, s/he can refuse to see a person named in the order even without applying to the court. As a result, the child will only need to apply to the court where there is no other way of avoiding contact. The local authority only has to get the court's consent to refuse contact to those persons in respect of whom it has a duty to maintain contact (that is, those persons listed in s.34(1), and above). So, it can refuse contact to others, for example grandparents, without the need to obtain an order.

If the court makes an order for contact, the local authority may refuse to comply for seven days, provided it is satisfied that this is necessary to safeguard or promote the child's welfare and it is a matter of urgency.[47] The *Guidance* describes this as a "serious step which should not be undertaken lightly".[48] When an authority has decided to refuse contact, otherwise required either by s.34(1) or by court order, it has "as soon as the decision has been made" to notify the child, if s/he is of sufficient understanding, the parents, any guardian, persons in whose favour there was a residence order before the care order was made, a person who had care by virtue of an order made by the High Court exercising its inherent jurisdiction, and any other person whose wishes and feelings the authority considers relevant.[49]

There is also provision in the Regulations for a local authority to depart from the terms of a court order when all concerned are agreeable to the new arrangement.[50] This provision allows for "flexibility and partnership in contact arrangements",[51] and obviates the need to go back to court when all concerned agree a new arrangement.

The court's powers are governed by s.1. It must therefore regard the child's welfare as paramount,[52] consider the checklist of factors in s.1(3), and make an order only where it is better for the child than not making an order.[53] The application of the paramountcy principle is far from straightforward when more than one child is involved.[54] In *Birmingham City Council v H*,[55] both the mother, who was 15, and the child were in care. The mother sought contact with the baby. It was in her best interests that contact should be allowed, in his that it should be stopped, and a permanent placement sought for him. The House of Lords ruled that, since s.34(4) made it clear that the subject-matter of the application is the child in care in respect of whom the order is being sought, it was the baby's welfare, and not the mother's, which was paramount. But what if a child in care seeks contact with another child, for example a sibling? There is a dictum in *Birmingham* to the effect that the applicant's welfare would still be paramount,[56] through it is not easy to see why. But in *Re F (Contact: Child in Care)*,[57] in which a child in care sought contact with four younger siblings who were not in care but were living with their parents who were opposed to such contact, it was held that an application (under s.34(2)) was misplaced because the parents could not be forced to permit the contact. The appropriate remedy was to seek a s.8 contact order.[58] The judge (Wilson J.) made further observations of which note may be taken.[59] They demonstrate the over-complexity of the issues. First, if the child is seeking contact with children who are not in care and are willing to see him—not the case here—it is the interests of the applicant child that are paramount, if the application is made under s.34(2), but the interests of the other children if it is sought under s.8. Wilson J. did not consider the position where both the applicant child and the other children are in care. Following the *Birmingham* analysis, it would seem that it is the children in respect of whom the order is sought whose interests are paramount. This has been criticised (see Douglas, 1994) for requiring paramountcy to be determined by who brought the application. But in this context is there a better approach?

CHALLENGING THE LOCAL AUTHORITY

We have already seen two ways in which local authority decision-making as regards children in care may be challenged. Decisions about contact may be challenged under s.34.[60] It is also possible to apply for the discharge of a care order under s.39.[61] The ideal, as we have seen, is partnership,[62] but partnerships are not always easy to achieve, and they may break down.

What courses of action are then open to aggrieved parents (and others)?

(i) Representations and complaints

First, there are procedures to hear representations and complaints.[63] All local authorities must have a formal representation or complaints procedure. Complaints may be made by:

"any child who is being looked after ... or who is not being looked after ... but is in need; a parent of his; any person ... [with] parental responsibility for him; any local authority foster parent; or such other person as the authority considers has a sufficient interest to warrant his representations being considered".

Young people can also complain if they consider the authority has not given them adequate preparation for leaving care or adequate after-care.[64] Representations and complaints are thus open to a wide range of people: this must surely include the wider family (*cf.* Bainham, 2005, p.86) and teachers (*cf.* Williams and Jordan 1996, p.338). Children making complaints now have access to an independent advocacy service.[65]

The Act requires that the authority establishes a procedure which provides "an accessible and effective means of representation or complaint where problems cannot otherwise be resolved".[66] The procedure must contain an independent element.[67] What may be complained about? The *Guidance* says included are complaints about day care, services to support children within their family home, accommodation of a child, after-care and decisions relating to the placement of a child or the handling of a child's case. It has now been extended to care, supervision and emergency protection. The placing of a child's name on a Child Protection Register does not have to be included within the scheme.[68] The procedure is discussed elsewhere (Freeman, 1992, pp.143–144; Lowe and Douglas, 2006, p.800). A panel decision is not strictly binding on the authority. However, it would be "an unusual case when a local authority acted otherwise than in accord with the panel's recommendations and the independent person's views".[69] An authority which ignored recommendations or failed reasonably to consider them would expose itself to judicial review.[70]

A complaints procedure is not a substitute for good practice, but should constitute part of good practice. Nor is it a substitute for challenging practices in court through judicial review. Perhaps, rather unfortunately, the courts themselves consider the complaints procedure an adequate substitute for court surveillance.[71] Whether it is, depends on the use made of the complaints mechanism. We know that children are reluctant to complain (Williams and Jordan, 1996), and we know that some serious allegations were, and perhaps still are, ruled outside the remit of complaints procedures (Lindsay, 1991).

(ii) Default powers

Second, there are default powers.[72] If the Secretary of State is satisfied that any local authority has failed, without reasonable excuse, to comply with any of the duties imposed on it by the Act, an order may be made declaring the authority to be in default. Directions may then be given to ensure the duty is compiled with, and they may be enforced by an application to the High Court for judicial review. It is envisaged that this power will only be used in "extreme circumstances"; for example where a local authority "fails to make requisite provision for a class of children".[73] The default powers are unlikely to assist the aggrieved individual.

(iii) Commissioner for Local Administration

Third, complaints may be made to the Commissioner for Local Administration ("the local government ombudsman"). Complaints must relate to maladministration. But "the central concern is with procedural propriety and not the child's welfare" (Lowe and Douglas, 2006, p.803). It is thus of little value in respect of children in care and, not surprisingly, is not much used.

(iv) Wardship and inherent jurisdiction

Fourth, it is necessary to consider wardship and inherent jurisdiction. Before the Children Act 1989, it was held in *A v Liverpool City Council* that local authority decision-making about children in their care could not be challenged through wardship.[74] In *A v Liverpool City Council* itself the House of Lords refused to interfere with a local authority's decision to restrict a mother's contact with her child in care to a monthly one-hour visit at a day nursery. Since the Children Act, it has been impossible for a child to be both in care and a ward of court.[75] *A fortiori*, the principle established in *A v Liverpool City Council* must continue to apply. And, if a challenge were attempted using the High Court's inherent jurisdiction, the courts would surely come to the same conclusion.

(v) Habeas corpus

Fifth, mention should be made of habeas corpus since an attempt was made to invoke this in a recent case.[76] However, Munby J. deprecated its use where care proceedings are "on foot and where the purpose of the application is to challenge the exercise by the local authority of its powers".[77] He also emphasised that habeas corpus protects against unlawful detention or imprisonment: the children in this case were, of course, not "in detention", but simply living with their foster carers.[78]

(vii) Judicial review

Sixth, there is judicial review. Applications are made to the Administrative Court. The focus of the court's investigation is not with the *merits* of the local authority's case but rather with the more limited question of the *legality* of the local authority's decision-making process.[79] Judicial review has been used to question decisions such as to place a child's name on a Child Protection Register,[80] to refuse to accommodate a child,[81] to remove a child from foster parents,[82] to apply for an emergency protection order in respect of a newborn baby,[83] to challenge a local authority's care plan,[84] to decide not to place a child at home on trial with parents.[85] Alternative remedies to judicial review are often thought preferable: for example, the courts encourage recourse to the complaints procedure,[86] and prefer challenges to take place in care proceedings in family courts rather than by invoking public law remedies in the Administrative Court.[87] The same reasoning, we will see, has been adopted in Human Rights Act challenges.[88]

(viii) Suing in negligence

Seventh, there is the possibility of suing in negligence. Those who work in the child protection system are not immune from claims in negligence. The courts have retreated from the position they took in *X (Minors) v Bedfordshire County Council*, in which it was held that the careless performance of a statutory duty did not give rise to any cause of action in the absence of either a right of action for breach of statutory duty or for breach of a common law duty of care.[89] The European Court of Human Rights subsequently held that the striking out of the negligence claims by the House of Lords did not breach Art.6 of the Convention[90] (though, as we shall see,[91] other Articles were breached). Nevertheless, in *Barrett v Enfield LBC*[92] the House of Lords held that a local authority owed a duty of care in negligence to a claimant who had been in their care for 17 years and as a result of a catalogue of errors was deeply disturbed. A distinction was drawn between the decision to take a child into care, which is not normally justiciable, and looking after a child in care, when it might be easier to establish a breach of duty. The *Barrett* decision was followed in *S v Gloucestershire County Council, Tower Hamlets LBC and Havering LBC*.[93] May L.J. stated the law as follows:

"(a) A claim in common-law negligence may be available to a

person who claims to have been damaged by failings of a local authority who were responsible ... for care and upbringing...

(b) the claim will not succeed if the failings alleged comprise actions or decisions by the local authority of a kind which are not justiciable. These may include, but will not be necessarily limited to, policy decisions and decisions about allocating public funds;

(c) the border line between what is justiciable and what is not may in a particular case be unclear...

(d) there may be circumstances in which it will not be just and reasonable to impose a duty of care of the kind contended for...

(e) in considering whether a discretionary decision was negligent, the court will not substitute its view for that of the local authority upon whom the statute has placed the power to exercise the discretion, unless the discretionary decision was plainly wrong. But decisions of ... social workers are capable of being held to have been negligent by analogy with decisions of other professional people ...".[94]

These actions were bought by children who alleged that foster fathers with whom they had been placed had sexually abused them and that in consequence they had suffered physical and long-term psychological damage. Each of the foster fathers was later convicted of sexual offences with children. The Court of Appeal held that Gloucestershire had failed to respond to the abuse by the father after being informed of it, and that this was actionable. More recently, in the case of *W v Essex County Council*,[95] the Court of Appeal allowed children of foster carers who had been sexually abused by a foster child, known by the social worker to be an active sexual abuser, to sue the local authority in negligence. However, it struck out the claim by the foster parents: the House of Lords reinstated this claim. In its view it was not unarguable.[96] The most recent decision is *D v East Berkshire Community Health NHS Trust; MAK v Dewsbury Healthcare NHS Trust; RK v Oldham NHS Trust*.[97] Parents alleged that medical professionals had negligently misdiagnosed child abuse rather than the actual cause of the child's health problems, that this had disrupted family life and had caused the parents psychiatric injury. They sought damages in negligence against the NHS Trusts. They failed. The House of Lords held that healthcare and other child care professionals did not owe a common law duty of care to parents not to make negligent allegations of child abuse. Such a duty would result in a conflict of interest: the doctor was under an obligation to act in the best interests of the child, rather than in the interests of the parent, and if his suspicions were aroused he had to be able to act single-mindedly in the child's interests without regard to the possibility of a claim by the parent. The seriousness of child abuse demanded that professionals should not be subjected to conflicting duties when deciding whether a child might have been abused, and what further steps to take. Lord Rodger was concerned that if parents could sue, then so could other members of the family and teachers and child-minders—anyone who might come under suspicion of having abused the child.[98] But Lord Bingham, in a powerful dissent, reminded us that these actions would succeed in France and Germany.[99] *East Berkshire* may be seen as an attempt to rein in liability, but it may be over-alarmist in its concerns about an opening of the floodgates. Following *East Berkshire*, it has recently been held that the local authority did not owe a duty of care to the parents of a child who was the subject of a child abuse investigation.[100]

(viii) Suing for breach of human rights

Eighth, the local authority can be sued for breach of human rights. To succeed it must be shown that a Convention right has been breached: the two most obvious are Arts 6 and 8, though other articles, for example Art.3, may also be relevant.

Local authorities are "public authorities" for the purposes of the Human Rights Act 1998, and must therefore act in a way which is compatible with the Convention.[101] Any person who is the victim of an unlawful act of a local authority may bring an application under s.7 of the Human Rights Act. Free-standing applications are discouraged. Certainly, where the complaint arises before the making of a final care order that the local authority's proposals infringe the human rights of either the child or anyone else, it "can and normally should be dealt with within the context of care proceedings". Only in a "wholly exceptional case" would it even be appropriate "to make a separate or free-standing Human Rights application in such a case".[102]

Claims not so arising should be brought in an "appropriate court or tribunal".[103] This is no definition of this: Hale J. was of the opinion that a claim against a local authority might be brought "as an ordinary civil claim in the county or the High Court".[104] The claimant must show s/he is a "victim", that is a person directly affected by the act or omission.[105] Being a secondary victim is insufficient—the father of the boy beaten with a garden cane by his step-father was not, therefore, a victim.[106] And there must be no other appropriate remedy. The action must be brought within one year of the act complained about.[107]

There have been many free-standing applications under s.7. One was brought in *Re M (Care: Challenging Decisions by Local Authority)*.[108] Whether, given the ruling referred to above,[109] it should have been free-standing, rather than an issue raised in the discharge of care proceedings, may be doubted. The case concerned a child of 18 months, whose parents were alcohol and drug abusers, who had been in care since she was ten days old. Her parents separated when she was two months old. The care plan proposed she should live with her mother. If that broke down, with her father, if he co-operated with the drugs team. Only if both these options failed was adoption to be considered. It may be wondered why adoption was not the initial plan. After the mother became desperately ill from drug and alcohol poisoning, the child was placed with foster parents. A permanency planning meeting then took place in the absence of the parents and their solicitors. The conclusion was reached that there was no prospect of the child living with either parent, and adoption was now to be considered. The parents claimed the decision was incompatible with their right to family life under Art.8(1), and that it was unlawful by virtue of s.6, and that the combined effects of ss 6, 7 and 8 required that the current plans of the authority should be reviewed and sanctioned by the court. The parents also applied under s.39 of the Children Act for discharge of the care order. It was held that the authority had acted unlawfully by not involving the parents sufficiently to protect their interests. The local authority's decision was quashed. In addition, there was no doubt that the local authority had made a fundamental change of plan, and that in such a situation the local authority's acts or proposed acts could be examined by the court in free-standing proceedings under the Human Rights Act. The court then had the power under s.8(1) to grant any relief or remedy or make an order, while ensuring that any extension of function was used sparingly and not for the perpetuation of adversarial issues. The judge gave directions for a full hearing of the review issues and of the applications for the discharge of the care order. Nice points of legality were thus observed, as they should be, but where were the interests of the child in this? Could there ultimately be a better conclusion for her than adoption? Children have human rights too—though this is sometimes rather easily overlooked.

11
UNDERSTANDING ADOPTION AND SPECIAL GUARDIANSHIP

INTRODUCTION

Adoption was only established in England in 1926.[1] It had been resisted. Informal adoptions, which had no legal effect, took place, on what scale it is not known, for many years before adoption was introduced.[2] It was the large numbers of children orphaned by the First World War which finally convinced Parliament that the institution of adoption was needed.

Adoption became a very popular institution. In 1968 there were 24,831 orders. There has been a steep decline since. 1968 saw the introduction of "legal" abortion,[3] the mid to late 1960s the increased availability of contraception particularly the pill. It also became easier for single mothers to keep their children: there were better employment prospects, and less stigma attached to illegitimacy. By 2003 there were only 5,354 adoption orders. The decline is attributable to the availability of many fewer babies for adoption: in the late 1960s 40 per cent of children adopted were under 12 months old; by 2003 only 213 babies under a year old (4 per cent) were adopted.[4] The infertile have turned instead to assisted conception with one cycle of IVF treatment being offered on the NHS.[5]

There has also been a decline in the number of adoptions by birth parents and their new partners.[6] These have been discouraged since the early 1970s:[7] in 1971 there were 10,751 step-parent adoption orders, by 2004 there were only 1,107 such orders. The introduction of special guardianship[8] is expected to reduce the number further.

Most adoptions today are of older children. Many have special needs, many have been damaged by abuse or neglect. Adoption today is a child care service focused more on the needs of children than on the desires of adults to become parents.

Apart from the parental order,[9] adoption is the only institution which severs the legal relationship between birth parents and their child and establishes a new one between the child and the adoptive parent.[10] It is the only mechanism by which parents can lose their parental responsibility. It is permanent—the only child-related order that lasts for life—and irrevocable (subject to one minor exception[11]). This latter point is illustrated by the case of *Re B (Adoption: Jurisdiction to Set Aside)*.[12] A child of mixed English Catholic and Muslim Kuwaiti origins was adopted by a Jewish couple and brought up as a Jew. Thirty-five years later he applied to have the adoption order set aside. The Court of Appeal held that there was no inherent power in the court to set aside an adoption order.

"To allow considerations such as those put forward ... to invalidate an otherwise properly made adoption order would ... undermine the whole basis on which adoption orders are made, namely that they are final and for life".[13]

ADOPTION AND HUMAN RIGHTS

It would be possible to construct models of adoption which were incompatible with Art.8 of the European Convention on Human Rights. But English law unquestionably complies with it. Hale L.J. in *Re B (Adoption by One Natural Parent to Exclusion of Other)*[14] conceded that adoption orders were interferences by a public authority with exercises of the right to respect for family life: "the most drastic interference with the right which is permitted by the law".[15] On the other hand, she observed, it is a "most valuable way of supplying a child with the 'family for life' to which everyone ought to be entitled and of which some children are so tragically deprived".[16] Provided the law is complied with—for example the consents of parents with parental responsibility are obtained or properly dispensed with—human rights challenges are unlikely to be upheld. Thus, in *Scott v United Kingdom*,[17] an alcoholic mother complained that her Art.8 rights had been infringed when she was not invited to a meeting at which the decision not to persist with rehabilitation and to pursue adoption was taken, and when the court subsequently dispensed with her consent to adoption. The European Court of Human Rights ruled that interference with her family life was justified in the child's interests. The European Court agreed with the English court's finding that it was unacceptable to expose a child suffering from foetal alcohol syndrome to further uncertainty and the risk of suffering (yet more) serious harm.

The European Court of Human Rights has also ruled that there is no right to adopt. French law, which denied a single homosexual man such a right, was held not to violate the Convention.[18]

THE PROFESSIONALISATION OF ADOPTION

When adoption was first introduced it was largely unregulated. Until 1982 there was no restriction on individuals placing children for adoption: private arrangements through doctors or solicitors were common practice—the Houghton Committee noting that babies were sometimes placed for adoption with casual acquaintances.[19] The Children Act 1975 outlawed independent placements,[20] unless the proposed adopter was a relative of the child or was acting pursuant to a court order. The ban has been strengthened in the latest legislation.[21] For example, it is no longer confined to domestic placements. But the Act does not stop private fostering placements, nor does it prevent such foster parents from subsequently applying to adopt.[22]

Adoption has now been "professionalised" (Lowe, 2000, p.325). Persons who wish to adopt a non-relative must be approved by an adoption agency.[23] They go through a screening process by an adoption panel.[24] This examines their commitment to, and motive for, wishing to adopt. It must decide whether the prospective adopter(s) is a suitable person to adopt the child. It must also consider and make recommendations as to whether the child should be placed for adoption.[25]

Every local authority must maintain a service designed to meet the needs, in relation to adoption of:

"(a) children who may be adopted, their parents and guardians,
 (b) persons wishing to adopt a child,
 (c) adopted persons, their parents, natural parents and former guardians".[26]

There is a duty to provide adoption support both pre-and post-adoption.

ADOPTION AND THE CHILD'S BEST INTERESTS

Courts have always had to be satisfied that an adoption order was in the best interests of the child. The Houghton Committee suggested in its Working Paper that the long-term welfare of the child should be the first and paramount consideration in resolving conflicts over adoption.[27] But in its final report, it thought that "the law should recognise that there are a number of interests to be considered and put the interests of the child first among them".[28] The legislation which followed—the first in adoption legislation to give any weighting to the child's welfare—directed courts and adoption agencies to give "first consideration", not paramount consideration, to the need to safeguard and promote the welfare of the child throughout his childhood.[29] This remained the law for over a quarter of a century. It was defended as recognition that there were other interests of which regard should be taken. The character of adoption—its permanence, its irrevocability—distinguished it from other decisions relating to children. But from the child's point of view, decisions about adoption and, for example, residence were both decisions about upbringing and his/her welfare should count in exactly the same way. There were attempts to divide adoption decisions, so that some of them, in particular the decision to dispense with parental consent, should be excluded from the paramountcy principle.[30] Ultimately, this compromise was rejected, and the 2002 Act states that, in coming to a decision relating to the adoption of a child, "the paramount consideration of the court or adoption agency must be the child's welfare, throughout his life".[31] The words "throughout his life" are additional to the paramountcy principle in the Children Act, and reflect the long-term nature of adoption.

The paramountcy principle in the 2002 Act is fleshed out with the statutory checklist,[32] modelled on that in s.1(3) of the Children Act 1989.[33] But this is supplemented by the requirement to consider:

"(c) the relationship which the child has with relatives, and with any other person in relation to whom the court or agency considers the question to be relevant, including—

  (i) the likelihood of any such relationship continuing and value to the child of its doing so,

  (ii) the ability and willingness of any of the child's

relatives, or of any such person, to provide the child
with a secure environment in which the child can
develop, and otherwise to meet the child's needs.
(iii) the wishes and feelings of any of the child's relatives,
or of any such person, about the child."[34]

The emphasis on paramountcy should make it easier to facilitate the adoption process. This is certainly what the Government
intends: it says it is hoping that there will be a 40 per cent
increase in the number of "looked after" children who are
adopted.

Three other considerations may be noted.

First, agencies placing a child for adoption must give "due
consideration to the child's religious persuasion, racial origin
and cultural and linguistic background".[35]

Second, an order should only be made when it is better for the
child than not doing so.[36]

Third, courts and adoption agencies are to bear in mind that,
in general, "any delay in coming to the decision [about adoption]
is likely to prejudice the child's welfare".[37]

WHO MAY BE ADOPTED?

Who may be adopted? Unlike some legal systems, which permit
adults to be adopted,[38] English law only allows children to be
adopted (though if an application is made as regards a person
under 18 an adoption order may be made until the person is
19).[39] The adopted person must be single and have never been
married or entered into a civil partnership.[40]

WHO MAY ADOPT?

The adopter(s) must be 21—if one of them is a parent it is sufficient that one of them is 21, provided the other is 18. The law
does not prescribe a maximum age.[41] Where prospective adopters are older—for example, they are the child's grandparents—
the court will have to consider age when deciding whether an
adoption order is for the child's benefit.

Adoption applications may be made by a couple or by one
person. Before the 2002 Act only a couple who were married to
each other could make a joint adoption application. The 2002 Act
provides that joint applications are permitted by spouses, civil

partners and by "two people (whether of different sexes or the same sex) living in an enduring family relationship".[42] Although a married couple and civil partners do not have to be in an "enduring family relationship", adoption agencies must have regard to the need for stability and permanence in their relationship.[43]

With the exception of a step-parent application (discussed below), an adoption order may not be made on the sole application of a married person, or civil partner, unless the spouse or partner cannot be found or is by reason of ill health (physical or mental) incapable of making an application for an adoption order, or, if the spouses or partners have separated, are living apart and the separation is likely to be permanent.[44]

STEP-PARENTS AND ADOPTION

Whether the law should allow step-parent adoptions has long been controversial. The Houghton Committee was concerned with the large number of them.[45] They could distort family relationships and damage the child. It recommended that step-parents should apply to become guardians. The Adoption Act 1976 directed courts to dismiss applications for adoption by step-parents after a divorce if they considered that the matter would be better dealt with by an application for a custody order.[46] This was initially taken to be clear discouragement of step-parent adoptions.[47] But in *Re D (Minors) (Adoption by Step-Parents)*, the Court of Appeal held that an application for an adoption order should be dismissed only if it could be shown that the matter could be better dealt with by a joint custody order.[48] These provisions did not survive the Children Act 1989. Step-parent adoption was questioned again during the Adoption Law Review:[49] one idea which was mooted was that a step-parent adoption should be revocable where the new marriage ended in divorce or death before the child was 18.[50] This idea was dropped. A second one, that step-parents should be able to acquire parental responsibility by agreement or court order, was taken up and, as we have seen,[51] is in the Adoption and Children Act 2002.

The 2002 Act has not banned step-parent adoptions. Since there is unlikely to be further adoption reform for some time, this question is not going to be re-opened soon. There are some cases where it may be appropriate—where the other birth parent has

died, or perhaps where the child wants it[52]—but in most cases
parental responsibility should be status enough for the step-
parent.

ADOPTION BY RELATIVES

Adoption by relatives also raises concerns.[53] Most such prospective adopters are grandparents. Age is clearly a concern, but
distortion of relationships perhaps a greater one, if not as great
as it was. It was as a result of concerns voiced by the Houghton
Committee that custodianship was created.[54] Although grandparents did apply for this,[55] the institution did not take on and it
was abolished by the Children Act 1989. Special guardianship,
introduced by the Adoption and Children Act 2002, is not dis-
similar.[56] On an application for adoption courts are able to make
a special guardianship order of their own motion.[57] Special
guardianship will suffice for many relatives, but it is thought that
for some relatives, particularly where the parents are dead or
abroad and inaccessible, adoption will remain the preferable
option. There is nothing in the legislation ruling out adoption by
relatives. It is perhaps surprising that they cannot acquire parental responsibility by agreement or court order.[58]

THE NEED FOR CONSENT

Before an adoption order can be made the court must be satisfied
that each parent or guardian consents or consented to a placement order and does not oppose the adoption order or their
consent is dispensed with by the court on a statutory ground.[59]
The new system of placement endeavours to ensure that parental
consent is dealt with before the child has been placed with the
prospective adopters.[60] The new system replaces a procedure
known as "freeing the child for adoption", which was not
judged a success (Lowe and Murch, 2001).

Section 18(1) of the 2002 Act provides that an adoption agency
can only place a child for adoption with prospective adopters
where each parent or guardian has consented to the placement.
Where the agency is a local authority it can do this where it has
obtained a placement order. Before any placement for adoption
may be made the agency must be satisfied that the child should
be placed for adoption.[61] The birth parent(s) retain parental

responsibility: they share this with the adoptive agency and the prospective adopters.[62]

An adoption agency may place a child for adoption where it is satisfied that each parent with parental responsibility or guardian (including special guardian) has consented to the child being placed for adoption and that this consent has not been withdrawn.[63] They may consent to placements with "identified" prospective adopters or any prospective adopters. Adoption law has always been cautious about mothers giving up their babies too soon after birth, and the 2002 Act reflects this policy. The mother's consent remains ineffective if given less than six weeks after the child's birth.[64] However, placements are allowed before this time provided she consents, informally, to this.[65]

At the time of consenting to the placement, a parent may also consent to the making of the adoption order. This consent can be withdrawn. A parent may also give notice to the agency that s/he does not wish to be informed when an application for an adoption order is made.[66] If notice is given, it may be withdrawn. Given the consequences of consenting, the signing of consent to a placement must be witnessed by a CAFCASS officer whose responsibility it is to decide that consent is freely and unconditionally given with full understanding of its consequences.[67]

THE PLACEMENT ORDER

A placement order is an order by a court authorising a local authority to place the child with any prospective adopters who may be chosen by the authority.[68] Local authorities must apply for a placement order if the child is placed for adoption by them or is provided with accommodation by them; no adoption agency is authorised to place the child for adoption; the child has no parent or guardian or the authority considers that the threshold conditions in s.31(2) of the Children Act 1989 are met; and the authority is satisfied that the child ought to be placed for adoption.[69] The court may only make a placement order if the child is subject to a care order or is satisfied that the threshold conditions for making a care order are satisfied or the child has no parent or guardian.[70] The court must be satisfied that each parent or guardian has consented to the placement of the child with any prospective adopters and has not withdrawn that consent or consent has been dispensed with. The paramountcy principle applies. Regard must be had to the checklist. And the court must be satisfied that making the placement order is better for the child than not doing so.[71]

The new placement regime has only been in operation for a short time. Whether it is successful remains to be seen. There is, however, general consensus that it is an improvement over the "freeing" model. No longer should children remain in legal limbo. The rights of birth parents are clearer. Requiring local authorities to obtain a placement order whenever adoption is part of the care plan is also obviously sensible and further integrates adoption into child care. Concern has been expressed that, as with freeing, the process will be slow.[72] This obviously is to the detriment of children. Speeding up the process, while giving due attention to all the interests involved, may require a cultural shift. Is it one the courts are prepared to take (or allow others to take)? There should at least not be human rights concerns: as already indicated,[73] the adoption regime is European Convention compliant.

To re-emphasise, before an adoption order can be made by a court—and only a court may make an adoption order—it must be satisfied "in the case of each parent or guardian of the child":

"(a) that the parent or guardian consents to the making of the adoption order,

(b) that the parent or guardian has consented under section 20 (and has not withdrawn the consent) and does not oppose the making of the adoption order, or

(c) that the parent's or guardian's consent should be dispensed with".[74]

WHOSE CONSENT?

The law requires the consent of each parent or guardian. This is so even if another person or even the local authority also has parental responsibility.[75] "Parent" means a parent with parental responsibility.[76] The unmarried father who has not acquired parental responsibility is not, therefore, a parent.[77] If he acquires parental responsibility after the mother has consented to the child's placement for adoption, he is deemed to have given consent.[78]

"Parent" does not include step-parent, who is not a "parent", even one who has acquired parental responsibility.

"Guardian" embraces guardians formally appointed by individuals or by a court, and special guardians.[79]

(i) The child

The child's consent is not required.[80] It was recommended that an adoption order should not be made in relation to a child of 12 or over unless the court was satisfied either that the child has consented or was incapable of so doing.[81] The 2002 Act did not include any such provision. Its omission is surely wrong. However, since the checklist requires courts and adoption agencies to have regard to "the child's ascertainable wishes and feelings" regarding the adoption decision in the light of the child's understanding[82] (note there is no mention of "age"),[83] it is unlikely than an adoption order will be made against the wishes of an older child. In *Re M (Adoption or Residence Order)* a residence order was made rather than an adoption order because the 11-year-old child objected to being adopted.[84] This decision antedates any obligation to have regard to the child's wishes and feelings. *A fortiori*, one would expect a similar decision to-day.

(ii) The unmarried father

The unmarried father without parental responsibility is, we have seen, not a "parent". His consent is therefore not required, and he is not automatically a party to the proceedings. The courts have discretion to make him a party.[85] Whether they do so or not, both they and adoption agencies must consider the wishes and feelings of relatives, and this includes fathers.[86] Mothers will sometimes want to hide adoption proceedings from fathers. While in some cases this may be understandable, it has now been ruled that as a matter of practice fathers should be informed of the proceedings unless there is a good reason for not so doing.[87] Where there has been a relationship between the mother and the father, in particular where there is commitment towards the child, the father has Art.8 rights, so that to place the child for adoption without giving him notice would constitute a violation of those rights.[88] Contrast the situation where there has not been cohabitation, no family life for which there could be respect. In such a case it is not necessary that the father be informed of the adoption proceedings.[89]

(iii) Unconditional consent

Consent must be unconditionally given. Until the Adoption Act 1976 it was possible to make consent conditional on the child being brought up in a particular religion.[90] Today, adoption agencies must give "due consideration to the child's religious persuasion, racial origin and cultural and linguistic back-ground".[91] The signing of consent is witnessed by a reporting officer appointed by the court. The officer ensures, so far as is reasonably practical, that the parent is giving consent unconditionally and will have full understanding of what is involved.

(iv) Dispensing with consent

Consent may be dispensed with. There are now just two grounds; there were previously seven, most of them fault-based. The 2002 Act lays down two grounds, one of which is entirely new, the other being closely modelled on the previous law. In applying the new grounds, the court is bound by the para-mountcy principle in the 2002 Act, and must have regard to the checklist in s.1(4).[92]

The first ground, which has already been amended by the Mental Capacity Act 2005 in relation to lack of capacity to consent,[93] enables consent to be dispensed with when the parent or guardian cannot be found or lacks capacity within the meaning of the Mental Capacity Act 2005 to give consent.[94]

It is not easy to establish that a parent or guardian "cannot be found"; all reasonable and proper steps must be taken, including seeking the assistance of government bodies and local government. On the other hand, the ground has been liberally interpreted where the parent could be found but it would be embarrassing or dangerous to them to make contact. Thus, in *Re R (Adoption)* the parents were in a totalitarian state,[95] and in *Re A (Adoption of a Russian Child)* they were in Russia and it was contrary to Russian law to make contact with the mother.[96]

Dispensing with consent on the grounds of incapacity requires it to be established that the parent is unable to understand the information relevant to the decision, to retain that information, and to use or weigh it as part of the process of making the decision or communicating it.[97] A person is not to be treated as unable to make a decision merely because s/he makes an unwise decision.[98] Someone who can retain information only for short periods of time, for example someone in the early stages of Alzheimer's disease, may still have capacity.[99] That a person is mentally ill, for example suffers from paranoid schizophrenia, does not mean s/he lacks mental capacity.[100]

The other ground for dispensing with consent is that the welfare of the child requires the consent to be dispensed with. This constitutes a major shift in the law. As Bridge and Swindells (2003, p.152) point out, "whereas parents (under the former law) could take a different view of their child's welfare and not be unreasonable, the courts will now be able to impose its view on them". It is their view (*ibid.*) that unless courts are vigilant, it "has the potential for bringing a strong flavour of social engineering against the birth family and gives rise to the question whether the balance has shifted too far". However, the checklist does emphasise the likely effect on the child of having ceased to be a member of the birth family,[101] and the court is also directed to consider the "relationship which the child has with relatives ... including the likelihood of any such relationship continuing and the value to the child of its doing so, the ability and willingness of any of the child's relatives to provide the child with a secure environment in which the child can develop, and the wishes and feelings of the child's relatives ...".[102] This should enable a balance to be struck between the interests of the parents and that of the child. And the Human Rights Act 1998 should not be forgotten: adoption must be a proportionate response.[103] This also chimes with social work practice which regards adoption as a last resort. But if we are going to err on one side, should it not be to promote the child's welfare? Do not children have the right to a permanent placement, to love and security which in nearly all the contested cases decided under the previous law parents were unable to provide? We should not forget that consent can only be dispensed with when the child's welfare "requires" it, and not, therefore, where it would merely be better for the child if an adoption order was made.[104] As yet there are no reported interpretations of this new provision.

A HOME WITH THE ADOPTERS

Before an adoption order may be made, the child must have spent a sufficient amount of time with the prospective adopters. The amount of time needed to satisfy the test depends on the nature of the applicants.[105]

If the adoption is arranged by an adoption agency, the child must have lived[106] with the applicants for at least ten weeks.

In the case of a non-agency application by local authority foster parents it is one year.

If the adoption is non-agency and the applicant is a relative of the child or a private foster parent the child must have lived with the applicant for not less than three years in the preceding five-year period. Under the pre-2002 law only 13 weeks was required. The massive increase is intended to encourage such applicants to seek alternatives to adoption.

Where a child has not been placed for adoption by an adoption agency, the applicant must, not more than two years or less than three months before the order, give written notice to the local authority within whose area the child has his home of the intention to apply for an adoption order.[107] The local authority then has the task of investigating and looking in particular at the suitability of the applicants before it submits a report to the court.[108]

OTHER OPTIONS

The courts have a number of functions and powers which may conveniently be addressed together.

The court must be satisfied that an adoption order is for the child's welfare. It must consider other options. It may be that a residence order is better for the child, perhaps where the child does not want to be adopted,[109] or a special guardianship order,[110] or an enhanced residence order.[111] Where adoption is sought for an ulterior purpose, for example to enable a child, particularly one nearing majority, to acquire UK citizenship, it may be refused.[112]

The court must also be satisfied that parents have consented or that their consent should be dispensed with. This has already been considered.[113]

Since adoption applications are family proceedings, courts have the power, upon application or of their own motion, to make s.8 orders, and special guardianship orders. Section 1(6) of the 2002 Act imposes an obligation on courts hearing adoption applications to consider all their powers. If one of these, for example a special guardianship order, better serves the child's interests, it should be made instead of an adoption order.

CONTACT AFTER ADOPTION

Before making an adoption order, the court must consider "whether there should be arrangements for allowing any person contact with the child; and for that purpose ... must consider any existing or proposed arrangements and obtain the views of the parties to the proceedings".[114] Once adoption was a closed and secretive process. Today "open adoption" is common with the child maintaining links with his/her birth family (Mullender, 1991). It is estimated that 70 per cent of children who have been adopted retain contact—direct or indirect—with their birth families (Department of Health, 2002b, p.15). Contact may be questionable where there has been abuse or where it might undermine the adopters. But, in its favour, it may be said to give the children greater security, and it may encourage their birth families to be supportive. It was held as long ago as 1973 that contact post-adoption was possible in the "exceptional case where a court is satisfied that by so doing the welfare of the child may be best promoted".[115] The courts have been reluctant to impose contact on unwilling adopters. As Lord Ackner explained in *Re C*:

"Where no agreement is forthcoming the court will, with very rare exceptions, have to choose between making an adoption order without terms or conditions as to access, or to refuse to make such an order and seek to safeguard access through some other machinery such as wardship. To do otherwise would be merely inviting future and almost immediate litigation".[116]

But, it was held in a later case, that where adopters agreed to indirect contact, they could not simply resile from it without explanation.[117] It remains to be seen whether courts will take a more pro-contact stand now that post-adoption contact is formally recognised in statute.

ACCESS TO BIRTH RECORDS

Openness in adoption is also reflected in the provision which enables adopted persons once they reach the age of 18 to investigate their origins and make contact with their birth family.[118] Access to birth records has existed in Scotland since the inception of adoption there in 1930 (Triseliotis, 1973). It was first

introduced in England by the Children Act 1975.[119] An adoption
contact register was first established by the Children Act 1989.[120]
The 2002 Adoption and Children Act contains further
developments.

In brief, an adopted child can at 18 obtain a copy of his/her
original birth certificate.[121] The Registrar General has a duty to
maintain a register of adoptions—the Adopted Children Register.[122] He also has a duty to enable connections to be made
between entries in birth registers, records which have been
marked "Adopted", and any corresponding entry in the Adopted Children Register.[123] The Adoption Contact Register can put
adopted persons and their birth parents or other relatives in
touch with each other where this is what they both want.[124] As
the *Guidance* explains, it "provides a safe and confidential way
for both parents and other relatives to assure an adopted person
that contact would be welcome and give a contact address".[125]
This register is in two parts: one has names and addresses of
adopted persons over 18 who have copies of their birth certificate
and want to contact a relative; the other has the current address
and identifying details of relatives who wish to contact an
adopted person.[126]

Curiosity about one's origins is understandable, and the
machinery is therefore important. Relatively few take advantage
of it (Eekelaar, 2003a, p.255). Where contact is made a relationship may continue, though the evidence is that this happens in
about half the cases only (Howe and Feast, 2000). American
research (Sachdev, 1992) suggests adopted persons are more
interested in tracing their mothers than their fathers.

EFFECTS OF AN ADOPTION ORDER

What are the effects of an adoption order? It constitutes a legal
transplant. Parental responsibility is transferred to the adop-
ter(s), and those who had parental responsibility have it extin-
guished.[127] From the date of the adoption "an adopted person is
to be treated as if born as the child of the adopters or adopter".[128]
If not already a UK citizen the adopted person becomes one if
one of the adopters is.[129] The adopters may, and usually do,
change the child's surname to their own. The adopted child and
his adoptive parents are deemed to come within the prohibited
degrees of consanguinity, so that they may not intermarry or
enter into a civil partnership.[130] Rather surprisingly—for surely

there are social objections—an adopted child is permitted to marry or enter into a civil partnership with his/her adoptive sibling, but not, of course, with any person who could have come within the prohibited degrees had there been no adoption.[131] Adoption has other consequences in relation to maintenance, property, pensions, etc.[132]

ADOPTION OF CHILDREN FROM OVERSEAS

Adoptions of children from overseas raise their own problems. Public attention focused on intercountry adoptions in the early 1990s when the plight of children in Romanian orphanages caught our attention. It would be all too simple to think that merely facilitating rescue and adoption by comfortable families in the West is a solution. On one level it is: who can pretend that a baby neglected in an orphanage in Romania would not be better off with a loving family in Hampshire? But there must be concern also that vulnerable families in poor countries are not exploited, that children do not lose their identity and that the right people become the adopters (or at the very least, that the children do not fall into the wrong hands).

The Hague Convention on Intercountry Adoption of 1993 came into force in the UK in 2003, as a result of the Adoption (Intercountry) Aspects Act 1999. The Convention has three aims:[133]

(i) to establish safeguards to ensure that intercountry adoptions only take place after the best interests of the child have been properly assessed and in circumstances which protect his/her fundamental rights;

(ii) to establish a system of co-operation among Contracting States to ensure these safeguards are respected, and so to prevent the abduction, sale of, or traffic in children;

(iii) to ensure the recognition in Contracting States of adoptions made in accordance with the Convention.

The Convention draws a distinction between "States of Origin" and "Receiving States". The State of Origin must establish the child is adoptable, and that intercountry adoption is in the child's best interests.[134] It must ensure the requisite consents have been obtained, freely and without financial inducement, and that the child, having regard to age and maturity, has been counselled and informed of the effects of adoption.[135] The Receiving State must determine that the prospective adoptive parents are suitable and that the child is or will be authorised to enter and reside permanently in that State.[136] States are to set up Central Authorities.[137] Persons who wish to apply to adopt a child habitually resident in another Contracting State must apply to the Central Authority in their own country.[138] This will transmit the request to the Central Authority of the State of Origin.[139] Both States must agree that adoption should proceed.[140] An adoption certified by the competent authority of the State of adoption as having been made in accordance with the Convention is to be recognised by operation of law in the other Contracting States.[141] Recognition may be refused if the adoption "is manifestly contrary to its public policy, taking into account the best interests of the child".[142] The Children and Adoption Act 2006 allows the Secretary of Sate to suspend intercountry adoptions from countries (including Convention countries) where he determines that it would be contrary to public policy to further the bringing into the UK of children by British residents from that country, for example where there is concern about child trafficking.[143]

In addition, there is s.83 of the 2002 Act. This applies to any person habitually resident in the British Islands who, except where the child is intended to be adopted under a Convention adoption order,

"(a) brings, or causes to bring, a child who is habitually resident outside the British Islands into the United Kingdom for the purpose of adoption by the British resident, or
 (b) at any time brings, or causes to bring, into the United Kingdom a child adopted by the British resident under an external adoption effected within the period of [twelve][144] months ending with that time".

This makes it more difficult for intercountry adopters to circumvent restrictions on bringing children to the UK for adoption. The Adoption with a Foreign Element Regulations 2005 requires prospective adopters to be assessed and approved as suitable by an adoption agency and to have obtained a certificate of approval by the Secretary of State. Failure to comply with these provisions is a criminal offence.

SPECIAL GUARDIANSHIP

Special guardianship has been created to offer an alternative to adoption.[145] Special guardianship orders offer new parents greater security than a residence order without, as adoption does, extinguishing the legal relationship between the child and his or her birth family. Special guardians are different from guardians who only take office on the parent's death.[146] Unlike guardians, special guardians are appointed by the court. Special guardianship is thought particularly appropriate when children need permanence without severance of ties. It may be particularly appropriate for older children who do not wish to be adopted. It offers an alternative to adoption also where there are cultural or religious objections to the institution of adoption.[147] But there is nothing in the legislation which limits the making of a special guardianship order (or an adoption order) to any given set of circumstances.[148]

The following persons are entitled to apply for a special guardianship order: any guardian of the child; any individual in whose favour there is a residence order; a person who has the consent of all those persons who have a residence order; any person with whom the child has lived for three out of the previous five years, provided s/he has the consent of any person with parental responsibility, any person with a residence order, or the local authority if the child is in care; a local authority foster parent with whom the child has lived for at least one year immediately preceding the application.[149] The applicant cannot be a parent of the child.[150] Other persons can only apply with the leave of the court.[151] The same considerations apply as for leave applications under s.8 of the Children Act 1989.[152] Children themselves can apply with leave of the court: this may only be granted if the court is satisfied that the child has sufficient understanding to make the proposed application.[153] The court can also make a special guardianship order of its own motion in any family proceedings, which includes adoption proceedings.[154]

When considering whether to make a special guardianship order the court must apply the paramountcy principle,[155] have regard to the checklist in s.1(3) of the Children Act 1989,[156] and only make the order if it is better for the child than not making the order. Before making the order it must consider whether a contact order should be made at the same time.[157] The significance of this should not be overlooked: contact with parents and other family members is upheld as relatively normal. Before

making a special guardianship order the court must also consider whether any s.8 order which is in force should be varied or
discharged.[158] It may be thought that a residence order will
normally be discharged since it is difficult to see a special
guardianship order and a residence order continuing in tandem.

On making a special guardianship order the court may give
leave for the child to be known by a new surname.[159] It is too
early to say whether this provision will encourage applications
or what the attitudes of the courts will be. Presumably, leave will
not be given where there is opposition by the child. The court can
also give permission for the child to be removed from the UK.[160]

Special guardians have parental responsibility, which they are
entitled to exercise to the exclusion of any other person with
parental responsibility (apart from another special guardian).[161]
It is not entirely clear what this means but it cannot give a special
guardian power to exercise responsibility independently where
the consent of all parties with parental responsibility is
required.[162] They can consent to the child's adoption, but the
parents must still consent (or have consent dispensed with).[163]
They cannot cause a child to be known by a new surname,[164] or
remove the child from the UK for more than three months,[165]
while a special guardianship order is in force. They also have the
power to appoint a guardian to act in their stead upon their
death.[166] There are provisions for the variation and discharge of
special guardianship orders.[167]

Local authorities must make arrangements for the provision of
special guardianship support services to provide counselling,
information and advice. Other services such as financial support
are prescribed by regulations.[168]

Whether special guardianship is to succeed will depend upon
whether those most eligible for it—long-term foster parents and
relatives looking after children—are prepared to apply for it.
Custodianship, a strikingly similar institution, did not take on.[169]
Special guardianship may prove a more attractive package: the
name is less off-putting, it is simpler, and there are support
services which may encourage potential applicants. But the
auguries are not good. Smith and Logan (2002) found that 78 per
cent of their adoptive mother respondents and 65 per cent of
their adoptive father respondents would not apply for special
guardianship. In their minds, it did not "construct parenthood"
in the way adoption did. They did not think it would give
enough control to "enable effective parenting, security and stability for the child" (*ibid.*, p.297). Much will depend on the

courts' attitudes and this may be influenced by human rights considerations. As the Court of Appeal emphasised in *Re S (A Child) (Special Guardianship Order)*,[170] "the statute implicitly envisages an order being made against the wishes of the parties". Special guardianship orders have not replaced adoption orders in cases where children are placed permanently within their wider families. The Court of Appeal has said that the question of likely distortion of family relationships by an adoption should not be overplayed.[171]

12

UNDERSTANDING CHILD SUPPORT

THE OBLIGATION TO MAINTAIN

Parents have an obligation to maintain their children. They do not have to care for their children in any physical sense, but they must support them financially. If we ask why, the simple answer is that they brought the children into the world. The state didn't. Nor did anyone else, grandparents for example.[1] That the parent didn't intend to bring the child into existence, for example the father who was falsely led to believe that his sexual partner, the mother, was using contraception, is not an acceptable excuse.[2] There may be cases where this conclusion looks unjust—the *Leeds Teaching Hospitals* case,[3] discussed in Chapter 6, where a man only became the father of twins because the fertility clinic had used his sperm to fertilise the wrong woman is an egregious example. A reading of this case suggests that the mother is unlikely to call upon the father for support. But were she to do so, he would be legally liable. But, of course, he did not bring the children into existence: this was the result of an act of negligence by the fertility clinic. The father might well have a claim in negligence.

It should be stressed that we don't impose financial liability on the absent parent—who is usually the father—in order to punish him.[4] We want him to fulfill his responsibilities. A well-functioning legal system is said (Cane, 2002, p.60) to be "one in which non-compliance with ... responsibilities ... [is] minimized". As we will see, judged by this criterion the system introduced in 1993 is an absolute failure. When this was introduced, it was officially because "children came first".[5] The real reason, as Eekelaar (1990) immediately observed, was to protect the public purse: his comment was aptly entitled "taxpayers come first".[6] But children should come first, and there is a case for seeing financial support from parents as a child's entitlement, both morally and legally.[7] An efficient child support system must be seen as part of a strategy to conquer child poverty.[8]

The parental obligation to maintain children does not end when the parental relationship breaks down, and the child ceases to live with one (or both) of the parents. Many parents will make private maintenance arrangements, and this is now to be encouraged.[9] But most child maintenance disputes come within the remit of the Child Support Agency (CSA) (or when in operation its successor C-MEC[10]). However, the courts retain a residual role, and only the courts can make orders for capital sums and property orders for children.

THE FORMER SYSTEM AND ITS PROBLEMS

The current system, as amended, was brought into operation in 1993.[11] Before then disputes about child maintenance were heard by the courts. The system was described as "unnecessarily fragmented, uncertain in its results, slow and ineffective. It is based largely on discretion".[12] The White Paper quoted research[13] which found that only 30 per cent of lone mothers received regular payments of maintenance for their children; maintenance formed less than 10 per cent of lone parents' total net income, with 45 per cent of this coming from income support. The White Paper proposed that responsibility for assessing claims for child maintenance should be removed from the courts. The Prime Minister said that "complicated cases" might still be referred to the courts, but this concession did not find its way into the legislation.[14]

THE CHILD SUPPORT AGENCY

The Child Support Act 1991 established the Child Support Agency[15] which was to be responsible for the assessment of all child maintenance payments. It created a universally applicable and highly complex formula to calculate liability. It required all "parents with care"[16] claiming means-tested income support, family credit or disability working allowance to authorise the Secretary of State to recover maintenance from the "absent parent" (now called the non-resident parent), to co-operate with the CSA in tracing an "absent parent", assessing and collecting any maintenance owed.[17] Only where the "parent with care" could demonstrate reasonable grounds for believing that this would cause her or a child to suffer "harm or undue distress" was this requirement to be waived.[18] A "parent with care" who refused to co-operate without being able to demonstrate this was to have her personal allowance element of the benefit reduced by 20 per cent for six months and 10 per cent for a further year.[19] This was increased in 1996 to 40 per cent to last for three years, with the penalty renewed if the parent with care is still on benefit and refusing to co-operate. The co-operative "parent with care" on income support gained nothing, since maintenance recovered was deducted from their benefit (though those on family credit had £15 maintenance "disregarded" in calculating their entitlement).[20]

EARLY CRITICISMS

Coming from a Conservative Government bent on "privatising" more or less everything,[21] the Child Support Act 1991 was an anomaly—in effect it nationalised. It came under attack almost immediately. It was said by non-resident parents to be unfair. There were complaints from fathers in particular that they were expected to support even when denied contact with the children.[22] That this criticism is wide of the mark has been addressed in Chapter 8.[23] Parents with care also complained of unfairness, with rather more justification.[24] It was (and is) a system designed to save the Treasury money, rather than alleviate the poverty of lone parents.[25] Criticism was also voiced at the inflexibility of the system. The case of *Crozier v Crozier*[26] illustrated this well. A husband had transferred his interest in the former matrimonial home to his wife on the basis that his child maintenance liability would be £4 a week. His assessment under the Child Support Act was £29 a week. He was not allowed to appeal out of time[27] against the original order (which was made before the Act). The state was not bound by a private agreement.[28] A further criticism, which continues despite subsequent reforms, is that the CSA gets its assessments wrong. Early reports suggested as many as half of the assessments were wrong.[29] In part this is attributable to the complexity of the formula, but it was due also to incorrect information furnished by the parents. The high level of errors is still being criticised.[30] The CSA was also soon perceived to be inefficient. It spends most of its time assessing maintenance and perhaps only 10 per cent collecting it. Most of those assessed do not pay the full amount due: as many as a third pay nothing.[31] They may reason that money paid will not actually benefit their child. The CSA has had to write off unpaid child support—£2 billion in 2002—and another £850 million of its current debt of £3.5 billion is due to be written off in the near future.[32]

THE CHILD SUPPORT ACT 1995

A number of changes were made by the Child Support Act 1995. The legislation introduced discretion to "depart" from the formulaic assessment to take account of special hardship.[33] In addition, the formula was adjusted to take account of the needs of second partners and children, earlier property adjustment settlements, and the absent parent's travel-to-work costs.[34] The 1995 Act also enabled lone parents on income support or jobseeker's allowance to build up what were called "maintenance credits" of £5 a week, repaid as a lump sum when they started working more than 16 hours a week.[35]

THE CHILD SUPPORT, PENSIONS AND SOCIAL SECURITY ACT 2000

The system was further reformed by the Child Support, Pensions and Social Security Act 2000, which came into operation in March 2003. The general rule now is that the weekly rate of child support maintenance is the "basic rate" unless a "reduced rate", a "flat rate" or a "nil rate" apply.[36] The basic rate is a percentage of the non-resident parent's net weekly income: 15 per cent for one qualifying child, 20 per cent for two, and 25 per cent where there are three or more.[37] There are two qualifications to this. First, there is a cap on the amount of income to which those rates apply. Anything above £2000 a week is ignored.[38] This advantages the wealthy non-resident parent but, as we shall see, the courts retain a top-up jurisdiction where this is thought appropriate.[39] Second, responsibilities for step-children (and the children of cohabitants) are taken into account: 15 per cent is allowed for the first of such children, 20 per cent for the second and 25 percent where there are three or more relevant such children.[40] A non-resident father with three children by a new partner will thus only have 40 per cent of his net weekly income available from which to maintain his children of his previous relationship. The first family no longer gets priority.

The reduced rate is payable where the non-resident parent's net weekly income is more than £100 and less than £200.[41] This operates on a sliding scale. The flat rate of £5 applies where the non-resident parent's net weekly income is £100 or less and he is receiving prescribed benefits (or his partner is), provided the nil rate does not apply.[42] This applies where the non-resident parent is a child under 16, a student, a prisoner, a patient in hospital or is in a residential care home or nursing home, and net weekly income is less than £5.[43]

SHARED CARE

The new scheme is also more responsive to the needs of non-resident parents who share care with the "parent with care". The amount payable is reduced to reflect the number of nights the child spends with the non-resident parent: for example, the rate is reduced by a seventh if the child spends between 52 and 103 nights a year with him. It is reduced by a half once the child spends 175 nights a year with him.[44] The acknowledgment of shared care is significant. It is a reaffirmation of the normativity of continuing parental responsibility—though it should be emphasised again that parental obligation to support is not dependent on the possession of parental responsibility and thus applies to all fathers—and may encourage fathers to want meaningful contact with their children.

VARIATIONS

The system allows for what are now called "variations" (these were introduced in 1995 as "departure directions"[45]). This recognises that there are a small number of exceptional cases where justice demands adjustment to the rigid formula. The Secretary of State—in reality the CSA—may agree a variation if he is satisfied that the case falls within those specified and in his opinion it would be "just and equitable to agree to a variation".[46] He must have regard in particular to the welfare of any child likely to be affected by a variation.[47] There are also factors he must, and factors he must not, take into account. An example of a factor he must take into account is whether a variation would be likely to result in a relevant person ceasing paid employment: as Bainham (2005, p.389) observes, "a clear indication of the priorities which the Government attaches to work as opposed to welfare dependency". Examples of what must not be taken into account are equally revealing: they include that the qualifying child was unplanned, responsibility for the breakdown of the relationship, the formation of a new relationship, and whether contact arrangements are being adhered to.

The cases "specified", where there may be variation, include such situations as "special expenses"[48], for example those incurred in maintaining contact with a child. There are also, what are known as, "additional cases",[49] where the non-resident parent has assets in excess of £65,000, a lifestyle inconsistent with declared income or where he has unreasonably reduced the income taken into account in making the calculation.

THE WELFARE RECIPIENT

Whether the CSA gets involved at all depends upon whether the person with the care of the child is in receipt of welfare benefits.[50] If not, the agency will only get involved if the person with care applies to it for a maintenance calculation against the non-resident parent. The legislation does not stop parents making their own financial arrangements:[51] indeed, under the new proposals this will be further encouraged.[52] But if the person with care is in receipt of income support, income-based jobseeker's allowance or another prescribed benefit, she will be treated as having applied for a maintenance calculation unless she specifically requests the Secretary of State not to act.[53] She must, so far as she reasonably can, provide information to enable the non-resident parent to be identified or traced, and the amount of child support to be calculated and recovered from him.[54] A refusal to give information, or to submit to a scientific test to determine paternity, will lead to the parent being served with a notice to give reasons.[55] It is then the duty of the Secretary of State to consider whether there are reasonable grounds for believing that, were the parent to comply, there would be "a risk of her, or of any children living with her, suffering harm or undue distress as a result of taking such action, or her complying or taking the test".[56] If he is not satisfied, he has the discretion to make a "reduced benefit decision".[57]

MAINTENANCE AGREEMENTS

Parents, as already noted, can agree on the financial arrangements to be made for their children. But the existence of a maintenance agreement does not prevent any party to the agreement, or any other person, from applying for a maintenance calculation with respect to any child to whom or for whose benefit periodical payments are to be made, or secured, under the agreement. Any provision in the agreement purporting to restrict the right of any person to apply for a maintenance calculation under the Act is void.[58]

THE HUMAN RIGHTS ACT

The original scheme has thus been reformed several times, but criticism, even ridicule, remains. The 2000 Act was heavily criticised by the House of Commons Select Committee on Work and Pensions in 2005.[59] That huge sums were uncollectible was described as an astonishing state of affairs. One possible solution, to involve private debt collection firms in the task of collecting child maintenance, has been condemned as morally unacceptable, but it is distinctly possible that it will be tried in the near future.[60] There is no doubt that the CSA is resented by both parents with care and non-resident parents.

A challenge under the Human Rights Act was inevitable but, surprisingly—and wrongly, in my opinion—it failed.[61] The non-resident father had failed to make payments of child maintenance to the mother. Enforcement measures taken by the CSA had failed. The mother brought judicial review proceedings, seeking a declaration of incompatibility on the basis that the enforcement provisions of the Act were incompatible with Art.6 of the European Convention, because they prevented a parent from bringing enforcement proceedings in her own name or on behalf of her children. She additionally sought a declaration that delay by the CSA constituted a breach of her Art.6 rights. She claimed damages under s.7 of the Human Rights Act. The House of Lords found against her. It held[62] that the scheme under the Child Support Act 1991 was not incompatible with Art.6. The parent with care had no right to recover maintenance from the absent parent, that right having been removed by the Child Support Act 1991, and vested in the CSA. It reasoned that because these was no "civil right" in respect of such enforcement, Art.6(1) of the ECHR, which provided guarantees with regard to "civil rights and obligations", was not engaged. Since Art.6(1) was not engaged, the CSA could not be said to have acted unlawfully, and so the parent with care had no remedy.

There is a powerful and convincing dissent by Baroness Hale. As she notes, "neither the private nor the public law obligation, nor the corresponding right of the child to the benefit of that obligation, has been taken away".[63] It is therefore "obvious"[64] that the obligation of a parent to maintain his child, and the right of the child to have the benefit of that obligation, are "not wholly contained in the 1991 Act".[65] And, that being the case:

"... it is clear ... that children have a civil right to be maintained by their parents which is such as to engage Art.6. ... Their rights are not limited to the rights given to the parent with care under the 1991 Act...

The system ... is trying to enforce children's rights. It is sometimes ... lamentably inefficient in so doing. It is safe to assume that there are cases ... where the children's carer would be much more efficient in enforcing the children's rights. ... A promise that the CSA is doing its best is not enough. Nor is the threat or reality of judicial review...

The children's civil right to the benefit of the parental obligations survives the 1991 Act...

But if I am right that the children's civil rights to be properly maintained by their parents are engaged, it follows that the public authority which is charged by Parliament with securing the determination and enforcement of their rights is under a duty to act compatibly with their Art.6 rights to the speedy determination and effective enforcement of those rights. ... Just as the courts, as public authorities, have to act compatibly with the European Convention rights, so does the CSA".[66]

Baroness Hale is the only one of the Lords to as much as mention children's rights, and yet it is difficult to see how the question of the parental obligation to support can be seen outside such a context (and see Fortin, 2004). Even she neglects to cite the United Nations Convention on the Rights of the Child under which the UK is obligated to "take all appropriate measures to secure the recovery of maintenance for the child from the parents".[67] The UK clearly falls far short of meeting this obligation. The challenge in *Kehoe* should have succeeded, and it is possible that a further one might.

THE WELFARE OF THE CHILD

The closest the legislation itself gets to ackowledging the centrality of children is in the general principle enunciated in s.2.

This requires the Secretary of State in considering the exercise of any discretionary power under the Act to "have regard to the welfare of any child likely to be affected by his decision". It is noteworthy that this refers to "any child" and not just the child in question, because any exercise of discretion could affect all children. But no indication is given as to what weight attaches to the child's welfare or on how a balance should be struck between the interests of children. And, certainly, the welfare of the child is neither paramount[68] nor first[69] nor even, so it has been said, "particularly significant".[70] Section 2 was invoked by an aggrieved father in *R. v Secretary of State for Social Security Ex p. Biggin*.[71] He argued that the amount assessed to be enforced against him meant that he would not be able to afford to have contact with his sons. He failed. Thorpe J. said it was "manifest that [s.2] has no influence on the quantification of liability",[72] and admitted that the heading words of the section "seem hollow indeed".[73] This must be right: calculation of assessment under the formula is not discretionary, and the welfare principle only applies to the exercise of discretionary powers, of which there are few.[74] Section 2 echoes the title of the White Paper "Children Come First", but its emphasis on children's welfare, like its progenitor, is sadly disingenuous.

COURTS' RESIDUAL JURISDICTION

Courts retain residual jurisdiction in nine situations.

They can make a periodical payments if the maximum child maintenance assessment is in force.[75] A "top-up" order is only likely to be made where the court is satisfied that the assessed maintenance is inadequate, and only then where the non-resident parent is very wealthy or the child has special needs.

Second, they can make an order if the child is, will or, if the order were to be made, receiving education or undergoing training for a trade, profession or vocation to meet the costs of this.[76]

Third, where the child is disabled[77] (even where a disability living allowance is not being paid) the court can order periodical payments to be made or secured to meet some or all of the expenses attributable to the child's disability. This may be useful since there is no liability to support a child over 18 under the Child Support Act 1991.[78]

Fourth, where the child is not a "qualifying child",[79] as defined by s.55. Examples are dependants of 17 and 18 who are not in full-time education.

Fifth, where there is a maintenance agreement in writing, it can be enforced.[80] But such an agreement cannot prevent a person applying to the CSA for an assessment,[81] and the court does not have jurisdiction to vary the agreement if the CSA would have jurisdiction to make the assessment.[82] The court also has the power to convert an agreement made between the parties into an order.[83]

Sixth, the court can still make a lump sum order[84] (unless it is in effect a capitalised maintenance order) and a property adjustment order in favour of a child under the Children Act 1989.[85]

Seventh, the court retains jurisdiction to make an order where maintenance is sought from the parent with care.[86]

Eighth, where maintenance is sought for a step-child, the Child Support Act does not apply, and only the courts have jurisdiction. The step-parent has an obligation to support any "child of the family", that is any child "treated" by both parties to a marriage or civil partnership as a member of the family.[87] Whether a child has been so treated is a question of fact, and is to be tested objectively. It has been held that a child can be a "child of the family" even through a maintenance order against the biological father remains in force.[88] There must be a family of which the child may be treated as a member.[89] It is legally impossible to treat a child as a member of a family until s/he is born.[90]

Ninth, the courts will retain the power to make orders in any other situation where the CSA has no jurisdiction to make a maintenance calculation. An example is where the parent is not habitually resident in the UK.

HOW COURTS EXERCISE THEIR JURISDICTION

During a marriage or civil partnership orders can be sought in both the family proceedings courts and county court. Such orders are rarely sought, first, because during an ongoing relationship it is unusual to seek court intervention and second, because child maintenance will normally fall within the province of the CSA. Either spouse or civil partner can apply to either court on the grounds that the other spouse or civil partner has failed to provide, or make a proper contribution towards, reasonable maintenance for any child of the family.[91] In the county court the criteria in s.25 of the Matrimonial Causes Act 1973 which apply to ancillary relief on divorce apply; in the family proceedings court similar criteria apply, with the additional requirement that magistrates must consider whether to exercise any of the powers they have under the Children Act, for example to make a residence or contact order.[92] Both courts may make periodical payments orders and lump sum orders: the family proceedings court is limited to awarding lump sums of £1,000.

There is also jurisdiction under the Children Act 1989. Under s.15 and Sch.1 paras 1 and 2, family proceedings courts, county courts and the High Court can make periodical payments orders, lump sum orders and property adjustment orders for children (and sometimes for those over 18).[93] The court can do this of its own motion when varying or discharging a residence order[94] or if the child is a ward of court.[95] Otherwise, it requires an application. This may be made by a parent, a guardian, a special guardian or by any person in whose favour a residence order is in force with respect to the child. It cannot be made by the child.

The orders—periodical payments, lump sum, settlement of property, transfer of property—can be made in favour of the applicant for the benefit of the child or in favour of the child, except a settlement of property order, which can only be made for the benefit of the child. The family proceedings court has limited powers. It cannot order the transfer and settlement of property, cannot make secured periodical payments orders and is limited to lump sum orders of £1,000.

A "child" over 18 can apply for a periodical payments order and a lump sum order against one or both parents if the "child" is, will be, or, if an order were made, would be receiving instruction at an educational institution or undergoing training for a trade, profession or vocation, whether or not while in gainful employment. An order cannot be made if the applicant's parents are living with each other in the same household.

The discretion to make an award is governed by statutory criteria, similar to those in s.25 of the Matrimonial Causes Act 1973, with the addition of "the manner in which the child is being, or is expected to be, educated or trained" and some necessary adaptations to make the criteria child-focused. The child's standard of living is not mentioned. Where the court is exercising its powers under para.1 against a person who is not the child's mother or father, for example against a step-parent, the court must also consider:

"(a) whether that person has assumed responsibility for the child's maintenance and, if so, the extent to which and the basis on which that responsibility was assumed and the length of the period during which he met that responsibility;

(b) whether he did so knowing that the child was not his child;

(c) the liability of any other person to maintain the child".

An examination of the case law reveals the governing principles. The welfare of the child is "not just" one of the relevant circumstances but in most cases "a constant influence".[96] It is not, however, the paramount consideration.[97] As already pointed out, the court is not specifically required to have regard to the family's standard of living. The court can nevertheless do so but, where the parents have never lived together, the question necessarily arises as to whose standard is to be looked to. In many of the cases, hardly surprisingly, the father's financial position is stronger than the mother's and she is the child's carer. The courts have recognised this and tied the child's standard of living to that of the father.[98] Of course, this also advantages the mother who if unmarried, has no entitlement to any financial provision in her own right. But it is not possible or desirable to pitch the child's standard of living at a higher level than the mother's.

The leading case is *Re P (Child: Financial Provision)*.[99] The father was an immensely successful international business man who was "fabulously wealthy". The mother came from a wealthy background and was dependent upon her parents for her standard of living. The Court of Appeal held that where a parent was very wealthy the court should first consider the kind of home he should provide for the child—in this case £1 million for a house in an appropriate part of London. Then an appropriate sum should be added to furnish and decorate such a property—£100,000 in this case. Finally, the court should

"recognise the responsibility, and often the sacrifice, of the unmarried parent (generally the mother) who is to be the primary carer for the child. In order to discharge this responsibility, the carer must have control of a budget that reflects her position and the position of the father, both social and financial".[100]

To reflect this, the court also awarded periodical payments of £70,000 per year: this would be over and above the child support assessment. Thorpe L.J. acknowledged that "this represents a liability of approximately £1,500 a week for a 2-year-old child". However, this is "a distortion of reality that £70,000 is a budget to enable the mother to run the home for [the child] and to provide her additional needs". And it is worth remarking in a post-*White* and *Miller/McFarlane* era, had she been married the award would have been very much greater. Even if women can be penalised for cohabiting rather than marrying—of course the mother in this case did neither—is it fair to make their children suffer?

The home is, we have just seen, central to the courts' thinking, but this is to enable the child's financial position to be secured during dependency. For this reason, an settlement of property order (a *Mesher* order[101]) is commonly used. This settles the home on the carer for the benefit of the child, with the property reverting to the other party on the child's majority or completion of full-time education.[102] Even where, as in *Re P*, the non-resident parent is fabulously wealthy, an outright transfer of the home to the other parent is unusual.[103] The Court of Appeal also has accepted that he has the right to veto "an unsuitable investment".[104] He can make a windfall; the child cannot.

These awards are for the benefit of the child, not his mother. The courts are thus wary of claims purporting to be for the benefit of the child but which are in reality for the benefit of the mother who is caring for the child.[105] Such claims are more likely to be advanced where the mother herself has no entitlement to support. But as long ago as 1980 it was held that it was not wrong for the court to augment an order for a child to include an allowance for the mother, particularly if her child-care responsibilities prevented her from working.[106]

REFORMING THE CHILD SUPPORT AGENCY

The system centred on the Child Support Agency is acknowledged by everyone now as an abysmal failure. A Government Minister described it as a "shambles".[107] Its victims are the poor—most applicants for maintenance assessments are claiming income support or income-based job-seekers allowance—and most are women—95 per cent of non-resident parents are male, a quarter of whom have partners, and 86 per cent of parents with care, mostly mothers, remain lone parents. That the CSA collects less than half of the maintenance due on its calculations has been described by the House of Commons Select Committee on Work and Pensions as "nothing less than a severe breach of trust".[108] And because what it collects is based on the non-resident parent's net income, not the child's needs, the amount assessed is woefully low.[109] Assessments are often unduly delayed, as state of affairs described by Ward L.J. in one case brought to his attention as "appalling".[110]

A major stumbling block is the enforcement of maintenance assessments. The CSA is a collection service. Parents with care on benefit must use it, those not on benefit may make their own arrangements about payment.[111] Where the collection service is used, the CSA will usually give the non-resident parent the option of paying by direct debit or standing order, or by voluntary deduction from earnings.[112] If the non-resident parent does not pay the amount due, a penalty payment of up to 25 per cent of the amount payable may be imposed,[113] but this money does not go to the parent with care. If a non-resident parent in employment does pay, the CSA[114] can make a deduction from earnings order.[115]

If the non-resident parent fails to pay and it is "inappropriate" to make a deduction from earnings order, for example because he is not in regular employment, or if the deduction order is ineffective, the CSA may apply to the magistrates' court for a liability order.[116] The magistrates are not permitted to question the CSA's maintenance assessment.[117] Liability orders can be enforced by distress,[118] a garnishee order or a charging order.[119] The use of liability orders is not, it has been held, an interference with the non-resident parent's rights under Art.8 or Protocol 1, Art.1 of the ECHR or, if it is, it is proportionate as a way of seeking to ensure parents fulfill their responsibilities to support their children.[120]

If these enforcement measures fail, more severe ones can be imposed. The non-resident parent may be committed to prison for up to six weeks or disqualified from holding or obtaining a driving licence for up to two years,[121] but only if the court is of the opinion that there has been wilful refusal or culpable neglect to pay.[122] Such drastic measures might be effective were they used, but in the first three and three-quarter years of the existence of these sanctions only four driving licences were removed and only 15 prison sentences were imposed.[123]

Yet tougher sanctions are now to be introduced. The

Government stands firm in its belief that there can be "no question of allowing parents who are able to pay to escape their responsibilities".[124] And so the non-paying parent is now to be threatened with losing his passport (but what if he has a non-UK passport?), and with being curfewed and, presumably, though this is not stated, tagged. The possibility of introducing powers to collect maintenance directly from bank and building society accounts is being explored.[125] The possibility of removing the requirement to apply to the courts for a charging order or for a driving licence or passport to be given up is also being examined. The Government concedes that there are "very strong powers that are not normally used to collect civil debts", but responds "we must put the needs of children first".[126] Naming and shaming is also proposed: the names of parents who are successfully prosecuted or have a successful application made against them in court will, if these proposals are implemented, be published on the Agency's website (and on that of C-MEC when this is established).[127] A new power to factor debts using "specialist organisations", that is debt collection agencies, is also proposed. This is "to provide money for more children",[128] but it is also to increase the profits of such organisations. Whether this is morally acceptable is dubious. Questions also need to be raised about how many of the proposed new powers are human rights compliant. If they fail—and we cannot really have confidence that they will succeed—what next? Public flogging, perhaps!

One suggested change, which Resolution proposed in 2005, has not been taken up. It recommended the introduction of a Child Maintenance Arbitrator system to promote settlements. Its other main proposal in that report, to introduce a special enforcement body separate from the CSA, can be seen in the proposed establishment of C-MEC, though this will replace rather than complement the CSA.[129]

An interesting proposal to emerge from the government, and one which will affect the parent–child relationship more generally, is actively to promote joint birth registration.[130] It is proposed that current laws should change so that both parents' names are registered following the birth of their child, unless it would be unreasonable to do so. Is this a proposal by the back door to confer parental responsibility on all fathers?[131] And if so, will it be contested? How will feminist groups react? Will there be concerns that undeserving men, fathers who have shown no commitment,[132] will acquire power over women and children without the need for agreement or a court order? The proposal,

ostensibly to further children's rights, may be seen as a concession to the fathers' lobby which wishes to tie maintenance in to
contact.[133]

The government also proposes to encourage parents to make
their own arrangements. Whether this will be better for children
remains to be seen. No longer will parents with care who claim
benefits be treated as applying for child maintenance. Parents
with care will have the right to keep up to £10 of their child
maintenance a week before it affects their benefits.[134] But if the
relief of child poverty is a major consideration, why not allow
them to keep all maintenance without it affecting their benefit?
Most maintenance assessments are very low. We are also promised a more efficient and streamlined maintenance assessment
process. This includes a system of fixed-term awards of one year,
with some exceptions for a significant change of circumstances.[135]
Is there no concern that this can be manipulated, for example by
ensuring salary increases come shortly after the yearly award?

ALTERNATIVES

A return to a system based on court awards may be favoured by
some lawyers—it had some support from Resolution (the Solicitors' Family Law Association) in 2005—but it is unrealistic to
believe a return to the pre-1991 position is a feasible option.
When the courts were in charge, the evidence suggested that
their awards lacked rationality: Eekelaar found that rather than
using any guideline to determine awards, registrars (now district
judges) preferred to rely upon "common knowledge" about how
much it cost to raise children. Where guidelines were used, they
tended to use income support levels (Eekelaar, 1991c). He also
found registrars who rejected National Foster Care Association
rates because they were regarded as unrealistically high (Eekelaar, 1991c, p.95). In a post-*White* era[136] they might be expected to
act differently, and guidelines could be set.

For a more radical solution we need to turn the clock back
even further, to 1974 when the Finer Report on One-Parent
Families was published. This questioned whether child support
should be seen as a private matter. It argued rather for the state
assuming a degree of responsibility for assisting one-parent
families living in poverty. It recommended a "guaranteed
maintenance allowance" as a non-contributory fixed benefit to be
paid to all one-parent families as a substitute for maintenance

payments. The concept was resurrected by the House of Commons Select Committee on Work and Pensions in its report on the "Performance of the Child Support Agency" in 2005. It recommended an allowance which it called "guaranteed child support". The government gave this short shift.[137] It saw it as destabilising. It would "undermine the principle that parents should provide financial support for their children", and parents on this benefit would lose their incentive to comply with the Agency. But the Government is committed to eradicating child poverty—it says by 2020—and sees reforms to the child support system a part of the strategy to achieve this. Tinkering with the child support system will not achieve this: "guaranteed child support" might. As Fineman (2004, p.204) points out:

"It may also be that we want to establish and collect child support orders for reasons other than that they can in fact substitute for governmental or collective assistance to children in poverty, but in doing so, we should not delude ourselves that we are solving the larger problem".

13

UNDERSTANDING CHILDREN'S RIGHTS

CHILDREN AS PROPERTY

For most of our history children were regarded as little more than an item of property (Mason, 1994). Pinchbeck and Hewitt (1973, Vol.II, p.348), commenting upon the status of children in Victorian England, describe children as "legally the property of their parents". "They were used by them as personal or family assets ... among the poor, the labour of children was exploited; among the rich their marriages were contrived; all to the economic or social advantage of the parents". There was complacency regarding their exploitation, explained, Pinchbeck and Hewitt argue (1973, Vol.II, p.357), by the ideology

"supported by religious sanctions, that in society there was a place for everyone, and everyone should remain in his place. Hence, the knowledge that for some that place could be unpleasant was merely confirmation that they belonged to lesser and lower orders of creation".

And this was linked to notions of parental rights. Nineteenth-century reformers had to confront the view of parental rights which identified patriarchal decision-making with family stability, and this with societal cohesion.[1]

It would be idle to pretend that children are not treated better today. But we live with the legacies of these attitudes. Writing in 1980, Mia Kellmer-Pringle detected an understanding that "a baby completes a family, rather like a TV set or fridge ... that a child belongs to his parents like their other possessions over which they may exercise exclusive rights" (1980, p.156). We know that far too many children are returned to abusive parents, or not removed from them, because of an overemphasis on preserving family integrity. Once this was in the name of the "blood-tie";[2] today democratic values and human rights dominate the debates and there is concern that they may marginalise the lives of children.[3] It is hardly surprising that children's rights do not feature prominently in influential books on children which preach rather family autonomy.[4]

THE BEGINNINGS OF CHILDREN'S RIGHTS

The beginnings of a children's rights movement can be traced back to the middle of the nineteenth century. In France, Jean Vallès attempted to establish a league for the protection of the rights of children in the aftermath of the Paris Commune.[5] The late nineteenth century saw the birth of the child-saving movement (Tiffin, 1982; Platt, 1969), the growth of the orphanage, the development of schooling (compulsory only from 1870), and the construction of separate institutions, including the juvenile court. At the end of the century there was also the first child protection legislation.[6] But it was left to writers like Kate Douglas Wiggin in the USA,[7] Ellen Key in Sweden,[8] and most significantly Janusz Korczak in Poland[9] to begin to expound children's rights, as we understand them to-day. Korczak's main thesis was that you cannot possibly love a child—your own or anyone else's—until you see him as a separate being with the inalienable right to grow into the person he was meant to be. From his writings we can draw up a charter of children's rights.[10] Two of these are foundational: the right to love and the right to respect. He emphasised both protection and welfare, and the child's right to autonomy and participation. He wrote of the child's right to justice, freedom, dignity and equality.

Wiggin, Key and Korczak all wrote before the first international recognition of children's rights in the Geneva Declaration of 1924.[11] Contrasted with Korczak's ideas and practices, this was more limited in its aspirations. In its preamble, it states that "mankind owes to the Child the best it has to give". Its five terse principles emphasise welfare: the requisite means for normal development, food and medicine, relief in times of distress, protection against exploitation, and socialisation to serve others. It was another 35 years before children's rights received international recognition again. The coverage of the United Nations Declaration of the Rights of the Child of 1959 is broader than its predecessor, though the emphasis was still firmly on protection and welfare and on what has been called, the "investment motive" (Meyer, 1973). There was no recognition of a child's autonomy, of the importance of a child's views, nor any appreciation of the concept of empowerment.

THE CHILD LIBERATION MOVEMENT

With the growth in consciousness of the evils of discrimination, a child's liberation movement emerged in the 1970s, spearheaded by John Holt (1975) and Richard Farson (1978). Ollendorf (1972)—in a collection subtitled "Toward the Liberation of the Child"—called for the adolescent's right to self-determination. It was self-determination that Farson saw as at the root of all other rights that children were entitled to claim. Responding to the anticipated criticism that such rights might not be "good" for children—"children's rights" we have seen, had hitherto been directed towards furthering the "good" for children—Farson argued:

"...asking what is good for children is beside the point. We will grant children rights for the same reason we grant rights to adults, not because we are sure that children will then become better people, but ... because we believe that expanding freedom as a way of life is worthwhile in itself. And freedom, we have found, is a difficult burden for adults as well as children" (1978, p.31).

Farson enumerated nine rights, all derived from the right to self-determination. If they do no more than capture the spirit of "enlightened" thinking 30 years ago, they are worth pondering upon.

First, the right to alternative home environments: a child's "choice in living arrangements" (1978, p.62).[12] Second, the right to information accessible to adults (for example, the ability to inspect records kept about them). Third, the right to educate oneself: freedom from indoctrination, with children choosing their "belief systems" (1978, p.110). Fourth, the right to sexual freedom.[13] Fifth, the right to economic power including the right to work (1978, p.154). Sixth, the right to political power, including the right to vote.[14] Nothing he suggests, indicates that children will "vote less responsibly than adults" (1978, p.182). Seventh, the right to responsive design.[15] Eighth, the right to freedom from physical punishment.[16] Ninth, the right to justice.

Holt devised a similar list but included the right to travel, to drive and to use drugs, as well as the rights in Farson's list.

Though ripe for reconsideration, the Farson–Holt thesis has clear limitations. The liberation school is nonetheless important in making us address discrimination and recognising the importance of autonomy. It has come to be realised that the dichotomy between protecting children and protecting their rights is false. Children who are not protected, whose welfare is not advanced, will not be able to exercise self-determination; on the other hand, a failure to recognise the personality of children is likely to result in an undermining of their protection with children reduced to objects of intervention.

THE UN CONVENTION ON THE RIGHTS OF THE CHILD

This is to some extent recognised by the United Nations Convention on the Rights of the Child. Significantly, the United Kingdom questioned the need for a Convention. It saw the project as "premature". It took ten years, from 1979, when Poland proposed there ought to be a Convention, until 1989 when it emerged. It became the most swiftly ratified of all international conventions, and only two countries, Somalia and the USA have not now ratified it. The Convention has been described (Veerman, 1992, p.184) as "an important and easily understood advocacy tool". Perhaps the most important Article of the Convention is Art.12. This states:

"1. States Parties shall assure the child who is capable of forming his or her own views the right to express those views freely in all matters affecting the child, the views of the child being given due weight in accordance with the age and maturity of the child.
 2. For this purpose, the child shall in particular be provided the opportunity to be heard in any judicial and adminis-trative proceedings affecting the child, either directly, or though a representative or an appropriate body, in a manner consistent with the procedural rules of the national law".[17]

This right is significant not only for what it says, but because it recognises the child as a full human being, with integrity and personality, and with the ability to participate fully in society.

The Convention's articles are often broken down into the so-called three "Ps": those concerned with the protection of children from harm; those which promote participation by children in decisions about their own lives; and those designed to set out provision for children (Van Bueren, 1995). The Convention addresses a wide range of concerns: non-discrimination (Besson, 2005), the best interests of the child to be a primary consideration in all matters (Freeman, 2007),[18] the right to life (Nowak, 2005).[19] It targets violence, abuse and exploitation,[20] health and development.[21] There are provisions on education,[22] employment,[23] juvenile justice[24] and leisure, art and culture.[25] There are rights for refugee children[26] and disabled children.[27] The Convention has not been incorporated into English law. There is no court to enforce its provisions. Nevertheless, its provisions are influential. They can be seen as a benchmark, and English courts cite them as authoritative statements.[28] The Convention established a Committee on the Rights of the Child: this monitors the implementation of the Convention in the states which are parties to it.[29] The Committee can be critical of the laws and practices of a particular country, and has the capacity to stimulate reform. The UK has submitted two reports to the Committee—a third is imminent—and the Committee's responses, the latest in 2000, have pinpointed matters of concern: child poverty (which has since been addressed); the treatment of child offenders; corporal punishment by parents (which, we have seen, has been responded to, if rather weakly); and the inadequate opportunities afforded children to participate in legal proceedings.[30]

It should be emphasised that the Convention recognises the importance of the family and that of parents in the upbringing of their children. Thus, the responsibilities, rights and duties of parents to provide appropriate direction and guidance in the exercise by children of their rights is to be respected.[31] The state is to use its best efforts to ensure recognition of the principle that both parents have common responsibilities for the upbringing and development of their children, and the "primary responsibility" for bringing them up.[32] Further, parents and others responsible for children have the "primary responsibility" to secure the living conditions necessary for the child's development.[33]

CHILDREN AND THE EUROPEAN CONVENTION ON HUMAN RIGHTS

In 1950 when the ECHR was formulated children were an object of concern—one and a half million had been murdered in the Nazi Holocaust—but no one thought of children as rights-holders.[34] It is accordingly not surprising that there is nothing specifically on children's rights in the Convention. There was therefore justifiable concern when the Human Rights Act 1998 was enacted that it might have a deleterious effect on children (Fortin, 1999). What would the impact be of Art.8 with the endorsement of respect for private and family life? This has not happened: indeed, as Fortin (2003, p.61) points out, the "Convention's ability to promote children's rights has been strengthened through the notion of positive obligations attaching to many of its provisions". For example, to protect children from inhuman and degrading treatment under Art.3.

The jurisprudence of the European Court of Human Rights "inevitably recognises the paramountcy principle".[35] In *Yousef v Netherlands* the European Court of Human Rights concluded that where under Art.8 the rights of parents and those of the child are at stake, "the child's rights *must* be the paramount consideration".[36] The Court has said that

"a fair balance must be struck between the interests of the child and those of the parent and that in striking such a balance, particular importance must be attached to the best interests of the child which, depending on their nature and seriousness, may override those of the parent".[37]

In particular, a parent cannot be entitled under Art.8 to have such measures taken as would harm the child's health and development.[38]

Nevertheless, when disputes about children are fought against the background of Art.8, it is very easy to overlook the rights that children themselves have. Perhaps the best example of this, though it was Art.9 and Protocol 1, Art.2 that the parents invoked, is the case of *R (Williamson) v Secretary of State for Education and Employment*.[39] The case was brought by fundamentalist Christian parents (and teachers at fundamentalist Christian schools) who claimed that education legislation[40] prohibiting corporal punishment in schools infringed their right to manifest their religion and to educate their children in conformity with their own religious convictions.[41] It took Baroness Hale to point out that:

"...this is, and always has been, a case about children, their rights and the rights of their parents and teachers. Yet there has been no one here or in the courts below to speak on behalf of the children. No litigation friend has been appointed to consider the rights of the pupils involved separately from those of the adults. ... The battle has been fought on ground selected by the adults".[42]

Her judgment is, she says, "for the sake of the children".[43] The House of Lords held that Art.9 did protect the parents' belief that their children should be exposed to corporal punishment at school and the Education Act infringed this right, but the interference was justified under Art.9(2). As Baroness Hale explained: "if a child has the right to be brought up without institutional violence, as he does, that right should be respected whether or not his parents and teachers believe otherwise".[44]

In the context of Art.8 the courts make some reference to the rights of children. An example is *Re B (Care: Interference with Family Life)*[45] in which it was said that a care order should not be made "in modern times" without considering the Art.8 rights of the "adult members of the family and of the children of the family".[46] The parents in this case had been denied the opportunity to challenge the evidence of a psychiatrist, to whom evidence of sexual abuse by the 81-year-old grandfather had been communicated by an adult daughter. Another example is *Re C and B (Care Order: Future Harm)*:[47] care orders had been made some years before on two children and care orders were now sought on two more because of the risk of future harm. The Court of Appeal held it had been wrong to make the new care orders: the action taken needed to be a proportionate response to the nature and gravity of the feared harm. Other options should have been explored. The court emphasised that the principle of proportionality dictated that the local authority worked to support and eventually to reunite the family unless the risks were so high that the child's welfare required alternative care. Hale L.J. stressed that under Art.8 "both the children and the parents have the right to respect for their family and private life".[48] And "cutting off all contact and the relationship between the child ... and their family is only justified by the overriding necessity of the interests of the child".[49]

The invisibility of the child's rights is just as apparent in private law disputes. As we will see,[50] children are rarely represented in such disputes and this may be a reason why their profile is low. The child's right may be ignored entirely or briefly mentioned in passing. An interesting example is the recent male circumcision case of *Re S (Specific Issue Order: Religion: Circumcision)*.[51] The Muslim mother and Jain Hindu father could not agree on the circumcision of their son, aged 8½. Baron J.'s judgment which ruled against the mother is fascinating—for students of comparative religion—but there is no reference whatsoever to rights, the Convention and certainly not to children's rights. The nearest the judge gets to talking in children's rights concepts is when she suggests that at puberty the boy will be *Gillick*-competent and thus be able to make his own decision.[52] This is a pity because circumcision raises so many rights issues (and see Freeman, 1999).

One of these is the child's right to an identity. In one of the rare cases in which rights are discussed this right is very much to the fore. In *Re T (Paternity: Ordering Blood Tests)*,[53] the applicant claimed he was the father of a seven-year-old boy and wanted DNA tests to establish this as a preliminary to seeking a parental responsibility and a contact order. Bodey J. held this to be a case where tests to establish paternity were in the child's best interests. The paternity issue was discussed in Chapter 6.[54] What is of note is the way the judge dealt with competing Convention rights. The mother and her husband (who was of course presumed to be the father)[55] had a right to respect for their private and family life, a right which was not to be intruded upon except as may be necessary to give effect to the child's rights and those of the applicant, if he has any. The child also had a right to respect for his private life "in the sense of having knowledge of his identity, which encompasses his true paternity" and "a right to respect for his family life with each of his natural parents". He also has

" 'competing' rights to respect for his private and family life, in the *other* sense that the stability of his present de facto family life should not be put at risk, except as may otherwise be held to be in his interests, and pursuant to Art.8.2".[56]

Bodey J., following settled jurisprudence, had no doubt that the weightiest of the rights belonged to the child, that is the right to know "his true roots and identity".[57]

Courts also grapple with children's rights when applications are brought by, or on behalf of, children. One example of the corporal punishment case of *A v United Kingdom*, discussed in chapter 7.[58] Another is *Z and Others v United Kingdom* brought by children who had suffered abuse: the European Court of Human Rights held the UK government to be in breach of the Convention since the children had suffered inhuman and degrading treatment and had lacked an effective remedy.[59] As a result, the Court of Appeal has held that local authorities have a common law duty of care towards children at risk.[60]

A particularly good example is the case of *R (Howard League for Penal Reform) v Secretary of State for the Home Department.*[61] The league, the leading non-governmental organisation concerned with penal issues, was successful in its application for a declaration that an assertion in the Prison Service Order that the Children Act 1989 did not apply to under 18-year-olds in prison establishments was wrong in law. So the duties a local authority owes to a child under s.17 and s.47 do not cease to be owed merely because the child is detained in a Young Offender Institution. Since very many such children are clearly "in need" and many are suffering or likely to suffer significant harm,[62] this is a ruling of considerable importance. This case was not bought on behalf of an aggrieved child. It was fought in the abstract. But Munby J. warned that if it were the case that children were being subjected to "degrading, offensive and totally unacceptable treatment ... then it can only be a matter of time ... before an action is bought under the Human Rights Act 1998 by or on behalf of a child detained in a YOI ...". His view was that it would "very likely succeed".[63]

CHILDREN AND THE EUROPEAN CHARTER

Among the human rights documents to which Munby J. refers is the Charter of Fundamental Rights of the European Union of 2000. Article 24 of this states that

"(1) Children shall have the right to such protection and care as is necessary for their well-being....
(2) In all actions relating to children, whether taken by public institutions, the child's best interests must be a primary consideration".

Munby J. points out that this, like the UN Convention on the Rights of the Child, though not a source of law in the strict sense, can "properly be consulted insofar as they proclaim, re-affirm or elucidate the content of those human rights that are generally recognised throughout the European family of nations, particular the nature and scope of those fundamental rights that are guaranteed by the European Convention".[64]

THE GILLICK DECISION AND ITS AFTERMATH

The *Gillick* decision is a watershed in the history of children's rights in England.[65] It arose out of a challenge by Mrs Gillick to a DHSS circular which advised doctors that they could prescribe contraceptives to under-age girls.[66] Noting that the law must be "sensitive to human development and social change", Lord Scarman said that "a minor's capacity to make his or her own decision depends on the minor having sufficient understanding and intelligence to make the decision and is not to be determined by reference to any judicially fixed age limit". He saw the "underlying principle" of the law as that "parental right yields to the child's right to make his own decisions when he reaches a sufficient understanding and intelligence to be capable of making up his own mind on the matter requiring decision".[67]

Though the ruling in *Gillick* was about the legality of a government circular on contraception, the implications of the decision have a much wider effect both within healthcare decisions (where it is most often raised[68]) and beyond. For example, can a *Gillick*-competent child be corporally punished? Or seek alternative accommodation? Or leave school? Or refuse to wear school uniform? In *Re Roddy (A Child) (Identification: Restriction on Publication)*,[69] the *Gillick* principle was applied to the question whether a child could exercise her right of freedom of expression under Art.10 of the European Convention on Human Rights, and choose to waive her right to privacy under Art.8. Munby J. emphasised that it was the duty of the court "to *defend* the *right* of the child who has sufficient understanding to make an informed decision to make his or her own choice".[70]

Why? As Munby J. observed, "this is not mere pragmatism".[71] Nolan L.J. explained in *Re W (A Minor) (Medical Treatment: Court's Jurisdiction)*, "it would not only be wrong in principle but also futile and counter-productive for the court to adopt any different approach".[72] And Balcombe L.J., in the same case, accepted that "a court should 'respect' a child's integrity as a human being and not lightly override its [*sic*] decision on such a personal matter as medical treatment".[73] So, in *Re Roddy*, Munby J. reasoned "we do not recognise Angela's dignity and integrity as a human being—we do not respect her rights under Arts 8 and 10[74]—unless we acknowledge that it is for her to make her own choice, and not for her parents or a judge or any other public authority to seek to make the choice on her behalf".[75]

Gillick was applied recently in the *Axon* case.[76] Mrs Axon sought declarations: (i) that medical professionals were under no obligation to keep confidential advice and treatment provided to children under 16 in respect of contraception, sexually trans-mitted infections and, particularly, abortion, and should there-fore not provide such advice and treatment without a parent's knowledge unless to do so might prejudice the child's physical or mental health, so that it was in the child's best interests not to do so; and (ii) that Department of Health guidance was unlawful because it misrepresented the House of Lords' decision in *Gillick*. She failed. *Gillick* was determinative of these issues and the *Guidance* was not unlawful. Though the *Gillick* guidelines were designed for contraception they applied to questions relating to advice and treatment in all sexual matters equally. It was also held that a parent does not have an Art.8 right to family life where (i) the child is "almost 16 ... and does not wish it"; or (ii) where the parent no longer has the right to control the child, and this right only exists "for the benefit of the child" and is justified only insofar as it enables the parent to perform duties towards the child; or (iii) where the child "has sufficient understanding of what is involved to give a consent valid in law".[77]

Supporters of children's autonomy will be much heartened by the *Roddy* and *Axon* decisions (but see Fortin, 2004 and 2006). *Gillick* was beginning to look like "a false dawn" (Lowe and Douglas, 2006, p.364). The case was, of course, about consent to medical treatment. In 1985, when it was decided, it was taken for granted—the question was not even raised—that the reasoning of the Lords applied equally to *Gillick*-competent children who refused to consent to medical treatment. But first in *Re R (A Minor) (Medical Treatment)*[78] and subsequently in a string of other cases, notably *Re W (A Minor) (Medical Treatment: Court's Jur-isdiction)*,[79] courts have retreated from *Gillick* and held it enables a *Gillick*-competent to consent to treatment but not to refuse treatment.[80]

Thus, in *Re R*, a 15-year-old girl with a serious mental illness was in an adolescent psychiatric unit.[81] She was refusing to give her consent to the administration of medication. The unit caring for her made it clear that, if she were to remain there, they required a free hand to administer drugs to her, against her will if necessary. The local authority was reluctant to authorise the administration of drugs to her against her will and applied in wardship for her to be given treatment without her consent.[82] The Court of Appeal considered she was not *Gillick*-competent: she had neither the ability to understand the nature of the proposed treatment, nor a full understanding of the consequences of the treatment and the anticipated consequences of a failure to treat. Her mental state fluctuated from day to day. But, even if she had been competent, it was held the court would still have had the power to override her refusal. The court was also of the opinion that a *Gillick*-competent child's refusal to have treatment could be overridden if a person with parental responsibility gave consent. In *Re W*, where the child was a 16-year-old anorexic, the Court of Appeal held the court had inherent jurisdiction to override a *Gillick*-competent child's refusal to consent to treatment, despite s.8(1) of the Family Law Reform Act 1969 (which provides in unambiguous language that "the consent of a minor who has attained the age of sixteen ... shall be as effective as it would be if he were of full age"). Lord Donaldson M.R. stated:

"No minor of whatever age has power by refusing consent to treatment to override a consent to treatment by someone who has parental responsibility for the minor and *a fortiori* a consent by the court. Nevertheless, such a refusal is a very important consideration in making clinical judgments and for parents and the court in deciding whether themselves to give consent. Its importance increases with the age and maturity of the minor".[83]

The courts are coming to this conclusion for two reasons. One—and this is very clear from Lord Donaldson's judgment in both *Re R* and *Re W*—is to protect the medical profession from subsequent litigation.[84] This may be understandable, but it is difficult to see how removing legitimate expectations from rights-conscious adolescents is going to forestall litigation. Quite the reverse. Second, as Nolan L.J. explained in *Re W*:

"In general terms the present state of the law is that an individual who has reached the age of 18 is free to do with his life what his wishes, but it is the duty of the court to ensure so far as it can that children survive to that age".[85]

Re R and *Re W* have been followed a number of times.[86] The 15-year-old Jehovah's Witness in *Re S (A Minor) (Consent to Medical Treatment)*[87] said compelling her to undergo blood transfusions was "like rape".[88] She prayed for a miracle and for God to save her. But this suggested to the judge that she was not *Gillick*-competent, though many adults in S's position would also pray for a miracle. Of course, a finding of *Gillick* incompetence is an easy way out, and one accordingly that has regularly been taken, and not just by the courts but also by doctors who are the gatekeepers of treatment. The 14-year-old in *Re L (Medical Treatment: Gillick Competency)*[89] carried an Advance Directive but lacked, so it was held, "the constructive formulation of an opinion which occurs with adult experience".[90] Treatment was authorised by the court despite strong opposition.[91] The case is particularly significant because the judge acknowledged that L had not been given "all the details which it would be right and appropriate to have in mind when making ... a decision" to write an advance directive.[92] Of course, if you withhold information from a child it is less likely they can make an informed decision. Competence should be understood in terms of capability of understanding, rather than in terms of what the child actually understands. In *Re M (Medical Treatment: Consent)*,[93] the judge conceded that to impose a heart transplant on a young woman—she was 15—against her wishes is "very serious indeed". There was no suggestion that the girl was not *Gillick* competent. Was she making a "dangerous mistake"[94] and, if so, does society have an interest in protecting her (Fortin, 2003), or was she capable of making "a competent, maximally autonomous choice" (Lewis, 2001). If so, respecting her choice is difficult, but it is preferable to "arbitrary discrimination on the basis of age alone" (Lewis, 2001). If we are to take rights seriously, we may have to accept this includes the right to make, what we consider are, mistakes (Dworkin, 1977).

The most recent of the refusal cases is also highly significant. In *Re P (Medical Treatment: Best Interests)*,[95] the child was nearly 17 and a committed Jehovah's Witness. In the light of his problems, it was likely that an episode might occur—one already had—requiring the administration of blood or blood products if he were to survive. The hospital was seeking leave to administer blood if his situation became life-threatening. It knew he would

object: he already had, and had done so independently of his
parents. The order was made. The judgment makes no reference
to *Gillick* or to the 1969 Act. There is no discussion of whether the
patient is competent, though from what we can glean he clearly
is. However, the judge did at least think that:

"... there may be cases as a child approaches the age of 18 when
his refusal would be determinative. A court will have to consider
whether to override the wishes of a child approaching the age of
maturity when the likelihood is that all that will have been
achieved will have been deferment of an inevitable death and for
a matter only of months".[96]

The underlying jurisprudence of these cases may be that a
child can agree to treatment because treatment is beneficial, but a
refusal involves a rejection of what "doctor thinks best" and
harm may be a likely consequence. As formulated the law makes
a clear distinction between accepting and refusing treatment, but
the distinction itself is not clear. For example, it may be that there
are alternative treatments and the child wishes to agree to one
form of treatment but the doctor wishes to treat differently.
Perhaps the child is prepared to consent to experimental treatment, but the doctor is not prepared to take this risk and offers
only conventional treatment which the child refuses to accept.
The law discriminates and does so on grounds of age when the
clear intention of the House of Lords was to adopt a functional,
rather than a status-based, approach. It means that an elderly
paranoid schizophrenic in Broadmoor can refuse treatment,[97] but
an intelligent 15-year-old girl cannot.[98] The retreat from the
implications of *Gillick* also runs counter to the philosophy of the
Children Act 1989, which, in specified areas, makes it clear that
competent children can object to medical and psychiatric
examination, assessment and treatment.[99]

Can the courts' refusal to take seriously a child's refusal to
accept treatment be defended? Lowe and Juss (1993) and Douglas
(1993) point to what I wrote in 1983 (Freeman, 1983, p.57):

"What sorts of action or conduct would we wish, as children, to
be shielded against on the assumption that we would want to
mature to a rationally autonomous adulthood and be capable of
deciding our own system of ends as free and rational beings? We
would choose those principles that would enable children to
mature to independent adulthood. Our definition of irrationality

would be such as to preclude action and conduct which would frustrate such a goal ...".

Lowe and Juss (1993, p.865) argue that it is "surely right for the law to be reluctant to allow a *child* of whatever age to be able to veto treatment designed for his or her benefit, particularly if a refusal would lead to the child's death or permanent damage". And Douglas (1993, p.868) presumes that if my "liberal paternalism" approach is adopted, the child patient can be held to be "not mature", and her decision accordingly overridden.

But would it not be better to see a 15-year-old like the girl in *Re M* (the heart transplant case) as already "capable of deciding own system of ends as [a] free and rational being"? Or to conclude similarly with the 16-year-old anorexic in *Re W*? It is surely the case that someone so capable is actually *beyond* what is required to satisfy *Gillick* competence. We are right to be sceptical about the autonomy of a child but not where competence can be established. One lesson which can be drawn from the retreat from *Gillick* is that *Gillick* itself may need to be reformulated, with an emphasis less on what children know and understand and more on how the decisions they reach further their goals and cohere with their system of values.

THE CHILDREN'S COMMISSIONER

The concept of an ombudsperson for children was first advocated in 1987 (Freeman, 1987, pp.315–316). There was already one in Norway, established in 1981 (Flekkøy, 1991). There were further calls for a "children's rights commissioner" including in a major report in 1991 (Rosenbaum and Newell, 1991 and Newell, 2000), and the United Nations Committee on the Rights of the Child urged the creation of a commissioner in its reports on the United Kingdom in 1995 and 2002. The Government resisted,[100] but after devolution Wales in 2001[101] and Scotland in 2003[102] went ahead, and Northern Ireland also created a Commissioner in 2003.[103] A Children's Commissioner for England was eventually established by the Children Act 2004 and the first Commissioner, Al Aynsley-Green, started in post in March 2005.

Section 2(1) of the 2004 Act confers on the Children's Commissioner a mandate to promote awareness of the views and interests of children. He may in particular "(a) encourage persons exercising functions or engaged in activities affecting children to take account of their views and interests;

(b) advise the Secretary of State on the views and interests of children;

(c) consider or research the operation of complaints procedures so far as relating to children;

(d) consider or research any other matter relating to the interests of children".

The Commissioner has a narrow remit. Other Commissioners in the United Kingdom are required to promote and safeguard the *rights* of children; by contrast the English Commissioner is to promote "awareness of the views and *interests* of children". Even though s.2(11) directs the Commissioner, when considering what constitutes the interests of children, to have regard to the United Nations Convention on the Rights of the Child, it is regrettable that the rather tame expression "interests" is substituted for rights in the general mandate. Even in s.2(11) the word "rights" is avoided: reference is made instead to the "interests of child".

The commissioner's hands are tied in other ways too. He may undertake an investigation on his own initiative but he must first consult with the Secretary of State.[104] He may also be directed by the Secretary of State to launch an investigation.[105] In each case the trigger is a child, through he is not permitted to conduct an investigation into an individual child as such. The Scottish Commissioner is similarly constrained, not so their counterparts in Wales and Northern Ireland.[106]

The Commissioner may be able to raise the profile of children, though there is not a lot of evidence of this thus far, but whether he will be able to advance children's rights is more doubtful. Those who campaigned for a commissioner must be concerned that children's rights are not on the agenda. Indeed, Clucas (2005) is surely right to observe that "the excision of children's rights from the Act suggests a view that children are less-than-full persons". She comments: "to move away from a rights discourse and back to concern for welfare and compassion is a retrograde step". Will the establishment of a Children's Commissioner be seen as an opportunity lost?

THE MINISTER FOR CHILDREN

The creation of a Minister for Children was advocated first by Brian Jackson in 1983 (Jackson and Jackson, 1981) and subsequently by Joan Lestor MP in 1995 (Lestor, 1995). Writing in 1987 I commented that it was "a concept which only partially attracts me" (Freeman, 1987, p.314). I was concerned that it would just add to bureaucracy, would be impervious to any input of ideas from children and would not generate new ideas. I did not, however, doubt its symbolic importance.

We now have one. The post of Minister for Children and Young People was created in 2003. It is based in the Department for Education and Skills. The Minister is responsible for children's services, child care and provision for children under five, as well as family policy (which includes parenting support and family law). The new post is an integrating measure: it involves the transfer of responsibilities away from the Department of Health, the Home Office and what was the Lord Chancellor's Department (now Minister for Justice). It has done nothing—and is likely to do nothing—to promote children's rights. Nor is this very likely when the Minister can voice the outrageous opinion that the Government (which has after all ratified the UN Convention) does not agree with it (and see Fortin, 2006). We now have both a children's commissioner and a Minister for Children, but no one in government is responsible for co-ordinating the implementation of the Convention.

CHILDREN AS PARTIES IN LEGAL PROCEEDINGS

Since children have been objects of concern rather than subjects in their own right, it is hardly surprising that their participation in legal proceedings has been so limited. It took the Maria Colwell case in 1973–1974 to draw attention to a system which assumed even an abusive parent could represent his/her child's case. In public law proceedings children now have an automatic right to representation, with a guardian (an officer of CAFCASS) and a solicitor together to protect their interests and ensure their case is put. By contrast, in private law proceedings—a dispute about residence or contact for example, there is no automatic right of representation, through increasingly older children have been given greater rights to participate in proceedings which affect them. Article 12(2) of the United Nations Convention on the Rights of the Child emphasises the importance of the child "be[ing] provided the opportunity to be heard in any judicial and administrative proceedings affecting the child, either directly, or though a representative or an appropriate body ...". Nor should we overlook Art.6 of the European Convention on Human Rights: children must with adults be ensured a "fair trial". And Art.8: if there is no obligation to consider a child's views, as is the case where a s.8 application is uncontested, is this a breach of a child's right to have family life respected? Lyon (2000, p.70) goes further and argues that the way children are treated in private law proceedings may be a breach of Art.14 which prohibits discrimination on any ground. She argues "a child's or young person's case could certainly be included within this". Hitherto, the European Court of Human Rights has not been receptive to these arguments, but in *Sahin's* case the child concerned was only five. The compatibility of a child's status in private law proceedings with European norms has yet to be tested in a case concerning an older child.

There is a sense that the courts should be, and perhaps now are, more receptive to the need of the child to be separately represented. In *Re A (Contact: Separate Representation)*[107] Dame Elizabeth Butler-Sloss P., after observing that children are not like "a package"[108] to be handed from one parent to the other, referred to the European Convention on Human Rights to support the view that guardians in private law cases would be increasingly used. Nethertheless, the *CAFCASS Practice Note*[109] insists that "in most private law cases ... a child's interests will be sufficiently safeguarded" by a welfare report.[110] It gives examples of where the child may need party status and legal representation: where there is a foreign element; a need for expert medical or other evidence; where a child wants to instruct a solicitor directly but has been refused leave; an application to seek contact with an adopted child; and where "there are exceptionally difficult, unusual or sensitive issues making it necessary for the child to be granted party status".[111]

L v L (Minor) (Separate Representation)[112] was described by Butler-Sloss L.J. as "a clear case for children to have their own representation".[113] The children were nearly 14, 12 and 9; the family was Australian. The parents had separated, the mother had formed a new relationship, and the children were with the father. It was likely that he would take them back to Australia. There was a dispute as to contact with the mother. There was a concern that the father, "a dominant personality", may have been silencing the children's views. These, the court held, needed separate representation. Although their views could appear in a welfare report, the welfare officer herself was of the view that she could not adequately reflect the children's views in court.

These cases approach separate representation from essentially a paternalistic position. Shouldn't the emphasis rather be on children's rights to participation, a right embedded in the UN Convention on the Rights of the Child? *Mabon v Mabon*[114] recognises this, and it may be predicted points the way forward. The Court of Appeal overturned a refusal to allow three brothers, aged 17, 15 and 13, separate representation. Thorpe L.J. recognised there is "a keener appreciation of the autonomy of the child and the child's consequential right to participate in decision-making processes that fundamentally affect his family life".[115] He realised that "unless we ... are to fall out of step with similar societies as they safeguard Art.12 rights, we must, in the case of articulate teenagers, accept the right to freedom of expression and participation outweighs the paternalistic judgment of welfare".[116] Of course, this is not to say that welfare has no place. Thorpe L.J. explained:

"If direct participation would pose an obvious risk of harm to the child ... and, if the child is incapable of comprehending that risk, then the judge is entitled to find that sufficient understanding has not been demonstrated. But judges have to be equally alive to the risk of emotional harm that might arise from denying the child knowledge of and participation in the continuing proceedings".[117]

On the facts, it was "simply unthinkable" to exclude these young men from proceedings that affected them so fundamentally.[118]

This may be contrasted with the status of the child in public law proceedings. Thus, in care and supervision proceedings the court must appoint a children's guardian (an officer of CAF-CASS) unless "it is not necessary" for one to be appointed to "safeguard" the child's interests.[119] The guardian must safeguard the child's interests.[120] Among the guardian's duties are to ascertain the child's wishes and to advise on whether the child has sufficient understanding for any purpose including the child's refusal to submit to a medical or psychiatric examination or other assessment that the court has the power to require, direct or order.[121] The guardian is required to appoint a solicitor to act for the child (unless she has already been appointed). The guardian instructs the solicitor. But if the child wishes and is able to give instructions him or herself, the solicitor has to take instructions from the child.[122]

The guardian cannot promise that information received from the child will not be disclosed to the court. The guardian may also disclose information to social workers involved in the case, but not to the police without the leave of the court.[123] It has been said that guardians, in safeguarding the child's interests, may choose whether or not they are to believe what the child says.[124] The guardian's report, like a welfare report, is influential and recommendations in it are not to be departed from without reasons being given.[125]

The system has been described as a "Rolls-Royce" model and as the envy of many other jurisdictions.[126] Wall L.J. believes the "tandem model" of representation serves the interests of children very well. The child gets the input of expertise from two disciplines—law and social work. He concedes, though, that the system is "paternalistic", though it works well "even in cases where the child has sufficient understanding to participate in the proceedings concerned without a guardian".[127] It may be that the tandem model will not survive cutbacks in legal expenditure. It is possible, indeed probable, that guardians will cease to be legally represented. While the system is not beyond improvement,[128] this is not a reform calculated to enhance the status of children.

ENDNOTES

CHAPTER 1

1 As in the Adoption and Children Act 2002 s.144(4) and the Human Tissue Act 2004.
2 Article 8(1).
3 See Hart (1994, ch.7) for a discussion of the "open texture" of law.
4 A good account is Flandrin, 1979.
5 They wrote of the "coercion of privacy". See also Olsen, 1985, and Davidoff *et al.*, 1976.
6 Perhaps 10% of one-parent families were male-headed, but there is no doubt that the problem was considered "the unmarried mother".
7 Section 28; this was eventually repealed in 2003.
8 And extended to the children who were "illegitimate".
9 First seen as a social problem in the early 1960s but barely recognised until the Maria Colwell case of 1973–1974.
10 The monograph by Pizzey, 1974, brought this to public attention.
11 *Diwell v Farnes* [1959] 2 All E.R. 379, 384.
12 [2001] 1 A.C. 27: see further Diduck, 2001.
13 There is a powerful dissent by Ward L.J.
14 [1976] Q.B. 503.
15 *Ibid.* 511.
16 The Lords said they were deciding the meaning of "family" for the purposes of the Rent Act only, but it is far-fetched to assume that others will limit it in this way.
17 But see *Karner v Austria* [2003] 2 F.L.R. 623.
18 *Fretté v France* [2003] 2 F.L.R. 9. *Cf.* the Adoption and Children Act 2002 s.49, discussed below, pp.320–321.
19 [2004] 2 A.C. 557.
20 The "non-discrimination" principle.
21 The right to respect for one's home.
22 Rent Act 1977 Sch.1, para.2(2), as amended by the Housing

Act 1988. Note the reference is to "a person". Other legislation referred to "a man and a woman" and has since been amended to "two persons". See Family Law Act 1996 s.62(1) and now Domestic Violence, Crime and Victims Act 2004 s.3 (and Civil Partnership Act 2004 Sch.9, para.13).

23 On gay marriage see below, p.21.

24 A trend noted as regards cohabitation by Deech, 1998 and Freeman and Lyon, 1983.

25 See *Wilkinson v Kitzinger* (No.2) [2007] 1 F.L.R. 295: a gay marriage in British Columbia recognised as a civil partnership. The couple were both domiciled in England.

26 [1971] P. 83.

27 Matrimonial Causes Act 1973 s.11(c).

28 Other details are discussed below, pp.20–21.

29 See Department of Health, *Adoption—A New Approach* Cm. 5017, 2000.

30 Section 49.

31 See the definition of "couple" in s.144(4) of the 2002 Act, as amended by the Civil Partnership Act 2004 s.79.

32 See *Re AB (Adoption: Joint Residence)* [1996] 1 F.L.R. 27 and *Re W (Adoption: Homosexual Partner)* [1997] 2 F.L.R. 406.

33 About 4% of adoptions are handled by Catholic adoption agencies.

34 See the leading article in the *Guardian*, January 25, 2007, p.34, and Bunting, 2007, p.32.

35 Abortion Act 1967 s.4 and Human Fertilisation and Embryology Act 1990 s.38(1).

36 See Baroness Hale's comment—not *à propos* this question—that "Race discrimination was always wrong, long before the world woke up to that fact. Sex discrimination was always wrong, long before the world woke up to that fact" (*Secretary of State for Work and Pensions v M* [2006] 2 F.L.R. 56, 91).

37 If an ECHR challenge were mounted, would it succeed? *Cf. Fretté v France*, above n.18.

38 More so than European Union institutions including the European Court of Justice (see Stalford, 2002).

39 *K and T v Finland* [2000] 2 F.L.R. 79.

40 [2004] 2 F.L.R. 463.

41 *Ibid.*, 471.

42 *Ibid.*, quoting *Kroon and Others v The Netherlands* (1995) 19 E.H.R.R. 263.

43 (1988) 11 E.H.H.R. 322.

44 *Ibid.*, 329.

45 *Marckx v Belgium* (1979) 2 E.H.R.R. 330.

46 *Boyle v United Kingdom* (1995) 19 E.H.R.R. 179.

47 *Selmouni v France* (2000) 29 E.H.R.R. 403.

48 See below, pp.7, 62.

49 See above, n.25, 329.

50 In *R v R* [1992] 1 A.C. 599.

51 But see the investigation of its origins in Freeman, 1985.

52 And see below, p.103.

53 For similar comments in relation to class see Thompson, 1975, p.262.

54 *Wachtel v Wachtel* [1973] Fam. 72, 94.

55 They also protect men but, as I indicate below, p.60, violence against men is not the social problem.

56 See above, n.50.

57 See below, p.63.

58 According to the latest "compromise" in s.58 of Children Act 2004. See below, p.197.

59 Children Act 1989 s.31(2).

60 Graphically illustrated in *Re H (Minors) (Sexual Abuse: Standard of Proof)* [1996] A.C. 563. See below, p.286, and Hayes, 1997.

61 This is well-illustrated in the Sir Roy Meadow case and the evidence that paediatricians are now reluctant to give evidence in cases of suspected child abuse.

62 This is explained below, p.362.

63 *Re R (A Minor) (Wardship: Medical Treatment)* [1992] Fam. 11, and *Re W (A Minor) (Medical Treatment: Court's Jurisdiction)* [1993] Fam. 64. See below, p.363–365.

64 Which they would if a parent or court consented on behalf of a recalcitrant child.

65 See above, n.25, 329.

66 *Ibid.*

67 So described by the petitioner in *Wilkinson v Kitzinger (No.2)* n.25, above, 299 and 300.

68 *Brown v Board of Education* 349 U.S. 483 (1954).

69 The case for gay marriages is argued below, pp.21–26.

70 See below, p.336.

71 Though it is increasingly so. See below, pp.180–188.

72 Ironically, some rapists (husbands) have parental status and thus parental responsibility automatically: see below, p.181.

73 See below, p.168.

74 See below, p.237.
75 I questioned the need for a Family Court in Freeman, 1984b.
76 See [1986] Fam Law 247.
77 Respectively *A Single Civil Court?* and *Focusing Judicial Resources Appropriately*, both 2005.
78 See below, pp.85–87.
79 Administration of Justice Act 1970 s.1.
80 There are six female judges in the Family Division.
81 Matrimonial Causes Act 1967.
82 Matrimonial and Family Proceedings Act 1984 ss.33 and 34.
83 Children Act 1989 s.92(1).
84 Matrimonial and Family Proceedings Act 1984 ss.33(3), 36A(6).
85 Children (Allocation of Proceedings) Order 1991 s.3. Unless proceedings are brought following a s.37 direction, on which see below, p.247.

CHAPTER 2

1 Since 1994; the Marriage Act 1994 inserted s.46A into the Marriage Act 1949.
2 The formalities for marriage in Scotland were eventually modernised in 1977: see Marriage (Scotland) Act 1977.
3 For the latter part of this history see Stone, 1992.
4 Article 12.
5 Marriage Act 1949 s.2.
6 Matrimonial Causes Act 1973 s.11(a)(ii).
7 Put, for example, to the Latey Committee on the *Age of Majority*, Cmnd 3342: see para.102.
8 In 2003 6,860 women aged 16 to 19 married. Only 1800 men did so. See *Population Trends* 119 (2005), Table 5.
9 For history of the change see Cretney, 2003, pp.57–62.
10 In 1970 the Law Commission rejected the proposal that underage marriages should be made voidable, as they had been until 1929 (Report on *Nullity of Marriage*, Law Com 33, paras 16–20).
11 Unless there is a residence order (see below, p.175), in which case only the parents with parental responsibility and a residence order need consent: Marriage Act 1949 s.3, as amended.
12 If the relevant person is absent, inaccessible or under a disability: *ibid*.

13 Marriage Act 1949 s.3(1)(b). In 1988, the Law Commission rejected the view that the consent requirement be repealed, seeing it "of doubtful benefit to the very children whom it is trying to help" (*Review of Child Law*, No.172, para.7.11).

14 The underage person would necessarily have had to deceive the registrar, and probably therefore to have committed a crime.

15 *Social Trends.*

16 Many fertility clinics impose a maximum age: challenges to such tests have failed (*R v Sheffield AHA Ex p. Seale* (1995) 25 B.M.L.R. 1).

17 Marriage Act 1949 Sch.1, as amended.

18 On the genetic risks of inbreeding see Kilbrandon report, *The Marriage Laws of Scotland* Cmnd. 4011 (1969).

19 On this see H.D. Krause, *Family Law*, 1990, p.38. But the law of incest does not apply: see American Law Institute, *Model Penal Code* §230.2, 410–411 (1980).

20 See *Cheni v Cheni* [1965] P.85.

21 See *Catalano v Catalano* 170 A 2d 726 (1961).

22 Marriage Act 1949 Sch.1.

23 Leviticus 18: 22 and 20: 13. But was this the Israelite abhorrence of Egyptian practices, including same-sex marriage?

24 Family Law Act 1975.

25 Genesis 2: 24.

26 Deceased Wife's Sister's Marriage Act 1907. It only became lawful to marry a deceased brother's widow in 1921. The extension followed World War I which had left many widows.

27 The Valerie Mary Hill and Alan Monk (Marriage Enabling) Act 1985. There were two further examples, but none since the 1986 Act came into operation.

28 *No Just Cause: Affinity: Suggestions for Change*, 1984.

29 *Ibid.*

30 Marriage (Prohibited Degrees of Relationship) Act 1986 s.1(1).

31 Probably about £2000. Legal aid is not available to obtain a personal Act of Parliament.

32 *B and L v United Kingdom* [2006] 1 F.L.R. 35.

33 The announcement (in November 2005) has not yet led to the promised legislation.

34 Provided she is not his half-sister or he her half-brother.

Further, children can intermarry—this has seemingly never been questioned.

35 On the meaning of polygamy see *Lee v Lau* [1967] P. 14.

36 *Hyde v Hyde* (1866) L.R. 1 P. & D. 130.

37 The African Protocol on Women's Rights 2003 Art.6(b) encourages monogamy as "the preferred form of marriage" (and see Banda, 2005, pp.70–71)

38 Polyandry—women with a plurality of husbands—commands less attention. No case has ever been the subject of litigation in the UK. It tended once to be found in parts of the world where the male role in procreation was not understood.

39 See the discussion of Kaganas and Murray (1991) *Acta Juridica* 116, 119, 121. But in relation to South Africa see now Recognition of Customary Marriages Act 1998.

40 And see J. McMurty, "Monogamy: A Critique" (1972) 56 *The Monist* 587.

41 Particularly Pakistan and Bangladesh, but also the Muslim Middle East.

42 *Mohamed v Knott* [1969] 1 Q.B. 1, 13–14. See further Clarkson and Hill, *Jaffey on the Conflict of Laws*, London, Butterworths, 2002, p.375. So, for example, the children are legitimate and spouses qualify as spouses for succession purposes.

43 Matrimonial Proceedings (Polygamous Marriages) Act 1972 (now Matrimonial Causes Act 1973 s.47).

44 *Chetti v Chetti* [1909] P. 67.

45 *A-M v A-M (Divorce: Jurisdiction: Validity of Marriage)* [2001] 2 F.L.R. 6, 23.

46 *Re Bethell* (1887) 38 Ch.D. 220; *Ali v Ali* [1968] P. 564.

47 *Radwan v Radwan* (No.2) [1973] Fam. 35.

48 Which the court said was France: of course this is contrary to normal international law understanding.

49 *Lord Advocate v Jaffrey* [1921] 1 A.C. 146. The rule changed in 1974: Domicile and Matrimonial Proceedings Act 1973 s.1.

50 See *Radwan v Radwan* [1993] Fam. 24.

51 See now Domicile and Matrimonial Proceedings Act 1973 s.16(1).

52 They had contemplated permanent residence in Egypt and Mary had converted to Islam.

53 Matrimonial Proceedings (Polygamous Marriages) Act 1972 (now s.47 of Matrimonial Causes Act 1973). *Hyde v Hyde*, above n.36, denied a polygamous spouse matrimonial relief.

54 For example, Karsten, 1973; Pearl, 1973; Wade, 1973.
55 To this effect see Hart, 1967, p.10.
56 They spent 5 years in Egypt and 14 years in England.
57 Matrimonial Causes Act 1973 s.11(d).
58 Matrimonial Causes Act 1973 s.14(1).
59 Because polygamous marriages are not permitted under English domestic law.
60 *Hussain v Hussain* [1982] 3 All E.R. 369.
61 Private International Law (Miscellaneous Provisions) Act 1995 s.5(1).
62 Of course, it may be void for another reason, for example, failure to comply with formalities.
63 In effect the prohibition on taking a second wife could only be effective if the first marriage could not be dissolved.
64 There is an excellent assessment of this in D'Onofrio, 2005. See also Tracy, 2002.
65 *Bibi v United Kingdom* (App. No.19628/92) (a challenge to English law's failure to recognise second marriage of a polygamous marriage).
66 Offences Against the Person Act 1861 s.47.
67 Even where there is deception it is rare for a prison sentence of more than three years to be imposed.
68 But the position can be regularised if the couple go through a new ceremony of marriage.
69 Matrimonial Causes Act 1973 s.11(c).
70 This was noted by the European Court of Human Rights in *Sheffield and Horsham v United Kingdom* [1998] 2 F.L.R. 928.
71 [1971] P.83.
72 The law has a tendency to dichotomise. On the dichotomy see Kennedy, 1988, ch.13, and Collier, 1995, p.130: basing marriage on a biological dichotomy ignores the "social" aspects of a marriage relationship. On persons who are intersex see Chau and Herring, 2002, 2004, and the case of *W v W (Nullity: Gender)* [2001] 1 F.L.R. 324.
73 See above n.71, 107.
74 *Ibid.*, 106.
75 *Rees v United Kingdom* [1987] 2 F.L.R. 111.
76 *Cossey v United Kingdom* [1991] 2 F.L.R. 492.
77 See above n.70.
78 [2002] 2 F.L.R. 487.
79 [2002] 2 F.L.R. 518.
80 But it reinforces the pathology of gender dysphoria. See also Diduck, 2003, p.204.

81 *Bellinger v Bellinger* [2003] 2 A.C. 467 and see Cowan, 2004.
82 The Act does not affect the law on capacity to marry.
83 Gender Recognition Act 2004 s.1(1), (3). On children and dysphoria see Giordano, 2007.
84 Gender Recognition Act 2004 s.9(1).
85 Gender Recognition Act 2004 s.2(1).
86 Gender Recognition Act 2004 s.3(3).
87 Gender Recognition Act 2004 s.4.
88 Gender Recognition Act 2004 Sch.4.
89 Gender Recognition Act 2004 s.4(3).
90 Gender Recognition Act 2004 s.5.
91 In 2002.
92 In 2001.
93 In 2005. Other countries to allow same-sex marriage include Canada (see Civil Marriages Act 2005 and Wright, 2006) and in the USA, Massachusetts (see *Goodridge v Department of Health* 798 N.E. 2d 941 (2003)), Vermont, New York and California.
94 These are set by the state. Contrast the French *Pacte Civil de Solidarité* where the parties register a contract, rather than a relationship. It is open to heterosexual couples as well, and is different from marriage, thus giving them a choice.
95 DTI Women and Equality Unit, *Civil Partnerships: A Framework for the Recognition of Same-Sex Couples*, 2003, para.1.2.
96 See H. Muir in the *Guardian*, August 8, 2006—"6,500 Couples Opt for Civil Partnerships but Ceremony Creates New Problems".
97 And see Curry-Sumner (2006).
98 1996, p.8. It is not his view.
99 Boswell (1994) cites examples, and quotes texts of same-sex enfraternisation rituals carried out by Roman Catholic and Greek Orthodox Churches.
100 "It is revolting to have no better reason for a rule of law than it was laid down in the time of Henry IV", noted Oliver Wendell Holmes (see (1897) 10 *Harvard Law Review* 457, 459).
101 St Augustine had no problem with this: see above n.98, pp.96–97. And see Ormrod J. in *Corbett v Corbett*, above, n.71, at 106.
102 Women over 50 can cope with motherhood, according to a study reported in the *Guardian*, October 23, 2006, pp.1, 2.

The oldest mother in England was a 63-year-old child psychiatrist. See the *Guardian*, May 5, 2006, p.3.

103 "The Closet Straight", *National Review*, July 5, 1993, pp.43, 45. This is reproduced in Sullivan, 1997, p.154. See also Arkes, 1993.

104 This argument, which Arkes, n.103, above, comes close to making, suffers from the standard objection to the "slippery slope argument".

105 1994, p.1067. For Finnis (1996) the common good of marriage is a "basic good" (and see Finnis, 1980).

106 So he argues (1994, p.1066).

107 Of course, many religious conservatives object to the use of contraception.

108 Thus, Harvey Mansfield "Saving Liberalism from Liberals", *Harvard Crimson*, November 8, 1993, p.2. On "shame" see Nussbaum, 2004.

109 Thus, Arkes, above, n. 103, 43.

110 Harry V. Jaffa. See "Our Ancient Faith: A Reply To Professor Anastaplo in *Original Intent and the Framers of the Constitution*, Washington, Regnery, 1994, pp.369 and 383.

111 In *Sex And Reason*, 1992, p.311.

112 See below, p.60.

113 Posner, 1992, p.313.

114 Posner, 1992, p.313.

115 See to this effect Diduck and Kaganas, 2006, p.69. See also Auchmuty, 2004.

116 So described by Carl Stychin, 2006.

117 Thus in above, n.95, para.1.3 it was said there were "no plans to introduce same-sex marriage".

118 Ettelbrick, 1996, p.115.

119 Thus a civil partnership is not voidable for non-consummation: Civil Partnership Act 2004 s.50. Inexplicably, it is also not voidable if the respondent is suffering from a communicable venereal disease.

120 Civil Partnership Act 2004 s.44. Harper *et al.*, 2005, are critical of the omission, but finding an equivalent—infidelity seems too vague—would be difficult.

121 Married Women's Property Act 1964 s.1.

122 This is rarely used today in relation to spouses but is hardly apt in the case of civil partners, where the assumption is that they are equals.

123 Civil Partnership Act 2004 s.72(3) and Sch.6.

124 Civil Partnership Act 2004 s.254 and Sch.24.

125 Civil Partnership Act 2004 Sch.5 Pt 6.
126 Civil Partnership Act 2004 s.71 and Sch.4.
127 Civil Partnership Act 2004 s.82 and Sch.9.
128 Civil Partnership Act 2004 s.72(2).
129 See his _Virtually Normal_, 1995, p.172. See also Sullivan, 1997, a most useful collection of materials on the debate.
130 Had Mill addressed the question, it is the response we would expect of him (see Mill, 1859).
131 Sullivan appears to accept this because he says, inter alia, that marriage is a mechanism for emotional stability and economic security: 1995, p.182.
132 See also Raz, 1986.
133 Eskridge, 1996, p.116.
134 Eskridge, 1996, p.8.
135 1996, p.9.
136 1996, p.9.
137 It is thought that recognition of same-sex partnerships is a key element in Sweden's successful anti-AIDS campaign (Henriksson and Ytterburg, 1992, pp.321–322). See also Eskridge and Weimer, 1994, pp.768–769 and Eskridge, 1996, p.120.
138 Eskridge, 1996, p.112.
139 See also Patterson, 1995; Flaks _et al._, 1995; Golombok _et al._, 1983. For a contrary view see Belcastro _et al._, 1993. Herek, 1991, offers a lawyer's guide to the research.
140 Eskridge, 1996, p.112.
141 Eskridge, 1996, p.118.
142 (1866) L.R. 1 P.&D. 130.
143 _P v P_ [1964] 3 All E.R. 919.
144 As in _Corbett v Corbett_, above, n.71.
145 And see Matrimonial Causes Act 1857 ss.2 and 22, and Cretney, 2003, pp.76–77.
146 (1845) 1 Rob. Eccl. 279.
147 Collier, 1995, 153. So penetration defines sexual intercourse in English law.
148 _R v R_ [1952] 1 All E.R. 1194.
149 _Dredge v Dredge_ [1947] 1 All E.R. 29.
150 It will not always be obvious to the petitioner which it is: it is therefore not unusual to petition in the alternative.
151 _Harthan v Harthan_ [1949] P. 115.
152 _S. v S. (otherwise C)_ [1956] P. 1.
153 [1971] P. 226.
154 _Ibid._, 232.

155 *Horton v Horton* [1947] 2 All E.R. 871, 874
156 *Ford v Ford* (1987) 17 Fam. Law 232.
157 *Ford v Ford.*
158 See *Jodla v Jodla* [1960] 1 W.L.R. 236, *Kaur v Singh* [1972] 1 W.L.R. 105, *A v J (Nullity Proceedings)* [1989] 1 F.L.R. 110.
159 *Baxter v Baxter* [1948] A.C. 274 (and see Gower, 1948).
160 *Ibid.*, 290.
161 *Cackett v Cackett* [1950] P. 253; *White v White* [1948] P. 330. Contrast *Grimes v Grimes* [1948] P. 323.
162 In the Nullity of Marriage Bill 1971. But the most experienced of all divorce judges at the time (Lord Hodson) favoured retaining the existing law.
163 The Lord Chancellor, Lord Hailsham "refused to budge" (Cretney, 2003, p.88).
164 Particularly those which cannot be regarded as "forced". See below, p.30. See Cretney, 2003, p.88.
165 Under the Matrimonial Causes Act 1973 s.1(2)(d).
166 See on the sources Johnson and Jordan, 2006.
167 The constitutional prohibition on divorce was removed in 1995.
168 See Matrimonial Causes Act 1973 s.12(c). Cretney *et al.* (2003, p.61) conceptualise drunkenness and under the influence of drugs as going to "mistake", but I think "or otherwise" is intended to cover such problems. Why else is it there?
169 *Per* Sir J. Hannen P. in *Durham v Durham* (1885) 10 P.D. 80, 82. See also Hodson L.J. in *Re Park* [1954] P. 112, 136.
170 [2005] 1 F.L.R. 965.
171 *Ibid.*, 1004.
172 *Ibid.*, 991.
173 *Ibid.* See also Karminski J. in *Re Park*, above n.169, at 107.
174 See *Re E*, above n.170, 991.
175 *Ibid.*
176 *Ibid.*, 993.
177 *Ibid.*, 994.
178 See *Re F* [1990] 2 A.C. 1, and *Re S* [2003] 1 F.L.R. 292.
179 "Annulment of marriage is a very serious step", *per* Sir J. Simon P. in *Szechter v Szechter* [1971] P. 286.
180 *Scott v Sebright* (1886) 12 P.D. 21. See also the US case of *Lee v Lee* 3 S.W. 2d 672 (1928): "if there had not been a wedding, there would have been a funeral".
181 *Buckland v Buckland* [1968] P. 296. The alleged offence was in Malta, where it was described as "minor corruption". It

was said of the bridegroom that, "fearing prison, he chose marriage".

182 *Szechter v Szechter* [1971] P. 286. The facts of this case, while touching the heart strings, strain credulity. But do read them.

183 And in assisting it. See, in addition to *Szechter*, *H v H* [1954] P. 258 and *Parojcic v Parojcic* [1958] 1 W.L.R. 1280.

184 See above, p.27.

185 (1981) 11 Fam. Law 152.

186 As was found in the "totalitarian" cases, above, p.30.

187 (1982) 4 F.L.R. 232.

188 *Ibid.*, 234.

189 *Ibid.*, 234.

190 [2003] 1 F.L.R. 661.

191 *Hirani* was followed in *NS v MI* [2007] 1 F.L.R. 44 and has also been followed in Scotland. See *Mahmood v Mahmood* 1993 S.L.T. 580 and *Mahmud v Mahmud* 1994 S.L.T. 599.

192 *P v R*, 666.

193 See *Re SK (Proposed Plaintiff) (An Adult by way of her Litigation Friend)* [2005] 2 F.L.R. 230 and *Re SA (Vulnerable Adult With Capacity: Marriage)* [2006] 1 F.L.R. 867.

194 In *Re SA*, above, n.194.

195 The Home Office had previously issued guidance to the police.

196 See Home Office and Foreign and Commonwealth Office, *Forced Marriage: A Wrong Not a Right*, Consultation Paper, September 2005. Forced Marriage (Civil Protection) Bill (debated in the House of Lords on January 26, 2007) is expected to become law. A new remedy of a civil injuction to which a power of arrest may be attached is included in this.

197 See the *Guardian*, June 8, 2006, p.13. It is interesting that there was support for the new offence among victims, but 74% of police, prosecutors and probation officers who responded to the Consultation Paper thought existing legislation was sufficient. On the question of whether schools are doing enough when Asian girls disappear from the classroom see Tickle, 2006.

198 But see the Australian case of *Allardyce v Mitchell* (1869) 6 W.W & A'B 45 (belief that H was a member of a particular family—he wasn't—was a mistake as to identity).

199 Particularly where the mistake has been induced by deception or fraud. A good example is *Moss v Moss* [1897]

P. 263 (a woman deceived her husband-to-be that she was pregnant by another man—she gave birth 18 days after the marriage ceremony). Pregnancy *per alium* at the time of the marriage is now a separate nullity ground (see below, p.33). It wasn't then, and Cretney reports (2003, p.76) the couple remained bound to one another until death terminated the marriage (he doesn't say when).

200　*Alfonso-Brown v Milwood* [2006] 2 F.L.R. 265 (exuberant traditional engagement in Ghana in Ga language: no intention to marry despite placing a ring on woman's finger).

201　*Kelly (otherwise Hyams) v Kelly* (1932) 49 T.L.R. 99 (a Jewish woman thought register office ceremony was a betrothal, believing marriages could only take place in a synagogue).

202　*Mehta v Mehta* [1945] 2 All E.R. 690 (Englishwoman marrying in India believing it was a ceremony to convert her to the Hindu faith: it was, but it was also a marriage ceremony).

203　*Hall v Hall* (1908) 24 T.L.R. 756 (an Englishwoman thought marriages could only be celebrated in church and thus believed register office ceremony was the registration of her name).

204　Matrimonial Causes Act 1973 s.12(d), as amended by the Mental Health Act 1983, Sch.4, para.34.

205　*Bennett v Bennett* [1969] 1 W.L.R. 430, 434.

206　*Ibid.*

207　That is those of unsound mind and those with mental disorder.

208　On divorce and mental illness, see below pp.94–95, 97.

209　Matrimonial Causes Act 1973 s.12(e). This was introduced as much to promote "the interests of morality" as to protect the petitioner from the possibility of contamination.

210　On other solutions see Closen *et al.*, 1994.

211　As in *Moss v Moss*, above n.199.

212　It seems the concern is not with men's sexuality.

213　Matrimonial Causes Act 1973 s.12(h).

214　Matrimonial Causes Act 1973 s.12(g).

215　See above, p.12.

216　For example, in Cretney *et al.*, 2003. ch.1.

217　It is still possible to enter into a common law marriage but only in limited circumstances, and abroad. Marriages in war-torn countries which do not comply with the formalities of local law (the *lex loci celebrationis*) may be upheld in

England as a common law marriage, though the last thing the parties can have intended was to comply with English law as it existed until 1753! For an example see *Taczanowska (otherwise Roth) v Taczanowski* [1957] P. 301.

218 By the Clandestine Marriages Act 1753 (Lord Hardwicke's Act), on which see Gillis, 1985 and Parker, 1987 and 1990. The Act did not apply to the Royal Family, Jews or Quakers.

219 The Chelmsford Royal Commission (see Cretney, 2003b, pp.15–19).

220 Report of the Royal Commission on the Laws of Marriage, 1868, p.35.

221 Law Com. No.53.

222 See Annex to Law Com. No.53, para.72.

223 Law Com. No.53. And see Cretney, 2003, pp.26–27.

224 According to *The Times*, May 11, 2001. But is it a building?

225 See Cretney, 2003, p.28.

226 *Report of the Efficiency Scrutiny of the Registration Service*, 1985.

227 *Ibid.*, para.41.1.

228 Marriage Act 1949 s.46A.

229 The Marriages (Approved Premises) Regulations 1995 SI 510/1995.

230 *Hansard*, H.C. vol.250, col.1339. In fact Debussy wrote this!

231 *Ibid.*

232 *R v Registrar-General Ex p. Segerdal* [1970] 2 Q.B. 697, which concerns the Church of Scientology. The Court of Appeal denied this was a religion, but had difficulty, indeed was embarrassed, at positing that religion required reverence to a deity, because this might require Buddhism to be rejected.

233 Cretney, 2003b, p.31.

234 *Hansard*, H.C. vol.250, col.1330.

235 Marriage Act 1949 s.47 (Quakers), s.26(1)(d) (Jews).

236 Section 24. See also Reporting of Suspicious Marriages and Registration of Births, Deaths and Marriages (Miscellaneous Amendments) Regulations 2000, SI 2000/3164.

237 Sections 160 and 161.

238 But such a regime has not been held to be in breach of the European Convention: see *R (On the Application of Baiai) v Secretary of State for Home Dept.* [2006] 2 F.C.R. 131.

239 And see *R v IAT Ex p. Kumar* [1986] Imm. A.R. 446.

240 Though English law does not recognise the concept of a "sham" marriage: see *Vervaeke v Smith* [1983] 1 A.C. 145.

241 See Haskey, 1987.
242 In 1999 38% of marriages were in a church or other place of religious worship.
243 See *Social Trends*.
244 See *Civil Registration: Vital Change*, 2002 and Consultation Paper, *Civil Registration: Delivering Vital Change*, Office for National Statistics, 2003.
245 In 2002.
246 On this see below, pp.107–108.
247 *Supporting Families: A Consultation Document* (London, Stationery Office), 4.15.
248 And see Deech, 1998, p.711.
249 See Closen *et al.*, 1994.
250 Matrimonial Causes Act 1973 s.12(e).
251 *Gandhi v Patel* [2002] 1 F.L.R. 603.
252 *A-M v A-M* [2001] 2 F.L.R. 6.
253 *Gereis v Yagoub* [1997] 1 F.L.R. 854. The church was not licensed for marriages, and the ceremony was conducted by a priest not licensed to conduct marriages.
254 Unreported, 1999: it is briefly discussed in above, n.252, 613–614. I am sure fuller reports can be found in *Hello!* or *OK* magazines!
255 [2000] 1 F.L.R. 8.
256 37 years in this case.
257 Section 25.
258 Matrimonial Causes Act 1973 ss.23 and 24.
259 [1995] 2 F.L.R. 268, 275 *per* Russell L.J. See, further, Cretney, 1996.
260 *J v S-T* [1997] 1 F.L.R. 402. The facts of the case are extraordinary: "she" had "intercourse" with her wife using a plaster of paris penis which she kept in a sock. The "wife's" suspicions were not aroused by noticing that her "husband" menstruated etc.
261 There is also a six-month bar where an interim gender recognition certificate has been issued. See Matrimonial Causes Act 1973 s.13(2A).
262 Matrimonial Causes Act 1973 s.13(2).
263 Matrimonial Causes Act 1973 s.13(3).
264 Matrimonial Causes Act 1973 s.13(1).
265 [1979] Fam. 70.
266 Legitimacy Act 1976 s.1(1).
267 An illegitimate child cannot at present succeed to a title of honour. See further Cretney, 2003, ch.15.

268 The agreement does not have effect as a contract: Civil Partnership Act 2004 s.73.
269 Law Reform (Miscellaneous Provisions) Act 1970 s.1(1).
270 *Mossop v Mossop* [1988] 2 F.L.R. 173, 176.
271 See s.3(2), and *Cohen v Sellar* [1926] 1 K.B. 536; *Jacobs v Davis* [1917] 2 K.B. 532.
272 See Family Law Act 1996, s.62(3)(e).
273 See, above, n.269, s.2(2).
274 This has been under attack since *Pettitt v Pettitt* [1970] A.C. 777, 793 (Lord Reid).
275 See Matrimonial Proceedings and Property Act 1970 s.37.
276 Michael Douglas, having paid $40 million to his previous wife, is reported to have entered into a pre-marital agreement with Catherine Zeta Jones.
277 See *White v White* [2001] 1 A.C. 596 and *Miller v Miller/ McFarlane v McFarlane* [2006] 1 F.L.R. 1186, and below, p.130.
278 *K v K* [1995] 2 F.L.R. 45.
279 *Financial Provision on Divorce: Clarity and Fairness—Proposals for Reform.*
280 (1981) 2 F.L.R. 19.
281 *Ibid.*, 25.
282 [2002] 1 F.L.R. 508.
283 *Ibid.*, 536, approving Lord Nicholls in *White v White* [2001] 1 AC 596, 599 (and see below, p.130).
284 *Ibid.*, 537.
285 In *Edgar v Edgar* above, n.280.
286 See above, n.282, 537.
287 *Ibid.*
288 Under Matrimonial Causes Act 1973 s.25(2)(g).
289 [2002] 1 F.L.R. 654.
290 [2003] 1 F.L.R. 120.
291 Under the Matrimonial Causes Act 1973 s.25(1) the child's welfare is the "first consideration". See below, p.137.
292 *A More Certain Future—Recognition of Pre-Marital Agreements in England and Wales*, November 2004.
293 The European Commision is looking at this.
294 *The Marriage Contract* (New York, Free Press, 1975).
295 *The Neutered Mother, the Sexual Family and other Twentieth Century Tragedies* (New York, Routledge, 1995).
296 "Contract Marriage—The Way Forward or Dead End?" (1996) 23 *Journal of Law and Society* 234, 237.
297 *Book of Common Prayer*: "Betrothal".

298 The divorce rate in Arkansas is more than twice the national average (6.5 per 1000 as opposed to 4.2).

299 Arizona Revised Statutes ss.25–901 to 25–906. The change took effect on August 21, 1998.

300 See Laura A. Sanchez, Steven L. Nook and James D. Wright, "The Implementation of Covenant Marriage in Louisiana" (2000) 9 *Virginia Journal of Social Policy and Law* 192–223 and Katherine Spaht and Symeon C. Symeonides, "Covenant Marriage and Conflict of Laws" (1999) 32 *Creighton Law Review* 1085–1120.

301 There have been Bills to introduce covenant marriage in many more US States. Such legislation has passed one House, but not both, in Oregon, Georgia, Texas and Oklahoma.

302 See *R v R (Rape: Marital Exemption)* [1991] 4 All E.R. 481.

303 "Just Marriage" in (ed.) Mary Lyndon Shanley, *Just Marriage* (New York, Oxford University Press, 2004), p.16.

304 "Afterword" in *ibid.*, 114. A classic source is John Stuart Mill: see *On Liberty*, Cambridge, Cambridge University Press, 1989 (Originally published in 1859), pp.105–108.

305 According to Etzioni, "A Communitarian Position for Civil Unions" in above, n.304, 63. One of the first advocates of same sex-marriage (Milton Regan) reasoned that marriage would "extend institutional support to those who desire to proclaim their commitment to each other" (1993, 152).

306 *Ibid.*, p.64.

307 *Per* Drucilla Cornell, "The Public Supports of Love", above n.303, p.81.

308 See above, n.297, pp.242–243.

309 "The Division of Marital Assets Following Divorce" (1998) 25 *Journal of Law and Society* 336, 337 and 363.

310 See, for example, Rasmusen and Stake, 1998, who argue the case for allowing the private construction of grounds of divorce.

311 "The Economics of Wifing Services: Law and Economics on the Family" (1991) 18 *Journal of Law and Society* 206, 215–216.

312 And see Abrams, 1998.

313 "Bargaining In The Shadow of the Market: Is there a Future for Egalitarian Marriage?" (1998) 84 *Virginia Law Review* 509, 669. See also Hirshman and Larson, 1998.

314 "Marriage: An Unneccessary Legal Concept" in (eds.) J.

Eekelaar and S. Katz, *Marriage and Cohabitation in Contemporary Societies* (Toronto, Butterworths, 1980), pp.71–81.

315 *The Neutered Mother, the Sexual Family and Other Twentieth Century Tragedies* (New York, Rouledge, 1995), p.229.

316 *The Autonomy Myth* (New York, The New Press, 2004), p.123.

317 *Ibid.*

318 Above, n.304, p.112.

319 *Ibid.*, p.113.

320 See above, n.316, p.133.

321 In Europe, Belgium, the Netherlands and Spain. In the USA, Massachusetts.

322 See above, n.316, p.134.

323 See above, n.302.

324 *R v Jackson* [1891] 1 Q.B. 671, 682 and see below, p.63.

325 See below, p.60.

326 See *White v White* [2001] 1 A.C. 596; *Miller v Miller; McFarlane v McFarlane* [2006] 1 F.L.R. 1186, and below, p.130.

327 See above, n.316, p.135.

328 Protection from Harrassment Act 1997.

329 See Freeman, 1984.

330 See Morgan, 1995.

331 *The Ties That Bind* (London, Routledge, 1984).

332 For a recent challenge see *Wilkinson v Kitzinger* (No.2) [2007] 1 FLR 295.

333 "Marriage and the Construction of Reality" (1964) 46 *Diogenes* 1, 16.

334 "Marriage: A Sacred or Profane Love Machine?" (1993) 1 *Feminist Legal Studies* 75.

335 *Ibid.*, 78.

336 *Ibid.*, 80.

337 *Ibid.*, 82.

338 "Married and Unmarried Cohabitation: The Case of Sweden, with some Comparisons" (1975) 37 *Journal of Marriage and the Family* 677–682, 677.

339 *Dyson Holdings Ltd v Fox* [1975] 3 All E.R. 1030.

340 An assimilation noted by Freeman and Lyon in the early 1980s (1983, p.206).

341 Though parish registers give some insight into children born of non-marital relationships. See Laslett *et al.* (1980). On the problems of measuring "cohabitation" see Murphy, 2000.

342 As few as 3% of women were thought to be cohabiting in 1980. It was about 12% in Denmark and Sweden.

343 Office for National Statistics, *Census 2001*, Table s.006.

344 Office for National Statistics, *Social Trends* 36 (2006), 27; *Social Trends* 35 (2005), Table 2.10.

345 See Law Commission, *Cohabitation: The Financial Consequences of Relationships Breakdown*, Consultation Paper No.179 (2006), 2.10.

346 Such as H.G. Wells, Bertrand Russell and Bernard Shaw. Cretney (2003, p.516 n.2) cites also "George Eliot", though she could not marry the man she lived with for 25 years because he was married to another woman whose adultery he had condoned.

347 See Ermisch and Francesconi, 2000, pp.35–36.

348 Figures from General Household Survey, cited above n.346, 2.31.

349 Office for National Statistics, *Marriage, Divorce and Adoption Statistics*, Series FM2 No.31 (2006), table 3.38.

350 See above, n.347, p.27.

351 See Haskey, 1999, p.17.

352 The median duration of marriage at point of divorce in 2006 was 11.6 years. Many will have been living apart during the latter part of this period (the *Guardian*, August 31, 2007, p.3).

353 Though controlling for socio-economic and other variables, cohabitants are only 2–3 times more likely than spouses to separate: see Böheim and Ermisch, 1999, pp.7, 12–13.

354 And see Waite L.J. in *Fitzpatrick v Sterling Housing Association* [1998] Ch. 304, 308.

355 See Barlow *et al.*, 2001, table 2.2.

356 See Freeman and Lyon, 1983, pp.5–6 (noting that it was unlikely that "cohabitant" will easily or readily become part of common usage!).

357 In *Churchill v Roach* [2004] 2 F.L.R. 989 (believed that after 6 months' cohabitation, 7 days a week, partner would become common-law wife).

358 See above, n.356, pp.45–46.

359 See Hibbs *et al.*, 2001.

360 Consumer Credit Act 1974 s.184(5).

361 Pneumoconiosis (Workmen's Compensation etc) Act 1979 s.3(1)(c).

362 See *Brock v Wollams* [1949] 1 All E. R. 715 and *Hawes v Evenden* [1953] 2 All E.R. 737.

363 [1950] 2 All E. R. 140.

364 In *Dyson Holdings v Fox* [1976] Q.B. 503.

365 In *Fitzpatrick v Sterling Housing Association* [2001] A.C. 27 and subsequently in *Ghaidan v Godin-Mendoza* [2004] 2 F.L.R. 600.

366 Family Income Supplement Act 1970 s.1(1)(b).

367 *Davis v Johnson* [1979] A.C. 264.

368 See Freeman, 1996c.

369 Earl Russell described this as either "useless ... or penicious" (*Hansard*, H.L. vol.570, col.115). It was repealed in 2004 by the Domestic Violence, Crime and Victims Act 2004 s.2(1).

370 *R v SW London Appeal Tribunal Ex p. Barnett*, April 11, 1973, unreported (but see Freeman, 1976, p.106).

371 *Crisp v Mullings*, *The Times*, July 4, 1975 (Russell L.J.).

372 *Helby v Rafferty* [1978] 3 All E.R. 1016.

373 *Kokosinski v Kokosinski* [1980] Fam. 72.

374 *H v H*, *The Times*, May 16, 1981.

375 [1999] 1 F.L.R. 878, 883.

376 A fuller list of differences is in Herring, 2004, pp.60–66.

377 The Government goal, announced in 1999, is to abolish this by 2020.

378 [1984] Ch. 317. See also *Stack v Dowden* [2006] 1 F.L.R. 254; [2007] 1 F.L.R. 1858.

379 *Windeler v Whitehall* [1990] 2 F.L.R. 505.

380 He was alluding to the case of *Marvin v Marvin* 18 Cal. 3d 660 (1976).

381 In *The Enforcement of Morals*, Oxford, Clarendon Press, 1965.

382 *Law, Liberty and Morality*, 1963. And see "Social Solidarity and the Enforcement of Morality" (1967) 35 *University of Chicago Law Review* 1.

383 [1977] 1 All E.R. 1, 6.

384 *Ibid.*

385 Home Office, 1998, 4.12.

386 See Lewis, 2001, p.39.

387 In fact most end on death.

388 See below, p.120.

389 For example, Stamp L.J. in *Helby v Rafferty*, above n.372,: Sir Robert Megarry V.C. in *Re Beaumont* [1980] 1 All E.R. 266, 276; and Oliver L.J. in *Watson v Lucas* [1980] 3 All E.R. 647, 657.

390 1980, p.302.

391 "Formality and the Family—Reform and the Status Quo" (1980) 96 LQR 248, 279.

392 *Ibid.*

393 1980, p.304.

394 See Freeman and Lyon, 1983, pp.50–55.

395 See Foucault, 1980.

396 See further Barton, 1985; Barlow, 2001; Kingdom, 2000.

397 And see Freeman and Lyon above, n.394, pp.215–220.

398 *Walker v Perkins* (1764) 1 W.B. 517; *Benyon v Nettlefold* (1850) 3 Mac and G. 94; *Robinson v Cox* (1741) 9 Mod. 163.

399 *Fender v St John Mildmay* [1938] A.C. 1, 42.

400 See *Balfour v Balfour* [1919] 2 KB 571 and Freeman, 1996d.

401 See *Sutton v Mishcon De Reya and Gawor and Co* [2004] 1 F.L.R. 837 (the case was atypical: a sado-masochistic relationship between two men enacting a master–slave relationship).

402 It is wise to separate the financial terms from any sexual ones (and see Wilson, 2004).

403 Law Commission, *Sharing Homes*, Law Com. No.278.

404 But see *Oxley v Hiscock* [2004] 3 All E.R. 703.

405 Above, n.403, paras 2, 105–2, 112.

406 *Cohabitation: The Case for Clear Law.*

407 Both opposite-sex and same-sex.

408 This reform was proposed in Scotland in 1992.

409 See above, n.345.

410 *Ibid.*, para.6.50.

411 Introduction to *Marriage and Cohabitation: Regulating Intimacy, Affection and Care*, Aldershot, Ashgate, 2007, [6].

412 Law Commission, *Sharing Homes: A Discussion Paper*, Law Com. No.278, 2002 para.1.31(4).

413 Family Law Act 1996 s.62(3) (and see Reece, 2006). The definition was widened by the Domestic Violence, Crime and Victims Act 2004 ss.3 and 4.

414 This is widely defined: see s.62(1), (3).

415 This was added by the Domestic Violence, Crime and Victims Act 2004 s.4.

416 *Beyond Conjugality: Recognizing and Supporting Close Personal Adult Relationships*, 2002, and see Cossman and Ryder, 2001.

417 See Cossman, "Beyond Marriage; in above, n.303, p.97.

418 Above, n.416, ch.2. On autonomy see also Karst, 1980.

419 *Ibid.*

CHAPTER 3

1 Harmondsworth, Penguin, 1974.
2 Her later book, *Prone To Violence* (with Jeff Shapiro) was, by contrast, damaging to the cause of domestic victims. It pathologised them.
3 See Angela Weir, "Battered Women: Some Perspectives and Problems" in M. Mayo (ed.), *Women In the Community*, London, RKP, 1977, p.113.
4 The case in the latter part of the nineteenth century, and in the years immediately before the First World War (working-class suffragists in the north of England were particularly concerned about such violence).
5 "Violence and the Social Control of Women" in G. Littlejohn *et al.* (eds), *Power and the State*, London, Croom Helm, 1978, p.219.
6 *Safety and Justice*, Cm. 5847, 2003, p.6.
7 See M. Eaton, "Abuse By Any Other Name: Feminism, Difference and Intralesbian Violence" in M. Fineman and R. Myktiuk (eds), *The Public Nature of Private Violence*, London, RKP, 1994.
8 C. Mirrlees-Black, *Domestic Violence: Home Office Research Study* 191, 1999.
9 See Home Office, *British Crime Survey* 2001, 2002. See also E. Stanko, "The Day To Count" (2001) 1 *Criminal Justice* 215, and S. Walby and J. Allen, *Domestic Violence, Sexual Assault and Stalking: Findings from The British Crime Survey*, Home Office Research Study 276, 2004.
10 See E. Buzawa and C. Buzawa, *Domestic Violence: The Criminal Justice Response* London, Sage, 2003, p.13.
11 See above, n.8, p.61.
12 See R.E. Dobash and R.P. Dobash, "Women's Violence to Men in Intimate Relationships: Working on a Puzzle" (2004) 44 *Brit J. of Criminology* 324.
13 Council of Europe, *The Protection of Women Against Men: Recommendation (2002) 5 of the Committee of Ministers to Member States on the Protection of Women Against Violence*, Brussels, Council of Europe.
14 See above, n.9 (British Crime Survey).
15 See above, n.9 (Stanko).
16 See above, n.9 (British Crime Survey).
17 On child abuse see below, p.255.

18 See E. Stark and A. Flitcraft, *Women At Risk: Domestic Violence and Women's Health*, New York, Sage, 1996.
19 See M. Hester and L. Radford, *Domestic Violence and Child Contact Arrangements in England and Denmark*, Bristol, Policy Press, 1996, pp.10–11. Domestic violence and contact is discussed below, p.234.
20 A good discussion of these is S. Steinmetz and M. Straus, 1974, pp.6–17.
21 But Pizzey, above n.1, gives many examples of professional men battering wives. See also Freeman, 1979b, pp.134–135 on "sub-culture of violence".
22 In *The Mountain Arapesh*, Muller, 1972. For a comparison with the Gusii see Freeman, above, n.21, p.135.
23 above, n.20, p.14. It is found in Freud.
24 So argued by Ferreira, 1968.
25 The work of Gayford, 1975, was initially very influential.
26 A useful statement is the Discussion Document of the British Association of Social Work on Home Violence, 6 *Social Work Today* 409, 1975.
27 As the psycho-pathological model gave us "sick society" (McGrath, 1979, p.17).
28 See the important study by Jakes, 1999.
29 On the social control of women see Smart and Smart, 1978.
30 "Like children's bodies, women's bodies have been legally defined as legitimate objects of corporal punishment" (Smart, 1989, p.93). See also Siegel, 1996.
31 "A man's laying hands on a woman can be seen as necessary discipline, proof of manhood, a felony or hideous sin, depending on the relationship (wife, slave, stranger) which itself is socially constructed" (Klein, 1979, p.28).
32 Questioned by Dobash and Dobash. But they describe the period from the 16th to 19th centuries as the "great age of flogging" (1980, p.56). That it was also believed in by judges until very recently is illustrated by Freeman, 1979b, p.178.
33 *R v Jackson* [1891] 1 Q.B. 671.
34 In *Davis v Johnson* [1979] A.C. 264.
35 *R v R* [1992] 1 A.C. 599.
36 On the origins of the immunity see Freeman, 1985a, pp.128–134.
37 Law Reform (Married Women and Tortfeasors) Act 1935.
38 See above, n.35.
39 *Ibid.*

40 So argues Eva Figes, *Patriarchal Attitudes*, London, Panther, 1972, p.39. See Jakes' continuum of controls in Jakes, above n.28, p.103.

41 Dobash and Dobash also found this (see 1998, 167): "Men's accounts of their use of violence ... were usually animated by anger and supported by rationales", for example "she was in my face".

42 See Freeman (1984, p.72) calling for a challenge to patriarchal ideology if violence against women is to be conquered. Note Wilson (1983, p.240) arguing for a "re-examination of our moral system". See also Jasinski and Williams, 1998; Hester *et al.*, 1996. For a feminist (or pseudo-feminist) argument which suggests that most domestic violence is not serious see Mills, 2003.

43 Matrimonial Causes Act 1878. This was advocated by Frances Power Cobbe in her famous pamphlet, *Wife Torture*.

44 The Women's Charter of 1909 contained a section on violence against women. In 1935 Bertrand Russell wrote of husbands as a "downtrodden race" because they had lost rights they once had!

45 But until 1962 a spouse was not allowed to sue the other in tort.

46 House of Commons Select Committee on *Violence In the Family*, Minutes, 1975, p.366. It added "every effort should be made to re-unite the family": *ibid.*, p.369.

47 Domestic Proceedings and Magistrates Courts Act 1978.

48 See *Vaughan v Vaughan* [1973] 1 W.L.R. 1159; *Horner v Horner* [1982] Fam. 90; *George v George* [1986] 2 F.L.R. 347; and *Johnson v Walton* [1990] 1 F.L.R. 350.

49 The 1976 Act applied to a man and a woman living with each other in the same way as husband and wife. The 1978 Act was limited to parties to a marriage (see s.16). I criticised this (Freeman, 1978, p.viii).

50 *B v B* [1978] 1 All E.R. 821; *Cantliff v Jenkins* [1978] 1 All E.R. 836.

51 See above, n.34.

52 *Davis v Johnson* [1978] 1 All E.R. 841, 849.

53 *Wiseman v Simpson* [1988] 1 W.L.R. 35, 44; *Blackstock v Blackstock* [1991] 2 F.L.R. 308.

54 Domestic Violence and Matrimonial Proceedings Act 1976 s.2.

55 *Lewis v Lewis* [1978] 1 All E.R. 729, 731, *Widdowson v Widdowson* (1983) 4 F.L.R. 121, 125.

56 In 1989 only 29% of 1976 Act injunctions had powers of arrest attached: see Law Commission, *Domestic Violence and Occupation of the Family Home*, Law Com. 207, 1992, p.44 n.23.

57 [1984] 1 A.C. 174.

58 See above, n.56.

59 Family Law Act 1996 s.42.

60 Family Law Act 1996 ss.33, 35, 36, 37, 38 (see s.39(1)).

61 Most applications are made to county courts.

62 Family Law Act 1996 s.45.

63 Family Law Act 1996 s.45.

64 Arrest for breach of an order is provided for by s.47 of the Family Law Act 1996.

65 Family Law Act 1996 s.60. and see Humphreys and Kaye, 1997 and Burton, 2003. Humphreys and Thiara (2003, p.203) found many women who would have preferred a third party to seek the order on their behalf to relieve them of dangers and responsibilities.

66 In 2004 23,357 non-molestation orders were granted; there were 9,075 occupation orders. See *Judicial Statistics* 2004 (2005), Table 5.9.

67 Family Law Act 1996 s.42(1).

68 *Horner v Horner*, above, n.48, 93.

69 *Spencer v Camacho* (1983) 4 F.L.R. 662.

70 *George v George*, above, n.48.

71 *Johnson v Walton*, above, n.48.

72 Family Law Act 1996 s.62(3).

73 See Reece, 2006 for an excellent critique.

74 Section 82 and Sch.8.

75 Section 4.

76 Family Law Act 1996 s.43.

77 [2000] 2 F.L.R. 533.

78 *Chechi v Bashier* [1999] 2 F.L.R. 489.

79 Family Law Act 1996 s.42(2)(a).

80 Family Law Act 1996 s.42(2)(b).

81 Family Law Act 1996 s.42(4A) and (4B), inserted by Sch.10 para.36 of the Domestic Violence, Crime and Victims Act 2004.

82 There is no reference to this in s.42(5): and see Law Commission report, above, n.56, para.3.6.

83 See *Wooton v Wooton* [1984] F.L.R. 871.

84 [1999] 1 F.L.R. 726.

85 *P v P (Contempt of Court: Mental Capacity)* [1999] 2 F.L.R. 897.

86 *Wookey v Wookey; Re S (A Minor)* [1991] Fam. 121, 136.

87 Family Law Act 1996 s.42(6).

88 Family Law Act 1996 s.42(7).

89 *Galan v Galan* [1985] F.L.R. 905, 918 (in relation to an ouster order).

90 See *Re B-J (Power of Arrest)* [2000] 2 F.L.R. 443.

91 Family Law Act 1996 s.42(8).

92 See below, p.234.

93 See above, n.63.

94 Family Law Act 1996 s.46(4).

95 Family Law Act 1996 s.46(3A), inserted by Domestic Violence, Crime and Victims Act 2004 Sch.10, para.37(3).

96 Family Law Act 1996 s.47.

97 Family Law Act 1996 s.42A(5)(a).

98 Family Law Act 1996 s.42A.

99 [2005] 2 F.L.R. 329.

100 [2006] 1 F.L.R. 365.

101 See below, pp.77, 83.

102 See above, n.98.

103 *Lomas v Parle* [2004] 1 W.L.R. 1643, and see Burton, 2004.

104 Family Law Act 1996 s.33(1)(a).

105 Family Law Act 1996 s.33(1)(b).

106 Family Law Act 1966 s.33(4), as amended.

107 Family Law Act 1966 s.33(3).

108 See *Burris v Azadani* [1995] 1 W.L.R. 1372 (250 yards from the home).

109 Section 31(2).

110 See below, p.282.

111 [1999] 1 F.L.R. 715, and see Kaganas, 1999.

112 Housing Act 1996 s.191(1).

113 Housing Act 1996 s.189(1).

114 *Chalmers v John* [1999] 1 F.L.R. 392, 396; *G v G (Occupation Order: Conduct)* [2000] 2 F.L.R. 36.

115 See *Judicial Statistics* 1996, 1997 Table 5.9 and compare *Judicial Statistics* 2003, 2004, Table 5.9.

116 *Practice Note* [1978] 1 WLR 1123.

117 Family Law Act 1996 s.33(10).

118 The press, particularly The *Daily Mail*, was tilting at windmills when it helped to kill the Family Homes and Domestic Violence Bill (the 1996 Act's predecessor).

119 Family Law Act 1996 s.36.

120 Family Law Act 1996 s.35.
121 Civil Partnership Act 2004 Sch.9 para.6, amending s.35 of the 1996 Act.
122 Family Law Act 1996 s.35(1)(c), as amended; s.36, as amended.
123 Family Law Act 1996 s.33(5).
124 Family Law Act 1996 s.36(6), as amended by Domestic Violence, Crime and Victims Act 2004 s.2(2) and Sch.10 para.34(3).
125 See above, p.49.
126 *Burns v Burns* [1984] Ch.317.
127 *Kokosinski v Kokosinski* [1980] Fam. 72.
128 Family Law Act 1996 s.35(10) and s.36(10).
129 Family Law Act 1996 s.38(6).
130 Family Law Act 1996 s.37, s.37(1A), and s.38.
131 Family Law Act 1996 s.40.
132 As happened in *Davis v Johnson*; above n.34.
133 *Nwogbe v Nwogbe* [2000] 2 F.L.R. 744.
134 Family Law Act 1996 s.42(4A) and (4B), inserted by Sch.10 para.36 of Domestic Violence, Crime and Victims Act 2004.
135 Family Law Act 1996 s.47, as amended by Domestic Violence, Crime and Victims Act 2004 Sch.10 para.38.
136 Family Law Act 1996 s.47.
137 On *ex parte* orders see *Ansah v Ansah* [1977] Fam. 138.
138 Family Law Act 1996 s.47(2).
139 *Re B-J (Power of Arrest)* [2000] 2 F.L.R. 443.
140 Family Law Act 1996 s.47(3).
141 Family Law Act 1996 s.47(6).
142 Family Law Act 1996 s.47(7).
143 [2001] 1 F.L.R. 641.
144 Family Law Act 1996 s.45(1).
145 Family Law Act 1996 s.45(2).
146 See above, p.76.
147 Protection from Harassment Act 1997 s.3(1).
148 Protection from Harassment Act 1997 s.3(2).
149 Protection from Harassment Act 1998 s.3(3).
150 Protection from Harassment Act 1997 s.3(6)–(8).
151 *R v McCann* [2003] 1 A.C. 787.
152 *Hipgrave v Hipgrave and Jones* [2005] 2 F.L.R. 174.
153 Supreme Court Act 1981 s.37 and County Courts Act 1984 s.38
154 See above, n.57.
155 [1996] 2 F.L.R. 506.

156 *Ibid.* 511.
157 For a discussion see Freeman, 1979b, pp.180–181.
158 Above n.35. R challenged this: see *CR v United Kingdom; SW v United Kingdom* [1996] 1 F.L.R. 434, on which see Ghandhi and James, 1997.
159 Criminal Justice and Public Order Act 1994 s.142. See now Sexual Offences Act 2003 s.1.
160 Police and Criminal Evidence Act 1984 s.80, and see Creighton, 1990.
161 See further Edwards, 1989 and 1996.
162 One was killed in England in May 2007 (*Guardian*, May 2007). Parnas, 1967 discusses this concern.
163 Home Office Circular 60/1990.
164 The "Minneapolis" study was very influential. See Sherman and Berk, 1984. See also Sherman *et al.*, 1992.
165 Home Affairs Committee, Third Report, *Domestic Violence* HC 245, paras 23–32.
166 Home Office Circular 19/2000.
167 HM Crown Prosecution Service Inspectorate, HM Inspectorate of Constabulary, *A Joint Inspection of the Investigation and Prosecution of Cases Involving Domestic Violence*, 2004, p.10.
168 *Ibid.*, para.2.28.
169 *Ibid.*, para.6.6.
170 *Ibid.*, para 6.10. See also Hester *et al.*, 2003, Humphreys and Thiara, 2003.
171 It "facilitates agency when it informs battered women of the social and legal options essential for sustained agency ..." (Hart, 1997). An excellent review of the issues is Sack, 2004.
172 On privacy as a double-edged sword for women, see Schneider, 2000, pp.87–97. See also Margulies, 1995, and MacKinnon, 1987, pp.101–102.
173 See above n.160.
174 There have been cases of battered women being gaoled for contempt when too frightened to give evidence, with the assailant going free.
175 See Morley and Mullender, 1992.
176 See Bennett and Williams, 2001, p.261.
177 See above n.167, para.7.53.
178 Crown Prosecution Service, 2005, paras 3.2–3.5.
179 *Ibid.*, para.5.3.
180 *Ibid.*, para.4.9

181 Above, n.160.
182 Criminal Justice Act 1988 s.23, and see Ellison, 2002a, 2002b.
183 Youth Justice and Criminal Evidence Act 1999 s.17.
184 Youth Justice and Criminal Evidence Act 1999 s.23.
185 Youth Justice and Criminal Evidence Act 1999 s.24.
186 Youth Justice and Criminal Evidence Act 1999 s.25(4)(b).
187 Youth Justice and Criminal Evidence Act 1999 s.28 (not yet in force).
188 See above n.167, para.7.68.
189 *Ibid.*, para.7.27.
190 *Ibid.*, para.6.11.
191 *R v Cutts, The Times* December 3, 1986.
192 Cretney and Davis (1996) found conviction to be less likely where the couple were still together, and where they were together the sentence tended to be lower. See also Gilchrist and Blissett, 2002.
193 *R v McNaughten* [2003] 2 Cr. App. R. (5) 142.
194 Sentencing Guidelines Panel, *Overarching Principles: Domestic Violence Consultation Guideline*, 2006, Section D.
195 Domestic Violence, Crimes and Victims Act 2004 s.10.
196 Family Law Act 1996 s.42A, and see Serious Organised Crime and Police Act 2005 s.110.
197 The first anti-stalking laws were passed in the USA.
198 Protection from Harassment Act 1998 s.7(3).
199 *Lau v DPP* [2000] 1 F.L.R. 799.
200 Protection from Harassment Act 1998 s.5.
201 Domestic Violence, Crime and Victims Act 2004 s.12.
202 Protection from Harassment Act 1997 s.5(3)(b).
203 Domestic Violence, Crime and Victims Act 2004 s.12(5).
204 *R v Liddle; R v Hayes* [1999] 3 All E.R. 816.
205 The government said it anticipated about 200 prosecutions a year. There were more than 6000 prosecutions in the Act's first full year of operation (Harris, 2000).
206 See Harris, 2000.
207 See above n.194, para.53.
208 *Ibid.*
209 Now recognised by the legal system: see further Wolak and Finkelhor, 1998, p.73, and Peled, 1996, p.125.
210 *Lomes v Parle* [2004] 1 W.L.R. 1642, 1652.

CHAPTER 4

1 Good histories of divorce are McGregor, 1957, and Stone, 1990 and 1993. See Anderson, 1984.

2 Discussed by Menefee, 1981 and O'Donovan, 1984. *The Times*, September 19, 1797 said that there was to be a sale of wives "soon at Christie's". For judicial criticism see *R v Delaval* (1763) 3 Burr. 1434, 96 E.R. 234.

3 Michael Henchard sold his wife for five guineas.

4 It was assumed that in the absence of such aggravation she suffered no "very material injury" and "ought not to resent her husband's unfaithfulness" (Cornish and Clark, 1989, p.379).

5 According to Menefee, above n.2, p.46 there were still wife sales at inns in 1890.

6 Particularly by radical suffragists: see Liddington and Norris, 1978.

7 Royal Commission on Divorce and Matrimonial Causes Cd. 6478, 1912.

8 The Minority thought extending divorce beyond female adultery was "against the express words of Christ".

9 Matrimonial Causes Act 1923.

10 Matrimonial Causes Act 1937. A.P. Herbert's novel *Holy Deadlock*, London, Methuen, 1934, remains an entertaining (and eye-opening) read.

11 Matrimonial Causes Bill. The debate is at *Hansard*, H.C. vol.485, col.926.

12 Royal Commission on Marriage and Divorce, Cmd. 9678, 1956.

13 *Ibid.*, para.3.

14 *Ibid.*, para.69.

15 *Ibid.*, para.70.

16 Matrimonial Causes and Reconciliation Bill 1962.

17 Particularly the Archbishop of Canterbury's lay secretary, Robert Beloe. See Cretney, 1998, pp.43–46.

18 Matrimonial Causes Act 1963 s.2.

19 Matrimonial Causes Act 1963 s.4. See also Abse, 1973, pp.162–171.

20 *Gollins v Gollins* [1964] A.C. 644; *Williams v Williams* [1964] A.C. 598.

21 Archbishop of Canterbury's Group, *Putting Asunder—A Divorce Law For Contemporary Society*, SPCK, 1966.

22 *Ibid.*, para.100(i).

23 *Ibid.*, para.104. The Report of the Matrimonial Causes Procedure Committee in 1985 also recommended this (see paras 4.6–4.11).

24 *Ibid.*, para.89.

25 Cmnd 3123.

26 *Ibid.*, para.15.

27 *Ibid.*, para.18.

28 See Lee, 1974, pp.235–240.

29 The three years' discretionary bar was reduced to a one-year absolute bar in 1984: see below, p.101.

30 *Richards v Richards* [1972] 3 All E.R. 693.

31 *Buffery v Buffery* [1988] 2 F.L.R. 365.

32 Matrimonial Causes Act 1973 s.1(2)(a).

33 *Dennis v Dennis* [1955] P. 153.

34 *Clarkson v Clarkson* (1930) 46 T.L.R. 623.

35 *Maclennan v Maclennan* 1958 S.L.T. 12 (a Scottish decision).

36 See above, n.43. See also *Sapsford v Sapsford* [1954] 2 All E.R. 373.

37 *Goodrich v Goodrich* [1971] 2 All E.R. 1340, 1342.

38 Faulks J. in *Dodds v Dodds*, unreported, but quoted in the *Daily Mirror*, March 20, 1974.

39 In above, n.47 and in *Roper v Roper* [1972] 3 All E.R. 668.

40 [1974] 1 All E.R. 498.

41 [1974] 1 All E.R. 1193.

42 According to Lord Denning M.R., above n.40, 501.

43 According to Stamp L.J. *ibid.*, 502.

44 Matrimonial Causes Act 1973 s.2(2).

45 Matrimonial Causes Act 1973 s.1(2)(b).

46 "A linguistic trap": *Bannister v Bannister* (1980) 10 Fam. Law 240. See also *Carew-Hunt v Carew-Hunt*, *The Times*, June 28, 1972.

47 *Ash v Ash* [1972] Fam. 135; *Pheasant v Pheasant* [1972] Fam. 202.

48 *Ash v Ash*, above, n.47, 139–140.

49 [1974] Fam 47, 54, approved in *O'Neill v O'Neill* [1975] 1 W.L.R. 1118.

50 See above, n.31.

51 See above, n.47.

52 *Bergin v Bergin* [1983] F.L.R. 344. See also *Rusic v Rusic*, *The Times*, December 20, 1975 (about as violent a marriage as is imaginable—cross-decrees were granted). But see *Galan v Galan* (1985) FLR 905 (wife failed to get a decree though husband broke her nose).

53 See above, n.47, 140.

54 In *Livingstone-Stallard v Livingstone-Stallard*, n.49, above.

55 *O'Neill v O'Neill*, above, n.49.

56 *Birch v Birch* [1992] 1 F.L.R. 564.

57 *Carter-Fea v Carter-Fea* [1987] Fam. Law 130.

58 *Wachtel v Wachtel (No.1)*, *The Times*, August 1, 1972.

59 *Katz v Katz* [1972] 3 ALL E.R. 219, 223.

60 *Ibid*.

61 *Stevens v Stevens* [1979] 1 W.L.R. 383.

62 The wife suffering from Alzheimer's disease in *Smith v Smith* (1973) 118 S.J. 184, for example.

63 See above, n.59.

64 [1976] Fam 32.

65 Matrimonial Causes Act 1973 s.1(2)(c).

66 *Hopes v Hopes* [1949] P. 227, 231. *Cf. Le Brocq v Le Brocq* [1964] 1 W.L.R. 1085.

67 *Pulford v Pulford* [1923] P. 18.

68 *Perry v Perry* [1963] 3 All E.R. 766; *Kaczmarz v Kaczmarz* [1967] 1 All E.R. 416.

69 *G v G* [1964] P. 133; *Lilley v Lilley* [1959] 3 All E.R. 283.

70 [1948] P. 302.

71 *Pardy v Pardy* [1939] P. 288; *Joseph v Joseph* [1953] 2 All E.R. 710.

72 *Glenister v Glenister* [1945] 1 All E.R. 513.

73 *Quoraishi v Quoraishi* [1985] F.L.R. 780.

74 Matrimonial Causes Act 1973 s.1(2)(d).

75 Matrimonial Causes Act 1973 s.2(6).

76 [1973] 2 All E.R. 650.

77 [1972] 1 W.L.R. 321.

78 [1972] Fam. 247.

79 See Matrimonial Causes Act 1973 s.2(5).

80 [1972] 1 All E.R. 362.

81 *Mason v Mason* [1972] 3 All E.R. 315.

82 Matrimonial Causes Act 1973 s.2(7).

83 Matrimonial Causes Act 1973 s.1(2)(e).

84 England was set to become "a philanderer's paradise". See *Hansard*, H.C., vol.784, col.2034.

85 So Finer J. commented in *Reiterbund v Reiterbund* [1974] 2 All E.R. 455.

86 *Talbot v Talbot* (1971) 115 S.J. 870.

87 *Mathias v Mathias* [1972] Fam. 287.

88 *Rukat v Rukat* [1975] Fam. 63, 73.

89 *Ibid*.

90 Matrimonial Causes Act 1973 s.5(3).
91 See above, n.85.
92 See below, p.125.
93 *Julian v Julian* (1972) 116 S.J. 763.
94 [1972] 1 All E.R. 410.
95 *Lee v Lee* (1973) 117 S.J. 616.
96 (1975) 5 Fam. Law 48.
97 [1973] 3 All E.R. 45.
98 *Banik v Banik (No.2)* (1973) 3 Fam. Law 174.
99 Looked at from the judge's perspective. Does this impose an ethnocentric test?
100 *Parghi v Parghi* (1973) 117 S.J. 582.
101 *Ibid.*
102 Matrimonial Causes Act 1973 s.5(1).
103 *Brickell v Brickell* (1973) 3 All E.R. 508.
104 *Allan v Allan* (1974) 4 Fam. Law 83.
105 See above, n.87, 299.
106 See above, nn.87 and 88.
107 See above, n.103.
108 See above, n.87, 300. See also n.85, above, 464.
109 Matrimonial Causes Act 1973 s.10(2), (3).
110 *Parkes v Parkes* [1971] 3 All E.R. 870.
111 *Garcia v Garcia* [1992] 1 F.L.R. 256.
112 See below, p.126.
113 Matrimonial Causes Act 1973 s.1(3).
114 The history is explained by Cretney, 2003b, p.178.
115 Matrimonial Causes Act 1973 s.1(5).
116 Matrimonial Causes Act 1973 s.9(2).
117 *Wickler v Wickler* [1998] 2 F.L.R. 326.
118 *Manchanda v Manchanda* [1995] 2 F.L.R. 590.
119 *Re G (Decree Absolute: Prejudice)* [2003] 1 F.L.R. 870.
120 *Bhaiji v Chauhan, Queen's Proctor Intervening (Divorce: Marriages Used For Immigration Purposes)* [2003] 2 FLR 485.
121 Matrimonial Causes Act 1973 s.3(1).
122 Matrimonial Causes Act 1937 s.1.
123 Matrimonial and Family Proceedings Act 1984 s.1.
124 [1949] 2 All E.R. 127.
125 By the Law Commission, 1982, Law Com. No.116.
126 See below, p.113.
127 Matrimonial Causes Act 1973 s.2(1).
128 Matrimonial Causes Act 1973 s.2(2).
129 Matrimonial Causes Act 1973 s.2(3).
130 [1973] 3 All E.R. 750.

131 Matrimonial Causes Act 1973 s.2(4), (5).
132 Matrimonial Causes Act 1973 s.6(1).
133 Matrimonial Causes Act 1973 s.6(2).
134 See Walker and McCarthy, 2004
135 Continuation of co-residence does not necessarily mean the marriage has been "saved". See Walker and McCarthy, 2004.
136 See above, n.25.
137 *Ibid.*, para.16.
138 It is very easy to make allegations of behaviour and easy to establish the adultery fact, particularly once it was held that a causal link did not need to be established between the adultery and finding it intolerable to live with the adulterer (above nn.40 and 41).
139 See above, p.93.
140 See *Le Brocq v Le Brocq* [1964] 3 All E.R. 464.
141 Both *Putting Asunder*, above n.21, para.78, and *Field of Choice*, above n.25, para.19 favoured its retention.
142 *Ibid.*
143 *Ibid.*, para.15. It added a third requirement—"divorce law should be understandable and respected" (para.18).
144 By 1977 this applied to all undefended divorces.
145 The preference for fault-based grounds is in large part due to the speed with which such divorces may be obtained.
146 69% of divorces are granted to wives. See *Population Trends*, Spring 2006.
147 But only 37% of marriages end in divorce. The number of divorces is declining: 132,562 in 2006, 143,393 in 2005, 153,689 in 2004.
148 See above, n.23. These included joint applications including for a divorce.
149 "Facing the Future: A Discussion Paper on the Grounds for Divorce", Law Com No.170.
150 Law Com. No.192.
151 *Ibid.*, para.2.11.
152 *Ibid.*, paras 2.13–2.14.
153 *Ibid.*, para.2.15.
154 *Ibid.*, para.2.16.
155 *Ibid.*, para.2.17.
156 *Ibid.*, para.2.19.
157 *Ibid.*, para.3.1.
158 For two reasons: (i) the law cannot really assess fault; (ii) it is an ineffective way of promoting good marital conduct.

159 Law Com No.192, para.3.12.
160 *Ibid.*, para.3.13.
161 *Ibid.*, paras 3.20–3.25.
162 It recommended one year: *ibid.*, paras 5.27, 5.69 and 5.79.
163 Cm. 2424, para.4.1.
164 *Ibid.*, para.5.24.
165 But if its success rate is only 60%, as Bevan and Davis (1999) found, it may not prove as cost effective as supposed.
166 See above, n.163, para.5.2.
167 See Freeman, 1997.
168 Above, n.163, para.4.26.
169 Family Law Act 1996, Part II.
170 Section 1.
171 Section 8.
172 Section 8(2).
173 Section 7(6).
174 Section 7(3)
175 Section 7(11), (13).
176 Section 7(10).
177 But it was not to be extended where there was an occupation order or non-molestation order or where delaying the order would be significantly detrimental to a child of the family.
178 Section 3.
179 Section 10.
180 Section 9(2).
181 Section 11(4).
182 See Matrimonial Causes Act 1973 s.41. Its weakness is discussed by Douglas *et al.*, 2000.
183 See Walker *et al.*, 2001, and Davis, 2001.
184 See Davis *et al.*, 2001, and Davis, 2001.
185 And see Bevan *et al.*, 2001.
186 See above, n.78.
187 In "Foreword" to above, n.163, p.iii.
188 See Legal Services Commission, *The Funding Code: Restructured Family Guidance*, 2004, para.20.2.1.
189 Civil Partnership Act 2004 s.37.
190 Civil Partnership Act 2004 s.44(5).
191 Civil Partnership Act 2004 s.45(2).
192 Civil Partnership Act 2004 s.47.
193 Civil Partnership Act 2004 ss.37(2)(a), 38(1)(a).
194 Civil Partnership Act 2004 s.39.
195 Civil Partnership Act 2004 s.45

196 Civil Partnership Act 2004 s.47.
197 Civil Partnership Act 2004 s.37(2).
198 Civil Partnership Act 2004 s.39.
199 A duty which was enforceable until 1970 by an order for restitution of conjugal rights.
200 Matrimonial Causes Act 1973 s.17.
201 Matrimonial Causes Act 1973 s.18 (in relation to marriage).

CHAPTER 5

1 An important American study (Weitzman, 1985; also 1986) found that one year after divorce men experienced a 42% improvement in their standard of living, and women a 73% decline. Weitzman comments (1986, 100): "divorce is a financial catastrophe for most women". For England see Eekelaar and Maclean, 1986, Arthur *et al.*, 2002, and Douglas and Perry, 2001.
2 *White v White* [2001] 1 A.C. 596; *Miller v Miller; McFarlane v McFarlane* [2006] 1 F.L.R. 1186.
3 Pensions Act 1995 s.166, and Welfare Reform and Pensions Act 1999 Schs 3 and 4.
4 Despite the Equal Pay Act 1970, women still earn on average 83% of what men earn.
5 Little is known of its practice though, in relation to alimony, it is here that the "one-third" rule developed. See Barton in Graveson and Crane, 1957.
6 Matrimonial Causes Act 1857 s.32.
7 Matrimonial Causes Act 1907 s.1.
8 Matrimonial Causes Act 1963 s.5.
9 *Davis v Davis* [1967] P. 185. Similar statements continued to be made right up to the reforms of 1969 and 1970. See *von Mehren v von Mehren* [1970] 1 All E.R. 153, 156.
10 See above, p.97.
11 Matrimonial Property Bill 1969. See *Hansard*, H.C. vol.776, col.894.
12 Matrimonial and Family Proceedings Act 1984.
13 *Minton v Minton* [1979] A.C. 593, 608.
14 The court is "no rubber stamp", but nor is it a "forensic ferret" *per* Ward L.J. in *Harris v Manahan* [1997] 1 F.L.R. 205, 213.
15 [1999] 1 F.L.R. 683.
16 [1985] A.C. 424.

17 Section 7, inserting s.33A into Matrimonial Causes Act 1973.
18 Family Proceedings Rules 1991 s.2.61.
19 *Pounds v Pounds* [1994] 1 F.L.R. 775, 779 *per* Waite L.J.
20 [1995] 2 F.L.R. 45.
21 *Ibid.*, 69.
22 Family Proceedings (Amendment No.2) Rules 1999, SI 1999/3491.
23 *Clibbery v Allan and Another* [2002] Fam 261.
24 See Bird, 2002, ch.16 and Gerlis, 2001 to which Bird (2002b) responds.
25 *Rose v Rose* [2002] 1 F.L.R. 978, 988 *per* Thorpe L.J.
26 Matrimonial Causes Act 1973 s.22.
27 *Hawkes v Hawkes* (1828) 1 Hag. Ecc. 526.
28 *A v A (Matrimonial Pending Suit: Provision of Legal Fees)* [2001] 1 F.L.R. 377.
29 *Ibid.*, 386.
30 *F v F (Ancillary Relief: Substantial Assets)* [1995] 2 F.L.R. 45, 49.
31 Matrimonial Causes Act 1973 s.23(1)(a), (b).
32 Matrimonial Causes Act 1973 s.25A(3).
33 Matrimonial Causes Act 1973 s.25A(2) and s.28A(1).
34 It would terminate on the payee's death: Matrimonial Causes Act 1973 s.28(1)(b).
35 See *Pearce v Pearce* [2004] 1 W.L.R. 68.
36 *AMS v Child Support Officer* [1998] 1 F.L.R. 955, 964 *per* Thorpe J.
37 Matrimonial Causes Act 1973 s.28(1)(a), (b).
38 [1988] Fam. 93.
39 *Fleming v Fleming* [2004] 1 F.L.R. 667.
40 Matrimonial Causes Act 1973 s.23(1)(c).
41 Matrimonial Causes Act 1973 s.23(1)(d).
42 Matrimonial Causes Act 1973 s.23(3)(c).
43 Matrimonial Causes Act 1973 s.23(3)(a), (b).
44 See above, p.119.
45 [1973] Fam. 72.
46 *Ibid.*, 91.
47 *Ibid.*, 93.
48 [1973] Fam. 134.
49 *Ibid.*, 140.
50 *O'D v O'D* [1976] Fam. 83.
51 *P v P* [1978] 3 All E.R. 70
52 *Martin v Martin* [1976] Fam. 335.

53 *Calderbank v Calderbank* [1976] Fam. 93.
54 *Ibid.*, 103.
55 [1992] Fam. 40.
56 *Westbury v Sampson* [2002] 1 F.L.R. 166.
57 *D v D (Lump Sum Order: Adjournment of Application)* [2001] 1 F.L.R. 633.
58 [1986] 2 F.L.R. 389.
59 *Ibid.*, 397.
60 *Re G (Financial Provision: Liberty to Restore Application for Lump Sum)* [2004] 1 F.L.R. 997.
61 Pensions Act 1995 s.166.
62 *R (Smith) v Secretary of State for Defence and Secretary of State for Work and Pensions* [2005] 1 F.L.R. 97, 102.
63 Welfare Reform and Pensions Act 1999.
64 Matrimonial Causes Act 1973 s.24(1)(a).
65 [2006] 1 F.L.R. 1263.
66 *Hamlin v Hamlin* [1986] Fam. 11.
67 Matrimonial Causes Act 1973 s.24(1)(b).
68 First used in *Mesher v Mesher* [1980] 1 All E.R. 126 (decided in 1973).
69 The courts have often criticised the order: for example, *Mortimer v Mortimer-Griffin* [1986] 2 F.L.R. 315, 319 (no longer "the bible" *per* Parker L.J.).
70 See below, p.130.
71 See above, *White*, n.2, 605.
72 [2003] 2 F.L.R. 285.
73 *Martin v Martin* [1978] Fam. 12.
74 [1991] 1 All E.R. 340.
75 *Ibid.*, 344.
76 Matrimonial Causes Act 1973 s.24(1)(c).
77 *Prinsep v Prinsep* [1929] P. 225; *Prescott v Fellowes* [1958] 3 All E.R. 55. And see Ormrod L.J.'s criticism in *Guerrera v Guerrera* [1974] 1 W.L.R. 1542.
78 [1996] A.C. 375.
79 [2003] 2 F.L.R. 493.
80 In *Guerrera v Guerrera*, above, n.77.
81 Above n.78, 392.
82 Matrimonial Causes Act 1973 s.24A.
83 *Orders for Sale of Property Under the Matrimonial Causes Act 1973*, Law Com. 99.
84 Matrimonial Homes and Property Act 1981 s.7.
85 Though the new partner's assets are relevant; see *Macey v Macey* (1981) 3 F.L.R. 7.

86 *Crittenden v Crittenden* [1990] 2 F.L.R. 361.
87 *Milne v Milne* (1981) 2 F.L.R. 286.
88 *Mullard v Mullard* (1981) 3 F.L.R. 330.
89 In *Wachtel v Wachtel*, n.45, above.
90 [2001] 1 A.C. 596.
91 [2006] 1 F.L.R. 1186.
92 See above n.90, 600.
93 *Ibid.*, 599.
94 *Ibid.*, 605.
95 *Ibid.*
96 *Ibid.*
97 *Ibid.*, 606.
98 *Ibid.*
99 *Ibid.*, 615.
100 Above, n.91, 1191.
101 *Ibid.*, 1221.
102 *Ibid.*, 1193.
103 *Ibid.*, 1219.
104 *Ibid.*, 1219.
105 *Ibid.*, 1192.
106 *Ibid.*, 1220.
107 [1986] 2 F.L.R. 34.
108 Above, n.91, 1221.
109 Even after *White and Miller/McFarlane*: see *Charman v Charman* (No.2) [2007] 1 F.L.R. 593.
110 Above, n.91, 1222.
111 [2001] 2 F.L.R. 192.
112 [2003] Fam. 103.
113 [2002] 1 F.L.R. 642 (wife awarded only 37% because husband was exceptionally gifted in business).
114 Above, n.112, 122.
115 Above n.91, 1202.
116 [2006] 1 F.L.R. 497.
117 [2003] 2 F.L.R. 108.
118 [2004] 2 F.L.R. 236.
119 Above, n.91, 1224.
120 [2003] 2 F.L.R. 299.
121 See above n.91, 1192.
122 *Ibid.*, 1194.
123 See above, n.90, 599; n.91, 1191.
124 Matrimonial Causes Act 1973 s.25(2)(g) and below, p.142.
125 [2006] 1 F.L.R. 151.
126 See above, n.91, 1202.

127 See Lord Denning M.R. in *Wachtel v Wachtel*, n.45 above, 90.
128 [2004] 2 F.L.R. 893.
129 And see Lord Nicholls in n.91, above, 1191.
130 Bennett J.'s judgment is reported as *J v J* [2004] Fam. Law 404.
131 See above n.128, 920.
132 See above, n.91, 1207.
133 See above, n.128, 912.
134 See above, n.91, 1208.
135 *Ibid.*, 1218.
136 [2007] 1 F.L.R. 790.
137 *Ibid.*, para.24.
138 [2007] E.W.H.C. 459 (Fam.), [2007] All E.R.(D) 99 (Apr.), and Brown and Edwards, 2007.
139 A view expressed by Cretney, 2003a, but rejected by Bennett J. in above, n.116, 514.
140 Matrimonial Causes Act 1973 s.25(1).
141 Children Act 1989 s.1(1); Adoption and Children Act 2002 s.1(2).
142 *Suter v Suter and Jones* [1987] 2 F.L.R. 232.
143 *E v E* [1990] 2 F.L.R. 233, 249.
144 *Waterman v Waterman* [1989] 1 F.L.R. 380.
145 *M v B (Ancillary Proceedings: Lump Sum)* [1998] 1 F.L.R. 53.
146 [2002] 1 F.L.R. 555.
147 [1996] 2 F.L.R. 617.
148 At first instance: [1994] 2 F.L.R. 1051, 1054.
149 Matrimonial Causes Act 1973 s.25(2)(a).
150 See above, n.94.
151 See above, n.91, 1193.
152 *Ibid.*, 1223.
153 See above, n.90.
154 *P v P (Inherited Property)* [2005] 1 F.L.R. 576. See Francis and Fisher, 2005.
155 *McEwan v McEwan* [1972] 2 All E.R. 708.
156 *Klucinski v Klucinski* [1953] 1 All E.R. 683.
157 *Hardy v Hardy* [1981] 1 F.L.R. 321 (husband worked for his father for much less than he could have earned elsewhere).
158 *Leadbetter v Leadbetter* [1985] F.L.R. 789. *Cf. Mitchell v Mitchell* [1984] F.L.R. 387.
159 *Barrett v Barrett* [1988] 2 F.L.R. 516.
160 *Atkinson v Atkinson* [1995] 2 F.L.R. 356.
161 *Macey v Macey* (1981) 3 F.L.R. 7.
162 *Ibid.* See also *Brown v Brown* (1981) 3 F.L.R. 161.

163 Matrimonial Causes Act 1973 s.25(2)(b).
164 For example, *Preston v Preston* [1982] Fam.17; *Dart v Dart* [1996] 2 F.L.R. 286.
165 See *F v F (Ancillary Relief: Substantial Assets)* [1995] 2 F.L.R. 45, where Thorpe J. said this was not reasonable.
166 *Conran v Conran* [1997] 2 F.L.R. 615.
167 *Duxbury v Duxbury* [1992] Fam. 62n.
168 So noted by Holman J. in *White v White*, cited by Lord Nicholls, above n.90, 609.
169 *Ibid.*
170 *Ibid.*
171 For whom there is "life after divorce" (see *Delaney v Delaney* [1990] 2 F.L.R. 457). See also *Ashley v Blackman* [1988] 2 F.L.R. 278.
172 [1968] 3 All E.R. 479.
173 *W H-J v W H-J* [2002] 1 F.L.R. 415.
174 Matrimonial Causes Act 1973 s.25(2)(c).
175 See above, n.164.
176 [1994] 2 F.L.R. 309.
177 [1998] 2 F.L.R. 180.
178 Matrimonial Causes Act 1973 s.25(2)(d).
179 *Krystman v Krystman* [1973] 3 All E.R. 247.
180 [1980] Fam. 72.
181 *Co v Co (Ancillary Relief: Pre-Marital Cohabitation)* [2004] 1 F.L.R. 1095.
182 *Ibid.*, 1002.
183 Matrimonial Causes Act 1973 s.25(2)(e).
184 *C v C (Financial Provision: Personal Damages)* [1995] 2 F.L.R. 171.
185 Matrimonial Causes Act 1973 s.25(2)(f).
186 Matrimonial and Family Proceedings Act 1984 s.3.
187 See above, n.45.
188 See above, n.94.
189 See above, p.132.
190 [1975] Fam. 9.
191 *Ibid.*, 16. See also *E v E (Financial Provision)* [1990] 2 F.L.R. 233.
192 Matrimonial Causes Act 1973 s.25(2)(g).
193 *S(BD) v S(DJ)* [1977] 1 All E.R. 656, and *Re K* [1977] 1 All E.R. 647.
194 Matrimonial Proceedings and Property Act 1970 s.5.
195 See above n.45, 90.
196 *Ibid.*

197 *W v W* [1976] Fam. 107, 110.
198 *Bailey v Tolliday* (1983) 4 F.L.R. 542.
199 *Cuzner v Underdown* [1974] 2 All E.R. 353.
200 Matrimonial and Family Proceedings Act 1984 s.3.
201 [2001] 2 F.L.R. 790.
202 [1989] 1 F.L.R. 351.
203 *Ibid.*, 255.
204 [1988] Fam. 145.
205 *H v H (Financial Relief: Attempted Murder as Conduct)* [2006] 1 F.L.R. 990. See also *H v H (Financial Provision: Conduct)* [1994] 2 F.L.R. 801, and *Jones v Jones* [1975] 2 All E.R. 12.
206 *Clark v Clark* [1999] 2 F.L.R. 498.
207 *Al Khatib v Masry* [2002] 1 F.L.R. 1053.
208 *Martin v Martin* [1976] Fam. 335, 342 *per* Cairns L.J.
209 *Tavoulareas v Tavoulareas* [1998] 2 F.L.R. 418. But Thorpe L.J. agreed that s.25(2)(g) is "aimed at marital misconduct".
210 Family Law Act 1996 Sch.8 para.9(3)(b).
211 Matrimonial Causes Act 1973 s.25(2)(h).
212 See above, pp.125–126.
213 See above, n.48.
214 See above, n.13, 608.
215 Section 3, as amended by the Welfare Reform and Pensions Act 1999 Sch.3 para.6.
216 Matrimonial Causes Act 1973 s.25A(1).
217 Matrimonial Causes Act 1973 s.25A(2).
218 Matrimonial Causes Act 1973 s.25A(3).
219 Matrimonial Causes Act 1973 s.31(7A)–31(7G).
220 *Cf. Suter v Suter and Jones*, above n.142.
221 *M v M (Financial Provision)* [1987] 2 F.L.R. 1; *SRJ v DWJ (Financial Provision)* [1999] 2 F.L.R. 176.
222 *Fisher v Fisher* [1989] 1 F.L.R. 423.
223 *Fournier v Fournier* [1998] 2 F.L.R. 990.
224 An example is *Seaton v Seaton* [1986] 2 F.L.R. 398.
225 See above, n.91.
226 *Ibid.*, 1213.
227 Matrimonial Causes Act 1973 s.31(1), (2).
228 Matrimonial Causes Act 1973 s.31(2)(d).
229 *Richardson v Richardson* [1994] 1 F.L.R. 286; *N v N (Consent Order: Variation)* [1993] 2 F.L.R. 868, 883.
230 Matrimonial Causes Act 1973 s.31(7)(a).
231 Matrimonial Causes Act 1973 s.31(10).
232 Matrimonial Causes Act 1973 s.31(78), inserted by Family Law Act 1996. In *Cornick v Cornick (No.3)* [2001] 2 F.L.R.

1240 it was said courts could use the principles in *White v White* in exercising this power.

233 Matrimonial Causes Act 1973 s.31(7B)(a)–(c).

234 Law Com No.192, paras 6.8–6.10.

235 [2004] 1 W.L.R. 68.

236 *Ibid.*, 81.

237 Matrimonial Causes Act 1973 s.31(7)(a).

238 Matrimonial Causes Act 1973 s.31(7)(b).

239 *Flavell v Flavell* [1997] 1 F.L.R. 353.

240 *B(GC) v B(BA)* [1970] 1 All E.R. 913.

241 Matrimonial Causes Act 1973 s.37.

242 *Cf. Woodley v Woodley* [1992] 2 F.L.R. 417, 423.

243 Under s.282(1)(a) of the Insolvency Act 1986.

244 Matrimonial Causes Act 1973 s.37(5).

245 *Kemmis v Kemmis (Welland Intervening)* [1988] 1 W.L.R. 1307: it does not have to be his only intention.

246 *G v G* [1985] 1 W.L.R. 647.

247 [1999] 2 F.L.R. 763, 785.

248 [1988] A.C. 20.

249 *Smith v Smith (Smith Intervening)* [1992] Fam. 69.

250 *Wells v Wells* [1992] 2 F.L.R. 66 (decided in 1980); *Willians v Lindley* [2005] 2 F.L.R. 710.

251 *S v S (Financial Provision) (Post Divorce Cohabitation)* [1994] 2 F.L.R. 228.

252 [2003] Fam. 1. *White v White* was a "Barder event".

253 [1989] 2 F.L.R. 56.

254 See for example *Rundle v Rundle* [1992] 2 F.L.R. 80.

255 [1994] 2 F.L.R. 530.

256 *Maskell v Maskell* [2003] 1 F.L.R. 1138.

257 [1992] 2 F.L.R. 71.

258 *Livesey v Jenkins* [1985] A.C. 424, 445 *per* Lord Brandon.

259 Home Office, *Supporting Families*, 1998, ch.4.

260 *Ibid.*, para.4.49.

261 *Ibid.*, para.4.49.

262 *Ibid.*, paras 4.20–4.22.

263 *Financial Provision on Divorce: Clarity and Fairness—Proposals For Reform*, 2003.

264 *Ibid.*, 15.

265 See above, n.90.

266 See above n.263, 15.

267 *Ibid.*

268 See Wilson J., "Ancillary Relief Reform: Response of the

Judges of the Family Division to Government Proposals" [1999] 29 Fam Law 159 at 162–163.

269 *A More Certain Future—Recognition of Pre-Marital Agreements in England and Wales.*

270 Accounts can be found in Hamilton and Perry, 2002.

271 See above, n.268.

272 See above, n.269.

273 See above, n.263.

274 See Diduck and Kaganas, 2006, pp.272–273.

275 And see Lord Hope in *Stack v Dowden* [2007] 1 F.L.R. 1858, 1862.

276 Consultation Paper 179, *Cohabitation: The Financial Consequences of Relationship Breakdown*, 2006.

277 *Ibid.*, para.3.36.

278 *Ibid.*

279 *Ibid.*, para.1.16.

280 This mirrors the shift away from needs (reasonable requirements) in ancillary relief decisions, above, p.139.

281 See above, n.276, para.3.91.

282 *Ibid.*, para.1.16.

CHAPTER 6

1 For a collection of essays debating this see Tittle, 2004.

2 See Campion, 1995.

3 See below, p.279.

4 A good account (in the US context) is Bartholet, 1993. See, further, below: p.318.

5 See Jackson, 2002 and, more generally, Peters, 2004.

6 See *R v Sheffield AHA Ex p. Seale* [1994] 25 B.M.L.R. 1.

7 See *Re B (A Minor) (Wardship: Sterilisation)* [1988] A.C. 199 and *Re F (Mental Patient: Sterilisation)* [1990] 2 A.C. 1. A critique of *Re B* is found in Freeman, 1988.

8 Originally understood as her best medical interests, this is now interpreted more broadly to include other best interests such as social and psychological ones.

9 *Re D (Wardship: Sterilisation)* [1976] Fam. 185. For evidence that the practice long-existed see Trombley, 1988.

10 *Re A (Medical Treatment: Male Sterilisation)* [2000] 1 F.L.R. 549.

11 *R v Secretary of State for the Home Department Ex p. Mellor* [2001] 2 F.L.R. 1158

12 *Dickson v Premier Prison Service Ltd, Secretary of State for the Home Department* [2004] E.W.C.A. Civ. 1477, para.8.

13 On reproductive health and human rights more generally see Cook *et al.*, 2003.

14 See also the Universal Declaration of Human Rights Art.16, emphasising that this is "without any limitation due to race, nationality or religion".

15 Abortion Act 1967 (the grounds were amended by the Human Fertilisation and Embryology Act 1990 s.37).

16 See Sheldon, 1997.

17 *Paton v British Pregnancy Advisory Services Trustees* [1979] Q.B. 276; *Paton v United Kingdom* [1980] 3 E.H.R.R. 408; *C v S* [1988] Q.B. 135.

18 And in *Paton v United Kingdom*, above, n.17, the European Commission prioritised her Art.8 rights.

19 In *Vo v France* [2004] 2 F.C.R. 577, and *Evans v United Kingdom* [2006] 2 F.L.R. 172, 186.

20 The question had previously arisen in the USA in *Davis v Davis* 842 S.W. 2d 588 (1992), *Kass v Kass* 673 N.Y.S. 2d 350 (1998) and *Litowitz v Litowitz* 48 P. 3d 261 (2002), and in Israel in *Nachmani v Nachmani* (1995) 50(4) P.D. 661.

21 Human Fertilisation and Embryology Act 1990 Sch.3, para.2(4).

22 *Evans v Amicus Healthcare* Ltd [2004] 2 F.L.R. 766.

23 *Ibid.*, 788

24 *Ibid.*, 786.

25 *Ibid.*, 796.

26 *Evans v United Kingdom* [2006] 2 F.L.R. 172.

27 *Ibid.*, 189.

28 *Ibid.*, 191.

29 A full chamber of the European Court of Human Rights dismissed Ms Evans' appeal in 2007: [2007] 2 F.C.R. 5.

30 On the history see Lewis, 1980. On the context see Fox-Harding, 1996.

31 It is now a little over 20% of the population.

32 In the UK in 2003 it was 1.71 per woman; 40 years earlier it was 2.95.

33 *Child Poverty Review*, London, Stationery Office, 2004, para.2.55.

34 Estimates put it at about one in seven in the population.

35 A cycle of IVF costs about £3000.

36 By the National Institute for Clinical Excellence.

37 Contrast France, where there is generous access for couples of child-bearing age. See Latham, 2002.

38 And see McMillan, 2003.

39 And see Bradshaw, 2002, and Hirsch, 2006.

40 According to UNICEF; 27% are defined by the Child Poverty Action Group as living in income poverty. And see Flaherty *et al.*, 2004.

41 This was announced in the Pre-Budget Report on December 6, 2006, but the change will not come into effect until April 2009.

42 It is governed by the Social Security Contributions and Benefits Act 1992.

43 Family allowance was only paid for second and further children.

44 As the person "responsible" for the child. See above, n.42, s.141.

45 *cf. Hockinjos v Secretary of State for Social Security* [2005] 1 F.C.R. 286.

46 See *R (Barber) v Secretary of State for Work and Pensions* [2002] 2 F.L.R. 1181.

47 It is a derisory 10p a week!

48 See Tax Credits Act 2002.

49 But only if s/he works for 30 hours a week and is 25 or over.

50 The maximum amount of the allowance is thus £240.

51 Also governed by the Tax Credits Act 2002.

52 See below, p.230.

53 See n.41, above.

54 Initiated by the Child Poverty Action Group.

55 So argued by One Parent Families, quoted in the *Guardian*, December 7, 2006.

56 A number which increases as medical advances save children who once would have died.

57 And see *Monitoring Poverty and Social Exclusion in the UK 2006*, Joseph Rowntree Foundation, 2006. A special issue of *Disability Now* (January 2007) focused on the disabled and poverty.

58 See *Every Child Matters* Cm 5860, London, Stationery Office, 2003.

59 Hence a campaign stated in 2006 called "Every Disabled Child Matters". See *Poverty* no.125, 2006, p.6.

60 A Private Member's Bill was debated in January 2007.

61 Lord Laming, *The Victoria Climbié Report*, London, Stationery Office, 2003, para.1. 30.

62 Above, n.58, Executive Summary, p.4.

63 *Ibid.*, para.1.10.

64 *Every Child Matters: Next Steps*, London, Stationery Office, 2004, paras 3.5 and 3.6.

65 Children Act 2004 s.10 (s.25 for Wales).

66 Health and emotional well-being, protection from harm and neglect, education, training and recreation.

67 Section 10(2)(e).

68 Section 10(3).

69 See above, n.58.

70 National Audit Office, 2000.

71 See Jackson, 2001, and Freeman, 2004.

72 See Matrimonial Causes Act 1973 s.52 and Children Act 1989 s.105(1).

73 See *Re Thain* [1926] Ch. 676; *Re C (MA) (An Infant)* [1966] 1 All E.R. 838.

74 For example, *Re M (Child's Upbringing)* [1996] 2 F.L.R. 441, and note *Re O (Family Appeals: Management)* [1998] 1 F.L.R. 431.

75 See Human Fertilisation and Embryology Act 1990 s.28(6) and below, p.169.

76 See below, p.175.

77 The *Ampthill Peerage Case* [1977] AC 547, 577.

78 As in the Californian case of *Johnson v Calvert* 851 P. 2d 776 (Cal.1993). A court in Ohio in *Belsito v Clark* 644 N.E. 2d 760 (Ohio Com. Pl. 1994) rejected the intention-based test on the ground that it is often difficult to prove. It favoured the genetic test.

79 *Report of Inquiry into Human Fertilisation and Embryology*, Cmnd. 9314, para.8.16.

80 The view of some psychologists and anthropologists (Robin Fox, 1992 is an example). See also Baroness Hale in *Re G (Children)* [2006] 2 F.L.R. 629, 641.

81 So argued by Kandel, 1994.

82 In Germany, where there were proposals to introduce anonymous birth, there are now baby boxes where unwanted babies can be deposited (Willenbacher, 2004). These are illegal but 50–70 exist nevertheless (as at 2004).

83 In 2002 French law was modified to allow details of birth to be revealed at the child's request and with the assent of the mother. But in my view it remains incompatible. The

decision of the European Court in *Jäggs v Switzerland* 2006 E.C.H.R. suggests it might not follow *Odièvre*.

84 *Odièvre v France* [2003] 1 F.C.R. 621.
85 See the recent case of *Re G (Children)* [2006] 2 F.L.R. 629.
86 Said in *Re D (Children and Parental Responsibility: Lesbian Mothers and Known Father)* [2006] 1 F.C.R. 556, para.57; see also Diduck, 2007.
87 See above, n.85.
88 *Ibid.*, 631.
89 See for example Kandel's discussion, above n.81, of the Efe of Zaire where there is "multiple caretaking" by all women of the camp.
90 See Smart, 1987, p.99.
91 *Banbury Peerage Case* (1811) 1 Sim. & St. 153.
92 Family Law Reform Act 1969 s.26.
93 [2002] 1 F.L.R. 1145.
94 *C v C and C (Legitimacy: Photographic Evidence)* [1972] 3 All E.R. 577.
95 In 2005 42.8% (Babb *et al.*, 2006).
96 *Brierley v Brierley* [1918] P. 257 and Births and Deaths Registration Act 1953 s.34(2).
97 See below, p.183.
98 Ontario, New South Wales and Tasmania.
99 *Illegitimacy*, Law Com. 118, 1982, para.10.54.
100 Births and Deaths Registration Act 1955 s.2.
101 Births and Deaths Registration Act 1955 s.10(1)(a).
102 Perhaps even a presumption of paternity (Lowe and Douglas, 2006, p.323).
103 See above, n.92.
104 Family Law Reform Act 1969 s.20(1).
105 Balcombe L.J. in *Re F (A Minor) (Blood Tests: Parental Rights)* [1993] Fam. 314, 318, on which see Fortin, 1996.
106 Article 7.
107 [1997] Fam. 89.
108 *S v S; W v Official Solicitor* [1972] A.C. 24.
109 Above, n.93.
110 An example is *K v M (Paternity: Contact)* [1996] 1 F.L.R. 312.
111 Family Law Reform Act 1969 s.21(1).
112 Family Law Reform Act 1969 s.23(1).
113 [1997] 1 F.L.R. 360, 366.
114 [1994] 2 F.L.R. 463, 473.
115 Family Law Reform Act 1969 s.21(3).

116 Family Law Reform Act 1969 s.21(3)(b), added by the Child Support, Pensions and Social Security Act 2000 s.82.

117 Above, n.108, *per* Lord Reid.

118 Bodey J. in *Re T (Paternity: Ordering Blood Tests)* [2001] 2 F.L.R. 1190.

119 *Ibid.*, 1194.

120 Human Fertilisation and Embryology Act 1990 s.28(2).

121 [2003] 1 F.L.R. 1091.

122 Children Act 1989 s.8, below p.230.

123 They were twins.

124 Human Fertilisation and Embryology Authority (Disclosure of Donor Information) Regulations 2004 (SI 2004/1511), reg.2(3).

125 This has happened here too. Only 119 sperm donors registered in the first months following the legislative change: about 500 are needed each year. See the *Guardian*, November 10, 2006.

126 A poll of more than 4000 people by YouGov found 58% believing that donors should have the right to give sperm or eggs anonymously. See *ibid.*, and S. Jeffries, "Who's The Daddy?", the *Guardian* November 18, 2006, p.31.

127 *R v Human Fertilisation and Embryology Authority Ex p. Blood* [1999] Fam. 151.

128 Human Fertilisation and Embryology Act 1990 s.28(5A)–(5B), inserted by Human Fertilisation and Embryology (Deceased Fathers) Act 2003.

129 But knowledge of paternity is a child's right: See UN Convention on the Rights of the Child Art.7(1), and *Re O (A Minor) (Blood Tests: Constraint)* [2000] Fam. 139, 144.

130 Children born as a result of sperm donation were usually "treated as a child of the marriage", so there were few practical differences.

131 Family Law Reform Act 1987 s.27.

132 Code of Practice, para.7.

133 See above, p.170.

134 Above, n.121, 1098.

135 Human Fertilisation and Embryology Act 1990 s.28(3).

136 In *Re R (A Child) (IVF: Paternity of Child)* [2003] Fam. 129. This was approved in the House of Lords by Lords Hope and Walker: [2005] 2 F.L.R. 843.

137 For example, *Re Q (Parental Order)* [1996] 1 F.L.R. 369; *U v W (Attorney-General Intervening)* [1997] 2 F.L.R. 282.

138 *Re B (Parentage)* [1996] 2 FLR 15, approved in above, n.127,

179, and by Lord Walker in *Re R (IVF: Paternity of Child)* [2005] 2 F.L.R. 843, 853.

139 As in the *Leeds Teaching Hospitals* case, above n.121.

140 Above, ns 22 and 26.

141 See *Re R*, above, n.138.

142 See below, Chapter 11.

143 Passed in response to *Re W (Minors) (Surrogacy)* [1991] 1 F.L.R. 385.

144 See generally Jackson, 2001. See also Freeman, 1989.

145 Above, p.165.

146 Human Fertilisation and Embryology Act 1990 s.28(2).

147 See above, n.135.

148 And see *Re D (A Child)* [2005] 2 F.C.R. 223.

149 Human Fertilisation and Embryology Act 1990 s.28(6).

150 Births and Deaths Registration Act 1953 s.2.

151 HFEA, *Code of Practice* (6th edn, 2003, p.144) states that the surrogate's husband or partner should "normally" be registered as the father.

152 Children Act 1989 s.4(1)(a), (1a).

153 The only way where the child was conceived by sexual intercourse, as happened in *Re Adoption Application (Payment for Adoption)* [1987] Fam. 81.

154 Under s.30 of Human Fertilisation and Embryology Act 1990.

155 Adoption and Children Act 2002 s.95.

156 Adoption and Children Act 2002 s.95.

157 See above, n.153. See also *Re WM (Adoption: Non Patrial)* [1997] 1 F.L.R. 132. These authorisations were under previous legislation, differently constructed, and may not be followed.

158 Human Fertilisation and Embryology Act 1990 s.30(1).

159 Human Fertilisation and Embryology Act 1990 s.30(1)(b).

160 Human Fertilisation and Embryology Act 1990 s.30(2).

161 Human Fertilisation and Embryology Act 1990 s.30(3).

162 Human Fertilisation and Embryology Act 1990 s.30(5).

163 See below, p.327.

164 Proceedings under s.30 are family proceedings: see s.30(8)(a) and Children Act 1989 s.8(3), (4) and below, p.232. A contact order—for example in favour of the surrogate— could also be made.

165 In *Re Q (Parental Order)* [1996] 1 F.L.R. 396, £8,280; in *Re C (Application by Mr and Mrs X)* [2002] Fam. Law 351, £12,000 (the surrogate was also claiming income support).

166 Parental Orders (Human Fertilisation and Embyology) Regulations 1994, SI 1994/2757 Sch.1.
167 Adoption and Children Act 2002 s.1(2).

CHAPTER 7

1 See Frank, 1990.
2 Parental Rights and Duties and Custody Suits, London, Stevens, 1975. I sat on the committee.
3 Law Com. No.172, para.2.4.
4 *Gillick v West Norfolk and Wisbech AHA* [1986] A.C. 112.
5 Scots Law Com, Discussion Paper No.88, *Parental Responsibilities and Rights, Guardianship and the Administration of Children's Property* (1990), para.2.3.
6 Children (Scotland) Act 1995.
7 These are important when judging whether a parent has fallen below the standard expected of a parent: see the test in s.31(2) of the Children Act 1989, below, p.289.
8 See below, pp.210, 276–278.
9 See Brazier, 1999 and Freeman, 1997, p.178, and 2008 (forthcoming).
10 See above, n.4.
11 *Hansard*, H.L. vol.502, col.1451.
12 See Eekelaar, 1991b.
13 See below, pp.330–331.
14 See above, pp.172–174.
15 Children Act 1989 s.33(3)(b), (4).
16 Law Commission, Working Paper No.96, *Custody*, 1986, para.7.16.
17 Children Act 1989 s.1(1).
18 United Nations Convention on the Rights of the Child, 1989, Art.3(1), on which see Freeman, 2007.
19 Most clearly articulated by Lord MacDermott in *J v C* [1970] AC 668, 710.
20 As an example see *Yousef v The Netherlands* (2003) 36 E.H.H.R. 20.
21 *Re KD (A Minor) (Access: Principles)* [1988] 2 F.L.R. 139, 141. And see *Re G (Children)*, above, p.166.
22 In *Stanley v Illinois* 405 U.S. 645, 651 (1972).
23 As late as the tenth century, a parent could sell a child under seven into slavery. Rights over property, services and earnings lasted into recent times.

24 Unfit parents may have rights terminated (by adoption): property owners may abuse their property with impunity.

25 I ignore the cloned child who is genetically related to only one parent.

26 See above, p.163.

27 As in the Natallie Evans litigation, above, pp.157–158.

28 On which see Meyer, 1997, p.61.

29 Intention includes recklessness.

30 An extreme example would be the rapist.

31 Differences of intention, questions about whether intention continues, disputes over abortion, etc.

32 See Dickens, 1981 and Bainham, 2005, p.119.

33 See Beck *et al.*, 1978; Scott and Scott, 1995.

34 See *Re B* [1981] (Down's Syndrome child with intestinal blockage). The court overruled the parents. Contrast *Re T* [1997] 1 F.L.R. 502 (toddler needed a liver transplant). The court supported the parents' decision. See below, p.202.

35 *Re T*, above, n.34. I say "clearly" but it was not clear to the Court of Appeal.

36 See Schneider, 1995, and also Herring, 2004, p.355.

37 See Vallentyne, 2002.

38 And see Finnis, 1980.

39 Not only in dystopias like Plato's *Republic*, Huxley's *Brave New World*, Orwell's *1984*, but in totalitarian societies like Nazi Germany, Soviet Russia and the North Korea of today.

40 See Becker, 1977.

41 Kelsen, 1967.

42 Children Act 1989 s.2(5).

43 Children Act 1989 s.2(6).

44 See above, p.177.

45 Children Act 1989 s.2(1), (2).

46 Children Act 1989 s.2(1).

47 Children Act 1989 s.2(2).

48 And they were dissatisfied, frequently referring to child support. They tended to feel strongly that fathers should have rights if they were expected to bear responsibilities: see Pickford, 1999, p.152.

49 It is now a criminal offence.

50 See Bainham, 1989, p.231.

51 See below, p.336.

52 Under the Human Rights Act 1998.

53 *B v United Kingdom* [2000] 1 F.L.R. 1. See also *McMichael v United Kingdom* (1995) 20 E.H.R.R. 205.

54 Article 8 of the European Convention on Human Rights.
55 However, see *M v United Kingdom*, *The Times*, September 15, 2005 (tax deductions to married fathers, but not to unmarried fathers, violated Art.14, in conjunction with Art.1 of the First Protocol (protecting property)).
56 Article 18.
57 Douglas's view, 2004, p.106.
58 See Fortin, 2003.
59 Article 7.
60 Article 9(3).
61 Scots Law Com No.135, *Report on Family Law*, 1992.
62 *Ibid.*, para.2.48.
63 In the Children (Scotland) Act 1995. See Family (Scotland) Act 2006 s.23 in relation to birth registration.
64 1. *Court Proceedings for the Determination of Paternity*; 2. *The Law on Parental Responsibility for Unmarried Fathers*, paras 3a *et seq.*
65 See below, pp.184–187.
66 Children Act 1989 s.2.
67 Children Act 1989 s.4(1)(a) and (1A), as amended by the Adoption and Children Act 2002.
68 Children Act 1989 s.4(1)(b).
69 Children Act 1989 s.4(1)(c).
70 Children Act 1989 s.12(2).
71 Children Act 1989 s.12(1).
72 Children Act 1989 s.5(6).
73 Adoption and Children Act 2002.
74 Adoption and Children Act 2002.
75 Children Act 1989 s.4(2A).
76 Children Act 1989 s.1(1).
77 Children Act 1989 s.1(5). And see *Re P (Parental Responsibility)* [1998] 2 F.L.R. 96, 107.
78 *Re P (Terminating Parental Responsibility)* [1995] 1 F.L.R. 1048.
79 Office for National Statistics, *Social Trends*, 31.
80 *Judicial Statistics*, Table 5.3.
81 Form C (PRA 1).
82 Which was a concern.
83 About 3,600 in 1996. There are no later figures.
84 See above, n.76.
85 Above, n.77.
86 *Re H (Parental Responsibility)* [1988] 1 F.L.R. 855.
87 *Judicial Statistics* 2004, Table 5.3. In 2000 6% were refused.

88 See below, pp.186–187.
89 [1991] Fam 151.
90 *D v Hereford and Worcester CC* [1991] 1 F.L.R. 205, 212.
91 [1992] 1 F.L.R. 1, 8.
92 *Re H (Parental Responsibility)* [1998] 1 F.L.R. 855.
93 *Ibid.*
94 Quoted in *ibid.*, 857.
95 [1993] 2 F.L.R. 450.
96 [1998] 2 F.L.R. 96.
97 A prohibited steps order could have been added to a par-
    ental responsibility order—see below p.241—but the court
    did not think this would contain him.
98 [1997] 2 F.L.R. 722.
99 Ward J. at *ibid.*, 726.
100 [1999] 2 F.L.R. 737.
101 See above, p.185.
102 [2001] 2 F.L.R. 342.
103 [1999] 1 F.L.R. 784.
104 In addition, part of the motivation for the application—
    concern about the mother's involvement with drugs—no
    longer existed.
105 [2001] 2 F.C.R. 134.
106 [1995] 2 F.L.R. 648, 657.
107 *Re C and V (Contact and Parental Responsibility)* [1998] 1
    F.L.R. 392, 397.
108 *Re H (Parental Responsibility: Maintenance)* [1996] 1 F.L.R.
    867, 868.
109 *Ibid.*, 869–870.
110 And see below, p.336.
111 See the *Guardian*, December 2006.
112 See also *Re T (A Minor) (Parental Responsibility: Contact)*,
    above, n.95.
113 *D v Hereford and Worcester CC*, above, n.90.
114 *Re H (Minor) (Local Authority: Parental Rights) (No.3)*, above,
    n.89 (which was a freeing for adoption). In *Re D (Contact
    and Parental Responsibility: Lesbian Mothers and Known
    Father)* [2006] 1 F.C.R. 556, parental responsibility was
    given to a sperm donor. He was "the child's father".
115 See *Re H (A Minor) (Contact and Parental Reponsibility)* [1993]
    1 F.L.R. 484.
116 By virtue of birth regulation or an agreement.
117 Under s.8 of the Children Act 1989.
118 Children Act 1989 s.12(1).

119 Children Act 1989 s.34.
120 See Masson, 1984.
121 Special guardianship is discussed below, pp.249–250, 333–335.
122 See below, p.230.
123 See below, pp.320–321.
124 Article 8.
125 If s/he has sufficient understanding.
126 Children Act 1989 s.1(1), (5).
127 See above, p.185.
128 The checklist in the Children Act 1989 s.1(3) is not applicable.
129 Bartlett (1984, p.914) was of the view that step-parents should acquire parental "rights" on marriage, and forfeit them on divorce.
130 Children Act 1989 s.4(2A), (3), (4). See *Re P (Terminating Parental Responsibility)* [1995] 1 F.L.R. 1048.
131 Or others, of course.
132 See *B v B (Grandparent: Residence Order)* [1992] 2 F.L.R. 327.
133 See below, p.334.
134 Children Act 1989 s.13.
135 Above, p.175.
136 On whether there is a right to contact see below, pp.190–192.
137 See *Elsholz v Germany* [2000] 2 F.L.R. 486 and *Sahin v Germany; Sommerfeld v Germany* [2003] 2 F.L.R. 67a.
138 See below, pp.356–362.
139 In *Hewer v Bryant* [1970] 1 Q.B. 357, 369.
140 Famously in *Re Agar-Ellis* (1883) 24 Ch.D. 317.
141 Child Abduction Act 1984 s.2.
142 In s.1(5).
143 Children Act 1989 s.13(2).
144 Under Children Act 1989 s.8. The child could also be made a ward of court.
145 See *R v Tameside MBC Ex p. J* [2000] 1 F.L.R. 942.
146 [1988] A.C. 806, 827.
147 Children Act 1989 s.34(1).
148 Children Act 1989 s.44(13).
149 *M v M (Child: Access)* [1973] 2 All E.R. 81. See also *Re S (Minors: Access)* [1990] 2 F.L.R. 166; *Re R (A Minor: Contact)* [1993] 2 F.L.R. 762 *Re F (Contact: Restraint Order)* [1995] 1 F.L.R. 956.

150 *Kosmopoulou v Greece* [2004] 1 F.L.R. 800; *Hokkanen v Finland* [1996] 1 F.L.R. 289; *Ciliz v Netherlands* [2000] 2 F.L.R. 469.

151 [2000] 2 F.L.R. 334. This case is fully considered below, p.235.

152 *Ibid.*, 264.

153 *Ibid.*

154 *Ibid.*

155 [2005] 3 F.C.R. 93. In *Hansen v Turkey* [2004] 1 F.L.R. 142, coercive measures against children were not ruled out.

156 [2005] 2 F.L.R. 897.

157 *Re S (Contact: Promoting Relationship with Absent Parent)* [2004] 1 F.L.R. 1279, 1288, 1287.

158 [2006] 1 F.L.R. 627.

159 Not just for parents or those with parental responsibility. The offence can be committed by anyone of 16 who has "responsibility", that includes those with parental responsibility, but also those legally liable to maintain the child (e.g. a step-parent who has treated the child as a child of the family or a foster parent) and anyone who has "care" (a teacher or a babysitter).

160 Children and Young Persons Act 1933 s.1(1).

161 Children and Young Persons Act 1933 s.1(2)(a).

162 *R v Sheppard* [1981] A.C. 394.

163 Children and Young Persons Act 1933 s.1(2)(b).

164 Children and Young Persons Act 1933 s.4.

165 This offence is discussed more fully in Ch.9, below.

166 An example is *Pereira v Keleman* [1995] 1 F.L.R. 428.

167 *Surtees v Kingston-Upon-Thames BC* [1991] 2 F.L.R. 559, 584. The case related to a foster parent, but it is clear is indistinguishable from that of a parent.

168 But see *R v D* [1994] A.C. 778 and *R v Rahman* [1985] 81 Cr. App. R. 349.

169 Children Act 1989 s.31(2)(b)(ii).

170 *R. v Hopley* (1860) 2 F. & F. 202. On the meaning of "reasonable" see *R v H (Assault of Child: Reasonable Chastisement)* [2001] 2 F.L.R. 431.

171 See *R. (on the Application of Williamson) v Secretary of State for Education and Employment* [2002] 1 F.L.R. 493 (*per* Elias J.).

172 If it was not, the parent (teacher etc.) could be convicted of occasioning actual bodily harm (or even a more serious offence). An example is *R v Derrivière* (1969) 53 Cr. App. Rep. 637 (brutal assault by father on 12-year-old son); father given 6 months. Another—from a much earlier era—is *R v*

Griffin (1869) 11 Cox C.C. 402 (father convicted of man-slaughter of two-and-a-half-year-old daughter whom he beat with a strap for "some childish fault").

173 *Tyrer v United Kingdom* (1978) 2 E.H.R.R. 1 (the case related to the Isle of Man: birching was abolished on the mainland in 1948).

174 *Campbell and Cosans v UK* (1982) 4 E.H.R.R. 293.

175 See Art.19 of the UN Convention on the Rights of the Child.

176 *Costello-Roberts v United Kingdom* (1996) 19 E.H.R.R. 1 (though slippering a 7-year-old over his clothed buttocks was held by 5–4 not to be degrading).

177 See Newell (1972).

178 Education (No.2) Act 1986 s.47. It applied also to state-funded pupils in independent schools, thus a nonsense (and a joke) that pupils in public schools could be divided into caning and non-caning streams!

179 School Standards and Framework Act 1998 s.131.

180 Children's Homes Regulations 2001 (SI 2001/3967), reg.17(5)(a).

181 Fostering Services Regulations 2002 (SI 2002/57) reg.28(5)(b). Foster parents must make a written agreement not to use corporal punishment.

182 Day Care and Child Minding (National Standards) (England) Regulations 2003 (SI 2003/1996), reg.5. For earlier controversy see *L.B. of Sutton v Davis* [1994] 1 F.L.R. 737.

183 Education Act 1996 s.550A.

184 It commenced the process as early as 1957, when it removed from the Penal Code the corporal punishment defence to criminal assault unless the punishment was mild. This is roughly where the UK, 50 years later, is at!

185 See Freeman, 1999.

186 *Protecting Children, Supporting Parents: a Consultation Document on the Physical Punishment of Children*, 2000, para.1.

187 The best critique is Newell, 1989.

188 That is, a contradiction in terms.

189 There was an attempt to bring back the cane as a judical punishment for 10–18-year-olds in 1996. See Corporal Punishment (Re Introduction) Bill 1996, discussed in the *Independent* June 7, 1996. It was lost by 153 votes to 58.

190 See M. Straus, 2000, who gets much the better of a debate with Larzelere (2000).

191 Zigler (1980, p.27) argues that "well over half of all

instances of child abuse appear to have developed out of disciplinary action taken by the parent".

192 The Swedish Ministry of Justice produced a pamphlet entitled "Can You Bring Up Children Successfully without Smacking and Spanking?" (1979).

193 In Sweden, for example, prosecutions of parents are rare. The ban is seen as an educational tool. The goal is social engineering.

194 This research (in 1999) was commissioned by Children Are Unbeatable!

195 See Freeman, 1974, p.64. On Sweden and anti-spanking laws see Durrant, 1999.

196 See for example Colombotos's study of Medicare in New York (1969).

197 A view supported by the police, see above, p.79.

198 See above, n.185.

199 In Sweden.

200 But they may become sexually deviant, see King *et al.*, 2003.

201 [1998] 2 F.L.R. 959 (see Bainham, 1999a and Barton, 1999).

202 Article 19.

203 See above, pp.194–195.

204 *Analysis of Responses to the Protecting Children, Supporting Parents Consultation Document*, 2001.

205 6th Report of the House of Commons Health Committee— *The Victoria Climbié Inquiry Report*, H.C. 270, London, Stationery Office, 2003.

206 Proposed by David Hinchliffe MP.

207 As a result of Lord Lester's initiative in the House of Lords. On the history see Smith, 2004.

208 Children Act 2004 s.58(5).

209 Article 28(1).

210 Article 26(1).

211 Article 2, Protocol 1.

212 Education Act 1996 s.7.

213 This was introduced in 1988 and see now Education Act 2002.

214 Failure to do so is an offence: Education Act 1996 s.443.

215 Failure to do so is offence: Education Act 1996 s.444. These two offences can now lead to parents being imprisoned for three months and a parenting order being made. Parents can also be made to enter into a parenting contract under the Anti-Social Behaviour Act 2003.

216 And see Grenville, 1988.

217 For Christians, Ascension Day.
218 See *Rogers v Essex CC* [1986] 3 All E.R. 321, and *George v Devon CC* [1988] 3 All E.R. 2002.
219 On *Gillick*-competence see below, p.362.
220 Children and Young Persons Act 1969 s.1(2)(e). Care was sometimes used, unlawfully I would maintain, as a threat (see Hullin, 1985).
221 See DHSS, *Review of Child Care Law*, 1985, para.12–22.
222 Children Act 1989 s.31(2), and see *Re O (Care Proceedings: Education)* [1992] 1 W.L.R. 912.
223 Children Act 1989 s.36.
224 Children Act 1989 s.36(3).
225 Children Act 1989 Sch.3 para.12(1)(a).
226 See above, n.212.
227 *Crump v Gilmore* (1970) 68 L.G.R. 56.
228 Education Act 1996 s.9; European Convention on Human Rights Art.2 of 1st Protocol.
229 *R. (On the Application of Williamson) v Secretary of State for Education and Employment* [2005] 2 F.L.R. 374.
230 School Standards and Framework Act 1998 s.71.
231 Education Act 1996 s.241. Sex education must be balanced and objective: see *Kjeldsen v Denmark* (1986) 1 E.H.R.R. 711.
232 Education Act 1996 s.375(3).
233 School Standards and Framework Act 1998 s.70. This must be "wholly or mainly of a broadly Christian character": *ibid.*, Sch.20 para.3(2).
234 Education Act 1996 s.403(1A).
235 It must be arguable that *Gillick*-competent children can insist on these rights: as far as sex education is concerned, children over 16 must surely be entitled to sex education, whatever their parents wish.
236 See further Meredith, 2001 and Monk, 2001.
237 See below, p.240.
238 Children Act 1989 s.1(1).
239 *Re A (Specific Issue Order: Parental Dispute)* [2001] 1 F.L.R. 121.
240 *Re J (Specific Issue Orders: Muslim Upbringing and Circumcision)* [1999] 2 F.L.R. 678–685.
241 See *Re S (Access: Religious Upbringing)* [1992] 2 F.L.R. 313 and *Re P (A Minor) (Residence Order: Child's Welfare)* [2000] Fam. 15.
242 Children Act 1989 s.33(6)(a).
243 Adoption and Children Act 2002 s.1(5).

244 As was the case before: see Adoption Act 1976 s.7.

245 [1999] 2 F.L.R. 573.

246 See above, n.240.

247 See s.1(5) of Children Act 1989, discussed below pp.228–230.

248 [2000] 1 F.L.R. 571.

249 English law has no rule on this: see above, n.240, pp.681–682.

250 Despite s.2(7) of Children Act 1989, discussed below, p.206.

251 Since the Prohibition of Female Circumcision Act 1985. See now Female Genital Mutilation Act 2003.

252 *Re B (A Minor) (Wardship: Sterilisation)* [1988] A.C. 199, 205. There is still responsibility to bring the issue before the High Court: *Re HG (Specific Issue Order: Sterilisation)* [1993] 1 F.L.R. 587.

253 Family Law Reform Act 1969 s.8.

254 See *Gillick v West Norfolk and Wisbech AHA* [1986] A.C. 112, and below, p.362.

255 *Re R (Wardship: Consent to Treatment)* [1992] Fam. 11; *Re W (A Minor) (Medical Treatment: Court's Jurisdiction.)* [1993] Fam. 64, and see Freeman, 2005.

256 [1976] Fam. 185.

257 Now "Liberty".

258 [2001] Fam. 147.

259 [1997] 1 W.L.R. 242.

260 So the father did not have parental responsibility.

261 *Secretary, Dept of Health and Community Services v JWB and SMB* (1992) 175 C.L.R. 218 (usually known as "Marion's Case").

262 *Ibid.*, 295 *per* Deane J. It is in this way that male circumcision is justified. For a case study of what would not be justified—though it seemingly is in Washington State—see the discussion by E. Perkington, the *Guardian*, January 4, 2007, p.3 of "Pillow Angel".

263 Section 2.

264 Section 10(1), and Births and Deaths (Amendment) Regulations 1994, SI 1994/1948 (unmarried father is not required to give information concerning the birth).

265 Registration of Births, Deaths and Marriages Regulations 1987 reg.9(3)(a).

266 And see Bond, 1998.

267 *Re PC (Change of Surname)* [1997] 2 F.L.R. 730, 739.

268 [1999] 2 A.C. 308.

269 *Re R (Surname: Using Both Parents')* [2001] 2 F.L.R. 1358, 1362.

270 Children Act 1989 s.13(1)(a).

271 See above, n.267, p.739.

272 *Ibid.*, p.736.

273 Children Act 1989 s.8(1), and below, p.241.

274 Above, n.268.

275 Children Act 1989 s.1(1), and *Dawson v Wearmouth*, above, n.268.

276 *Re C (Change of Surname)* [1998] 2 F.L.R. 656.

277 *Re B (Change of Surname)* [1996] 1 F.L.R. 791 (teenagers forced to keep their father's surname to maintain link with him, despite their opposition).

278 [1999] 1 F.L.R. 672.

279 On which see below, p.362.

280 *Re P (Parental Responsibility: Change of Name)* [1997] 2 F.L.R. 722; *Re W, Re A, Re B (Change of Name)* [1999] 2 F.L.R. 930.

281 [2001] 2 F.L.R. 1005.

282 *Re H (Child's Name: First Name)* [2002] 1 F.L.R. 973.

283 In *Re M, T, P, K and B (Care: Change of Name)* [2000] 1 F.L.R. 645 (local authority given leave to change name of children in care because they lived in fear that parents would discover their whereabouts).

284 They normally exercise it, but can choose not to do so.

285 C.P.R. 1998, r.21.2(2).

286 *Woolf v Pemberton* [1877] 6 Ch.D. 19.

287 *Re Taylor's Application* [1972] 2 Q.B. 369.

288 Family Proceedings Rules 1991 r.9.2A, and see Sawyer, 1995.

289 Children Act 1989 s.3(3).

290 Children Act 1989 s.3(4)(b).

291 Administration of Estates Act 1925 Pt IV and Family Law Reform Act 1987 s.18(2).

292 *R v Gwynedd CC Ex p. B* [1992] 3 All E.R. 317.

293 Children Act 1989 s.2(5).

294 Law Com. No.172, para.2.07.

295 Children Act 1989 s.2(7).

296 Children Act 1989 s.2(8).

297 *Re G (A Minor) (Parental Responsibility: Education)* [1994] 2 F.L.R. 964.

298 *Re J (Specific Issue Orders) (Muslim Upbringing and Circumcision)* [2000] 1 F.L.R. 571.

299 *Re PC (Change of Surname)* [1997] 2 F.L.R. 730, and above pp.203–204.
300 *Re C (Welfare of Child: Immunisation)* [2003] 2 F.L.R. 1095, C.A.
301 Children Act 1989 s.2(8).
302 Even though the local authority requires parental responsibility.
303 Children Act 1989 s.2(9).
304 Children Act 1989 s.3(5).
305 Children Act 1989 s.20(8).
306 An example given by David Mellor MP in a debate on the Children Bill in 1989: Standing Committee B, col.148. See also *Hansard*, H.L. vol.503, col.1412 and vol.505, col.370.
307 [1994] 1 F.L.R. 578.
308 *Re C (Welfare of Child: Immunisation)* [2003] 2 F.L.R. 1054, 1088 (Sumner J.), p.1088.

CHAPTER 8

1 Children Act 1989 s.1(1).
2 See below, pp.215–225.
3 [1970] A.C. 668, 710.
4 The Preamble refers to "the inherent dignity and ... equal and inalienable rights of all members of the human family". There are also references to children in Art.5(1) (d) and in Art.6, and the 1st Protocol in 1952 forbids the denial of the right to education.
5 See, e.g. Fortin, 1999, and Herring, 1999.
6 (1982) 5 E.H.R.R. 223.
7 *Re L (A Child) (Contact: Domestic Violence)* [2001] Fam. 260, 277; *Payne v Payne* [2001] 1 F.L.R. 1052.
8 *Payne v Payne*, above, n.7, 1065.
9 *Yousef v Netherlands* [2003] 1 F.L.R. 210, 221–222.
10 In *CF v Secretary for the Home Department* [2004] 2 F.L.R. 556.
11 And see Fortin, 2003, p.57.
12 On which see Van Bueren, 1995.
13 On which see Freeman, 2007.
14 In *Payne v Payne*, above n.7, 1065, Thorpe L.J. wrongly states the paramountcy principle is "enshrined in Article 3(1) of the UN Convention".
15 1975, p.260.
16 *Ibid.*, p.235.

17 1995, p.50.
18 See Elster, 1987.
19 See Reece, 1996.
20 See Thèry, 1989, p.81. An excellent example is the Iowa decision of *Painter v Bannister* 140 N.W. 2d 152 (1966), discussed by Freeman, 1983, pp.202–204.
21 See Thorpe L.J.'s comment: the fact that a Dubai court had reached a different decision from that which an English court would have reached "does not mean that the welfare of the child is not the first consideration for the judge of the Sharia Court. It is the interpretation of child welfare, governed as it is by different religions, cultures and traditions, that produces such starkly different outcomes" (*Al-Habtoor v Fotheringham* [2003] 1 F.L.R. 951, 970–971).
22 See above, p.201.
23 *Re J (Specific Issue Orders: Muslim Upbringing and Circumcision)* [1999] 2 F.L.R. 678 and [2000] 1 F.L.R. 571. See also *Re S (Specific Issue Order: Religion: Circumcision)* [2005] 1 F.L.R. 236.
24 By Buchanan and Brock, 1989, p.247.
25 1975, p.260.
26 See 1 Kings 16–28.
27 Mnookin, 1975, p.258.
28 1973, p.51.
29 1958, pp.97–98.
30 1973, p.378.
31 See below, p.217.
32 See above, n.20.
33 Discussed by Freeman, 1983, pp.202–204.
34 See above, p.201.
35 [1986] 1 F.L.R. 325.
36 *Re W (Residence Order)* [1999] 1 F.L.R. 869.
37 [1999] 2 F.L.R. 573, and above, p.201.
38 *Ibid.*, 586, This was contested.
39 *B v B (Residence Order: Reasons for Decisions)* [1997] 2 F.L.R. 602.
40 *Re G (Children)* [2006] 2 F.L.R. 629, 642.
41 Children Act 1989 s.1(3)(a)
42 See Art.12.
43 Even magistrates may do this: *Re M (A Minor) (Justices' Discretion)* [1993] 2 F.L.R. 706.
44 [2005] Fam. 366.
45 That is CAFCASS.

46 *President's Direction: Representation of Children in Family Proceedings Pursuant to Family Proceedings Rules* 1991, r.9.5 [2005] 1 F.L.R. 1188.
47 Thorpe L.J. in *Mabon v Mabon*, above, n.44.
48 *Sahin v Germany; Sommerfeld v Germany* [2003] 2 F.L.R. 671.
49 Children Act 1989 s.7.
50 But only where it has involvement with the case anyway.
51 *R v R (Private Law Proceedings: Residential Assessment)* [2002] 2 F.L.R. 953.
52 *Re K (Contact: Psychiatric Report)* [1995] 2 F.L.R. 432.
53 By Thorpe L.J. in *Re M (Disclosure: Child and Family Reporter)* [2002] 2 F.L.R. 893, 901.
54 *Ibid.* See also *Re C (Section 8 Order: Court Welfare Office)* [1995] 1 F.L.R. 617, 619.
55 The *Thematic Inspection* in 1997 found children were seen alone in less than half the reports and not at all in nearly a sixth.
56 See *Re P* [1991] 1 F.L.R. 337.
57 *Cadman v Cadman* (1982) 3 F.L.R. 275; *Stephenson v Stephenson* [1985] F.L.R. 1140; *Re V (Residence: Review)* [1995] 2 F.L.R. 1010.
58 An example is *Re P (A Minor) (Inadequate Welfare Report)* [1996] 2 F.C.R. 285.
59 *Re T (Abduction: Child's Objections to Return)* [2000] 2 F.L.R. 193.
60 *Re S* [1967] 1 All E.R. 202, 210.
61 And see *M v M* [1977] 7 Fam. Law 17.
62 See below, pp.282–283.
63 [1995] 1 F.L.R. 274.
64 [1993] 2 F.L.R. 163.
65 And see *Re T (Minors) (Custody: Religious Upbringing)* (1975) 2 F.L.R. 239. but see *Re B and G (Minors) (Custody)* [1985] F.L.R. 493, and below, pp.362–367.
66 *Re T (Abduction: Child's Objections To Return)* [2000] 2 F.L.R. 192.
67 [2000] 2 F.L.R. 645. The case concerned children of travellers.
68 *Ibid.*, 652.
69 Supported by the guardian ad litem.
70 [2002] 1 F.L.R. 1156.
71 This case is one in which the so-called and discredited "parental alienation syndrome" was raised. And see *Re Bradford; Re O'Connell* [2007] 1 F.L.R. 530.

72 An illustration is *Re P (Minors) (Wardship: Care and Control)* [1992] 2 F.L.R. 681 (boys of 13 and 11).

73 See *C v C* [1991] 1 F.L.R. 223.

74 See above, n.36.

75 See above, n.35.

76 Popularised in Bowlby, 1953.

77 It did sometimes have this impact. See *Southgate v Southgate* [1978] 8 Fam. Law 246, on which see Freeman, 1978. See also *L v L* (1981) 2 F.L.R. 48, *M v M* [1980] 1 F.L.R. 380. Fathers 4 Justice argues that this continues to be the case. The Constitutional Affairs Select Committee in March 2005 found that the family justice system is not consciously biased against men. And see *Re Bradford; Re O'Connell*, n.71, above, p.562.

78 *Re S (A Minor) (Custody)* [1991] 2 F.L.R. 388, 390, 392; *Re A (A Minor) (Custody)* [1991] 2 F.L.R. 394, 399–400. A presumption would presumably be incompatible with the ECHR.

79 [1996] 2 F.L.R. 499. The case is a Scottish appeal to the House of Lords.

80 *Ibid.*, 505.

81 *Ibid.*

82 [1999] 1 F.L.R. 583.

83 On evidence of sexual abuse where girls are awarded to fathers see the disturbing research of Fretwell-Wilson, 2002.

84 Above, p.166.

85 See *Re KD (A Minor) (Ward: Termination of Access)*, quoted above p.190.

86 See above, p.163. And see Schaffer, 1990 and Weyland, 1997.

87 *Re D (Care: Natural Parent Presumption)* [1999] 1 F.L.R. 134 (conflict between father and maternal grandparents).

88 [1996] 2 F.L.R. 441.

89 An echo of the notorious reasoning of Eve J. in *Re Thain* [1926] Ch. 676.

90 See above n.88, pp.460–461.

91 [2002] 3 F.C.R. 277.

92 *Ibid.*, 284.

93 *Ibid.*, 285.

94 See also *Re O (Family Appeals: Management)* [1998] 1 F.L.R. 431: Thorpe L.J. said the CA in *Re M* had fallen into error.

95 *B v B (Custody of Children)* [1985] F.L.R. 166.

96 Cited by Bainham, 2005, pp.176–177 as such an example.

97   For example, the young child's need for a mother and a child's attachment to his/her family, above p.218.

98   *Re D* [2001] 2 F.C.R. 291.

99   *Per* Purchas L.J. in *C v C (Minors: Custody)* [1988] 2 F.L.R. 291, 302. But Douglas *et al.*, 2001 did not find this: they found friends to be more important.

100 See *B v B (Residence Order: Restricting Applications)* [1997] 1 F.L.R. 139.

101 *B v B (Minors) (Custody: Care Control)* [1991] 1 F.L.R. 402.

102 *Re O (Infants)* [1962] 2 All E.R. 10; *Angrish v Angrish (now Butcher)* (1973) 3 Fam. Law 108.

103 See above, pp.190–192 and below, p.232.

104 Above, n.20.

105 Above, n.35.

106 *Re C (HIV Test)* [1997] 2 F.L.R. 1004.

107 See Eekelaar and Clive, 1977, pp.13–14 to show the policy is long-standing.

108 [1983] Fam. 33, 41.

109 [1998] 1 F.L.R. 368.

110 *Per* Ormrod L.J. in *S v W* (1981) 11 Fam. Law 81, 82.

111 *Re B and G (Minors) (Custody)* [1985] F.L.R. 493.

112 See above, n.37.

113 Children Act 1989 s.1(2).

114 *Edwards v Edwards* [1986] 1 F.L.R. 187, 205.

115 *Baldrian v Baldrian* (1973) 4 Fam. Law 12. But it was not a rule: see *Aldous v Aldous* (1984) 4 Fam. Law 83.

116 *Brixey v Lynas*, above n.79.

117 *Re M (Section 94 Appeals)* [1995] 1 F.L.R. 546, 550.

118 See above, n.88. See also *Re B (Adoption: Child's Welfare)* [1995] 2 F.L.R. 895, where the child was from Gambia.

119 It is inconceivable that atheism would count against a parent. It once did, famously in *Shelley v Westbrooke* (1817) Jac. 266n (the poet Shelley was denied custody).

120 [1999] 2 F.L.R. 678.

121 See above, p.201.

122 [2005] 1 F.L.R. 236.

123 In the latter case a Muslim mother and Hindu father. The boys were being bought up as Hindus, with Islamic influences.

124 Above, n.64.

125 See above, p.217.

126 *Hoffman v Austria* (1993) 17 E.H.R.R. 293; *Palau-Martinez v France* [2004] 2 F.L.R. 810.

127 See above, n.111.
128 *Hewison v Hewison* (1977) 7 Fam. Law 207.
129 *Wright v Wright* (1980) 2 F.L.R. 276.
130 *Re S (A Minor) (Blood Transfusion: Adoption Order Conditions)* [1994] 2 F.L.R. 416.
131 This was highly significant in *Re M (Child's Upbringing)*, above n.88.
132 Which is, of course, unlawful. On culture generally see Macdonald, 1991.
133 [2001] 2 F.L.R. 1005.
134 See above, p.222.
135 Children Act 1989 s.31(9).
136 *Re H* [1989] 2 F.L.R. 174, 184–185.
137 For example, *L v L (Child Abuse: Access)* [1989] 2 F.L.R. 16 or *Re B* [1990] 2 F.L.R. 317 (the father was described as "warm" and "playful").
138 *Re L, V, M, H (Contact: Domestic Violence)* [2000] 2 F.L.R. 334.
139 Adoption and Children Act 2002 s.120.
140 *Re M and R (Child Abuse: Evidence)* [1996] 2 F.L.R. 195, 203 (and see Freeman, 2000b), Lord Nicholls finds this conclusion "attractive": *Re D (Minors) (Care: Preliminary Hearing)* [2004] 1 A.C.
141 Such as the father in *C v C* [1988] 1 F.L.R. 462, said to have indulged in "vulgar and inappropriate horseplay", who was allowed contact. Or the one in *L v L* [1989] 2 F.L.R. 16, where the five-year-old girl insisted on wearing trousers for "access" visits, so concerned was she that abuse might reoccur.
142 *Re L (Residence: Justices' Reasons)* [1995] 2 F.L.R. 445.
143 See above, n.36.
144 *Re P (Contact: Supervision)* [1996] 2 F.L.R. 314.
145 *S v S* [1978] 1 F.L.R. 143; *C v C* [1991] 1 F.L.R. 223; *B v B* [1991] 1 F.L.R. 402.
146 *Scott v Scott* [1986] 2 F.L.R. 320.
147 *Re D (Grant of Care Order: Refusal of Freeing Order)* [2001] 1 F.L.R. 862.
148 *Re K (Minors) (Children: Care and Control)* [1977] Fam. 179.
149 Children Act 1989 s.10(1)(b).
150 These are in Children Act 1989 s.31(2).
151 *Re K (Care Order or Residence Order)* [1995] 1 F.L.R. 675.
152 Children Act 1989 s.1(1).
153 *Re M (A Minor) (Secure Accommodation Order)* [1995] Fam. 108.

154 *S v S; W v Official Solicitor* [1972] A.C. 24.
155 *R (P) v Secretary of State for Home Department; R (Q) v Secretary of State for Home Department* [2001] 1 W.L.R. 2002.
156 [2005] 1 A.C. 593.
157 [2006] 1 F.L.R. 1.
158 *F v Leeds City Council* [1994] 2 F.L.R. 60.
159 *Birmingham City Council v H (A Minor)* [1994] 2 A.C. 212.
160 *Re A (Conjoined Twins: Surgical Separation)* [2001] 1 F.L.R. 1.
161 *Ibid.*, 54.
162 On least detrimental alternative see also Black and Cantor, 1989, p.140.
163 See Art.14 of the European Convention on Human Rights.
164 See Alston, 1994.
165 The UN Committee on the Rights of the Child.
166 By Goldstein *et al.*, above, p.227.
167 Article 3(1).
168 Article 12.
169 See below, pp.363–367.
170 Law Com No.172, pp.3.2–3.4.
171 See *Johansen v Norway* (1996) 23 E.H.R.R. 33.
172 It is possible that applications may be withdrawn, thus preventing a "no order". The evidence is sketchy.
173 *Re X and Y (Leave To Remove from Jurisdiction: No Order Principle)* [2001] 2 F.L.R. 118.
174 *Ibid.*, 147–148.
175 For example *Re H (Children) (Residence Order: Condition)* [2001] 2 F.L.R. 1277.
176 *Payne v Payne*, above, n.7.
177 *Re G (Children) (Residence: Making of Order)* [2005] E.W.C.A. Civ. 1283.
178 [1992] 2 F.L.R. 327.
179 [1996] 1 F.L.R. 1588.
180 Children Act 1989 s.8(1).
181 Or unmarried, where the father has parental responsibility.
182 Children Act 1989 s.2(8).
183 By Booth J. in *Re SC (A Minor) (Leave to Seek Section 8 Orders)* [1994] 1 F.L.R. 96.
184 Children Act 1989 s.11(4).
185 Before the Children Act 1989 it was said that, as a matter of principle, such as order could not be made; *Riley v Riley* [1986] 2 F.L.R. 429.
186 *Re H (A Minor) (Shared Residence)* [1994] 1 F.L.R. 717.
187 *A v A (Minors) (Shared Residence Order)* [1994] 1 F.L.R. 669.

188 [2001] 1 F.L.R. 495.
189 *Ibid.*, 501.
190 [2004] 1 F.L.R. 1195.
191 *Ibid.* Of course, if the relationship between the parents is harmonious, an order would not be needed at all (s.1(5)). And see *Re R (Residence: Shared Care: Children's Views)* [2006] 1 F.L.R. 491, 495.
192 [2003] 2 F.L.R. 397.
193 See *Re R*, above, n.191, 496 (the children were 9 and 7).
194 Children Act 1989 s.11(7).
195 [2004] 2 F.L.R. 979.
196 *Birmingham City Council v H* [1992] 2 F.L.R. 323.
197 *Per* Ward L.J. in *Re D (Residence: Imposition of Conditions)* [1996] 2 F.L.R. 281, 284.
198 See also *Re E (Minors) (Residence: Conditions)* [1997] 2 F.L.R. 638 (not impose condition that mother resided at a particular address).
199 That is with no notice being given to the respondent.
200 *Re G (Minors) (Ex p. Interim Residence Order)* [1993] 1 F.L.R. 910, 912.
201 *Ibid.*
202 *Re Y (A Minor) (Ex p. Residence Orders)* [1993] 2 F.L.R. 422.
203 *Judicial Statistics.*
204 A report to the Lord Chancellor by the Advisory Board on Family Law; Children Act Sub-Committee, 2002.
205 Children Act 1989 s.8(1).
206 Children Act 1989 s.10(2)(b).
207 It concerned Matthew Lucas and was reported (see *The Times*, April 16, 1993) as a decision by a county court judge in Southampton to transfer the matter to a High Court judge.
208 "The Voice of The Children", the *Guardian*, April 21, 1993, p.23.
209 1st Report, H.L. Paper 100–1/H.C. 400–1.
210 *Government Reply to the Report from the Joint Committee*, Cm. 6583 (June 2005).
211 [1999] 2 F.L.R. 893.
212 [2002] 1 F.L.R. 621, 636.
213 *Re C (Contact: No Order for Contact)* [2000] 2 F.L.R. 723 (child terrified of father, and destroyed his letters). A good example pre-Children Act is *Geapin v Geapin* (1974) 4 Fam. Law 188 (boy had severe asthmatic attacks after "access").
214 [1994] Fam. 18.

215 [1995] 1 W.L.R. 667.

216 Children and Adoption Act 2006, adding s.11L to Children Act 1989.

217 *Re O (Contact: Imposition of Conditions)* [1995] 2 F.L.R. 124, 129–130.

218 *Re D (Contact: Reasons for Refusal)* [1997] 2 F.L.R. 48, 53; *Re H (Contact: Domestic Violence)* [1998] 2 F.L.R. 42.

219 *Re H (Children) (Contact Order) (No.2)* [2000] 3 F.C.R. 385.

220 *Re M (Contact: Welfare Test)* [1995] 1 F.L.R. 274.

221 *Cf.* above, p.187 in relation to applications for a parental responsibility order.

222 *Re M (Contact: Violent Parent)* [1999] 2 F.L.R. 321, 333.

223 *Re S (Contact: Indirect Contact)* [2000] 1 F.L.R. 481.

224 [2001] Fam. 260.

225 Written by Dr Claire Sturge and Dr Danya Glaser: see (2000) 30 Fam. Law 615.

226 See above, n.224, 272. In *Re H (Contact: Domestic Violence)* [2006] 1 F.L.R. 943, the Court of Appeal was critical of a judge who had no regard to this decision or to the Sturge/Glaser report.

227 *Re G (Direct Contact: Domestic Violence)* [2000] 2 F.L.R. 865.

228 *Re M and B (Children) (Contact: Domestic Violence)* [2001] 1 F.C.R. 116.

229 They are conveniently found as an Annex to *Re H*, above, n.226, 986.

230 *Ibid.*, para.1.5.

231 Children Act 1989 s.1(3), and above, p.215.

232 Family Law Act 1996 s.42(2)(b), and above, p.67.

233 See above, n.229, para.1.G.

234 See above, n.224.

235 See above, pp.67–71.

236 *Re F (Contact: Enforcement: Representation of Child)* [1998] 1 F.L.R. 691.

237 *V v V (Contact: Implacable Hostility)* [2004] 2 F.L.R. 851, *per* Bracewell J.

238 *Re S (Contact Dispute: Committal)* [2005] 1 F.L.R. 812 (with interim residence order to father). In *A v N (Committal Refusal of Conduct)* the sentence was 42 days for persistent and repeated breaches.

239 *Re M (Contact Order)* [2005] 2 F.L.R. 1006: here the father was in breach—by 10 minutes! And we wonder why our prisons are overcrowded!

240 *Re K (Contact: Committal Order)* [2003] 1 F.L.R. 377.

241 See *V-P v V-P* (1978) 1 F.L.R. 336.

242 See above n.237.

243 Children Act 1989 s.16.

244 See *Re F (Minors) (Denial of Contact)* [1993] 2 F.L.R. 677.

245 Children Act 1989 s.16(4A), added by s.6(3) of the 2006 Act.

246 [2004] 1 F.L.R. 1279.

247 See below, p.247.

248 *Re M (Intractable Contact Dispute: Interim Care Order)* [2003] 2 F.L.R. 636.

249 See *Parental Separation: Children's Needs and Parents' Responsibilities*, Cm. 6273, 2004; *Parental Separation: Children's Needs and Parents' Responsibilities: Next Steps*, Cm. 6452 (2005). See also Masson and Humphreys, 2005.

250 Sch.A1, para.4 of Children Act 1989, added by Sch.1 of the 2006 Act.

251 Children Act 1989 s.11L.

252 See above, pp.232–233.

253 See below, p.239.

254 See above, p.237.

255 Children Act 1989 s.11O and 11P, added by the 2006 Act.

256 Children Act 1989 s.11A to G.

257 Children Act 1989 s.11A.

258 Children Act 1989 s.11A(5).

259 Children Act 1989 s.11C.

260 A strange contrast with contact activity directions, and not one that is readily explicable.

261 Children Act 1989 s.11H.

262 Children Act 1989 s.8(1).

263 *Re A (Specific Issue Order: Parental Dispute)* [2001] 1 F.L.R. 121.

264 *Re C (Welfare of Child: Immunisation)* [2003] 2 F.L.R. 1054, 1095.

265 *Re D (A Minor) (Child: Removal from Jurisdiction)* [1992] 1 W.L.R. 667.

266 *Re W, Re A, Re B (Change of Name)* [1999] 1 F.L.R. 930.

267 *Re K (Specific Issue Order)* [1999] 2 F.L.R. 280 (the application was unsuccessful).

268 *Re F (Specific Issue: Child Interview)* [1999] 1 F.L.R. 819.

269 [1993] 1 F.L.R. 587.

270 Permission is required: see *Re B (A Minor) (Wardship: Sterilisation)* [1988] A.C. 199, 205.

271 Whether a child went on holiday to Bulgaria was held not

to be such a matter: *Re C (A Minor) (Leave To Seek Section 8 Order)* [1994] 1 F.L.R. 26.
272 Halal meat was in issue in *Re J (Specific Issue Orders: Child's Religious Upbringing and Circumcision)* [2000] 1 F.L.R. 571; Kosher food in *Re P (Section 91(14) Guidelines) (Residence and Religious Heritage)* [1999] 2 F.L.R. 573.
273 *Judicial Statistics.*
274 Children Act 1989 s.8(1).
275 *Re H (A Minor) (Prohibited Steps Order)*, above, p.233.
276 *Re G (Parental Responsibility: Education)* [1994] 2 F.L.R. 964.
277 *Dawson v Wearmouth* [1999] 2 A.C. 308 (in the absence of a residence order).
278 *Re D* [1992] 1 All E.R. 892 (the child was already abroad).
279 *Judicial Statistics.*
280 *Croydon LBC v A (No.1)* [1992] 2 F.L.R. 341.
281 *Re Z (A Minor) (Identity: Restrictions on Publicity)* [1996] 1 F.L.R. 191.
282 See above, n.275.
283 See above, p.233. And see *Pearson v Franklin* [1994] 2 All E.R. 137.
284 See above, n.275.
285 Children Act 1989 s.9(5)(a).
286 [1994] Fam. 18.
287 *Re B (Minors) (Residence Order)* [1992] Fam. 162.
288 Children Act 1989 s.9(5)(b).
289 See below, p.279.
290 For another application see *Re S and D (Children: Powers of Court)* [1995] 2 F.L.R. 456.
291 Children Act 1989 s.9(7) and (6).
292 Children Act 1989 s.91(11).
293 Adoption and Children Act 2002 s.114, including: 12(5) in Children Act 1989. and see below, p.248.
294 Children Act 1989 s.91(1).
295 Children Act 1989 s.9(2).
296 *Re SC (A Minor) (Leave To Seek Residence Order)* [1994] 1 F.L.R. 96, 100.
297 Children Act 1989 s.10(1).
298 Children Act 1989 s.8(3), (4).
299 A local authority's application to invoke the High Court's inherent jurisdiction is not included.
300 On these orders see pp.270–272 and 272–274.
301 The court's power is constrained by international conventions, notably the Hague Abduction Convention.

302 Children Act 1989 s.10(1).

303 *Gloucestershire County Council v P* [2000] Fam. 1.

304 Children Act 1989 s.10(4), as amended.

305 Children Act 1989 s.10(5) and (5)(aa), added by the Civil Partnership Act 2004 s.77.

306 This has the support of the United Nations Convention on the Rights of the Child Art.12.

307 *Re C* [1994] 1 F.L.R. 26; *Re SC* [1994] 1 F.L.R. 96; *Re CT* [1993] 2 F.L.R. 278. See also *Kingsley v Kingsley* 623 So. 2d 780 (Fla. Dist. Ct. App. 1993).

308 Children Act 1989 s.10(8).

309 [1993] 2 F.L.R. 278, 281–282.

310 *Re C (A Minor) (Leave To Seek Section 8 Orders)* [1994] 1 F.L.R. 26, 27.

311 In *Re SC (A Minor) (Leave to seek on Residence Order)* [1994] 1 F.L.R. 96.

312 *Ibid.*, 100.

313 *Re H (Residence Order: Child's Application for Leave)* [2000] 1 F.L.R. 780.

314 *Cf. Re C*, above, n.310 and *Re SC*, above n.311.

315 *Re C (Residence) (Child's Application for Leave)* [1995] 1 F.L.R. 927.

316 Children Act 1989 s.10(9).

317 See above, p.241.

318 *Re A and W (Minors) (Residence Order: Leave To Apply)* [1992] Fam. 182.

319 *G v Kirklees MBC* [1993] 1 F.L.R. 805.

320 *Re M (Care: Contact: Grandmother's Application for Leave)* [1995] 2 F.L.R. 86, 98.

321 By Thorpe L.J. in *Re J (Leave to Issue Application for Residence Order)* [2003] 1 F.L.R. 114.

322 See e.g. *Re W (Contact) (Application by Grandparent)* [1997] 1 F.L.R. 793.

323 See above, n.321.

324 Children Act 1989 s.16.

325 An order can be made against an unwilling local authority: see *Re E Family Assistance Order)* [1999] 2 F.L.R. 512.

326 Department of Health, *Guidance and Regulation*: Court Orders vol.1, para.2.50.

327 Children Act 1989 s.16(3)(a).

328 Children and Adoption Act 2006 s.6(2).

329 Children Act 1989 s.16(6), inserted by s.6(5) of the 2006 Act.

330 Children Act 1989 s.16(4A), inserted by s.6(3) of the 2006 Act.

331 Section 37 of Children Act 1989.

332 The Court's importance was criticised in *Nottingham CC v P* [1994] Fam. 18.

333 *A v United Kingdom (Human Rights: Punishment of Child)* [1998] 2 F.L.R. 959 is a useful analogy. See above, pp.196–197.

334 *Re M (Intractable Contact Dispute: Interim Care Order)* [2003] 2 F.L.R. 636.

335 *Re H (A Minor) (Section 37 Direction)* [1993] 2 F.L.R. 541.

336 See above, p.211 (and Reece, 1996).

337 *Re L (Section 37 Direction)* [1999] 1 F.L.R. 984.

338 *Re P (Section 91(14) Guidelines) (Residence and Religious Heritage)* [1999] 2 F.L.R. 573.

339 *F v Kent CC* [1993] 1 F.L.R. 432.

340 See above, n.338.

341 Section 114.

342 Section 12(6).

343 Under Children Act 1989 s.9(6).

344 There is a residence order allowance: see Children Act 1989 Sch.1 para.15. The power to make it is "exercised haphazardly" (Lowe and Douglas, 2006, p.604, n.730).

345 Children Act 1989 ss.14A–G, inserted by the Adoption and Children Act 2002 s.115.

346 Muslims in particular.

347 Children Act 1989 s.14F.

348 Children Act 1989 s.14A(5).

349 Children Act 1989 s.14(A)(3).

350 See above, p.244.

351 Children Act 1989 s.14(A)(12).

352 Children Act 1989 s.14(A)(6).

353 Children Act 1989 s.14(B)(1).

354 Children Act 1989 s.14C.

355 Children Act 1989 s.91(5A).

356 Children Act 1989 s.14C(3) and (4).

357 See above, p.248. The special guardianship order is considered further in Chapter 11.

CHAPTER 9

1 Prevention of Cruelty to, and Protection of, Children Act 1889.
2 *Hansard*, H.C. vol.337, col.227.
3 *Ibid.*, col.229. It was assumed the legislation worked: the Home Office in 1923 was in no doubt—children of the poorer classes were being better cared for. See *Report of the Work of the Children's Branch*, pp.69–70.
4 London SPCC, *First Annual Report*; London, 1884, pp.5–6.
5 Criminal Law (Amendment) Act 1883.
6 Punishment of Incest Act 1908. There were few prosecutions: 516 in 1987, the year of "Cleveland" (Corby, 1993, p.162).
7 *Final Report*, Cd 8189, London, 1916.
8 *Lancet*, July 11, 1925, pp.101–102.
9 *Departmental Committee on Sexual Offences Against Young Persons*, Cmd. 2561, London, 1925.
10 *Report of the Inquiry into Child Abuse in Cleveland* 1987, Cm. 412, London, 1988, p.245.
11 See also Parton, 1970 and 1985, and Jenks, 1996, ch.4.
12 Invented in 1895.
13 See Pfohl, 1977.
14 And see Scheff, 1963.
15 See Rosenfeld and Newberger, 1977.
16 Of course, lawyers have become accustomed to working within a model of rehabilitation, in the criminal justice system notably.
17 See Becker, 1963.
18 See Freidson, 1966. See also Gelles, 1979, ch.3.
19 It was the "dominant underlying metaphor until 1987" (Parton, 2006, p.30).
20 See Kempe, 1962, p.19.
21 On appeal, the murder conviction was reduced to manslaughter, and he was sentenced to eight years' imprisonment.
22 Many other examples could be given; these are illustrations only.
23 Parton discusses the difference between the Colwell and Climbié cases in Parton, 2006, pp.48–50.
24 See below, p.255.
25 See above, p.252.
26 I first wrote about it in 1978 (Freeman, 1978), an article that

was to have appeared in a book, but was removed because the publishers thought it "unimportant"!

27 On "folk devils and moral panics" see Cohen, 1972.

28 For an account of two such cases (the "Norths" and the "Wests") see Freeman, 1997, pp.279–280.

29 They were physical abuse, physical neglect, failure to thrive and emotional abuse (a combined category), and children living in a household with, or which is regularly visited by, a parent or another person who has abused children and are considered at risk.

30 John Bowis, quoted in Lyon, 2000, pp.111–112.

31 Particularly a mandatory reporting law: see pp.268 and 451, n.140.

32 "Innocent" horseplay may be "sexual". But it is not always so construed: see *C v C* [1988] 1 F.L.R. 462.

33 See pp.63–68, particularly paras 5.135–5.138. The Second Report in 1999 says even less (see para.7.12).

34 See above, p.197.

35 Children Act 1989 s.31(2).

36 See below, pp.279–290.

37 The fourth version of this *Guidance*. See paras 1.29–1.35.

38 Now usually called "fabricated" or "induced" illness. See *ibid.*, para.6.4–6.6.

39 See further the Special Issue of the *Journal of Social Welfare Law*, 1988, particularly Wolkind, 1988, p.82.

40 On changes to attitudes to paedophilia see Jenkins, 1998 and 2001. See also Parton, 2006, ch.7.

41 Department of Health, *Child Protection: Messages from Research*, 1995, p.15.

42 *Ibid.*

43 Gelles (1973). See also Gelles, 1972, ch.1.

44 A good example is by Steele and Pollock, 1974.

45 One interesting research study traced physical abuse though five generations of social work records: Oliver, 1985.

46 See Gelles, 1973 (19 traits identified, but only 4 figured in more than two authors).

47 A view that can be traced to J.C. Flugel, 1926. Similar views were expressed in Sweden (see Sonder, 1936) and the USA (Guttmacher, 1951).

48 And statistics must be treated cautiously: the lives of the poor are more visible, and more exposed to public scrutiny and social control.

49 As with other violence against women: see Yllö and Bograd, 1988; Dobash and Dobash, 1998.

50 Nearly all surveys demonstrate this: there are a few female abusers.

51 See Home Office, *Protecting The Public; Strengthening Protection Against Sex Offenders, and Reforming The Law on Sexual Offences,* 2002.

52 See Freeman, 1983, pp.123–124.

53 1975, p.350.

54 Ariès, 1962.

55 And justified in religious terms: see Greven, 1991 and the recent *Williamson* case, below, pp.358–359.

56 It was the "system" which failed her, according to the *Report of the Inquiry into the Care and Supervision Provided in Relation To Maria Colwell,* London, HMSO, 1974, p.86.

57 *Re M (Child's Upbringing)* [1996] 2 F.L.R. 441, and above, pp.219–220.

58 *R (on the application of Williamson) v Secretary of State for Education and Employment* [2005] 2 F.L.R. 374, and below, pp.358–359.

59 As is the case with violence against women.

60 See above, p.193.

61 Children Act 2004 s.58. See above, p.197.

62 Section 25, replacing the crime of incest in the Sexual Offences Act 1956.

63 Section 26, replacing incitement to commit incest (in Criminal Law Act 1977 s.54).

64 Criminal Justice Act 1991 and Youth Justice and Criminal Evidence Act 1999. Such trials do not breach the defendant's Art.6 rights: see *R (on the Application of D) v Camberwell Youth Court* [2005] 1 F.L.R. 365.

65 It is estimated that only one in four trials leads to a conviction. See Spencer and Flin, 1993, 9.

66 See Keenan *et al.,* 1999.

67 It was in the Department of Health and Social Security, *Review of Child Care Law* that the word in the current context was first used (1985, para.2.8).

68 Department of Health, *Principles and Practice in Regulations and Guidance,* 1990, p.8. The example used is "taking compulsory measures". But there are cases where these obviously must be taken.

69 Children Act 1989 s.2(6). Its exercise may, however, be controlled by the local authority.

70   Children Act 1989 s.31(2).
71   Upon an application for a care order, a residence order, usually in favour of relatives, may be made. See below, p.293.
72   Department of Health, *Principles and Practice in Regulations and Guidance*, 1990, p.8.
73   Children Act 1989 s.17(1)(6).
74   Children Act 1989 Sch.2 para.15.
75   There is a full discussion in Freeman, 1992, ch.4.
76   Section 10.
77   Section 23(2).
78   That is to children in general, and not only to individual children.
79   Children Act 1989 s.17(1).
80   Children Act 1989 s.17(10).
81   Children Act 1989 s.17(11).
82   See *Guidance and Regulations* vol.2, 1991, para.2.4. See also White, 1991.
83   Children Act 1989 s.17(3).
84   *R(G) v Barnet LBC; R(W) v Lambeth LBC* [2004] 2 A.C. 208.
85   Children Act 1989 s.17(4A), inserted by s.53 of Children Act 2004.
86   Children Act 1989 s.17(6).
87   Children Act 1989 s.17A, inserted by Carers and Disabled Children Act 2000 s.7(1).
88   Children Act 1989 Sch.1 para.15.
89   Children Act 1989 Sch.2 para.1.
90   Children Act 1989 s.17(1)(b).
91   Children Act 1989 Sch.2 para.6.
92   Children Act 1989 s.18.
93   Since the Adoption and Children Act 2002 s.116(1).
94   The authority may prefer to seek a care order in order to acquire parental responsibility in such a case.
95   Child Care Act 1989 s.2.
96   Children Act 1989 s.20(4).
97   Children Act 1989 s.20(7). There is no need for anyone positively to consent.
98   Children Act 1989 s.20(9). The authority can act on an agreement with her. See *Guidance and Regulations* vol.3, 1991, para.2.65.
99   Children Act 1989 s.20(8).
100 *Guidance and Regulations* vol.2, para.3.38.
101 *Hansard*, H.L. vol.503, col.1412; vol.505, col.370.

102 See below, pp.270–272.
103 See below, pp.274–275.
104 On s.3(5) see above, p.207. *Nottinghamshire CC v J* (unreported, 26 November 1993) holds that it cannot be so used (see Lowe and Douglas, 2006, p.706).
105 Children Act 1989 s.20(3).
106 See above, pp.244–245.
107 Children Act 1989 s.9(2)
108 Neither s.20(7) nor s.20(8) apply where a child of 16 "agrees to being provided with accommodation" (s.20(11)).
109 See *Krishnan v LB of Sutton* [1970] Ch. 181.
110 Under Children Act 1989 s.100(3).
111 [1994] 1 F.L.R. 798.
112 *Re J (Specific Issue Order: Leave To Apply)* [1995] 1 F.L.R. 669.
113 See s.26 of the Children Act 1989.
114 *R v Tameside MBC Ex p. J* [2000] 1 F.L.R. 942.
115 *McL v Secretary of State for Social Security* [1996] 2 F.L.R. 748.
116 Department of Health, *Children Looked After By Local Authorities*, 2004, Tables 14 and 16.
117 Children Act Report 1992, para.2.21.
118 Children Act 1989 s.47.
119 See below, p.270.
120 See below, p.274.
121 Crime and Disorder Act 1998.
122 Children Act 1989 s.47(1)(b).
123 Including through Childline.
124 *Re S (Sexual Abuse Allegations: Local Authority Response)* [2001] 2 F.L.R. 776.
125 *Re O and Another (Minors) (Care: Preliminary Hearing); Re B (A Minor)* [2004] 1 A.C. 523.
126 Children Act 1989 s.47(1)(b).
127 As has happened in many of the well-known tragic cases such as Jasmine Beckford, Victoria Climbié and, most recently, "Child B" (see the *Guardian*, February 9, 2007).
128 Children Act 1989 s.47(6).
129 *D v D (County Court Jurisdiction: Injunctions)* [1993] 2 F.L.R. 802.
130 See above, p.241. I doubt if this has happened in many cases other than this reported one.
131 Including Special Health Authority, Primary Care Trust, NHS Trust or NHS Foundation Trust.
132 Children Act 1989 s.49(9), (11).

133 According to David Mellor, Children Bill Standing Committee B, col.342. See also Freeman, 1992, pp.177–178.

134 Children Act 1989 s.47(10).

135 See *W v Edgell* [1990] 1 All E.R. 855. In relation to the European Convention on Human Rights Art.8, see *Z v Finland* (1997) 25 E.H.R.R. 371 and *MS v Sweden* (1997) 45 B.M.C.R. 133.

136 The legal and ethical dilemmas are debated in *Tarasoff v Regents of University of California* 551 P. 2d 334 (1976).

137 *Working Together*, 1991, para.3.11.

138 It should be stressed that only appropriate authorities are "third parties". It would be a breach of confidence if a doctor was to tell a newspaper or friends in a pub: and see *W v Edgell*, above, n.135.

139 *D v NSPCC* [1978] A.C. 171.

140 Burgdorff (1981) notes only one-third of incidents were reported in the USA where there is mandatory reporting. See also Bell and Tooman, 1994.

141 *Working Together*, 1991, para.6.1.

142 *Ibid.*, para.6.5.

143 *Ibid.*, para.6.11

144 *R. v LB of Harris Ex p. D* [1989] 2 F.L.R. 51.

145 *Ibid.*, para.6.15.

146 *Ibid.*, para.6.3.

147 *Ibid.*, para.6.12.

148 *Ibid.*, para.6.36.

149 *Ibid,*

150 *Ibid.*, para.6.37.

151 *R. v Norfolk CC Ex p. X* [1989] 2 F.L.R. 120. See also *R. v Lewisham LBC Ex p. P* [1991] 2 F.L.R. 185.

152 *Working Together*, para.6.54.

153 Department of Health, *Guidance and Regulations* vol.1, para.4.78.

154 Children Act 1989 s.44(1).

155 See above, n.153, para.4.30.

156 See above, p.267.

157 Children Act 1989 s.47(6).

158 *X Council v B (Emergency Protection Orders)* [2005] 1 F.L.R. 341, 367.

159 Notorious examples centre on ritualistic (or "Satanic") abuse, inter alia, in Rochdale and the Orkneys in the early 1990s. See Brett, 1991.

160 This was until 1996 the only method. See Freeman, 1992, p.54.
161 Children Act 1989 s.44A.
162 Children Act 1989 s.44 A(5).
163 Children Act 1989 s.44(a).
164 Children Act 1989 s.44(1)(b).
165 Children Act 1989 s.44(1)(c).
166 Children Act 1989 s.1(1), (5).
167 Children Act 1989 s.44(4), (5).
168 Children Act 1989 s.45(1).
169 Children Act 1989 s.45(5).
170 See above n.158, p.367.
171 *Ibid.*
172 Children Act 1989 s.45(10) See *Re P (Emergency Protection Orders)* [1996] 1 F.L.R. 482 for an example of where this may cause concern.
173 There are 2,390 in 2004: see *Judicial Statistics for 2002–2004*, Table 5.2.
174 Vol.1, para.4.9.
175 Children Act 1989 s.43(1).
176 *Ibid.*
177 See above, pp.243–244.
178 Children Act 1989 s.43(3).
179 See above, pp.209 and 228.
180 See above, n.158, p.368.
181 Staurt Bell MP, *Hansard*, H.C. vol.158, col.594.
182 Children Act 1989 s.43(11).
183 Children Act 1989 s.91(14) and (15).
184 Children Act 1989 s.43(5).
185 See *Hansard*, H.L. vol.504. col.433.
186 Vol.1, para.4.12.
187 *Ibid.*
188 Children Act 1989 s.43(6)(a).
189 Children Act 1989 s.43(7).
190 Under Children Act 1989 s.44(1)(b).
191 Children Act 1989 s.43(8). It may be questioned whether the *South Glamorgan* decision, (*South Glamorgan CC v W and B* [1993] 1 F.L.R. 574), applies here: it was an "interpretation" of s.38(6) in flagrant breach of clear statutory language, and should not be extended to other provisions.
192 Children Act 1989 s.43(9).
193 Vol.1, para.4.15.
194 Children Act 1989 s.43(10).

195 See *Guidance,* vol.1, para.4.16.
196 The *Judicial Statistics* does not record numbers: only 55 orders were granted in 1993.
197 Children Act 1989 s.46(1)(a).
198 Children Act 1989 s.46(1)(b).
199 Children Act 1989 s.46(2).
200 Children Act 1989 s.46(6).
201 *Guidance,* vol.1, para.4.71.
202 Children Act 1989 s.46(4).
203 Children Act 1989 s.46(3)(e).
204 Children Act 1989 s.46(7).
205 Children Act 1989 s.46(5).
206 Children Act 1989 s.46(a)(a), (b).
207 See above, p.274.
208 But see n.191 above.
209 Article 19.
210 Human Rights Act 1998 s.6.
211 Human Rights Act 1998 s.2.
212 Human rights Act 1998 s.7.
213 [2004] 2 F.L.R. 39.
214 (1995) 14 E.H.R.R. 139.
215 *Re V (A Child) (Care Proceedings: Human Rights Claims)* [2004] 1 W.L.R. 1435 and *Westminster City Council v RA, B and S* [2005] 2 F.L.R. 1309.
216 [2000] 2 F.L.R. 79
217 *Ibid.,* 105.
218 *Ibid.*
219 [2000] 1 F.L.R. 134.
220 *Ibid.,* 141.
221 But Dyson L.J. in *Langley v Liverpool City Council* [2006] 1 F.L.R. 342, 360–361 did accord "a measure of deference or latitude to the judgment of [social workers]".
222 *Re V (A Child) (Care: Pre-birth Plans)* [2006] 2 F.C.R. 121.
223 *Venema v Netherlands* [2003] 1 F.C.R. 153.
224 *P, C, S v United Kingdom* [2002] 2 F.L.R. 631.
225 *C v Bury MBC* [2002] 2 F.L.R. 868.
226 [2003] 2 F.L.R. 160.
227 *Ibid.,* 168. See also Children Act 1989 s.1(2), and Finch, 2004.
228 *Re J (A Child) (Care Proceedings: Fair Trial)* [2006] 3 F.C.R. 107.
229 Children Act 1989 s.31(1), (9).
230 They can apply for an education supervision order under s.36 of the Children Act 1989.

231 Children Act 1989 s.31(6).
232 Children Act 1989 s.31(3).
233 For an example of its use see *Re SW (A Minor) (Wardship: Jurisdiction)* [1986] 1 F.L.R. 24.
234 F.P.R. 1991 p.4.7(1); F.P.C.A. 1991 p.7(1).
235 *Re B (Care Proceedings: Notification of Father Without Parental Responsibility)* [1999] 2 F.L.R. 408.
236 Children and Young Persons Act 1969 s.1(2).
237 The court can still make a s.8 order, for example a residence order, so that parents may not necessarily have their child returned to them.
238 *Hansard,* H.L. vol.502, col.488.
239 *Ibid.*
240 [2004] 1 A.C. 523.
241 See above, pp.276–278.
242 Children Act 1989 s.1(1). See also the checklist in s.1(3) and below, pp.290–292.
243 Children Act 1989 s.1(5).
244 Children Act 1989 s.31(2).
245 *Newham LBC v AG* [1993] 1 F.L.R. 281, 289.
246 Added by Adoption and Children Act 2002 s.120.
247 *C v C* [1988] 1 F.L.R. 462.
248 Formulated by the Standing Committee on Sexually Abused Children in 1984 (see Glaser and Frosh, 1988, p.9).
249 See above, p.197.
250 *Re M and R (Child Abuse: Evidence)* [1996] 2 F.L.R. 195.
251 And see Hobbs *et al.*, 1999.
252 See above, n.246.
253 Children Act 1989 s.31(9).
254 *Re O (A Minor) (Care Proceedings: Education)* [1992] 1 W.L.R. 912.
255 See *Mohamed v Knott* [1969] 1 Q.B. 1.
256 See above, p.30.
257 As in the Climbié case.
258 *Working Together to Safeguard Children,* 2006, para.10.9.
259 First passed in 1985. See now Female Genital Mutilation Act 2003.
260 See above n.258, para.6.15.
261 *Humberside CC v B* [1993] 1 F.L.R. 257, 263.
262 *Guidance and Regulations* vol.1, para.3.19.
263 [1990] 2 F.L.R. 317.
264 Children Act 1989 s.31(10).
265 *Hansard,* vol.503, col.354.

266 See above, n.262, para.3.20.
267 [1998] 28 Fam. Law 657. See also *Mohamed v Knott*, above, n.255.
268 But "a child's development is a continuing process. The present must be relevant in the context of what has happened in the past, and it becomes a matter of degree as to how far in the past you go" *per* Butler-Sloss J. in *M v Westminster CC* [1985] F.L.R. 325.
269 [1994] 2 A.C. 424.
270 *Ibid.*, 440.
271 *Ibid.*, 433.
272 *Northamptonshire CC v S* [1993] Fam. 136, 140; *Southwark LBC v B* [1998] 2 F.L.R. 1095, 1109 and *Re SH (Care Order: Orphan)* [1995] 1 F.L.R. 746.
273 See the facts of *D v Berkshire CC* [987] A.C. 317 (heroin addict harms child before it is born and as a result it suffers foetal drug withdrawal syndrome). But is harm done to a "child"?
274 Above n.262, para.3.22.
275 *Ibid.*
276 [1996] A.C. 563.
277 *Ibid.*, 585.
278 See above n.276, 586.
279 *Ibid.*, 581.
280 *Ibid.*, 572.
281 See above, n.262, para.3.23.
282 [2000] 2 A.C. 147.
283 *Ibid.*, 156.
284 *North Yorkshire CC v SA* [2003] 2 F.L.R. 849, 859.
285 See above, n.262, para.3.23.
286 According to Lord Mackay, the Lord Chancellor in 1989: *Hansard*, H.C. vol.512, col.756.
287 See above n.262, para.3.23.
288 Children and Young Persons Act 1969 s.1(2)(d), and see above n.262, para.3.25.
289 See above n.262, para.3.25. And see *Re O (A Minor) (Care Proceedings: Education)* above, n.254.
290 [1994] 2 F.L.R. 141.
291 *Ibid.*, 147.
292 See above, pp.276–278.
293 *Re O and Another (Minors) (Care: Preliminary Hearing); Re B (A Minor)* [2004] 1 A.C. 523, 539.

294 *Re R (Care: Disclosure: Nature of Proceedings)* [2002] 1 F.L.R. 755, 772.
295 See above n.293.
296 *Ibid.*, 540.
297 *Ibid.*
298 See above, p.287.
299 See above, n.284.
300 [1996] 2 F.L.R. 195.
301 *Ibid.*, 202.
302 See above, n.293, 542.
303 Children Act 1989 s.1(5).
304 It is now Children Act 1989 s.31(3A), inserted by the Adoption and Children Act 2002 s.121.
305 See *Manchester City Council v S* [1993] 1 F.L.R. 777.
306 *Re XL* [2001] 2 F.L.R. 555.
307 [2002] 2 A.C. 291.
308 *Ibid.*, 310.
309 *Re S (Parenting Skills: Personality Tests)* [2005] 2 F.L.R. 658.
310 See below, p.296.
311 Children Act 1989 s.31(1)(a).
312 Children Act 1989 s.33(1).
313 Children Act 1989 s.33(3)(a).
314 Children Act 1989 s.2(6).
315 Children Act 1989 s.33(3)(b).
316 Children Act 1989 s.33(6), (7), (8).
317 Children Act 1989 s.91(12).
318 Children Act 1989 s.39(1).
319 Children Act 1989 s.91(1).
320 Adoption and Children Act 2002 ss.29(2) and 46(2)(b).
321 Children Act 1989 s.31(1)(b).
322 Children Act 1989 s.35(1).
323 Children Act 1989 s.3, para.6(1).
324 Children Act 1989 Sch.3 para.6(3), (4).
325 Children Act 1989 Sch.3, para.2.
326 Children Act 1989 Sch.3 para.3.
327 Children Act 1989 Sch.3 paras 2(3) and 5.
328 Children Act 1989 Sch.3 paras 4 and 5.
329 Children Act 1989 Sch.3 paras 4(4)(a) and 5(5)(a). It has not been decided whether a refusal to give consent can be overridden.
330 Children Act 1989 s.22.
331 *Re S (J) (a Minor) (Care or Supervision Order)* [1993] 2 F.L.R. 919, 950.

332 *Oxfordshire CC v L (Care or Supervision Order)* [1998] 1 F.L.R. 70.
333 *Re S (Care or Supervision Order)* [1996] 1 F.L.R. 753.
334 *Re O (Care or Supervision Order)* [1996] 2 F.L.R. 755.
335 [1996] 1 F.L.R. 776.
336 *Judicial Statistics* 2004, Table 5.2.
337 *Re O (Supervision Order)* [2001] 1 F.L.R. 923, 928–929.
338 Children Act 1989 s.38(2).
339 *Re S (Minors) (Care Order: Implementation of Care Plan); Re W (Minors) (Care Order: Adequacy of Care Plan)* [2002] 2 A.C. 291, 323.
340 *Re G (Minors) (Interim Care Order)* [1993] 2 F.L.R. 839, 845.
341 *Hampshire CC v S* [1993] Fam. 158, 165.
342 See above, n.339, 323.
343 Children Act 1989 s.38(6).
344 [1993] 1 F.L.R. 569.
345 *Re C (a Minor) (Interim Care Order: Residential Assessment)* [1997] A.C. 489.
346 However, if the parents refer to co-operate they cannot be ordered to do so.
347 See above n.345, 501.
348 *Re G (A Minor) (Interim Care Order: Residential Assessment)* [2005] 3 W.L.R. 1166.
349 *Ibid.*, 1188. See Kennedy, 2006, and Cohen and Hale, 2005.
350 See particularly Lord Scott at 1176.
351 *South Glamorgan CC v W* [1993] 1 F.L.R. 574.
352 Children Act 1989 s.38(4), (5).
353 Children Act 1989 s.38A.
354 Children Act 1989 s.38A(5).
355 Children Act 1989 s.38B.
356 Children Act 1989 s.31B(2).
357 *W v A Local Authority* [2000] 2 F.C.R. 662.
358 Children Act 1989 s.39(1).
359 Children Act 1989 s.39(4).
360 Children Act 1989 s.39(5).
361 Children Act 1989 s.1(1).
362 Children Act 1989 s.39(2).
363 Children Act 1989 s.39(3).
364 Children Act 1989 s.100(1).
365 Children Act 1989 s.100(2)(a), (b).
366 Children Act 1989 s.100(3), (4).
367 *Practice Note (Minors and Mental Health Patients: Sterilisation)* [1993] 3 All E.R. 222.

368 *Re W (A Minor) (Medical Treatment: Court's Jurisdiction)* [1993] Fam. 64, and below, p.364.
369 *Re O (A Minor) (Medical Treatment)* [1993] 2 F.L.R. 149.
370 *Re J T (A Minor) (Wardship: Committal to Care)* [1986] 2 F.L.R. 107.
371 Children Act 1989 s.100(2)(d).
372 [1994] Fam. 169.
373 See also *Re M (Care: Leave To Interview Child)* [1995] 1 F.L.R. 825.

CHAPTER 10

1 Department of Education and Skills, Statistics of Education: Looked After Children Year Ending 31 March 2003, London, Stationery Office, 2004.
2 See above, pp.161–163.
3 See above, pp.263–264.
4 Children Act 1989 s.22(1).
5 Children Act 1989 s.33(3)(a), (b), (4).
6 Children Act 1989 s.22(3).
7 Children Act 1989 s.22(4).
8 *Guidance and Regulations*, vol.4, para.2.51.
9 Children Act 1989 s.22(5).
10 Children Act 1989 s.52.
11 There is not the same emphasis on religion, culture and language. See Freeman, 1992, p.75.
12 Children Act 1989 Sch.2 para.11.
13 Principle 21.
14 See above, n.8, paras 2.40–2.42.
15 *Ibid.*, para.2.41.
16 Children Act 1989 s.23(7)(b).
17 See above, n.8, para.2.42.
18 *Ibid.*
19 Children Act 1989 s.23(6).
20 Children Act 1989 s.23(7)(a).
21 Children Act 1989 s.23(7)(b).
22 Children Act 1989 s.22(6).
23 Children Act 1989 s.25, and *Re M (A Minor) (Secure Accommodation)* [1993] Fam. 108. The law has been upheld as Convention compliant: *Re K (A Child) (Secure Accommodation: Right To Liberty)* [2001] Fam. 377.
24 Children Act 1989 s.23(1).

25 Children Act 1989 s.23(2).
26 See above, p.276.
27 [2000] 2 F.L.R. 118, 139–140. See also *K and T v Finland* [2000] 2 F.L.R. 79.
28 *KA v Finland* [2003] 1 F.C.R. 230.
29 *Eriksson v Sweden* (1989) 12 E.H.R.R. 183.
30 Health and Social Services and Social Security Adjudication Act 1983, Sch.1, inserting ss.12A–12G into Child Care Act 1980.
31 *M v Berkshire CC* [1985] F.L.R. 257; *Re Y* [1988] 1 F.L.R. 299.
32 Department of Health and Social Security, *Review of Child Care Law*, London, HMSO, 1985, p.10.
33 Children Act 1989 s.34(1).
34 *Ibid.*
35 [1994] 1 FLR 146. See also *Re B (Minors) (Termination of Contact: Paramount Consideration)* [1993] Fam. 301, 311.
36 *Re E, ibid.*, 155.
37 But see *Re B*, above, n.35. "The proposals of the local authority ... must command the greatest respect and consideration from the court, but Parliament has given to the court, and not to the local authority, the duty to decide on contact between the child and the named in section 32(1)" *per* Butler-Sloss L.J. at 311.
38 See above, p.302.
39 Vol.1, para.3.75.
40 See above, pp.292–293.
41 Children Act 1989 s.34(7).
42 Children Act 1989 s.34(5).
43 Children Act 1989 s.34(10).
44 Children Act 1989 s.34(2).
45 Children Act 1989 s.34(3).
46 Children Act 1989 s.34(4).
47 Children Act 1989 s.34(6).
48 Vol.1, para.3.81.
49 Contact with Children Regulations 1991 reg.2.
50 *Ibid.*, reg.3.
51 *Guidance and Regulations*, vol.3, para.6.31.
52 Children Act 1989 s.1(1).
53 Children Act 1989 s.1(5).
54 See above, pp.226–227.
55 [1994] 2 A.C. 212.
56 *Ibid.*, 222 *per* Lord Slynn.
57 [1995] 1 F.L.R. 510.

58 Had the children been in care, s.9(1) would have prevented this.

59 See above, n.57, 513–514.

60 See above, p.306.

61 But a supervision order can be substituted: Children Act 1989 s.39(4).

62 See above, p.262.

63 Children Act 1989 s.26(3).

64 Children Act 1989 s.24(14), added by the Courts and Legal Services Act 1990 Sch.16 para.13.

65 Children Act 1989 s.26A, inserted by Adoption and Children Act 2002. And see *Get It Sorted: Providing Effective Advocacy Services for Children and Young People Making a Complaint under the Children Act 1989*, DFES, 2003.

66 *Guidance and Regulations*, vol.3, para.10.3.

67 Children Act 1989 s.26(4).

68 See above, n.65, para.10.8.

69 *R. v LB of Brent Ex p. S* [1994] 1 F.L.R. 203, 211 *per* Peter Gibson L.J.

70 *R. v Royal Borough of Kingston-upon-Thames Ex p. T* [1994] 1 F.L.R. 798, 814.

71 See, e.g. *R. v Birmingham City Council Ex p. A* [1997] 2 F.L.R. 841, and *R (BG) v Medway Council* [2006] 1 F.L.R. 663.

72 Children Act 1989 s.84.

73 Solicitor General, Standing Committee B on Children Bill 1989, col.492.

74 [1982] A.C. 363.

75 Children Act 1989 s.100(2)(c) and 91(4).

76 *Re S (Habeas Corpus); S v Haringey LBC* [2004] 1 F.L.R. 590.

77 *Ibid.*, 598.

78 *Ibid.*, 599.

79 As stated by Munby J. in *Re M (Care Proceedings: Judicial Review)* [2003] 2 F.L.R. 171, 178.

80 *R. v Norfolk CC Ex p. M* [1989] Q.B. 619; *R. v East Sussex CC Ex p. R* [1991] 2 F.L.R. 358. But *cf. R. v Harrow LBC Ex p. D* [1990] Fam 133: recourse to judicial review in respect of placing a name on a Child Protection Register ought to be rare.

81 *Re J* [1995] 1 F.L.R. 669: a specific issue order was sought but it was said the decision was amenable to judicial review. See also above n.70.

82 *R (CD) v Isle of Anglesey CC.* [2005] 1 F.L.R. 59.

83 See above, n.79.

84 *Re C (Adoption: Religious Observance)* [2002] 1 F.L.R. 1119.

85 *R. v Bedfordshire CC Ex p. C* [1987] 1 F.L.R. 239.

86 *R. v Birmingham City Council Ex p. A* [1997] 2 F.L.R. 841. See also above, n.70.

87 *A v A Health Authority and other; Re J and Linked Applications* [2002] Fam. 213, cited in above, n.76, 593. see also above, n.84.

88 See below, p.313.

89 [1995] 2 A.C. 633.

90 *Z v United Kingdom* [2001] 2 F.L.R. 612; *TP and KM v United Kingdom* [2001] 2 F.L.R. 549.

91 See below, p.313.

92 [2001] 2 A.C. 550.

93 [2000] 1 F.L.R. 825.

94 *Ibid.*, 848–849.

95 [1999] Fam. 90.

96 See also *A v Essex County Council* [2004] 1 F.L.R. 749.

97 [2005] 2 F.L.R. 284.

98 *Ibid.*, 322.

99 *Ibid.*, 305–306.

100 See *D v Bury MBC* [2006] 1 W.L.R. 917.

101 Human Rights Act 1998 s.6(3).

102 Above, n.79, 594, *per* Munby J. quoting himself in *Re L (Care Proceedings: Human Rights Claims)* [2003] 2 F.L.R. 160.

103 Children Act 1998 s.7(1)(a).

104 *Re W and B (Children: Care Plan), Re W (Children) (Care Plan)* [2001] 2 F.L.R. 582.

105 Children Act 1998 s.7(7).

106 *A v United Kingdom (Human Rights: Punishment of Child)* [1998] 2 F.L.R. 959; *A and B v United Kingdom* [1998] 1 E.H.R.R. 82.

107 Human Rights Act 1998 s.7(5) (the court has the discretion to admit later claims).

108 [2001] 2 F.L.R. 1300.

109 See above, p.313.

CHAPTER 11

1 Adoption of Children Act 1926; and see Lowe, 2000, p.307.

2 See *Humphreys v Polak* [1901] 2 K.B. 385.

3 Abortion Act 1967.

4 *Marriage, Divorce and Adoption Statistics* 2002, ONS series FM2 No.30 Table 6.26.
5 NICE recommended three. Provision is apparently patchy: see *The Times*, March 2, 2007, p.2.
6 *Judicial Statistics* 2004, Annual Report, Table 5.4.
7 *Houghton Report* Cmnd. 5107, para.115.
8 See below, p.333.
9 Human Fertilisation and Embryology Act 1990 s.30, above pp.172–174.
10 Adoption and Children Act 2002 s.46.
11 Where a person adopted by one parent alone is subsequently legitimated by his/her parents' marriage: Adoption and Children Act 2002 s.55.
12 [1995] 2 F.L.R. 1.
13 *Ibid.*, 8 *per* Swinton Thomas L.J.
14 [2001] 1 F.L.R. 589.
15 *Ibid.*, 599.
16 *Ibid.*
17 [2000] 1 F.L.R. 958.
18 *Fretté v France* [2003] 2 F.L.R. 9.
19 See above, n.7, paras 81–91.
20 See s.28.
21 Adoption and Children Act 2002 s.92.
22 Whether an adoption order can be made after an illegal placement is not clear. *Re G (Adoption: Illegal Placement)* [1995] 1 F.L.R. 403 held one could be. Is this still the case? See Lowe and Douglas, 2006, p.881.
23 See Adoption Agency Regulations 2005.
24 Regulation 3 requires a panel to be established.
25 Regulation 18.
26 Adoption and Children Act 2002 s.3. The original duty was in the Children Act 1995 s.1.
27 See pp.4–6, particularly proposition 2 on p.6.
28 See above n.7, para.216.
29 Children Act 1975 s.3 (subsequently Adoption Act 1976 s.6).
30 See *Adoption Law Review: Consultation Document* 1992, para.7.1ff.
31 Sections 1(1) and (2).
32 Adoption and Children Act 2002 s.1(4).
33 See above, pp.215–225.
34 Adoption and Children Act 2002 s.1(4). Note "relatives" includes birth parents: s.1(8)(a).

35   Adoption and Children Act 2002 s.1(5).
36   Adoption and Children Act 2002 s.1(6), modelled on s.1(5) of the Children Act 1989, above, p.228.
37   Adoption and Children Act 2002 s.1(3), modelled on s.1(2) of Children Act 1989.
38   An elderly Somerset Maugham (the English novelist) adopting his middle-aged male secretary in France is often cited.
39   Adoption and Children Act 2002 ss.47(9), 49(4).
40   Adoption and Children Act 2002 s.47(8) and (8A), added by the Civil Partnership Act 2004 s.79(3).
41   Adoption and Children Act 2002 ss.51 and 52.
42   Adoption and Children Act 2002 s.144(4), as amended by Civil Partnership Act 2004 s.79.
43   Suitability of Adopters Regulations 2005.
44   Adoption and Children Act 2002 s.51(3) and (3A), added by the Civil Partnership Act 2004 s.79(4).
45   10,000 plus in the early 1970s.
46   Section 14(3). See also s.15(4), where the application was by the step-parent alone. See also Children Act 1975 s.37(1).
47   *Re S (Infants) (Adoption by Parent)* [1977] Fam. 173.
48   (1980) 2 F.L.R. 102.
49   See above, n.30, para.19.
50   *Ibid.*, paras 19.4 and 19.8.
51   See above, pp.188–189.
52   The child's wishes and feelings are curiously neglected, particularly given the fact that many of these children will be adolescents.
53   Less so than once. See *Re C (A Minor) (Adoption Order: Condition)* [1989] A.C. 1.
54   Houghton called it "guardianship". See also above, p.250.
55   More than half the applications for custodianship were from grandparents: see Bullard *et al.*, 1991, Tables 24–28.
56   See below, pp.333–335.
57   Adoption and Children Act 2002 s.14A.
58   As step-parents can: see above, pp.188–189.
59   Adoption and Children Act 2002 s.47(2).
60   Adoption and Children Act 2002 s.18.
61   Adoption and Children Act 2002 s.18(2).
62   Adoption and Children Act 2002 s.25.
63   Adoption and Children Act 2002 s.19.
64   Adoption and Children Act 2002 s.52(3).
65   Adoption and Children Act 2002 s.18(1).

66 Adoption and Children Act 2002 s.20(4).
67 Family Procedure (Adoption) Rules 2005, rr. 20, 24, 27 and 28.
68 Adoption and Children Act 2002 s.21(1).
69 Adoption and Children Act 2002 s.22.
70 Adoption and Children Act 2002 s.21(2).
71 See above, pp.228–230.
72 On delay see Adoption and Children Act 2002 s.1(3).
73 See above, pp.317–318.
74 Adoption and Children Act 2002 s.47(2).
75 Children Act 1989 s.12(3) and s.33(6)(b).
76 Adoption and Children Act 2002 s.52(6).
77 *Re M (An Infant)* [1955] 2 Q.B. 479.
78 Adoption and Children Act 2002 s.52(9) and (10).
79 Adoption and Children Act 2002 s.144(4).
80 In Scotland the consent of children of 12 and over is.
81 See above n.30, para.9.5.
82 Adoption and Children Act 2002 s.1(4)(a).
83 *Cf.* Children Act 1989 s.1(3)(a).
84 [1998] 1 F.L.R. 370.
85 Family Procedure (Adoption) Rules 2005, r.23(3)(a).
86 Adoption and Children Act 2002 s.1(4)(f), (8).
87 *Re H, Re G (Adoption: Consultation of Unmarried Fathers)* [2001] 1 F.L.R. 646.
88 As in *Re H*, above n.87.
89 As in *Re G*, above, n.87.
90 See s.7 of Adoption Act 1976.
91 See above, p.320.
92 See above, pp.319–320.
93 Mental Capacity Act 2005 s.67 and Sch.6.
94 Adoption and Children Act 2002 s.52.
95 [1966] 3 All E.R. 613.
96 [2000] 1 F.L.R. 539.
97 Mental Capacity Act 2005 s.3(1).
98 Mental Capacity Act 2005 s.1(4).
99 Mental Capacity Act 2005 s.3(3).
100 See *Re C* [1944] 1 W.L.R. 290.
101 Adoption and Children Act 2002 s.1(4)(c).
102 Adoption and Children Act 2002 s.1(4)(f).
103 See above, pp.317–318. See also *P, C, S v United Kingdom* [2002] 2 F.L.R. 631.
104 In many of the cases the child will have been the subject of

a care order so that the threshold conditions will already
have been established.

105 Adoption and Children Act 2002 s.42.
106 The test is "home".
107 Adoption and Children Act 2002 s.44.
108 Adoption and Children Act 2002 s.42(5), (6).
109 As in *Re M*, above, n.84.
110 See below, pp.333–335.
111 See above, p.248.
112 *Re K (A Minor) (Adoption Order: Nationality)* (1994) 2 F.L.R. 557.
113 See above, pp.324, 326.
114 Adoption and Children Act 2002 s.46(6).
115 *Re J (A Minor) (Adoption Order: Conditions)* [1973] Fam. 106.
    And see *Re C (A Minor) (Adoption Order: Conditions)* [1989]
    A.C. 1.
116 *Ibid.*, 17–18. "Access" is now "contact".
117 *Re T (Adopted Children: Contact)* [1995] 2 F.L.R. 792, 797–798.
118 The Houghton Report, above, n.7, para.303, said it wished
    "to encourage greater openness about adoption". The
    current provision is Adoption and Children Act 2002 s.60.
119 Section 26.
120 Children Act 1989 Sch.10 para.21.
121 The Registrar General may refuse this on grounds of public
    policy: *R v Registrar General Ex p. Smith* [1991] 2 Q.B. 393.
122 Adoption and Children Act 2002 s.77.
123 Adoption and Children Act 2002 s.79.
124 Adoption and Children Act 2002 s.80.
125 *Guidance and Regulations* vol.9, para.32.
126 Adoption and Children Act 2002 s.80(2), (4).
127 Adoption and Children Act 2002 s.46(1), (2).
128 Adoption and Children Act 2002 s.67.
129 British Nationality Act 1981 s.1(5).
130 Marriage Act 1949 Sch.1 and Civil Partnership Act 2004 Sch.1.
131 Adoption and Children Act 2002 s.74(1)(a).
132 Discussed inter alia in Lowe and Douglas, 2006, pp.869–872.
133 Article 1.
134 Article 4(a) and (b).
135 Article 4(c).
136 Article 5.
137 Article 6.
138 Article 14.
139 Article 15.
140 Article 16.

141 Article 23.

142 Article 24.

143 Children and Adoption Act 2006 s.9.

144 It was 6 months. The Children and Adoption Act 2006 s.14 extended it.

145 As originally proposed, it was to be called "the child's inter vivos guardian".

146 Children Act 1989 s.5.

147 Muslims may have this.

148 *See Re S (A Child) (Special Guardianship Order), The Times* February 9, 2007.

149 Children Act 1989 s.14A(5).

150 Children Act 1989 s.14A(2)(b).

151 Children Act 1989 s.14A(3)(b).

152 Children Act 1989 s.14A(4) and see above, p.245.

153 Children Act 1989 s.14A(12).

154 Children Act 1989 s.14A(6)(b), and above, n.148.

155 *Re M-J (Adoption Order or Special Guardianship Order)* [2007] 1 F.L.R. 691, 697–698.

156 It is not necessary to go though it line by line: see *Re S (Adoption Order or Special Guardianship Order)* [2007] 1 F.L.R. 819.

157 Children Act 1989 s.14B(1)(a).

158 Children Act 1989 s.14B(2)(a), 14C(3)(a).

159 Children Act 1989 s.14B(2)(b), 14C(3)(b).

160 Children Act 1989 s.14B(2)(b), 14C(3)(b).

161 Children Act 1989 s.14C(1).

162 For example, sterilisation, male circumcision, changes in education. See above, p.206.

163 Children Act 1989 s.14C(2)(b).

164 Children Act 1989 s.14C(3)(a).

165 Children Act 1989 s.14C(3)(b), (4).

166 Children Act 1989 s.5(4), as amended by the Adoption and Children Act 2002 s.115(4)(b).

167 Children Act 1989 s.14D: on the details see Lowe and Douglas, 2006, pp.609–610.

168 Children Act 1989 s.14F(1) and (2). And see Special Guardianship Regulations 2005.

169 See above, p.250.

170 See above, n.148.

171 *Re AJ (Adoption Order or Special Guardianship Order)* [2007] 1 F.L.R. 507.

CHAPTER 12

1 Grandparents had this obligation until 1948: National Assistance Act 1948.

2 *Cf.* the approach in some American decisions, for example *Johnson v Calvert* 851 P. 2d 776 (1993). See above, p.165.

3 *Leeds Teaching Hospitals NHS Trust v A* [2003] 1 F.L.R. 1091, and above, p.170.

4 A suggestion that this may be one of the reasons why we do is found in Baker, 2004.

5 The title of the White Paper.

6 The *Independent*, November 2, 1990.

7 It has been argued that it is constitutive of a child's identity: see Carbone, 2005.

8 This is now, belatedly, acknowledged in Department of Work and Pensions, *A New System of Child Maintenance*, 2006, para.40.

9 *Ibid.*, paras 22–23.

10 The Child Maintenance and Enforcement Commission, due to be established in 2008: *ibid.*, para.19.

11 By the Child Support Act 1991. It was amended by the Child Support Act 1995, and the Child Support, Pensions and Social Security Act 2000.

12 *Children Come First*, Cm. 1264, London, HMSO, 1991.

13 See Bradshaw and Millar, 1991.

14 Mrs Thatcher, quoted in *The Times*, July 19, 1990. It is worth comparing the Australian system (see Harrison, 1991) and that in New Zealand (see Richardson, 1995). See also Oldham and Melli, 2000, and Altman, 2003.

15 This term as such is not in the legislation, which refers instead to the Secretary of State, whose functions are carried out by officers of the CSA.

16 See Child Support Act 1991 s.3(3).

17 Child Support Act 1991 s.6.

18 Child Support Act 1991 ss.6(8), 46(3).

19 Child Support Act 1991 s.46(5).

20 See Child Support (Maintenance Calculation Procedure) Regulations SI 2001/157 reg.11.

21 Including the family (in the Children Act 1989 and see Bainham, 1990) and, in one West End hit comedy (by Ben Elton) air!

22 See Davis *et al.*, 1998.

23 See above, p.234.

24 The formula's use of a child's age was justifiably ridiculed: do 11-year-olds really cost only 60% of 16-year-olds? And see Middleton *et al.*, 1997.

25 See Eekelaar, above, p.336, and Eekelaar and Maclean, 1997.

26 [1994] 1 F.L.R. 26.

27 On such appeals see above, pp.148–150.

28 Now a variation, formerly "departure direction" could be sought: see below, p.340.

29 See National Audit Office, 1994.

30 Though levels of accuracy have improved.

31 H.C. Work and Pensions Committee, *The Performance of the Child Support Agency* H.C. 44, 2005.

32 The *Guardian* December 14, 2006, p.10.

33 Child Support Act 1995 s.1.

34 Child Support Act 1995 s.5.

35 Child Support Act 1995 s.10.

36 See now Child Support Act 1991 Sch.1 para.1.

37 Child Support Act 1991, Sch.1 para.2.

38 Child Support Act 1991, Sch.1 para.10(3).

39 See below, p.344.

40 Child Support Act 1991 Sch.1 para.2(2).

41 Child Support Act 1991 Sch.1 para.3.

42 Child Support Act 1991 Sch.1 para.4.

43 Child Support Act 1991 Sch.1 para.5 and SI 2001/155 reg.4.

44 Child Support Act 1991 Sch.1, paras 6, 7, 8 and 9 and Child Support (Maintenance Calculations and Special Cases) Regulations 2001 reg.7A. See further Mitchell, 2003.

45 See Child Support Act 1991, Sch.4B and Child Support (Variations) Regulations 2000, SI 2001/156.

46 Child Support Act 1991 s.28F(1).

47 Child Support Act 1991 s.28F(2)(a).

48 Child Support Act 1991 Sch.4B para.2 and Child Support (Variations) Regulations 2000, regs 10–15.

49 Child Support Act 1991 Sch.4B para.4, and Child Support (Variations) Regulations 2000, regs 18–20.

50 Child Support Act 1991 s.6.

51 Child Support Act 1991 s.9(2).

52 See below, p.351.

53 Child Support Act 1991 s.6(3).

54 Child Support Act 1991 s.14.

55 Child Support Act 1991 s.46(2).

56 Child Support Act 1991 s.46(3).

57 Child Support Act 1991 s.46(5), (10).

58 Child Support Act 1991 s.9(4).
59 See above, n.31.
60 Below, p.350.
61 In *R (Kehoe) v Secretary of State for Work and Pensions* [2005] 2 F.L.R. 1249.
62 By four to one.
63 See above, n.61, 1274.
64 *Ibid.*, 1275.
65 *Ibid.*
66 *Ibid.*, 1275–1277. Wikeley, 2006, is critical of this judgment.
67 Article 27(3).
68 As in Children Act 1989 s.1(1), above, p.209 and Adoption and Children Act 2002 s.1(2), above, p.319.
69 As in Matrimonial Causes Act 1973 s.25(1), above, p.137.
70 In *Biggin's* case, below n.71, 854.
71 [1995] 1 F.L.R. 851.
72 *Ibid.*, 855.
73 *Ibid.*
74 See also *R. v Secretary of State for Social Security Ex p. Lloyd* [1995] 1 F.L.R. 856.
75 Child Support Act 1991 s.8(6).
76 Child Support Act 1991 s.8(7).
77 Child Support Act 1991 s.8(8). "Disabled" is defined in s.8(9), as in the Children Act 1989 s.17(11).
78 See *C v F (Disabled Child: Maintenance Order)* [1998] 2 F.L.R. 1.
79 See Child Support Act 1991 s.3(1).
80 Child Support Act 1991 s.8(5).
81 Child Support Act 1991 s.9(3), (4).
82 Child Support Act 1991 s.9(5).
83 See *Dorney-Kingdom v Dorney-Kingdom* [2000] 2 F.L.R. 853, 859.
84 See *Phillips v Peace* [1996] 2 F.L.R. 230 (a wealthy unmarried father with no income had nil assessment, but the court was able to order a lump sum to enable the mother to buy a home and furnish it).
85 Section 15.
86 Child Support Act 1991 s.8(10).
87 The concept is used in a number of statutes, e.g. Matrimonial Causes Act 1973 s.52.
88 *Carron v Carron* [1984] F.L.R. 805.
89 *M v M (Child of the Family)* (1980) 2 F.L.R. 39.
90 *A v A (Family: Unborn Child)* [1994] Fam. 6. This ruling is capable of working injustice: it would be better if it were not followed.

91 Domestic Proceedings and Magistrates Courts Act 1978 s.1(b); Matrimonial Causes Act 1973 s.27(1)(b); Civil Partnership Act 2004 s.72(1), (3), Schs 5 and 6.

92 Children Act 1989 s.8(3)(b), (4). Domestic Proceedings and Magistrates' Courts Act 1978 s.2(3).

93 Child Support Act 1989 Sch.1 para.2.

94 Child Support Act 1989 Sch.1 para.1(6).

95 Child Support Act 1989 Sch.1 para.1(7).

96 *Re P (Child: Financial Provision)* [2003] 2 F.L.R. 865, 874. And see now *Re C (A Child: Financial Provision)* (2007) 157 N.L.J. 516 (an award of twice that in *Re P*).

97 This is because s.105(1) of the Children Act 1989 excludes maintenance from the definition of upbringing. Nor is it the first consideration: there is no direction to this effect in Sch.1.

98 See a clear statement to this effect in *F v G (Child: Financial Provision)* [2005] 1 F.L.R. 261, 267.

99 See above n.96, 875–876.

100 *Ibid.*, 877.

101 See above, p.127.

102 See *T v S (Financial Provision for Children)* [1994] 2 F.L.R. 883; *J v C (Child: Financial Provision)* [1991] 1 F.L.R. 152.

103 *A v A (Financial Provision)* [1994] 1 F.L.R. 657.

104 See above, n.96, 875.

105 It may not be easy to determine whether a particular payment is for the child's benefit: see for example, *Re S (Child: Financial Provision)* [2005] 2 F.L.R. 94.

106 *Haroutunian v Jennings* (1980) 1 F.L.R. 62. See also above n.103.

107 David Blunkett MP, then Minister for Work and Pensions.

108 H.C. Select Committee on Work and Pensions, *The Performance of the Child Support Agency*, H.C. 44, 2005, para.31.

109 In 2005 £24 a week for one qualifying child: *ibid.*, para.135.

110 *Smith v Secretary of State for Work and Pensions* [2005] 1 F.L.R. 606.

111 Child Support Act 1991 s.4(1), (2).

112 Child Support Act 1991 s.29.

113 Child Support Act 1991 s.41A.

114 Note not a court, though there is an appeal to the magistrates' court (Child Support Act 1991 s.32(5)).

115 Child Support Act 1991 s.31.

116 Child Support Act 1991 s.33.

117 Child Support Act 1991 s.33(4).

118 Child Support Act 1991 s.35.

119 Child Support Act 1991 s.36.

120 *R (Denson) v Child Support Agency* [2002] 1 F.L.R. 938.
121 Child Support Act 1991 s.39A (inserted by s.16 of Child Support, Pensions and Social Security Act 2000).
122 Child Support Act 1991 s.40(3), (7).
123 See above n.31, para.168.
124 See above, n.8.
125 *Ibid.*, para.33.
126 *Ibid.*, para.29.
127 *Ibid.*, para.31.
128 *Ibid.*, para.32.
129 *Ibid.*, para.35.
130 *Ibid.*, para.37.
131 And see above, pp.181–182.
132 *Cf. Re H (Minors) (Local Authority: Parental Rights) (No.3)* [1991] Fam. 151, 158.
133 They would like to see such sanctions applied to mothers who impede contact.
134 The Henshaw Review, Cm. 6894, 2006 so recommended. And the government proposes "significantly" to increase the amount of maintenance that parents on benefit can keep before it affects the level of benefit they receive as from 2010–2011.
135 The government estimates that 40,000 parents could benefit from this: above, n.8 para.40.
136 See above, p.130.
137 See above, n.31, para.152.

CHAPTER 13

1 Exemplified in the case of *Re Agar-Ellis* [1883] 24 Ch. D. 317.
2 Maria Colwell, it was said (Howells, 1974) was killed by a misplaced emphasis on the blood-tie. See also the notorious case of *Re C (MA)* [1966] 1 All E.R. 838.
3 See below, p.358.
4 For example those by Goldstein *et al.* (1996) and Guggenheim (2005). See my critiques (Freeman, 1997 and 2006b).
5 His novel, *L'Enfant*, published in 1879, was dedicated to all oppressed children.
6 Prevention of Cruelty to, and Protection of Children, Act 1889. See further Behlmer, 1982.
7 See her *Children's Rights* (Wiggin, 1892).

8 See her *The Century of The Child* (Key, 1909; first published in Swedish in 1900).
9 On Korczak see Lifton, 1988.
10 A good summary of many of his ideas is Joseph, 2007. See also Freeman, forthcoming, 2008.
11 On this see Marshall, 1999.
12 *Cf.* above, p.244 on the so-called right to "divorce parents".
13 Sexual abuse had not really been discovered when he wrote.
14 On voting see Archard, 2004, p.98.
15 On which see Ward, 1978.
16 See above, p.193.
17 See Art.2, and also Arts 17(3), 20(3), 23, 28(1), 30 and 31.
18 Article 3(1). *Cf.* Children Act 1989 s.1(1).
19 Article 6. This begins at birth. The rights of the unborn child were one of several controversies at drafting stage (Johnson, 1992).
20 Articles 3(3), 19, 24(3), 25, 28(3), 33, 34, 36, 39.
21 Articles 3(3), 6, 17, 23, 24, 25, 36.
22 Articles 28, 29, 30.
23 Article 32.
24 Articles 37, 40.
25 Articles 13, 17, 31.
26 Article 22.
27 Article 23. And see *R (Spink) v Wandsworth BC* [2005] 1 F.L.R. 448.
28 For example, *R (Williamson) v Secretary of State for Education and Employment* [2005] 2 F.L.R. 374, 398–399 (Baroness Hale), and below, p.359; *Haringey LBC v C and E* [2005] 2 F.L.R. 47, 61 (Ryder J.); *Mabon v Mabon* [2005] 2 F.L.R. 1011, 1017 (Thorpe L.J.); *R (Thomson) v Secretary of State for Education and Skills* [2006] 1 F.L.R. 1751 (Munby J.); *R (Axon) v Secretary of State for Health and Family Planning Association* [2006] 2 F.L.R. 206, 231 (Silber J.).
29 Articles 43–45.
30 The Court of Appeal in *Mabon v Mabon*, n.28, above, 1017, does not agree with this criticism.
31 Article 5.
32 Article 18(1).
33 Article 27(2). See also Article 27(4), above, p.343.
34 The Convention was drafted against the background of the atrocities of the Second World War. Korczak, above p.354, himself accompanied some 200 children to their deaths in Treblinka (Lifton, 1988, p.338).

35 According to Thorpe L.J. in *Payne v Payne* [2001] 1 F.L.R. 1052, 1065.

36 [2003] 1 F.L.R. 210, 221–222.

37 *Hoppe v Germany* [2003] 1 F.L.R. 384, 394.

38 *Johansen v Norway* (1996) 23 E.H.R.R. 33, 72–73; *Elsholz v Germany* [2000] 2 F.L.R. 486, 497.

39 [2005] A.C. 246.

40 Education Act 1996 s.548(1), and above, p.194.

41 Corporal punishment is discussed fully above, pp.193–198.

42 See above n.39, 395.

43 *Ibid.*

44 *Ibid.*, 401.

45 [2003] 1 F.L.R. 813.

46 *Ibid.*, 821.

47 [2001] 1 F.L.R. 611.

48 *Ibid.*, 620.

49 *Ibid.*, 621.

50 See below, pp.369–372.

51 [2005] 1 F.L.R. 236.

52 *Ibid.*, 257. On Gillick competence see below, p.362.

53 [2001] 2 F.L.R. 1190 and see above, p.169.

54 See above, pp.167–169.

55 See above, p.167.

56 See above, n.53, 1197.

57 *Ibid.*, 1198.

58 See above, pp.196–197.

59 [2001] 2 F.L.R. 612.

60 In *D v East Berkshire Community Health NHS Trust; MAK v Dewsbury Healthcare NHS Trust; RK v Oldham NHS Trust* [2004] Q.B. 558. The duty does not extend to parents not to make negligent allegations of child abuse; see House of Lords' decision at [2005] 2 F.L.R. 284 and above, pp.312–313.

61 [2003] 1 F.L.R. 484.

62 There is bullying, self-harming and suicide.

63 See above n.61, 526. See also *R (on the application of BP) v Secretary of State for the Home Department* [2003] All E.R. (D) 310.

64 See above n.61, 495.

65 *Gillick v West Norfolk and Wisbech AHA* [1986] A.C. 112.

66 That is girls under 16.

67 See above n.65, 186.

68 It has been held to apply to decisions about abortion: see the *Axon* case, n.28 above and below, p.363.

69 [2004] 2 F.L.R. 949.
70 *Ibid.*, 968. The judge italicised "defend" and "right". Note also Munby J. in *Re E (By Her Litigation Friend The Official Solicitor) v Channel Four; News International Ltd and St Helens Borough Council* [2005] 2 F.L.R. 913, 929 (if an adult with a psychiatric condition has capacity her wishes are "determinative").
71 See above, n.69, 968.
72 [1993] Fam. 64, 93.
73 *Ibid.*, 88.
74 Of the European Convention on Human Rights.
75 See above, n.69, 968–969.
76 *R (On the Application of Axon) v Secretary of State for Health and Family Planning Association* [2006] 2 F.L.R. 206.
77 *Ibid.*, 249–250.
78 [1992] Fam. 11, and see Douglas, 1992.
79 [1993] Fam. 64.
80 *Cf.* adults who may, if competent, refuse treatment. See *Re C (Adult: Refusal of Treatment)* [1994] 1 W.L.R. 290 and Mental Capacity Act 2005 s.3(1).
81 It is not clear what her status was: she had originally been received into care (that is accommodated), and an interim care order had been made but it seems not a final care order.
82 See above, pp.299–300.
83 See above, n.79.
84 He uses the "key-holder" metaphor in *Re R*, above, n.78, and the "flak-jacket" metaphor in *Re W*, above n.79, to explain this.
85 See above, n.79.
86 *Re E (A Minor) (Wardship: Medical Treatment)* [1993] 1 F.L.R. 386 is earlier than *Re R*.
87 [1994] 2 F.L.R. 1065.
88 *Ibid.*, 1072.
89 [1998] 2 F.L.R. 810.
90 *Ibid.*, 812.
91 On whether a child is capable of making an advance directive see Jackson, 2006.
92 See above n.89, 813.
93 [1999] 2 F.L.R. 1097.
94 *Ibid.*, 1099.
95 [2004] 2 F.L.R. 1117.
96 *Ibid.*, 1119.
97 See *Re C*, above, n.80.

98 See *Re M*, above, n.93.
99 See above, p.274.
100 Even after the House of Commons Select Committee on Health in 1998 recommended a Commissioner.
101 Children's Commissioner for Wales Act 2001.
102 The Commissioner for Children and Young People (Scotland) Act 2003.
103 The Commissioner for Children and Young People (Northern Ireland) Order 2003, SI 2003/439 (NI 11).
104 Children Act 2004 s.3.
105 Children Act 2004 s.4.
106 See above, n.5, 101, 102, 103.
107 [2001] 1 F.L.R. 715.
108 *Ibid.*, 719.
109 [2004] 1 F.L.R. 1190.
110 *Ibid.*, 1191.
111 *Ibid.*, 1192.
112 [1994] 1 F.L.R. 156.
113 *Ibid.*, 160.
114 [2005] 2 F.L.R. 1011.
115 *Ibid.*, 1017.
116 *Ibid.*, 1018. And he quotes the New Zealand Care of Children Act 2004 ss.6 and 7.
117 *Ibid.*
118 *Ibid.*, 1016.
119 Children Act 1989 s.41.
120 Applications for the making or revoking of an adoption placement order also now require the appointment of a guardian. See Adoption and Children Act 2002 s.122(1)(a). Rules of Court may bring proceedings for the making, varying or discharge of a s.8 order within "specified proceedings". See *ibid.*, s.122(1)(b).
121 Children Act 1989 s.41(2)(b).
122 Family Proceedings Courts (Children Act) Rules 1991 r.12(1).
123 See *Oxfordshire County Council v P* [1995] Fam. 161 and *Re G (Minors) (Welfare Report)* [1993] 2 F.L.R. 293.
124 *Re N (Child Abuse: Evidence)* [1996] 2 F.L.R. 214.
125 *Re W (Minor) (Secure Accommodation)* [1993] 1 F.L.R. 692.
126 In *Mabon v Mabon*, above n.114, by Thorpe L.J., at 1017.
127 *Ibid.*, 1020.
128 See, for example, "Child Care Review Update" [2005] Fam. Law 844.

BIBLIOGRAPHY

Abrams, K. "Choice, Dependence and the Reinvigoration of the Traditional Family", *Indiana Law Journal* 1988, 73, 516.

Abse, L. *Private Member*. (London: Macdonald, 1973)

Adams, D. (1988) "Treatment Models of Men Who Batter: A Pro-Feminist Analysis". In K. Yllo and M. Bograd (eds), *Feminist Perspectives on Wife Abuse*. (Beverly Hills, CA: Sage, 1988)

Adcock, M. and White, R. *Significant Harm*. (Croydon: Significant Harm Publications, 1998)

Alston, P. *The Best Interests of the Child*. (Oxford: Clarendon Press, 1994)

Altman, S. "A Theory of Child Support", *International Journal of Law, Policy and the Family* 2003, 17, 173.

Anderson, S. "Legislative Divorce—Law for the Aristocracy". In G.R. Rubin and D. Sugarman (eds), *Law, Economy and Society: Essays in the History of English Law 1750–1914*. (Abingdon: Professional Books, 1984)

Archard, D. *Children: Rights and Childhood*. (London: Routledge, 1993)

Archard, D. *Children: Rights and Childhood*. (London: Routledge, 2004)

Ariès, P. *Centuries of Childhood*. (London: Jonathan Cape, 1962)

Ariès, P. "Marriage", *London Review of Books*, 1980, 2(20), 8.

Aris, R., Harrison, C. and Humphreys, C. *Safety and Child Contact*. (London: Lord Chancellor's Department, 2002)

Arkes, H. "The Closet Straight", *National Review*, 5 July 1993, 43.

Arthur, S. *et al. Settling Up: Making Financial Arrangements After Divorce or Separation*. (London: National Centre for Social Research, 2002)

Ashenden, S. *Governing Child Sexual Abuse: Negotiating the Boundaries of Public and Private Law and Science*. (London: Routledge, 2004)

Atkin, B. "Rights of Unmarried Couples in New Zealand—Radical New Zealand Laws on Property and Succession", *Child and Family Law Quarterly*, 2003, 12, 173.

Auchmuty, R. "Same-Sex Marriage Revived: Feminist Critique and Legal Strategy", *Feminism and Psychology*, 2004, 14, 101.

Babb, P. *et al. Social Trends.* (London: ONS, 2006)

Bailey-Harris, R. "Dividing the Assets on Family Breakdown: The Content of Fairness", *Current Legal Problems*, 2001a, 54, 533

Bailey-Harris, R. "Fairness in Financial Settlements on Divorce", *Law Quarterly Review*, 2001b, 117, 199.

Bailey-Harris, R. "Lambert v. Lambert—Towards the Recognition of Marriage as a Partnership of Equals", *Child and Family Law Quarterly*, 2003, 15, 417.

Bailey-Harris, R., Barrow, J. and Pearce, J. "Settlement Culture and the Use of the 'No Order' Principle under the Children Act 1989", *Child and Family Law Quarterly*, 1999, 11, 53.

Bainham, A. "When Is a Parent Not a Parent? Reflections on the Unmarried Mother, Father and his Child in English Law", *International Journal of Law and the Family*, 1989, 3, 208.

Bainham, A. "The Privatisation of the Public Interest in Children", *Modern Law Review*, 1990, 53, 206.

Bainham, A. *Children: The Modern Law.* (Bristol: Jordans, 1993)

Bainham, A. "Corporal Punishment of Children—A Caning for the United Kingdom", *Cambridge Law Journal*, 1999a, 58, 29.

Bainham, A. "Parentage, Parenthood and Parental Responsibility: Subtle, Elusive, yet Important Distinctions". In A. Bainham, S. Day Sclater and M. Richards (eds) *What Is A Parent?* (Oxford: Hart, 1999b)

Bainham, A. "Men and Women Behaving Badly: Is Fault Dead in English Family Law?", *Oxford Journal of Legal Studies*, 2001, 21, 219.

Bainham, A. *Children: The Modern Law.* (Bristol: Jordans, 2005)

Baker, K.K. "Bargaining Or Biology? The History and Future of Paternity Law and Parental Status", *Cornell Journal of Law and Public Policy*, 2004, 14, 1.

Banda, F. *Women, Law and Human Rights: An African Perspective* (Oxford: Hart, 2003)

Barlow, A. *Cohabitants and the Law.* (London: Butterworths, 2001)

Barlow, A. and James, G. "Regulating Marriage and Cohabitation in 21st Century Britain", *Modern Law Review*, 2004, 67, 143

Barlow, A., Callus. T. and Cooke, E. "Community of Property: A Study for England and Wales", *Family Law*, 2004, 34, 47.

Barlow, A. *et al. Cohabitation, Marriage and the Law* (Oxford: Hart, 2005)

Barmes, L. "Worlds Colliding: Legal Regulation and

Psychologists' Evidence about Workplace Bullying". In B.Brooks-Gordon and M.Freeman (eds), *Law and Psychology* (Oxford: Oxford University Press, 2006)

Bartholet, E. *Family Bonds: Adoption and the Politics of Parenting* (New York: Houghton Mifflin, 1993).

Bartlett, K. "Old Families into New: A Status for Step-Parents". In M. Freeman (ed.), *State, Law and Family*. (London: Tavistock, 1984)

Bartlett, K. "Re-Expressing Parenthood", *Yale Law Journal*, 1988, 98, 298.

Barton, C. *Cohabitation Contracts*. (Aldershot: Dartmouth, 1985)

Barton, C. "*A v United Kingdom*—The Thirty Thousand Pound Caning—An 'English Vice' in Europe", *Child and Family Law Quarterly*, 1999, 11, 63.

Barton, C. and Douglas, G. *Law and Parenthood*. (London: Butterworths, 1995)

Bawin-Legros, B and Gauthier, A. "Regulation of Intimacy and Love Semantics in Couples Living Apart Together", *International Review of Sociology*, 2001, 11, 39.

Beck, C. *et al*. "The Rights of Children: A Trust Model". *Fordham Law Review*, 1978, 46, 669.

Becker, H. *Outsiders*. (New York: Free Press, 1963)

Becker, L. *Property Rights: Philosophic Foundations*. (London: Routledge, Kegan Paul, 1977)

Behlmer, G. *Child Abuse and Moral Reform In England 1870–1908*. (Stanford, CA: Stanford University Press, 1982)

Belcastro, P. *et al*. "A Review of Data Based Studies Addressing the Effects of Homosexual Parenting on Children's Sexual and Social Functioning", *Journal of Divorce and Remarriage*, 1993, 20, 189.

Bell, C. and Newby, H. "Husbands and Wives: The Dynamics of the Deferential Dialectic". In D.L. Barker and S. Allen (eds), *Dependence and Exploitation in Work and Marriage*. (Harlow: Longman, 1976)

Bell, L. and Tooman, P. "Mandatory Reporting Laws—A Critical Overview", *International Journal of Law, Policy and the Family*, 1994, 8, 337.

Bellamy, C. and Lord, G. "Reflections on the Family Proceedings Rule 9.5" *Family Law*, 2003, 33, 265.

Bennett, B. "The Economics of Wifing Services: Law and Economics on the Family", *Journal of Law and Society*, 1991, 18, 206.

Bennett, L. and Williams, O. *Controversies and Recent Studies of*

Batterer Intervention Programs' Effectiveness. (VAW Applied Resource Forms, 2001)

Berger, P. and Kellner, H. "Marriage and the Construction of Reality". In M. Anderson (ed.), *The Sociology of The Family.* (Harmondsworth: Penguin, 1980)

Bessant, C. "Enforcing Non-Molestation Orders in the Civil and Criminal Courts", *Family Law* 2005, 35, 640.

Besson, S. "The Principle of Non-Discrimination in the Convention on the Rights of The Child", *International Journal of Children's Rights,* 2005, 13, 433.

Bevan, G. and Davis, G. "A Preliminary Exploration of the Impact of Family Mediation on Legal Aid Costs", *Child and Family Law Quarterly,* 1999, 11, 411.

Bevan, G. *et al.* "Can Mediation Reduce Expenditure on Lawyers?", *Family Law,* 2001, 31, 186.

Bird, R. "The Reform of Section 25", *Family Law,* 2002b, 32, 428.

Bitensky, S. *Corporal Punishment of Children—A Human Rights Violation.* (Ardsley, NY: Transnational Publishers, 2006)

Black, J. and Cantor, D. *Child Custody.* (New York: Columbia University Press, 1989)

Blackstone, Sir W. *Commentaries on the Laws of England.* (1765)

Böheim, R. and Ermisch, J. *Breaking Up—Financial Surprises and Partnership Dissolution,* Working Paper of Institute for Social and Economic Research, Paper 1999–09, University of Essex.

Bond, A. "Deconstructing Families—Changing Children's Surnames", *Child and Family Law Quarterly,* 1998, 10, 17.

Borkowski, A. "Police Protection and Section 46", *Family Law,* 1995, 25, 204.

Bourne, R. and Newberger, E.H. "Family Autonomy' or Coercive Intervention'", *Boston University Law Review,* 1977, 57, 870.

Bowlby, J. *Child Care and the Growth of Love.* (Harmondsworth: Penguin, 1953)

Boyd, S. "Is There an Ideology of Motherhood in (Post) Modern Child Custody Law?", *Social and Legal Studies,* 1996, 5, 495.

Bradshaw, J. *The Well-Being of Children.* (London: Save The Children, 2002)

Bradshaw, J. and Millar, J. *Lone Parent Families in the UK.* (London: HMSO, 1991)

Brazier, M. "Liberty, Responsibility, Maternity", *Current Legal Problems,* 1999, 52, 359.

Brett, R. "Orkney—Aberration or Symptom?" *Journal of Child Law,* 1991, 3, 143.

Bridge, C. and Swindells, H. *Adoption: The Modern Law*. (Bristol: Jordan Publishing, 2003)

Brophy, J. "'Race' and Ethnicity in Public Law Proceedings", *Family Law*, 2000, 30, 740.

Brophy, J. "Diversity and Child Protection", *Family Law*, 2003, 35, 674.

Brophy, J., Jhutti-Johal, J. and Owen, C. *Significant Harm: Child Protection Litigation in a Multi-Cultural Setting*. (London: Lord Chancellor's Department, Research Series 1/03, 2003)

Brown, J. and Edwards, J. "Divorce Law Update", *New Law Journal*, 2007, 157, 700.

Bryan, P. "Killing Us Softly: Divorce Mediation and the Politics of Power", *Buffalo Law Review*, 1992, 40, 441.

Buchanan, A. and Brock, D. *Deciding For Others*. (Cambridge: Cambridge University Press, 1989)

Bullard, E., Malos, E. and Parker, R. *Custodianship: Caring For Other People's Children*. (London: HMSO, 1991)

Bunting, M. "Retreat on Adoption and the Equality Act Will Crumble", *Guardian*, 25 January 2007, 32.

Burgdorff, K. *Recognition of and Reporting of Child Maltreatment from the National Study of Incidence and Severity of Child Abuse and Neglect*. (Washington, DC: National Center on Child Abuse and Neglect, 1981)

Burton, M. "Third Party Applications for Protection Orders in England and Wales: Service Providers' Views on Implementing Section 60 of the Family Law Act 1996", *Journal of Social Welfare and Family Law*, 2003, 25, 137.

Burton, M. "*Lomas v Parle*—Coherent and Effective Remedies for Victims of Domestic Violence: Time for an Integrated Domestic Violence Court", *Child and Family Law Quarterly*, 2004, 16, 317.

Burton, S. and Kitzinger, J. *Young People's Attitudes Towards Violence, Sex and Relationships: A Survey and Focus Group Study*. (Edinburgh: Zero Tolerance Charitable Trust, 1998)

Butler, I. *et al. Divorcing Children*. (London: Jessica Kingsley, 2001)

Buzawa, E. and Buzawa, C. *Domestic Violence: The Criminal Justice Response*. (London: Sage, 2003)

Campion, M.J. *Who's Fit To Be A Parent?* (London: Routledge, 1995)

Cane, P. *Responsibility in Law and Morality*. (Oxford: Hart, 2002)

Carbone, J. "The Legal Determination of Parenthood: Uncertainty at the Core of Family Identity", *Louisiana Law Review*, 2005, 65, 1295.

Case, P. *Compensating Child Abuse in England and Wales*. (Cambridge: Cambridge University Press, 2007)

Chau, P.L. and Herring, J. "Defining, Assigning and Designing Sex", *International Journal of Law, Policy and Family*, 2002, 16, 327.

Chau, P.L. and Herring, J. "Men, Women, People: The Definition of Sex". In B. Brooks-Gordon *et al*. (eds), *Sexuality Repositioned*. (Oxford: Hart, 2004)

Christopherson, J. "European Child Abuse Management Systems". In O. Stevenson (ed.), *Child Abuse*. (Brighton: Wheatsheaf, 1989)

Clarkson, C. and Hill, J. *Jaffey on the Conflict of Laws*. (London: Butterworths, 2002)

Clive, E. "Marriage: An Unnecessary Legal Concept?". In J. Eekelaar and S. Katz (eds), *Marriage and Cohabitation in Contemporary Societies*. (Toronto: Butterworths, 1980)

Closen, M., Gamrath, R. and Hopkins, D. "Mandatory Premarital HIV Testing:Political Exploitation of the AIDs Epidemic", *Tulane Law Review*, 1994, 69, 71.

Clucas, B. "The Children's Commissioner for England: The Way Forward?" *Family Law*, 2005, 35, 290.

Cobbe, F.P. "Wife Torture in England", 32 *Contemporary Review*, 1878, 32, 55.

Cobley, C. "Child Abuse, Child Protection and the Criminal Law", *Journal of Child Law*, 1992, 4, 78.

Cobley, C. "The Quest for Truth: Substantiating Allegations of Physical Abuse in Criminal Proceedings and Care Proceedings", *International Journal of Law, Policy and Family* 2006, 20, 317

Cohen, J. and Hale, C. "Treatment or Therapy: The House of Lords Decision in *Re G (Interim Care Order: Residential Assessment)*", *Family Law*, 2005, 36, 294.

Cohen, L. "Marriage, Divorce and Quasi Rents; or I Gave Him the Best Years of My Life'", *Journal of Legal Studies*, 1987, 16, 267.

Cohen, S. *Folk Devils and Moral Panics*. (London: MacGibbon and Kee, 1972)

Coker, D. "Crime Control and Feminist Law Reform in Domestic Violence Law: A Critical Review", *Buffalo Criminal Law Review*, 2001, 4, 801.

Collier, R. *Masculinity, Law and the Family*. (London: Routledge, 1995)

Collier, R. and Sheldon, S. *Fathers' Rights Activism and Law Reform In Comparative Perspective*. (Oxford: Hart, 2006)

Colombotos, J. "Physicians and Medicare: A Before-After Study of the Effect of Legislation on Attitudes", *Sociological Review*, 1969, 34, 378.

Cook, R., Dickens, B. and Fathalla, M. *Reproductive Health and Human Rights*. (Oxford: Clarendon Press, 2003)

Cooke, E. "Playing Parlour Games: Income Provision After Divorce", *Family Law*, 2004, 34, 906.

Cooke, E., Barlow, A. and Callus, T. *Community of Property: A Regime for England and Wales*. (London: Nuffield Foundation, 2006)

Corby, B. *Child Abuse—Towards A Knowledge Base*. (Buckingham: Open University Press, 1993)

Cornell, D. "The Public Supports of Love". In M.L. Shanley (ed.), *Just Marriage*. (New York: Oxford University Press, 2004)

Cornish, W. and Clark, G. *Law and Society in England 1750–1950*. (London: Sweet and Maxwell, 1989)

Cossman, B. and Ryder, B. "What is Marriage-like Like? The Irrelevance of Conjugality", *Canadian Journal of Family Law*, 2001, 18, 269.

Cowan, D. "On Need and Gatekeeping", *Child and Family Law Quarterly*, 2004, 16, 331.

Creighton, P. "Spouse Competence and Compellability", *Criminal Law Review*, 1990, 34.

Cretney, S. "Defining The Limits of State Intervention". In D. Freestone (ed.), *Children and the Law*. (Hull: Hull University Press, 1990)

Cretney, S. "Divorce Reform in England: Humbug and Hypocrisy or a Smooth Transition?". In M. Freeman (ed.), *Divorce: Where Next?* (Aldershot: Dartmouth, 1996)

Cretney, S. *Law, Law Reform and the Family*. (Oxford: Clarendon Press, 1998)

Cretney, S. "Black and White?", *Family Law*, 2001, 31, 3.

Cretney, S. "A Community of Property System Imposed by Judicial Decision", *Family Law*, 2003a, 33, 399.

Cretney, S. *Family Law In The Twentieth Century: A History*. (Oxford: Oxford University Press, 2003b)

Cretney, S. "Royal Marriages: The Law in a Nutshell", *Family Law*, 2005, 35, 317.

Cretney, S. "Royal Weddings, Legality and the Rule of Law", *Family Law*, 2007, 37, 159.

Cretney, A. and Davis, G. "Prosecuting Domestic Assult" *Criminal Law Review*, 1996, 162.

Cretney, S., Masson, J. and Bailey-Harris, R. *Principles of Family Law*. (London: Sweet and Maxwell, 2003)

Crown Prosecution Service *Policy for Prosecuting Cases of Domestic Violence*. (London: CPS, 2005)

Czpanskij, K. "Child Support and Visitation: Rethinking the Connections", *Rutgers Law Review*, 1989, 20, 619.

DH *The Children Act 1989: Guidance and Regulations*. (London: HMSO, 1991)

DH *Adoption and Permanence Taskforce: Second Report*. (London: Department of Health, 2002a)

DH *No Secrets* (London: Department of Health, 2002b)

DH *Working Together to Safeguard Children*. (London: Department of Health, 2006)

DHSS *Child Abuse: Central Register Systems*. (London: DHSS, 1980)

DHSS *Review of Child Care* Law (London: HMSO, 1985)

D'Onofrio, E. "Child Brides, Inegalitarianism and the Fundamentalist Polygamous Family in the United States", *International Journal of Law, Policy and the Family*, 2005, 19, 373.

Davidoff, L *et al.* "Landscape With Figures: Home and Community in English Society". In J. Mitchell and A. Oakley (eds), *The Rights and Wrongs of Women*. (Harmondsworth: Penguin, 1976)

Davis, G. "Informing Policy in the Light of Research Findings", *Family Law*, 2001, 31, 822.

Davis, G. and Roberts, S. "Mediation and the Battle of the Sexes" *Family Law*, 1989, 19, 305.

Davis, G., Bevan, G. and Pearce, J. "Family Mediation—Where Do We Go From Here?", *Family Law*, 2001, 31, 265.

Davis, G., Cretney, S. and Collins, J. *Simple Quarrels*. (Oxford: Clarendon Press, 1994)

Davis, G., Wikeley, N. and Young, R. *Child Support in Action* (Oxford: Hart, 1998)

Deech, R. "The Case Against Legal Recognition of Cohabitation". In J. Eekelaar and S. Katz, *Marriage and Cohabitation In Contemporary Societies*. (Toronto: Butterworths, 1980)

Deech, R. "The Rights of Fathers: Social and Biological Concepts of Parenthood". In J. Eekelaar and P. Sarcevic (eds), *Parenthood in Modern Society*. (Dordrecht: Martinus Nijhoff, 1993)

Deech, R. "Not Just Marriage Breakdown", *Family Law*, 1994, 24, 121.

Deech, R. "Family Law and Genetics", *Modern Law Review*, 1998, 61, 697.

Denfield, D. and Gordon, M. "The Sociology of Mate Swapping". In J.R. Smith and L.G. Smith (eds), *Beyond Monogamy*. (Baltimore, MD: Johns Hopkins University Press, 1974)

Devlin, P. *The Enforcement of Morals*. (Oxford: Clarendon Press, 1965)

Dewar, J. *Law and the Family*. (London: Butterworths, 1992)

Dey, I. and Wasoff, F. "Mixed Messages: Parental Responsibilities, Public Opinion and the Reforms of Family Law", *International Journal of Law, Policy and the Family*, 2006, 26, 225.

Dickens, J. "Assessment and the Control of Social Work: Analysis of Reasons for the Non-Use of the Child Assessment Order" *Journal of Social Welfare and Family Law*, 1993, 15, 88.

Dickens, J. "Being 'The Epitome of Reason': The Challenges for Lawyers and Social Workers in Child Care Proceedings", *International Journal of Law, Policy and the Family*, 2005, 19, 73.

Diduck, A. "A Family By Any Other Name ... or Starbucks Comes to England", *Journal of Law and Society*, 2001, 28, 290.

Diduck, A. *Law's Families*. (London: Butterworths, 2003)

Diduck, A. "Shifting Familiarity", *Current Legal Problems*, 2005, 58, 235.

Diduck, A. *Marriage and Cohabitation: Regulating Intimacy, Affection and Care*. (Aldershot: Ashgate, 2008)

Diduck, A. and Orton, H. "Equality and Support for Spouses", *Modern Law Review*, 1994, 57, 681

Diduck, A. and Kaganas, F. *Family Law, Gender and the State*. (Oxford: Hart, 2006)

Dingwall, R. and Eekelaar, J. *The Protection of Children*. (Oxford: Blackwell, 1983)

Dingwall, R. and Greatbatch, D. "Family Mediators—What Are They Doing? *Family Law*, 2001, 31, 379.

Dnes, A. "Cohabitation and Marriage". In A. Dnes and R. Rowthorn (eds), *The Law and Economics of Marriage and Divorce*. (Cambridge: Cambridge University Press, 2002)

Dobash, R. and Dobash, R. *Violence Against Wives: A Case Against the Patriarchy*. (London: Open Books, 1980)

Dobash, R. and Dobash, R. "Violent Men and Violent Contexts", in *Rethinking Violence against Women*. (Thousand Oaks, CA: Sage, 1988)

Dobash, R. and Dobash, R. *Rethinking Violence against Women*. (Thousand Oaks, CA: Sage Publications, 1998)

Dobash, R. and Dobash, R. "Women's Violence To Men In

Intimate Relationships", *British Journal of Criminology*, 2004, 44, 324.

Dodd, G. "Surrogacy and the Law in Britain: Users' Perspectives". In R. Cook and S.D. Sclater (eds), *Surrogate Motherhood: International Perspectives*. (Oxford: Hart, 2003)

Doggett, M. *Marriage, Wife-Beating and the Law in Victorian England*. (London: Weidenfeld and Nicolson, 1992)

Douglas, G. "The Retreat from *Gillick*", 55 *Modern Law Review*, 1992, 55, 569.

Douglas, G. "Assisted Reproduction and the Welfare of the Child", *Current Legal Problems*, 1993, 46, 53.

Douglas, G. "The Intention to Be a Parent and the Making of Mothers", *Modern Law Review*, 1994, 57, 636.

Douglas, G. *An Introduction To Family Law*. (Oxford: Clarendon Press, 2004)

Douglas, G. *An Introduction to Family Law*. (Oxford: Clarendon Press, 2005)

Douglas, G. and Ferguson, N. "The Role of Grandparents in Divorced Families", 2003, *International Journal of Law, Policy and the Family* 17, 41.

Douglas, G. and Perry, A. "How Parents Cope Financially on Separation and Divorce—Implications for the Future of Ancillary Relief", *Child and Family Law Quarterly*, 2001, 13, 67.

Douglas, G. *et al.* "Children's Perspectives and Experience of the Divorce Process", *Family Law*, 2001, 31, 373.

Douglas, G. *et al. Research into the Operation of Rule 9.5 of the Family Proceedings Rules 1991*. (London: DCA, 2006)

Dunne, G. "Opting into Motherhood: Lesbians Blurring the Boundaries and Transforming the Meaning of Parenthood and Kinship", *Gender and Society*, 2000, 14, 11.

Durrant, J. "Evaluating the Success of Sweden's Corporal Punishment Ban", *Child Abuse and Neglect*, 1999, 23, 435.

Durrant, J. "Legal Reform and Attitudes towards Physical Punishment in Sweden", *International Journal of Children's Rights*, 2003, 11, 147.

Dworkin, R. *Taking Rights Seriously*. (London: Duckworth, 1977)

Eaton, M. "Abuse By Any Other Name: Feminism, Difference and Intralesbian Violence". In M. Fineman and R. Myktiuk (eds), *The Public Nature of Private Violence*. (New York: Routledge, 1994)

Edwards, S.S.M. *Policing Domestic Violence*. (London: Sage,1989)

Edwards, S.S.M. *Sex and Gender in the Legal Process* (London: Blackstone, 1996)

Eekelaar, J. *Family Security and Family Breakdown*. (Harmondsworth: Penguin, 1971)

Eekelaar, J. *Family Law and Social Policy*. (London: Weidenfeld and Nicolson, 1978)

Eekelaar, J. *Family Law and Social Policy*. (London: Weidenfeld and Nicolson, 1984)

Eekelaar, J. "Taxpayers Come First", *The Independent*, 2 November 1990.

Eekelaar, J. "Are Parents Morally Obliged to Care for their Children?", *Oxford Journal of Legal Studies*, 1991a, 11, 51.

Eekelaar, J. "Parental Responsibility: State of Nature or Nature of the State?", *Journal of Social Welfare and Family Law*, 1991b, 37.

Eekelaar, J. *Regulating Divorce*. (Oxford: Clarendon Press, 1991c)

Eekelaar, J. "Should Section 25 Be Reformed?", *Family Law*, 1998, 28, 469.

Eekelaar, J. "Asset Distribution on Divorce—The Durational Element", *Law Quarterly Review*, 2001a, 117, 552.

Eekelaar, J. "Rethinking Parental Responsibility", *Family Law*, 2001b, 31, 426.

Eekelaar, J. "Beyond the Welfare Principle", *Child and Family Law Quarterly*, 2002, 14, 237.

Eekelaar, J. "Asset Distribution on Divorce: Time and Property", *Family Law*, 2003a, 33, 838.

Eekelaar, J. "Corporal Punishment, Parents' Religion, and Children's Rights", *Law Quarterly Review*, 2003b, 119, 370.

Eekelaar, J. "Children Between Cultures", *International Journal of Law, Policy and the Family*, 2004, 18, 178.

Eekelaar, J. "Shared Income After Divorce: A Step Too Far", *Law Quarterly Review*, 2005, 121, 1

Eekelaar, J. and Clive, E. *Custody After Divorce*. (Oxford: SSRC Centre for Socio-Legal Studies, 1977)

Eekelaar, J. and Maclean, M. *Maintenance After Divorce*. (Oxford: Clarendon Press, 1986)

Eekelaar, J. and Maclean, M. *The Parental Obligation*. (Oxford: Hart, 1997)

Ellis, A. "Group Marriage: A Possible Alternative?". In J.R. Smith and L.G. Smith (eds), *Beyond Monogamy*. (Baltimore, MD: Johns Hopkins University Press, 1970)

Ellison, L. "Responding to Victim Withdrawl in Domestic Violence Prosecutions", *Criminal Law Review*, 2002a, 760.

Ellison, L. "Prosecuting Domestic Violence Without Victim Participation, *Modern Law Reivew*, 2002b, 65, 834.

Elster, J. "Solomonic Judgments: Against the Best Interests of the Child", *University of Chicago Law Review*, 1987, 54, 1.

Elston, E., Fuller, J. and Murch, M. "Judicial Hearings of Undefended Divorce Petitions", *Modern Law Review*, 1975, 38, 609.

Ermisch, J. and Francesconi, M. "Patterns of Household and Family Formation" in R. Berthoud and J. Gershuny (eds) *Seven Years in the Lives of British Families* (Colchester: University of Essex, 2000)

Eskridge, W. *The Case For Same-Sex Marriage*. (New York: Free Press, 1996)

Eskridge, W. and Weimer, B. "The AIDS Epidemic in an Economic Perspective", *University of Chicago Law Review*, 1994, 61, 733.

Ettelbrick, P. "Wedlock Alert: A Comment on Lesbian and Gay Family Recognition", *Journal of Law and Policy*, 1996, 5, 107.

Etzioni, A. "A Communitarian Position for Civil Unions". In M.L. Shanley (ed.), *Just Marriage*. (New York: Oxford University Press, 2004)

Faller, K. *Child Sexual Abuse: An Interdisciplinary Manual for Diagnosis, Case Management and Treatment.* (New York: Columbia University Press, 1988)

Farson, R. *Birthrights*. (Harmondsworth: Penguin, 1978)

Ferreira, A. "Family Myth and Homeostasis". In N. Bell and E. Vogel (eds), *A Modern Introduction To The Family*. (New York: Free Press, 1968)

Figes, E. *Patriarchal Attitudes*. (London: Panther, 1972)

Finch, E. *Delays In Public Law Children Act Cases*. (London: DFES, 2004)

Fineman, M. "Dominant Discourse, Professional Language and Legal Change in Child Custody Decision Making", *Harvard Law Review*, 1988, 101, 727.

Fineman, M. *The Autonomy Myth*. (New York: New Press, 2004)

Finer, M. *Report of the Committee on One Parent Families*. (London: HMSO, 1974)

Finkelhor, D. *Child Sexual Abuse*. (New York: Free Press, 1984)

Finlay, H "Farewell to Affinity and the Celebration of Kinship", *University of Tasmania Law Review*, 1976, 5, 10.

Finnis, J. *Natural Law and Natural Rights*. (Oxford: Clarendon Press, 1980)

Finnis, J. "Law, Morality and Sexual Orientation", *Notre Dame Law Review*, 1994, 69, 1049.

Finnis, J. "Is Natural Law Theory Compatible with Limited

Government?". In R. George (ed.), *Natural Law, Liberalism and Morality*. (Oxford: Clarendon Press, 1996)

Fisher, L. "The Unexpected Impact of *White*—Taking Equality' Too Far", *Family Law*, 2002, 32, 108.

Fisher, M. *et al. In and Out of Care*. (London: Batsford, 1986)

Fiss, O. "Against Settlement", *Yale Law Journal*, 1984, 93, 1073.

Flaherty, J., Veit-Wilson, J. and Dornan, P. *Poverty: The Facts*. (London: Child Poverty Action Group 2004)

Flaks, D. *et al.* "Lesbians Choosing Motherhood: A Comparative Study of Lesbians and Heterosexual Parents and Their Children", 31 *Developmental Psychology*, 1995, 31, 220.

Flandrin, J.L. *Families in Former Times: Kinship, Household and Sexuality*. (Cambridge: Cambridge University Press, 1979)

Flekkøy, M.G. *A Voice for Children: Speaking Out as Their Ombudsman* (London: Jessica Kingsley, 1991)

Fletcher, R. *The Family and Marriage in Britain*. (Harmondsworth: Penguin, 1973)

Flugel, J. *The Psychoanalytic Study of The Family*. (London: Woolf, 1926)

Fortin, J. "The HRA's Impact on Litigation Involving Children and their Families", *Child and Family Law Quarterly*, 1999, 11, 237.

Fortin, J. *Children's Rights and the Developing Law*. (London: LexisNexis, 2003)

Fortin, J. "Children's Rights: Are the Courts Now Taking Them More Seriously?", *Kings College Law Journal*, 2004, 15, 253.

Fortin, J. "Children's Rights—Substance or Spin?", *Family Law*, 2006, 36, 759.

Forward, S. and Buck, C. *Betrayal of Innocence: Incest and Its Devastation*. (Harmondsworth: Penguin, 1981)

Foucault, M. *Power/Knowledge* (London: Harvester, 1980)

Fox, R. *Reproduction and Succession: Studies in Law, Anthropology and Society*. (London: Transaction, 1992)

Fox-Harding, L. "The Children Act 1989 in Context: Four Perspectives in Child Care Law and Policy", *Journal of Social Welfare and Family Law*, 1991, 179 and 285.

Fox-Harding, L. *Family, State and Social Policy*. (Basingstoke: Macmillan, 1996)

Frank, R. "Family Law and the Federal Republic of Germany", *International Journal of Law, Policy and the Family*, 1990, 4, 214.

Freeman, M. *The Legal Structure*. (Harlow: Longman, 1974)

Freeman, M. *Cracknell's Law Student's Companion—Family Law* (London: Butterworths, 1976a)

Freeman, M. "Divorce without Legal Aid", *Family Law*, 1976b, 6, 255.

Freeman, M. "The Sexual Abuse of Children", *Family Law*, 1978, 8, 222.

Freeman, M. "Bowlby Rides Again", *Justice of the Peace*, 1979a, 143, 574

Freeman, M. *Violence In The Home: A Socio-Legal Study*. (Aldershot: Gower, 1979b)

Freeman, M. "Violence Against Women: Does the Legal System Provide Solutions or Itself Constitute the Problem?", *British Journal of Law and Society*, 1980, 7, 215.

Freeman, M. *The Rights and Wrongs of Children*. (London: Frances Pinter, 1983)

Freeman, M. "Legal Ideologies, Patriarchal Precedents and Domestic Violence". In M.D.A. Freeman, *State, Law and the Family*. (London: Tavistock, 1984a)

Freeman, M. "Questioning the Delegalization Movement in Family Law: Do We Really Want A Family Court?". In J. Eekelaar and S. Katz (eds), *The Resolution of Family Conflict* (Toronto: Butterworths, 1984b)

Freeman, M. "Doing His Best to Sustain the Sanctity of Marriage". In N. Johnson (ed.), *Marital Violence*. (London: Routledge, Kegan Paul, 1985a)

Freeman, M. "Towards A Critical Theory of Family Law", *Current Legal Problems*, 1985b, 38, 153.

Freeman, M. *Law and Practice of Custodianship*. (London: Sweet and Maxwell, 1986)

Freeman, M. "Taking Children's Rights Seriously", *Children and Society*, 1987, 1.

Freeman, M. "Time To Stop Hitting Our Children", *Childright*, 1988, 51, 5.

Freeman, M. "Cleveland, Butler, Sloss and Beyond—How Are We to React to the Sexual Abuse of Children?" *Current Legal Problems*, 1989a, 42, 85.

Freeman, M. *Family, State and Social Policy*. (Basingstoke: Macmillan, 1989b)

Freeman, M. "Care After 1991". In D. Freestone (ed.), *Children and the Law*. (Hull: Hull University Press, 1990)

Freeman, M. *Children, Their Families and the Law*. (Basingstoke: Macmillan, 1992)

Freeman, M. "The Morality of Cultural Pluralism", *International Journal of Children's Rights*, 1995, 3, 1.

Freeman, M. "Can Children Divorce Their Parents?", In M.

Freeman (ed.) *Divorce: Where Next?* (Aldershot: Dartmouth, 1996a)

Freeman, M. "Children's Education: A Test Case For Best Interests and Autonomy". In R. Davie and D. Galloway (eds), *Listening To Children In Education.* (London: David Fulton, 1996b)

Freeman, M. *The Family Law Act 1996.* (London: Sweet and Maxwell, 1996c)

Freeman, M. "Contracting in the Haven: *Balfour v Balfour* Revisited". In R. Hallson (ed.), *Exploring the Boundaries of Contract.* (Aldershot: Dartmouth, 1996d)

Freeman, M. "Divorce Gospel Style", *Family Law*, 1997a, 27, 413.

Freeman, M. "The Best Interests of The Child? Is *The Best Interests of the Child* in the Best Interests of Children?", *International Journal of Law, Policy and the Family*, 1997b, 11, 360.

Freeman, M. "Children Are Unbeatable", *Children and Society*, 1999, 13, 130.

Freeman, M. "Can We Leave the Best Interests of Very Sick Children to their Parents?". In M. Freeman and A. Lewis (eds), *Law and Medicine.* (Oxford: Oxford University Press, 2000a)

Freeman, M. "The End of the Century of The Child?", *Current Legal Problems*, 2000b, 53, 505.

Freeman, M. "Whose Life is it Anyway?", *Medical Law Review*, 2001, 9, 259.

Freeman, M. "Human Rights, Children's Rights and Judgement", *International Journal of Children's Rights*, 2002, 10, 345.

Freeman, M. "Medically Assisted Reproduction". In A. Grubb (ed.), *Principles of Medical Law.* (Oxford: Oxford University Press, 2004)

Freeman, M. "Rethinking Gillick", *International Journal of Children's Rights*, 2005, 13, 201.

Freeman, M. "Review of Reece, *Divorcing Responsibly*", *Modern Law Review*, 2006a, 69, 120.

Freeman, M. "What's Right With Rights for Children", *International Journal of Law In Context*, 2006b, 2, 89.

Freeman, M. *CRC Commentary: Article 3—The Best Interests of The Child.* (Leiden: Martinus Nijhoff, 2007)

Freeman, M. "Do Children Have the Right to Responsible Parents?". In J. Bridgeman (ed.) *Family, Responsibility and the Law.* (Aldershot: Ashgate, 2008)

Freeman, M. "Janusz Korczak and Children's Rights" *International Journal of Children's Rights*, 2008, 16.

Freeman, M. and Lyon, C. *Cohabitation Without Marriage: An Essay In Law and Social Policy*. (Aldershot: Gower, 1983)

Freidson, E. "Disability As Social Deviance". In M. Sussman (ed.), *Sociology and Rehabilitation*. (New York: American Sociological Association, 1966)

Friedson, E. *The Profession of Medicine*. (New York: Dodd, Mead, 1970)

Fretwell, K. "How to Get a Good Divorce" *New Law Journal*, 2003, 153, 1877

Fretwell-Wilson, R. "Fractured Families, Fragile Children—The Sexual Vulnerability of Girls in the Aftermath of Divorce", *Child and Family Law Quarterly*, 2002, 14, 1.

Freud, A. "Child Observation and Prediction of Development", *Psychoanalytical Study of the Child*, 1958, 13, 97.

Frosh, S. "Issues for Men Working with Sexually Abused Children", *British Journal of Psychotherapy*, 1987, 3, 332.

Geach, H. and Szwed, E. *Providing Civil Justice for Children*. (London: Edward Arnold, 1983)

Geffner, R. and Pagelow, M. "Mediation and Child Custody in Abuse Relationships" *Behavioral Science and the Law*, 1990, 8, 152.

Geis, G. "Rape-in-Marriage: Law and Law Reform in England, the U.S. and Sweden", *Adelaide Law Review*, 1978, 6, 284.

Gelles, R. *The Violent Home*. (Beverly Hills, CA: Sage, 1972)

Gelles, R. "Child Abuse as Psychopathology: A Sociological Critique and Reformulation", *American Journal of Orthopsychiatry*, 1973, 43, 611.

Gelles, R. *Family Violence*. (Beverly Hills, CA: Sage, 1979)

Gelles, R. "Poverty and Violence toward Children", *American Behavioral Scientist*, 1992, 35, 258.

Gerlis, S. "Ancillary Relief—Progress or Decline?", *Family Law*, 2001, 31, 891.

Ghandi, P. and James, J. "Marital Rape and Retrospectivity—The Human Rights Dimensions at Strasbourg", *Child and Family Quarterly*, 1997, 9, 17.

Gil, D. *Violence Against Children*. (Cambridge, MA: Harvard University Press, 1970)

Gil, D. "Unraveling Child Abuse", *American Journal of Orthopsychiatry*, 1975, 45, 346.

Gilchrist, E. and Blissett, J. "Magistrates' Attitudes in Domestic Violence and Sentencing Options", *Harvard Journal*, 2002, 41, 348.

Gillis, J. *For Better or For Worse: British Marriage 1600 to the Present.* (Oxford: Oxford University Press, 1985)

Gilmore, S. "Parental Responsibility and the Unmarried Father— A New Dimension in the Debate", *Child and Family Law Quarterly*, 2003, 15, 21.

Gilmore, S. "The Nature, Scope and Use of The Specific Issue Order" *Child and Family Law Quarterly*, 2004, 16, 367.

Giordano, S. "Gender Atypical Organisation in Children and Adolescents: Ethico-Legal Issues and a Proposal for New Guidelines", *International Journal of Children's Rights*, 2007, 15, forthcoming.

Glaser, D. and Frosh, S. *Child Sexual Abuse.* (London: Macmillan, 1988)

Glass, N. "Sure Start: The Development of an Early Intervention Programme for Young Children in the United Kingdom" *Children and Society*, 1999, 13, 257.

Goldstein, J., Freud, A. and Solnit, A. *Beyond The Best Interests of the Child.* (New York: Free Press, 1973)

Goldstein, J., Freud, A. and Solnit, A. *Before The Best Interests of the Child.* (New York: Free Press, 1979)

Golombok, S. *et al.* "Children in Lesbian and Single Parent Households: Psychosexual and Psychiatric Appraisal", *Journal of Child Psychology and Psychiatry*, 1983, 24, 551.

Gower, L. "*Baxter v Baxter* in Perspective" *Modern Law Review*, 1948, 11, 176.

Graveson, R. and Crane, F.R. (eds) *A Century of Family Law.* (London: Butterworths, 1957)

Grenville, M. "Compulsory School Attendance and Children's Wishes" *Journal of Social Welfare Law*, 1988, 4.

Greven, P. *Spare the Child: The Religious Roots of Punishment.* (New York: Vintage, 1992)

Griffiths, D.L. and Moynihan, F.J. "Multiple Epiphyseal Injuries in Babies", *British Medical Journal*, 1963, 5372, 1558.

Grillo, T. "The Mediation Alternative: Process Dangers for Women", *Yale Law Journal*, 1991, 100, 1545.

Guggenheim, M. *What's Wrong With Children's Rights* (Cambridge, MA: Harvard University Press, 2005)

Guttmacher, M. *Sex Offenses.* (New York: Norton, 1951)

HM Government *Parental Separation: Children's Needs and Parents' Responsibilities.* (London: TSO, 2004)

Hale, M. *Pleas of the Crown.* (1736)

Hamilton, C. *Family, Law and Religion.* (London: Sweet and Maxwell, 1995)

Hamilton, C. "Rights of the Child—A Right to and a Right in Education". In C. Bridge (ed.), *Family Law Towards the Millennium*. (London: Butterworths, 1997)

Hanmer, J. "Violence and the Social Control of Women". In G. Littlejohn *et al.* (eds), *Power and the State*. (London: Croom Helm, 1978)

Hardiker, P. *et al.* "The Social Policy Contents of Prevention in Child Care", *British Journal of Social Work*, 1991, 21, 341.

Harding, J. "A Child Assessment Order: To Be or Not to Be?" *Community Care*, 1989, 758, 6.

Harper, M. and Landells, K. "The Civil Partnership Act 2004 in Force" *Family Law*, 2006, 36, 963.

Harris, J. *An Evaluation of the Use and Effectiveness of the Protection from Harassment Act 1997*. (London: Home Office, 2000)

Harrison, M. "Child Maintenance in Australia: the New Era". In L. Weitzman and M. Maclean (eds), *The Economic Consequences of Divorce*. (Oxford: Clarendon Press, 1991)

Hart, H.L.A. "Social Solidarity and the Enforcement of Moraliy", *University of Chicago Law Review*, 1967, 35, 1-13.

Hart, B.J. "Arrest: What's The Big Deal?", *William & Mary Journal of Women and the Law*, 1997, 3, 207.

Hart, H.L.A. *The Concept of Law* (Oxford: Clarendon Press, 1994).

Haskey, J. "Living Arrangements in Contemporary Britain: Having a Partner who Usually Lives Elsewhere and Living Apart Together", *Population Trends*, 2005, 122, 35.

Haskey, J. and Lewis, J. "Living Apart Together in Britain: Context and Meaning" *International Journal of Law in Context*, 2006, 2, 37.

Hasson, E. "Divorce Law and the Family Law Act 1996", *International Journal of Law, Policy and the Family*, 2003, 17, 338.

Haugaard, J. and Reppucci, N. *The Sexual Abuse of Children* (San Francisco, CA: Jossey Bass, 1988)

Hayes, M. "Cohabitation Clauses' in Financial Provision and Property Adjustment Orders—Law, Policy and Justice", *Law Quarterly Review*, 1994, 110, 124.

Hayes, M. "Reconciling Protection of Children with Justice for Parents in Cases of Alleged Child Abuse", *Legal Studies*, 1997, 17, 1.

Hearn, J. *The Violences of Men: How Men Talk about and How Agencies Respond to Men's Violence To Women*. (London: Sage, 1998)

Henriksson, B. and Ytterburg, H. "Sweden: The Power of the Moral(istic) Left". In D. Kirp and R. Bayer (eds), *AIDS and*

Industralized Democracies: Passions, Politics and Policies. (New York: Rutgers University Press, 1992)

Herek, G. "Myths About Sexual Orientation: A Lawyer's Guide to Social Science Research" *Law and Sexuality*, 1991, 1, 133.

Herring, J. "The Human Rights Act and the Welfare Principle in Family Law—Conflicting or Complimentary?", *Child and Family Law Quarterly*, 1999, 11, 223.

Herring, J. "Parents and Children". In J. Herring (ed.), *Family Law: Issues, Debates, Policy.* (Cullompton: Willan, 2001)

Herring, J. "Connecting Contact". In A. Bainham *et al.* (eds), *Children and Their Families.* (Oxford: Hart, 2003)

Herring, J. *Family Law.* (Harlow: Longman, 2004)

Hester, M. and Radford, L. *Domestic Violence and Child Contact Arrangements in England and Wales.* (Bristol: Policy Press, 1996)

Hester, M. *et al.* "Domestic Violence and Access Arrangements for Children in Denmark and Britain", *Journal of Social Welfare and Family Law*, 1992, 57.

Hester, M., Kelly, L. and Radford, L. (1996) *Women, Violence and Male Power.* (Buckingham: Open University Press, 1992)

Hester, M. et at. *Domestic Violence: Making it Through The Criminal Justice System,* (Sunderland: University of Sunderland Centre for Study of Violence and Abuse, 2003)

Hibbs, M., Barton, C., and Beswick, J. "Why Marry? Perceptions of the Affianced", *Family Law*, 2001, 31, 197

Hill, J. "What Does It Mean To Be a Parent'? The Claims of Biology as the Basis for Parental Rights", *New York University Law Review*, 1991, 66, 353.

Hirsch, D. "Ending Child Poverty", *Poverty*, 2006, 125, 11.

Hirshman, L. and Larson, J. *Hard Bargains: The Politics of Sex.* (New York: Oxford University Press, 1998)

Hobbs, C., Hanks, H. and Wynne, K. *Child Abuse and Neglect.* (London: Churchill and Livingstone, 1999)

Hodson, D. "The New Partner after Divorce", *Family Law*, 1990, 20, 27.

Hodson, D. *et al.* "*Lambert*—Shutting Pandora's Box", *Family Law*, 2003, 33, 37.

Holt, J. *Escape From Childhood.* (Harmondsworth: Penguin, 1975)

Howe, D. and Feast, J. *Adoption: Search and Reunion.* (London: Children's Society, 2000)

Howells, J. *Remember Maria.* (London: Butterworths, 1974)

Hullin, R. "The Leeds Truancy Project", *Justice of The Peace Notes*, 1985, 149, 488.

Humphreys, C. and Harrison, C. "Squaring The Circle—Contact and Domestic Violence", 33 *Family Law*, 2003a, 33, 419.

Humphreys, C. and Harrison, C. "Focusing on Safety—Domestic Violence and the Role of Child Contact Centres", *Child and Family Law Quarterly*, 2003b, 15, 237.

Humphreys, C. and Kaye, M. "Third Party Applications for Protection Orders: Opportunities, Ambiguities and Traps", *Journal of Social Welfare and Family Law*, 1997, 19, 403.

Humphreys, C. and Thiara, R. "Neither Justice Nor Protection: Women's Experience of Post Separation Violence", *Journal of Social Welfare and Family Law*, 2003, 25, 195.

Humphries, J. "Protective Legislation, the Capitalist State and Working Class Men: The Case of the 1842 Mines Regulation Act", *Feminist Review*, 1981, 7, 1.

Jack, G. "The Area and Community Components of Children's Well-Being", 20 *Children and Society*, 2006, 20, 334.

Jackson, B. and Jackson, S. *Childminder*. (Harmondsworth: Penguin, 1981)

Jackson, E. *Regulating Reproduction*. (Oxford, Hart, 2001)

Jackson, E. "Conception and the Irrelevance of the Welfare Principle", *Modern Law Review*, 2002, 65, 176.

Jackson, E. *Medical Law*. (Oxford: Oxford University Press, 2006)

Jacob, H. *Silent Revolution—The Transformation of Divorce Law In the United States*. (Chicago, IL: University of Chicago Press, 1988)

Jacob, H. "The Elusive Shadow of the Law" *Law and Society Review*, 1992, 26, 565.

Jakes, A. *Men Who Batter Women*. (London: Routledge, 1999)

Jasinski, J. and Williams, L. *Partner Violence: A Comprehensive Review of 20 Years of Research*. (Thousand Oaks, CA: Sage, 1998)

Jeffs, T. "Schooling, Education and Children's Rights". In B. Franklin (ed.), *The New Handbook of Children's Rights*. (London: Routledge, 2002)

Jenkins, P. *Moral Panic: Changing Concepts of the Child Monster in Modern America*. (New Haven, CT:Yale University Press. 1998)

Jenkins, P. *Paedophiles and Priests: Anatomy of a Contemporary Crisis*. (Oxford: Oxford University Press, 2001)

Jenks, C. *Childhood*. (London: Routledge, 1996)

Johnson, D. "Cultural and Regional Pluralism in the Drafting of the UN Convention on the Rights of the Child". In M. Freeman and P. Veerman (eds), *The Ideologies of Children's Rights*. (Dordrecht: Martinus Nijhoff, 1992)

Johnson, L.T. and Jordan, M.D. "Christianity". In D.S. Browning,

C. Green and J. Witte (eds), *Sex, Marriage and Family in World Religions*. (New York: Columbia University Press)

Joseph, S. *Loving Every Child*. (Chapel Hill, NC: Algonquin Books, 2007)

Justice, B. and Justice, R. *The Broken Taboo: Sex in the Family*. (London: Peter Owen, 1980)

Kaganas, F. "*B v B* (Occupation Order) and *Chalmers v John*: Occupation Orders under the Family Law Act 1996", *Child and Family Law Quarterly*, 1999, 11, 193.

Kaganas, F. "Domestic Violence, Men's Groups and the Equivalence Argument". In A. Diduck and K. O'Donovan (eds), *Feminist Perspectives on Family Law*. (London: Cavendish, 2006)

Kaganas, F. and Day Sclater, S. "Contact and Domestic Violence—The Winds of Change?", *Family Law*, 2000, 30, 630.

Kaganas, F. and Murray, C. "Law, Women and the Family: The Question of Polygyny in a New South Africa", *Acta Juridica*, 1991, 116.

Kaganas, F. and Piper, C. "Domestic Violence and Divorce Mediation", *Journal of Social Welfare and Family Law*, 1994, 16, 265

Kahan, B. *Growing Up in Care*. (Oxford: Blackwell, 1979)

Kahan, B. *Growing Up in Groups*. (London: HMSO, 1994)

Kahn-Freund, O. "Editorial Foreword". In J. Eekelaar (ed.), *Family Security and Family Breakdown*. (Harmondsworth: Penguin, 1971)

Kandel, R.F. "Which Came First: The Mother or the Egg? A Kinship Solution to Gestational Surrogacy", *Rutgers Law Review*, 1994, 47, 165.

Karst, K. "The Freedom of Intimate Association", *Yale Law Journal* 1980, 89, 624.

Karsten, I. "Capacity to Contract A Polygamous Marriage", *Modern Law Review*, 1973, 36, 291.

Kassel, V. "Polygyny After Sixty". In H. Otto (ed.), *The Family In Search of a Future*. (New York: Appleton-Century-Crofts, 1970)

Keenan, C. *et al.* "Interviewing Allegedly Abused Children With A View To Criminal Prosecution", *Criminal Law Review*, 1999, 863.

Kellmer-Pringle, M. *The Needs of Children* (London: Hutchinson, 1980)

Kelsen, H. *The Pure Theory of Law*. (Berkeley: University of California Press, 1967)

Kempe, C.H. "The Battered Baby Syndrome", *Journal of the American Medical Association*, 1962, 181, 17-24

Kempe, C.H. and Kempe, R. *The Common Secret: Sexual Abuse of Children and Adolescents*. (New York: W.H. Freeman, 1984)

Kennedy, I. *Treat Me Right*. (Oxford: Clarendon Press, 1988)

Kennedy, R. "Assessing Life After Re G", *Family Law*, 2006, 36, 379.

Key, E. *The Century of The Child*. (New York: Putnam's, 1909)

King, M. and Piper, C. *How The Law Thinks About Children*. (Aldershot: Arena, 1995)

King, N. , Butt, T. and Green, L. "Spanking and the Corporal Punishment of Children: The Sexual Story", *International Journal of Children's Rights*, 2003, 11, 199

Kingdom, E. "Cohabitation Contracts and the Democratization of Personal Relations", *Feminist Legal Studies*, 2000, 8, 5.

Kitch, A. "Conditioning Child Support Payments on Visitation Access: A Proposal", 5 *International Journal of Law and the Family*, 1991, 5, 318.

Klein, D. "Can This Marriage be Saved? Battery and Sheltering" *Crime and Social Justice*, 1979, 12, 19.

Krause, H. *Family Law*. (St Paul, MN: West, 1990)

Kurdek, L."Relationship Outcomes and their Predictors: Longitudinal Evidence from Heterosexual Married, Gay Cohabiting, and Lesbian Cohabiting Couples", *Journal of Marriage and the Family*, 1998, 60, 553.

Laming, Lord *The Victoria Climbié Inquiry*, Cm 5730. (London: Stationery Office, 2003)

Land, H."The Family Wage", *Feminist Review*, 1980, 6, 55.

Landau, B. Bartoletti, M. and Mesbur, R. *Family Mediation Handbook*, (Toronto: Butterworths, 1987)

Lasch, C. *Haven In a Heartless World*. (New York: Basic Books, 1977)

Laslett, P., Oosterveen, K. and Smith, R. *Bastardy and its Comparative History* (London: Edward Arnold, 1980)

Latham, M. *Regulating Reproduction*. (Manchester: Manchester University Press, 2002)

Lawson, A. *Adultery: An Analysis of Love and Betrayal*. (Oxford, Blackwell, 1988)

Leach, E. "Ourselves and Others", *The Listener* 30 October 1967, 695.

Lee, B. *Divorce Law Reform in England*. (London: Owen, 1974)

Lestor, J. "A Minister for Children". In B. Franklin (ed.), *The Handbook of Children's Rights*. (London: Routledge, 1995)

Levin, I. "Living Apart Together: A New Family Form", *Current Sociology*, 2004, 52.

Lewis, J. *The Politics of Motherhood: Child and Maternal Welfare in England 1900–1939*. (London: Croom Helm, 1980).

Lewis, J. "Debates and Issues Regarding Marriage and Cohabitation in the British and American Literature", *International Journal of Law, Policy and the Family*, 2001, 15, 169.

Lewis, J. "Adoption: The Nature of Policy Shifts in England and Wales 1972–2002", *International Journal of Law, Policy and the Family*, 2004, 18, 235.

Lewis, J. and Welsh, E. "Fathering Practices in Twenty-Six Intact Families and the Implications for Child Contact", *International Journal of Law in Context*, 2006, 1, 81.

Liddington, J. and Norris, J. *One Hand Tied Behind Us*. (London: Virago, 1978)

Lifton, B.J. *The King of Children*. (London: Chatto and Windus, 1988)

Lim, H. "Messages from a Rarely Visited Island: Duress and the Lack of Consent in Marriage", *Feminist Legal Studies*, 1996, 4, 195.

Lindsay, M. "Complaints Procedures and their Limitations in the Light of the Pindown' Inquiry", *Journal of Social Welfare and Family Law*, 1991, 432.

Lister, R. *As Man and Wife*. (London: Child Poverty Action Group, 1970)

Lowe, N. "English Adoption Law". In S. Katz, J.Eekelaar and M. Maclean (eds), *Cross Currents*. (Oxford: Oxford University Press, 2000)

Lowe, N. and Douglas, G. *Bromley's Family Law*. (Oxford: Oxford University Press, 2006)

Lowe, N. and Juss, S. "Medical Treatment—Pragmatism and the Search for Principle", 56 *Modern Law Review*, 1993, 56, 865.

Lowe, N. and Murch, M. "Children's Participation in the Family Justice System—Translating Principles into Practice", *Child and Family Law Quarterly*, 2001, 13, 137.

Lupton, D. and Barclay, L. *Constructing Fatherhood*. (London: Sage, 1997)

Lyon, C. "Children's Participation in Private Law Proceedings". In M. Thorpe and E. Clarke (eds), *No Fault or Flaw: The Future of the Family Law Act 1996*. (Bristol: Family Law, 2000)

Macdonald, S. *All Equal Under the Act?* (London: National Institute of Social Work, 1991)

MacKinnon, C. *Feminism Unmodified: Disccourses on Life and Law.* (Cambridge, MA: Harvard University Press, 1987)

Maclean, M. and Eekelaar, J. *The Parental Obligation: A Study of Parenthood across Households* (Oxford: Hart, 1997)

Maidment, S."Some Legal Problems Arising out of the Reporting of Child Abuse", *Current Legal Problems*, 1978, 31, 149.

Margulies, P. "Representation of Domestic Violence Survivors as a New Paradigm of Poverty Law: In Search of Access, Connection and Voice", *George Washington Law Review*, 1995, 63, 1071.

Marshall, D. "The Construction of Children as an Object of International Relations: The Declaration of Children's Rights and the Child Welfare Committee of the League of Nations", *International Journal of Children's Rights*, 1999, 7, 103.

Mason, M.A. *From Father's Property to Children's Rights.* (New York: Columbia University Press, 1994)

Masson, J. "Social Engineering in the House of the Lords: *Re M*", *Journal of Child Law*, 1994, 6, 17.

Masson, J. "Emergency Intervention To Protect Children: Using and Avoiding Legal Controls", *Child and Family Law Quarterly*, 2005, 17, 75.

Masson, J. and Humphreys, C. "Facilitating and Enforcing Contact: the Bill and the Ten Per Cent", *Family Law*, 2005, 35, 548.

Masson, J. and Morton, S. "The Use of Wardship by Local Authorities", *Modern Law Review*, 1989, 52, 762.

McGrath, C. "The Crisis of Domestic Order", *Socialist Review*, 1979, 43, 11.

McGregor, O. *Divorce in England.* (London: Heinemann, 1957)

McIntosh, M. "The Welfare State and the Needs of the Dependent Family". In S. Burman (ed.). *Fit Work for Women.* (London: Croom Helm, 1978)

McLennan, D. "Contract Marriage—The Way Forward or Dead End?", *Journal of Law and Society*, 1996, 23, 234.

McMurty, J. "Monogamy: A Critique", *The Monist*, 1978, 56, 587.

Mead, M. "Some Anthropological Considerations Concerning Natural Law", *Natural Law Forum*, 1961, 6, 61.

Mead, M. *The Mountain Arapesh.* (New York: Muller, 1972)

Menefee, S. *Wives for Sale.* (Oxford: Basil Blackwell, 1981)

Menkel-Meadow, C. "Toward Another View of Legal Negotiation: The Structure of Problem Solving", *UCLA Law Review*, 1984, 361, 754.

Meredith, P. "Children's Rights and Education". In J. Fionda (ed.), *Legal Concepts of Childhood*. (Oxford: Hart, 2001)

Meyer, C.L. *Politics and the Reproductive Rights of Women* (New York: New York University Press, 1997)

Meyer, P. "The Exploitation of the American Growing Class". In D. Gottlieb (ed.), *Children's Liberation*. (Englewood Cliffs, NJ: Prentice Hall, 1973).

Middleton, S., Ashworth, K. and Braithwaite, I.*Small Fortunes*. (York: Joseph Rowntree Foundation, 1997)

Mill, J.S. *On Liberty*. (1859)

Millham, S. *et al. Lost In Care*. (Aldershot: Gower, 1986)

Mills, L. *Insult to Injury: Rethinking Our Responses to Intimate Abuse*. (Princeton, NJ: Princeton University Press, 2003)

Mirrlees-Black, C. *Domestic Violence*. (London: Home Office, 1999)

Mirrlees-Black, C. and Bayron, C. *Domestic Violence: Findings from a New British Crime Survey Self-Completion Questionnaire*. (London: Home Office, 2000)

Mitchell, J. "Shared Care—Shared Benefits?", *Family Law*, 2003, 33, 321.

Mnookin. R. "Child-Custody Adjudication: Judicial Functions in the Face of Indeterminacy" *Law and Contemporary Problems*, 1975, 39, 226.

Mnookin, R. "Bargaining in the Shadow of the Law: The Case of Divorce", *Current Legal Problems*, 1979, 32, 65.

Mnookin, R. and Kornhauser, L. "Bargaining in the Shadow of the Law: The Case of Divorce", *Yale Law Journal*, 1979. 88, 950.

Monk, D. "New Guidance/Old Problems: Recent Developments in Sex Education", *Journal of Social Welfare and Family Law*, 2001, 23, 271.

Moor, P. and Le Grice, V. "Periodical Payment Orders following Miller and McFarlane", *Family Law*, 2006, 36, 655.

Morgan, P. *Farewell To The Family: Public Policy and Family Breakdown in Britain and the USA*. (London: IEA Health and Welfare Unit, 1995)

Morgan, P. *Marriage-Lite*. (London: Institute for Study of Civil Society, 2000)

Morley, R. and Mullender, A. "Hype or Hope? The Importance of Pro-Arrest Policies and Batterers' Programmes from North America to Britain as Key Measures to Preventing Violence to Women in the Home", *International Journal of Law and the Family*, 1992, 6, 265.

Mullender, A. *Open Adoption—The Philosophy and the Practice.* (London: BAAF, 1991)

Murphy, M. "The Evolution of Cohabitation in Britain", *Population Studies*, 2000, 54, 43

National Audit Office *Report on Accounts 1999–2000.* (London: National Audit Office, 2000)

Neale, B. and Smart, C. "Good and Bad Lawyers? Struggling in the Shadow of the New Law?", *Journal of Social Welfare and Family Law*, 1997, 19, 377.

Nelson, S *Incest: Fact and Myth.* (Edinburgh: Stramullion, 1987)

Neubeck, G. "Polyandry and Polygyny: Viable Today?". In H. Otto (ed.), *Search of a Future.* (New York: Appleton-Century-Crofts, 1970)

Newell, P. *The Last Resort.* (Harmondsworth: Penguin, 1972)

Newell, P. *Children Are People Too.* (London: Bedford Square Press, 1989)

Newell, P. *Taking Children Seriously.* (London: Calouste Gulbenkian Foundation, 2000)

Nowak, M. *Article 6: The Right to Life, Survival and Development.* (Leiden: Martinus Nijhoff, 2005)

Nussbaum, M. *Sex and Shame.* (Cambridge, MA: Harvard University Press, 2004)

O'Donovan, K. "Wife Sale and Desertion as Alternatives to Judicial Marriage Dissolution". In J. Eekelaar and S. Katz (eds), *The Resolution of Family Conflict.* (Toronto: Butterworths, 1984)

O'Donovan, K. "Marriage: A Sacred or Profane Love Machine?" *Feminist Legal Studies*, 1993, 1, 75.

O'Donovan, K. "Constructions of Maternity and Motherhood in Stories of Lost Children". In J. Bridgeman and D. Monk (eds), *Feminist Perspectives on Child Law.* (London: Cavendish, 2000)

O'Donovan, K. "'Real' Mothers for Abandoned Children", *Law and Society Review*, 2002, 36, 347.

O'Donovan, K. and Marshall, J. "After Birth: Decisions about Becoming a Mother". In A. Diduck and K. O'Donovan (eds), *Feminist Perspectives on Family Law.* (London: Cavendish, 2006)

O'Neill, G. and O'Neill, N. "Open Marriage: A Conceptual Framework". In J.R. Smith and L.G. Smith (eds), *Beyond Monogamy.* (Baltimore, MD: Johns Hopkins University Press, 1974)

Oakley, A. *Housewife.* (Harmondsworth: Penguin, 1974)

Oldham, J.T. and Melli, M. *Child Support: The Next Frontier.* (Ann Arbor, University of Michigan Press, 2000)

Oliver, J. "Successive Generations of Child Maltreatment" *British Journal of Psychiatry* 1985, 147, 484.

Olldendorf, R. "The Rights of Adolescents". In P. Adams *et al.* (eds), *Children's Rights.* (London: Granada, 1972)

Olsen, F. "The Family and the Market: A Study of Ideology and Legal Reform" *Harvard Law Review*, 1985, 96, 1497.

Outhwaite, R.B. *Clandestine Marriage in England 1500–1850.* (London: Continuum, 1995)

Overall, C. "Frozen Embryos and 'Father's Rights': Parenthood and Decision-Making in the Cryopreservation of Embryos". In J. Callahan (ed.), *Reproduction, Ethics and the Law: Feminist Responses.* (Bloomington: Indiana University Press, 1995)

Packman, J. *et al. Who Needs Care.* (Oxford: Blackwell, 1986)

Page, R. and Clark, G. *Who Cares?* (London: National Children's Bureau, 1977)

Paradine, K. and Wilkinson, J. *Research and Literature Review: Protection and Accountability: The Reporting, Investigation and Prosecution of Domestic Violence Cases.* (London: HMCPSI, 2004)

Parker, S. *Caring for Separated Children.* (London: Macmillan, 1980)

Parker, S. "The Marriage Act 1753: A Case Study In Family-Law Making", *International Journal of Law and the Family*, 1987, 1, 133.

Parker, S. *Informal Marriage, Cohabitation and the Law 1750–1989.* (Basingstoke: Macmillan, 1990)

Parkinson, L. "Child-Inclusive Family Mediation " , *Family Law*, 2006, 36, 483.

Parnas, R. "The Police Response to the Domestic Disturbance", *Wisconsin Law Review*, 1967, 914.

Parsons, T. "The American Family". In T. Parsons and R. Bales (eds), *Family, Socialization and Interaction Process.* (New York: Free Press, 1955)

Parton, N. "The Natural History of Child Abuse: A Study in Social Problem Definition" *British Journal of Social Work*, 1970, 9, 431.

Parton, N. *The Politics of Child Abuse.* (Basingstoke: Macmillan, 1985)

Parton, N. *Safeguarding Childhood.* (Basingstoke: Palgrave, 2006)

Patterson, C. "Children of Lesbian and Gay Parents: Summary of Research Findings". In A. Sullivan (ed.), *Same-Sex Marriage Pro and Con.* (New York: Vintage Books, 1997)

Pawlowski, M. "Property Rights of Home-Sharers: Recent

Legislation in Australia and New Zealand", *Nottingham Law Journal*, 2001, 10, 20.

Pearl, D. "Capacity for Polygamy", *Cambridge Law Journal*, 1973, 32, 43.

Peled, E. "Secondary' Victims No More: Refocusing Intervention with Children". In J.L. Edelson and Z.C. Eisikovits (eds), *Future Interventions with Battered Women and Their Families*. (Thousand Oaks, CA: Sage, 1996)

Pelton, L. "Child Abuse and Neglect: The Myth of Classlessness", *American Journal of Orthopsychiatry*, 1978, 48, 608

Perry, A. "Safety First? Contact and Family Violence In New Zealand", *Child and Family Law Quarterly*, 2006, 18, 1.

Perry, P. *et al. How Parents Cope Financially on Marriage Breakdown.* (London: Joseph Rowntree, 2000)

Peters, P.G., *How Safe Is Safe Enough?* (New York: Oxford University Press, 2004)

Pfohl, S. "The Discovery of Child Abuse", *Social Problems*, 1977, 24, 310.

Phillips, B. and Alderson, P. "Before Anti-Smacking': Challenging and Violence and Coercion in Parent-Child Relations, *International Journal of Children's Rights*, 2003, 11, 175.

Phillips, R. *Putting Asunder: A History of Divorce in Western Society.* (Cambridge: Cambridge University Press, 1988)

Pickford, R. "Unmarried fathers and the Law". In A. Bainham, S. Day-Sclater and M. Richards (eds), *What Is A Parent?* (Oxford: Hart, 1999)

Pinchbeck, I. and Hewitt, M. *Children In English Society.* (London: Routledge, Kegan Paul, 1973)

Piper, C, "Norms and Negotiation in Mediation and Divorce" in M. Freeman (ed.) *Divorce: Where Next?* (Aldershot: Dartmouth, 1996)

Pirrie, J. (2006) "Collaborative Divorce" *New Law Journal*, 2006, 156, 898

Pizzey, E. *Scream Quietly or the Neighbours Will Hear.* (Harmondsworth: Penguin, 1974)

Pizzey, E. and Shapiro, J. *Prone to Violence.* (London: Hamlyn, 1982)

Platt, A. *The Child Savers.* (Chicago, IL: University of Chicago Press, 1969)

Posner, R. *Sex and Reason.* (Cambridge, MA: Harvard University Press, 1992)

Poulter, S. "Polygamy—New Law Commission Proposals", *Family Law*, 1983, 13, 72.

Priest, J. and Whybrow, J. *Custody Law in Practice in the Divorce and Domestic Courts*. (London: HMSO, 1986)

Probert, R. "When We Are Married? Void, Non-Existent and Presumed Marriages", *Legal Studies*, 2002, 22, 398.

Probert, R. "How Would *Corbett v Corbett* be Decided Today", *Family Law*, 2005a, 35, 382.

Probert, R. "The Wedding of the Prince of Wales: Royal Privileges and Human Rights", *Child and Family Law Quarterly*, 2005b, 17, 363.

Radbill, S.Z. "A History of Child Abuse and Infanticide". In R. Heifer and C. Kempe (eds), *The Battered Child* (Chicago: University of Chicago Press, 1974)

Ramey, J.W. "Emerging Patterns of Innovative Behavior in Marriage". In J.R. Smith and L.G. Smith (eds), *Beyond Monogamy*. (Baltimore, MD: Johns Hopkins University Press, 1974)

Ramey, J.W. *Intimate Friendships*. (Englewood Cliffs, NJ: Prentice Hall, 1976)

Rasmusen, R. and Stake, J.E. "Lifting the Veil of Ignorance: Personalizing the Marriage Contract", *Indiana Law Journal*, 1998, 73, 452.

Raz, J. *Ethics In the Public Domain*. (Oxford: Clarendon Press, 1986)

Reece, H. "The Paramountcy Principle: Consensus or Construct?", *Current Legal Problems*, 1996, 46, 267.

Reece, H. *Divorcing Responsibly*. (Oxford: Hart, 2003)

Reece, H. "The End of Domestic Violence", *Modern Law Review*, 2006, 69, 770.

Regan, M. *Family Law and the Pursuit of Intimacy*. (New York: New York University Press, 1993)

Regan, M. *Alone Together: Law and the Meaning of Marriage*. (New York: Oxford University Press, 1999)

Richardson, N. "The New Zealand Child Support Act", *Child and Family Law Quarterly*, 1995, 7, 40.

Roberts, S. "Three Models of Family Mediation". In J. Eekelaar and R. Dingwall (eds) *Divorce, Mediation and the Legal Process*. (Oxford: Clarendon Press, 1988)

Roman, M. and Haddad, W. (1979) *The Disposable Parent: The Case for Joint Custody* (New York: Penguin).

Rose, W., Gray, J. and McAuley, C. "Child Welfare in the UK: Legislation, Policy and Practice". In C. McAuley, P. Pecora and W. Rose (eds), *Enhancing the Well-Being of Children and Families through Effective Interventions*. (London: Jessica Kingsley, 2006)

Rosenbaum, M. and Newell, P. *Taking Children Seriously*. (London: Gulbenkian Foundation, 1991)

Rosenfeld A.A. and Newberger, E. "Compassion versus Control: Conceptual and Practical Pitfalls in the Broadened Definition of Child Abuse", *Journal of American Medical Association*, 1977, 237, 2086.

Rubington, E. and Weinberg, M. *Deviance: The Interactionist Perspective*. (London: Macmillan, 1981)

Rubinstein, D. *Before the Suffragettes: Women's Emancipation in the 1890s*. (Brighton: Harvester, 1986)

Russell, D.E.H. *Sexual Exploitation: Rape, Child Sexual Abuse, Sexual Harassment*. (Beverley Hills: Sage Publications, 1984)

Russell, D.E.H. *The Secret Trauma: Incest in the Lives of Girls and Women*. (New York: Basic Books, 1986)

Ryan, W. *Blaming the Victim*. (New York: Vintage Books, 1976)

Sachdev, P. *Adoption, Reunion and After*. (Washington: Child Welfare, 1992)

Sack, E. "Battered Women and the State: The Struggle for the Future of Domestic Violence Policy", *Wisconsin Law Review*, 2004, 1658.

Saunders, H. *Making Contact Worse?* (Bristol: Women's Aid Federation of England, 2001)

Saunders, H. and Barron, J. (2003) *Failure to Protect? Domestic Violence and the Experiences of Abused Women and Children in the Family Courts* (Bristol: Women's Aid Federation of England).

Savas, D. "Parental Participation in Case Conferences", *Child and Family Law Quarterly*, 1996, 8, 57.

Sawyer, C. "The Competence of Children to Participate in Family Proceedings", *Child and Family Law Quarterly*, 1995, 7, 180.

Schaffer, R. *Making Decisions about Children: Psychological Questions and Answers*. (Oxford: Blackwell, 1990)

Scheff, T. "Decision Rules, Types of Error, and their Consequences in Medical Diagnosis", *Behavioral Science*, 1963, 8, 97.

Schneider, C. "Moral Discourse and the Transformation of American Family Law", *Michigan Law Review*, 1995, 83, 1803.

Schneider, E. *Battered Women and Feminist Law Making*. (New Haven, CT: Yale University Press, 2000)

Schuz, R. "When Is a Polygamous Marriage Not a Polygamous Marriage?", *Modern Law Review*, 1983, 46, 653.

Scott, E. and Scott, R. "Parents as Fiduciaries", *Virginia Law Review*, 1995, 81, 2401.

Shanley, M.L. *Just Marriage*. (New York: Oxford University Press, 2004)

Sheldon, S. *Beyond Control: Medical Power and Abortion Law*. (London: Pluto, 1997)

Sherman, L. *et al. Policing Domestic Violence: Experiments and Dilemmas*. (New York: Free Press, 1992)

Sherman, L.W. and Berk, R.A. "The Specific Deterrent Effects of Arrest for Domestic Assault" *American Sociological Review*, 1984, 49, 261.

Siegel, R. "The Rule of Love': Wife Beating as Prerogative and Privacy", *Yale Law Journal*, 1996, 105, 2117.

Sinclair, I. and Gibbs, I. *Children's Homes: A Study In Diversity*. (Chichester: Wiley, 1998)

Skolnick, A. *The Intimate Environment: Exploring Marriage and the Family*. (Boston, MA: Little Brown, 1973)

Smart, C. *The Ties That Bind*. (London: Routledge, 1984)

Smart, C. "'There Is, of Course, the Distinction Dictated by Nature': Law and the Problem of Paternity". In M. Stanworth (ed.) *Reproductive Technologies: Gender, Motherhood and Medicine*. (Cambridge: Polity, 1987)

Smart, C. *Feminism and the Power of Law*. (London: Routledge, 1989)

Smart, C. "A History of Ambivalence and Conflict in the Discursive Construction of the Child Victim' of Sexual Abuse", *Social and Legal Studies*, 1999, 8, 391.

Smart, C. "Reconsidering the Recent History of Child Sexual Abuse", *Journal of Social Policy*, 2000, 29, 55.

Smart, C. and May, V. "Why Can't They Agree? The Underlying Complexity of Contact and Residence Disputes", *Journal of Social Welfare and Family Law*, 2004, 26, 347.

Smart, C. and Neale, B. *Family Fragments?* (Cambridge: Polity Press, 1999)

Smart, C. and Smart, B. *Women, Sexuality and Social Control*. (London: Routledge, Kegan Paul, 1978)

Smart, C. Neale, B. and Wade, A. *The Changing Experience of Childhood*. (Cambridge: Polity Press, 2001)

Smith, C. and Logan, J. "Adoptive Parenthood as a 'Legal Fiction'—Its Consequences for Direct Post-Adoption Contact", *Child and Family Law Quarterly*, 2002, 14, 281.

Smith, J.V. and Smith, L.G. *Beyond Monogamy*. (Baltimore, MD: Johns Hopkins University Press, 1974)

Smith, R. "'Hands-Off Parenting': Towards a Reform of the

Defence of Reasonable Chastisement in the UK", *Child and Family Law Quarterly*, 2004, 16, 261.

Snare, A. and Stang-Dahl, T. "The Coercion of Privacy: A Feminist Perspective". In C. Smart and B. Smart (eds), *Women, Sexuality and Social Control*. (London: Routledge, Kegan Paul, 1978)

Sokoloff, N.J. and Dupont, I. "Domestic Violence at the Intersections of Race, Class and Gender", *Violence Against Women*, 2005, 11, 38.

Sonder, T. "Incest Crimes in Sweden and Their Causes", *Acta Psychologica and Neurologica*, 1936, 2, 379.

Spencer, J. and Flin, R. *The Evidence of Children*. (London: Blackstone, 1993)

Spencer, J. "Evidence In Child Abuse Cases—Too High a Price for Far Too High a Standard", *Journal of Child Law*, 1994, 6, 160.

Stalford, H. "Concepts of Family under EU Law—Lessons from the ECHR", *International Journal of Law, Policy and the Family*, 2002, 16, 410.

Stark, E. and Flitcraft, A. *Women at Risk: Domestic Violence and Women's Health*. (London: Sage, 1996)

Steele, B. and Pollock, C. "A Psychiatric Study of Parents Who Abuse Infants and Small Children". In R. Helfer and C. Kempe (eds), *The Battered Child*. (Chicago, IL: University of Chicago Press, 1974)

Stein, M. (1988) "Children of the State", *Social Work Today*, 1988, 10(28), 26.

Steinmetz, S. and Straus, M. *Violence in The Family*. (New York, Dodd, Mead, 1974)

Stoll, C. "Images of Man and Social Control", *Social Forces*, 1968, 47, 119.

Stone, L. *The Family, Sex and Marriage in England 1500–1800*. (London: Weidenfeld and Nicolson, 1977)

Stone, L. *Road to Divorce* (Oxford: Oxford University Press, 1990)

Stone, L. *Uncertain Unions: Marriage in England 1660–1753*. (Oxford: Oxford University Press, 1992)

Stone, L. *Broken Lives: Separation and Divorce in England 1660-1857* (Oxford: Oxford University Press, 1993)

Straus, M. *Beating The Devil Out of Them*. (New York: Lexington, 1994)

Straus, M. *et al*. *Behind Closed Doors—Violence in the American Family*. (Garden City, NY: Anchor, 1980)

Stychin, C. "Family Friendly? Rights, Responsibilities and

Relationship Recognition". In A. Diduck and K. O'Donovan (eds), *Feminist Perspectives on Family Law*. (London: Cavendish, 2006)

Sullivan, A. *Virtually Normal: An Argument About Homosexuality*. (New York: Alfred A. Knopf, 1995)

Sullivan, A. *Same-Sex Marriage Pro and Con*. (New York: Vintage Books, 1997)

Symes, P. "Indissolubility and the Clean Break", *Modern Law Review*, 1985, 48, 44.

Tatchell, P. "Civil Partnerships Are Divorced from Reality", *Guardian*, December 19, 2005.

Temkin, J. *Rape and the Legal Process*. (London: Sweet and Maxwell, 1987)

Théry, I. "The Interest of The Child' and the Regulation of the Post-Divorce Family". In C. Smart and S. Sevenhuijsen (eds), *Child Custody and the Politics of Gender*. (London: Routledge, 1989)

Thompson, E.P. *Whigs and Hunters*. (Harmondsworth: Penguin, 1975)

Thompson, R.A. "Developmental Research and Legal Policy: Toward a Two Way Street". In D. Cicchetti and S.L. Toth (eds), *Child Abuse, Child Development and Social Policy*. (Norwood, NJ: Ablex, 1993)

Tiffin, S. *In Whose Best Interest? Child Welfare Reform in the Progressive Era*. (Westport, CT: Greenwood, 1982)

Tittle, P. *Should Parents Be Licensed?* (Amherst, NY: Prometheus Books, 2004)

Tracy, K. *The Secret History of Polygamy*. (Naperville, IL: Sourcebooks, 2002)

Trinder, L., Beek, M. and Connolly, J. *Making Contact: How Parents and Children Negotiate and Experience Contact After Divorce*. (York: Joseph Rowntree, 2002)

Triseliotis, J. *In Search of Origins*. (London: Routledge, 1973)

Trombley, S. *The Right To Reproduce*. (London: Weidenfeld and Nicolson, 1988)

Vallentyne, P. "Equality and the Duties of Procreators" in D. Archard and C. Macleod, *The Moral and Political Status of Children* (Oxford: Oxford University Press, 2002)

Van Bueren, G. *The International Law on the Rights of the Child*. (Dordrecht: Martinus Nijhoff, 1995)

Varni, C. "An Exploratory Study of Spouse Swapping". In J.R. Smith and L.G. Smith (eds), *Beyond Monogamy*. (Baltimore, MD: Johns Hopkins University Press, 1974)

Veerman, P. *The Rights of The Child and the Changing Image of Childhood*. (Dordrecht: Martinus Nijhoff, 1992)

Wade, J. "Capacity to Marry: Choice of Law Rules and Polygamous Marriages", *International and Comparative Law Quarterly*, 1973, 223, 571.

Walby, S. and Allen, J. *Domestic Violence, Sexual Assault and Stalking*. (London: Home Office, 2004)

Walker, J. "FAInS—A New Approach for Family Lawyers?", *Family Law*, 2004, 34, 436.

Walker, J. and McCarthy, P. "Picking up the Pieces", *Family Law*, 2004, 34, 580.

Walker, J. *et al*. *Information Meetings and Associated Provisions within the Family Law Act 1996: Summary of Final Evaluation Report*. (London: TSO, Lord Chancellor's Department, 2001)

Wallbank, J. "Clause 106 of The Adoption and Children Bill: Legislation for the 'Good' Father?", 22 *Legal Studies*, 2002, 22, 276.

Wallerstein, J. and Kelly, J. *Surviving The Breakup*. (New York: Basic Books, 1980)

Walshok, M.L. "The Emergence of Middle-Class Deviant Subcultures: The Case of Swingers". In J.R. Smith and L.G. Smith (eds), *Beyond Monogamy*. (Baltimore, MD: John Hopkins University Press, 1974)

Ward, C. *The Child in the City*. (New York: Pantheon, 1978)

Wattenberg, E. "In a Different Light: A Feminist Perspective on the Role of Mothers in Father–Daughter Incest", *Child Welfare*, 1985, 64, 203.

Wax, A. "Bargaining in the Shadow of the Market: Is There a Future for Egalitarian Marriage?", *Virginia Law Review*, 1989, 84, 509.

Wedge, P. and Prosser, H. *Born To Fail?* (London: Arrow Books, 1973)

Weir, A. "Battered Women: Some Perspectives and Problems". In M. Mayo (ed.), *Women In The Community*. (London: Routledge, Kegan Paul, 1977)

Weitzman, L. *The Divorce Revolution*. (New York: Free Press, 1985)

Weitzman, L. "The Divorce Revolution and the Illusion of Equality: A View From the United States". In M. Freeman (ed.) *Essays in Family Law 1985*, (London: Stevens, 1986)

Weyland, I. (1997) "The Blood Tie: Raised to the Status of a Presumption", *Journal of Social Welfare and Family Law*, 1977, 19, 445.

White, R. "Assessing Children's Needs" *New Law Journal*, 1991, 141, 433

Wiggin, K.D. *Children's Rights*. (New York: Houghton Mifflin, 1892)

Wikeley, N. "A Duty But Not a Right: Child Support after *R. (Kehoe) v Secretary of State for Work and Pensions*", *Child and Family Law Quarterly*, 2006, 18, 97.

Willenbacher, B. "Legal Transfer of French Traditions? German and Austrian Initiatives to Introduce Anonymous Birth", 18 *International Journal of Law, Policy and the Family*, 2004, 18, 344.

Williams, C. and Jordan, H. *The Children Act 1989 Complaints Procedure: A Study of 6 Local Authority Areas*. (Sheffield: University of Sheffield, 1996)

Wilson, A. "Should We Have a Child Assessment Order? The Case for", *Childright*, 1989, 55, 12

Wilson, E. *What Is To Be Done About Violence against Women?* (Harmondsworth: Penguin, 1983)

Wilson, G. "*Sutton* in Practice", *Family Law*, 2004, 34, 202.

Wolak, J. and Finkelhor, D. "Children Exposed to Partner Violence". In J. Jasinski and L. Williams (eds), *Partner Violence: A Comprehensive Review of 20 Years of Research*. (Thousand Oaks, CA: Sage, 1998)

Wolkind, S. "Emotional Signs", *Journal of Social Welfare Law*, 1988, 82.

Wright, W.K. "The Tide in Favour of Equality: Same-Sex Marriage in Canada and England and Wales", *International Journal of Law, Policy and the Family*, 2006, 20, 249.

Yllo, K. and Bograd, M. *Feminist Perspectives on Wife Abuse*. (Thousand Oaks, CA: Sage)

Zaretsky, E. *Capitalism, the Family and Personal Life*. (New York: Harper Colophon, 1976)

Zedner, L. "Preventive Justice or Pre Punishment", *Current Legal Problems*, 2007, 60, forthcoming.

Zigler, E. "Controlling Child Abuse: Do We Have the Knowledge and/or the Will?". In G. Gerbner *et al.* (eds), *Child Abuse: An Agenda for Action*. (New York: Oxford University Press, 1980)

Zuckerman, A. "Formality and the Family—Reform and the Status Quo", *Law Quarterly Review*, 1980, 96, 248.

TABLE OF CASES

INDEX

LEGAL TAXONOMY
FROM SWEET & MAXWELL

This index has been prepared using Sweet and Maxwell's Legal Taxonomy. Main index entries conform to keywords provided by the Legal Taxonomy except where references to specific documents or non-standard terms (denoted by quotation marks) have been included. These keywords provide a means of identifying similar concepts in other Sweet & Maxwell publications and online services to which keywords from the Legal Taxonomy have been applied. Readers may find some minor differences between terms used in the text and those which appear in the index. Suggestions to *sweetandmaxwell.taxonomy@thomson.com*.

Adoption
adopted persons, 320
adoptive parents, 320–321
adoption agencies, 4, 318, 320, 322, 323
adoption orders, 323, 324
adoption support, 318
alternatives, 328
applications, 320, 321
birth records, 329–330
children's welfare, 327, 328
child's best interests, 317, 319–320
civil partners, 4, 320, 330, 331
cohabitants, 4
consanguinity, 330
consent
 children's welfare, 327
 child's consent, 325
 dispensing, with, 326–328
 freely given, 323
 guardians, 322–325
 incapacity, 326
 mental capacity, 326, 327
 missing parent, 326
 parental consent, 317, 322–324, 328
 timing, 323
 unconditional, 323, 326
 unmarried father, 325
court orders, 328
cultural background, 320

Adoption—*cont.*
delays, 320
effects, 316, 317
foster parents, 318
heterosexual couples, 4
home with adopters, 327–328
homosexual couples, 4
human rights
 child's best interests, 317
 interference with family life, 317
 parental consent, 317
 right to adopt, 318
informal adoptions, 316
inter-country adoption
 adoption agencies, 332
 adoption applications, 332
 child's best interests, 331, 332
 controls, 331, 332
 counselling, 332
 Hague Convention, 331
 public policy, 332
 requisite consent, 331
 trafficking, 332
introduction, 316
judicial powers, 328
legal relationships, 316, 317
linguistic background, 320
local authority services, 318
married couples, 4
paramountcy principle, 319–320
parental responsibility, 4, 323, 324